Edge Computing for Industrial IoT

Edge Computing for Industrial IoT

Prof. Dineshwari Bisen

ARCLER
PRESS

www.arclerpress.com

Edge Computing for Industrial IoT

Prof. Dineshwari Bisen

Arcler Press
4164 Lakeshore Road
Burlington, ON L7L 1A4
Canada
www.arclerpress.com
Email: orders@arclereducation.com

ISBN: 978-1-77956-984-4 (Hardcover)

ABOUT THE AUTHOR

Dineshwari Bisen, is presently working as an Assistant Professor in IT Department, Western College of Commerce and Business Management, Sanpada,Navi Mumbai, with 14 years of teaching experience. She has completed MCA, PGDCA andADCA. She has worked as a Member of Vigilance Committee, University of Mumbai. She filed and published 1 patent and 8 research papers presented forpublication in various conferences. The books authored and published by her are'Fundamentals of Database Management System, FYBSc IT, Semester-I, University of Mumbai','Open Source Technologies, Semester-1' and text books on'Data Science for Beginers' and'Machine learning Concept,Methodogy, Tools and Applications'.Her interest areas are Programming, Database, operating System, and Technology.

TABLE OF CONTENTS

LIST OF FIGURES

PREFACE

The development of the Industrial Internet of Things (IIoT) has transformed industries by enabling smart, connected systems that link machines, sensors, and advanced analytics. Through logistics and manufacturing to healthcare and energy, IIoT is transforming how companies manage operations, optimize resources, and improve productivity. But this rapid growth has also created new challenges. The high amounts of data generated inside the sites must be processed in real time but, relying solely on centralized cloud computing, proves to create unacceptable latencies, bandwidth congestion, and reliability problems. Delays of even a few hundredths of a second in real-time manufacturing environments can have serious safety and economic consequences.

Edge computing has been a robust solution for these issues by moving computation, data storage, and decision-making closer to the devices that data is being generated from. Instead of sending all data to a distant cloud to process, edge computing allows devices and local servers to process and react to data in real time. This approach reduces latency, enhances reliability, and supports mission-critical use cases such as predictive maintenance, autonomous machinery, and real-time quality control. By facilitating faster response times and lowering network congestion, edge computing is not just complementing the cloud but changing the design and deployment of IIoT systems.

The book *Edge Computing for Industrial IoT* aims to provide a comprehensive insight into how edge technologies meet IIoT to develop efficient, secure, and scalable systems. It explains fundamental concepts as well as advanced applications, giving readers insight into the hardware, software, communication protocols, and strategies behind industrial edge solutions. The books are designed to guide readers from basic concepts to practical deployments, highlighting the promise and challenges of applying edge computing in industrial environments.

Chapter 1 introduces Industrial IoT (IIoT). It explains the technological principles that drive IIoT, its significance in various industries, and how it revolutionizes current operations. The chapter explains how networked actuators, sensors, and intelligent systems lead to smarter factories, grids, and healthcare environments. It mentions the size, complexity, and real-time issues IIoT has to address, hence setting the stage for the edge computing role.

Chapter 2 focuses on the fundamentals of edge computing. It introduces the concept of edge computing, outlines its architecture, and contrasts it with cloud and fog computing. The chapter highlights the advantages of edge systems so far as minimization of latency, optimization of bandwidth, and increased autonomy are involved. Significant usage scenarios capture the reasons why edge computing has come to be used as a building block of today's IIoT infrastructure.

Chapter 3 discusses edge devices and hardware platforms. It discusses the range of devices for edge computing, ranging from industrial sensors and gateways to specialized edge servers. The chapter familiarizes readers with hardware requirements for processing, memory, connectivity, and power efficiency for industrial use. The chapter also demonstrates how hardware choice impacts scalability, cost, and system resiliency.

Chapter 4 provides a discussion on edge network architecture and communication protocols. It addresses how edge devices communicate with each other and with central systems via protocols such as MQTT, CoAP, OPC UA, and 5G. The chapter provides a review of different network topologies and how they are set up to cater to high reliability, low latency, and security requirements in industrial settings.

Chapter 5 discusses edge data processing. It demonstrates how data is filtered, collected, and analyzed in real-time to support decision-making. Items for discussion include stream processing, edge machine learning, and anomaly detection. The chapter emphasizes how local processing reduces cloud dependency, increases responsiveness, and enables real-time automation.

Chapter 6 explains edge-enabled mobile VR. It outlines how edge computing facilitates immersive technology like virtual reality (VR) and augmented reality (AR) in industrial scenarios. Remote training, real-time monitoring, and virtual prototyping are some examples. The chapter illustrates how offloading computationally expensive tasks onto edge devices improves the performance of VR by reducing latency and promoting interactivity.

Chapter 7 deals with security and privacy on the industrial edge of computing. The chapter discusses concerns such as distributed device security, security of industrial sensitive data, and compliance maintenance with the regulatory frameworks. The chapter outlines methods such as encryption, authentication, intrusion detection, and secure data sharing, with a focus on the importance of robust cybersecurity in decentralized systems.

Chapter 8 focuses on reliability, fault tolerance, and resilience. The chapter highlights the fact that edge systems must remain operational even in the face of failures, interruptions, or cyber attacks. The chapter explains fault-tolerant architecture, redundancy methods, and self-repair mechanisms that render industrial systems robust against interruptions and resilient with continued functionality.

Chapter 9 discusses cloud and legacy system integration. It explains edge computing's role in enhancing present cloud platforms and enabling interoperability with traditional industrial infrastructure. The reader finds out about hybrid edge-cloud architecture, legacy system adaptation, and the challenges in integrating edge into existing enterprise environments.

Chapter 10 concludes with industrial applications of edge computing. It shows real-world deployments by industries such as manufacturing, energy, healthcare, transportation, and logistics. The chapter shows how edge-powered IIoT ignites predictive maintenance, process optimization, worker safety, and sustainable resource management.

The book is suited for students, researchers, business professionals, and practitioners looking to blend edge computing and Industrial IoT. Undergraduate and graduate students of computer science, electrical engineering, and industrial systems engineering will find it as an introduction bridging theory and practice. Researchers and academics can use it as a guidebook for the current trends and challenges in IIoT and edge deployment. For industry practitioners—managers, engineers, and decision-makers—the book provides practical advice on designing, deploying, and operating industrial edge solutions. Policymakers and regulators may also find it helpful in terms of understanding technological foundations that guide standards, interoperability, and security policy in industry environments.

CHAPTER 1

INTRODUCTION TO INDUSTRIAL IOT (IIOT)

Contents

INTRODUCTION

The concept of Industrial Internet of Things or IIoT plays a key role in determining the convergence of technology and industrial processes. IIoT refers to an interconnected system of devices and sensors for collecting, analyzing, and transmitting information in industrial settings, leading to greater efficiency, reliability, and safety in various industries. This encompasses production, supply chain operations, and power generation, where interconnected machines cannot just communicate with each other but also with the master systems to ensure optimum performance. The capability to collect real-time data helps companies make intelligent choices, execute predictive maintenance plans, and reduce operational expenses significantly, thus transforming traditional operations into smart factories. With industries increasingly incorporating IIoT solutions, its effect on productivity and innovation is profound and sets the stage for additional development of intelligent and automated systems. One of the essentials of IIoT is the reliance upon data-driven intelligence that enables a seismic industrial sector transformation. Through the utilizations of cloud computing, big data analytics, and machine learning, IIoT can process vast volumes of data produced by industrial assets.

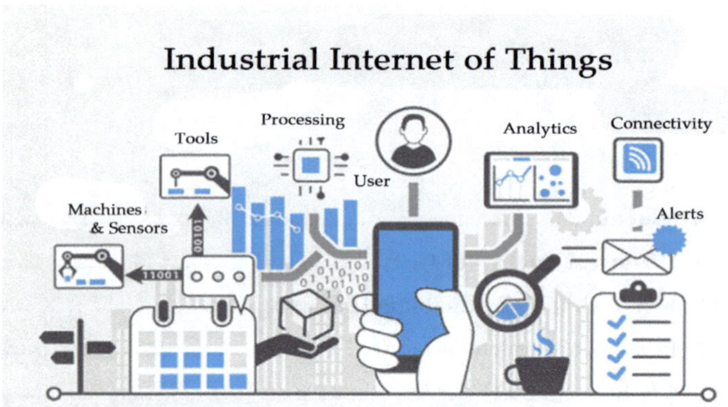

Figure 1.1. Industrial internet of things.

Source: https://external-content.duckduckgo.com/iu/?u=https%3A%2F%2Ftse4.mm.bing.net%2Fth%2Fid%2FOIP.TneQSlO9Y-TQUZX1-NPXVAHaEs%3Fr%3D0%26pid%3DApi&f=1&ipt=f9467a10003dbf98fb3bb2badff4fdb563d917a2d6a912962d6d839001a5e582.

This data not only enables equipment health monitoring but also supports predictive and prescriptive analytics for enhancing operational resiliency. The addition of Federated Learning (FL) to IIoT architectures presents new avenues for enhancing AI applications through solutions to privacy issues on data sharing. As explained in new research, FL applications have been promising in industries like smart industry and smart healthcare, leading to the future when intelligent systems will learn together without compromising integrity and confidentiality of data (Dinh et al., 2021). It is an indicator of increasing IIoT influence on the future of industrial operations. IIoT effects extend beyond business efficiencies; they carry huge impacts on human capital and labor dynamics. As businesses transform to technological revolutions led by IIoT and Industry 4.0, there is a consequent reconfiguration of occupational roles and skill profiles. Digital connectivity and automation demand a workforce with high technology and data analysis skills, thus creating challenges for training programs and schools to shift to evolving needs (Sima et al., 2020). Additionally, the manufacturing and retail sectors have new consumer behavior patterns driven by advanced data availability and digitalization. With these industries adopting IIoT-led methods, it is imperative to open up the nexus of technology and education to work towards creating capable professionals who are able to realize the potential of IIoT innovation in a rapidly changing economic scenario. This interactive cooperation requires emphasis on harmonizing people resources with technological innovations in the context of IIoT (Figure 1.1).

Explanation of IoT and Its Industrial Application

The Internet of Things (IoT) is an innovative paradigm first conceived for consumer environments but which has emerged as full of potential within industrial environments. Through the utilization of interconnected devices, sensors, and data analytics, IoT enables real-time monitoring and optimization of systems, a new capability for operational performance. In industry, the interconnectivity makes feasible seamless communication among equipment, facilitating accurate data gathering and transmission. Consequently, companies are able to make their decisions off large pools of data, optimizing productivity and reducing costs. This industrial IoT implementation underlies the broader drive toward the Industrial Internet of Things (IIoT), which promises to revolutionize processes in industries as diverse as manufacturing to logistics and resource management. Historically, partitioning between the outside world and industrial control systems provided some security; however, now that this partition has disintegrated, IoT integration into industrial systems has also introduced vulnerabilities. Traditionally, there were safety-oriented control systems in stand-alone environments to minimize risk, but the advent of IIoT technologies necessitated more open designs that, while efficient, are challenging to maintain cybersecurity. The improved connectivity also increases the potential for data analysis and strategic management, allowing high-level management to have close monitoring of production operations and flexible handling of resources. The emerging IIoT environment emphasizes the need to address aforementioned security issues, as seen in real-life experiences where the systems are compromised, necessitating a robust mechanism for safeguarding operational technology (Evangelopoulou et al., 2017). Furthermore, the onset of technologies such as fog computing has begun complementing IoT's capabilities for industrial use, promising enhanced data management and process efficiency. Through this integration, data can be processed locally, which would involve less bandwidth usage by central systems and less latency risk. These enhancements do come with additional security threats, particularly with the exponentially growing amount of data generated due to the myriad of IoT devices. The compatibility of IoT and fog computing also presents with it opportunities and challenges, hence the drive for ongoing research to devise strong cybersecurity solutions to safeguard industrial systems. As weaknesses continue to be identified in the networks through research, proactive security will be a key enabler to explore the IIoT potential while safeguarding critical infrastructure (Butun et al., 2018).

Key Components of IIoT Systems

The core of any Industrial Internet of Things (IIoT) consists of a series of key components that support its functionality and operation. Smart actuators and sensors form the core of these systems, collecting and transmitting real-time information from industrial environments. The sensors monitor multiple parameters such as temperature, pressure, and humidity, while actuators take action upon receiving the data. In communicating through protocols like Profibus and Modbus, the devices exchange information with Programmable Logic Controllers (PLCs) and other industrial automation equipment. The changeover from isolated "air gapped" systems to network configurations allows data to travel between operational technology and enterprise information systems unrestricted. Such interconnectivity not only enhances operational efficiency but also brings additional security vulnerabilities, for which effective steps need to be taken to defend against future cyber-attacks as reflected by the learning inferred from breaches on critical infrastructures (Evangelopoulou et al., 2017). Data analytics is yet another significant component of IIoT systems that enables organizations to tap into massive amounts of collected information to make better decisions. Through the application of advanced analytics techniques, including artificial intelligence and machine learning, businesses are able to derive actionable insights from flows of real-time data. The processing power allows predictive maintenance, cutting downtime by forecasting equipment breakdowns before they occur. Data analytics also allows manufacturing processes to be optimized by identifying inefficiencies and making informed changes based on data. However, using these analysis tools should be done cautiously considering the Security, Privacy, Dependability, and Interoperability (SPDI) needs because it is important to provide these elements in order to attain the maximum effective deployment of IIoT applications. SPDI realization and maintenance at run-time and system startup is a complex task that requires a formally specified framework and cautious addition of security protocols (Fysarakis et al., 2019). Finally, the interconnected nature of IIoT systems necessitates an efficient communications framework to facilitate seamless data transfer between machines and platforms. The communication framework is typically composed of gateways that ensure the bridge between operational technologies and cloud services for seamless sharing of data. The gateways facilitate various connectivity methods including Wi-Fi, cellular, and LPWAN (Low Power Wide Area Network), which brings greater flexibility to industrial use. Moreover, the ability of centralized control from a single point provides significant leverage in coordination and monitoring, leading to improved operational choices. Yet, such high connectivity is higher in vulnerabilities, and hence organizations need to deploy extensive security protocols and actively monitor for potential vulnerabilities. Overlooking these security concerns has the ability to undermine not just the integrity of the IIoT system but the overall industrial operations resilience as a whole (Evangelopoulou et al., 2017).

Differences Between IIoT and Traditional IoT

The contrast between Industrial Internet of Things (IIoT) and traditional Internet of Things (IoT) is more apparent in their respective purposes and functionalities. Traditional IoT generally serves consumer uses, including personal devices like intelligent household devices, wearable technology, and medical monitoring systems. These consumer devices focus on user convenience and data collection but operate in relatively unregulated environments. On the other hand, IIoT is based on industry segments with automation, efficiency, and interconnectivity of manufacturing processes being given priority. It involves advanced equipment, and thus more data reliability and real-time processing capability are needed to enhance the efficiency of operations. More complex industry environments have the need for expert hardware and software, which differ significantly from the simple frameworks of standard IoT, where devices could be supported with lower specifications. Moreover, the IIoT employs intricate analytics and machine learning algorithms to support decision-making procedures in industrial processes. Another significant difference lies in data processing methods; IIoT systems harvest enormous amounts of operating data from devices, sensors, and connected machines that support real-time analysis to optimize production streams. This stands in contrast to traditional IoT systems, which do not necessarily require intricate data algorithms and operate based on predetermined conditions. For instance, while smart refrigerators can merely notify consumers of low inventory levels, IIoT technology can utilize machine learning in the manufacturing sector to forecast equipment failures and optimize predictive maintenance strategies. By proposing novel frameworks that allow real-time cooperation, e.g., Collaborative Sensing Intelligence (CSI), IIoT shows its capability to integrate massive data streams from various industrial devices to achieve maximum operational efficiencies (Chen et al., 2025). Lastly, while both IIoT and traditional IoT seek to connect devices and maximize efficiencies, they are faced with distinct security threats — a key difference that reflects their varied environments.

Figure 1.2. Differences between IIoT and traditional IoT.

Source: https://external-content.duckduckgo.com/iu/?u=https%3A%2F%2Fd3tj4wnms16o5e.cloudfront.net%2Fs3fs-public%2Finline-images%2FIot%2520Vs%2520Iiot%2520blog-02_0.png&f=1&nofb=1&ipt=ee95de709ed0c66da1689e966e1e6ba5db472dc2c9cdb1848751a818756af50d.

Traditional IoT devices, often deployed within less secure home networks, may be subject to vulnerabilities that can be solved with consumer-grade security solutions. Conversely, IIoT systems operate in industrial settings that demand robust security protocols since they have more to lose in the form of operations downtime and safety risks. The IIoT must ensure data integrity in transactions between complex machines and logistics networks, especially since issues like energy wastage or manufacturing inefficiencies still persist. According to current research, employing frameworks with intelligent modeling and self-organizing configurations can significantly reduce challenges like manufacturing time and energy consumption (Guo et al., 2018). Therefore, the security features in the IIoT context further highlight the built-in differences in structure and applications between IIoT and the traditional IoT (Figure 1.2).

1.1. HISTORICAL CONTEXT OF IIOT

The history of the Industrial Internet of Things (IIoT) goes back to where information technology (IT) and operational technology (OT) converged in manufacturing environments. This convergence has been at the center of transforming traditional industrial processes, largely made possible by advancements in the Internet of Things (IoT). The emergence of Industry 4.0, also referred to as the fourth industrial revolution, is an indicator of huge technological progress encompassing IoT alongside cyber-physical systems (CPS) and big data analytics. As industries globally are shifting towards networked and automated systems, the adoption of smart manufacturing practices is an emerging trend in order to provide higher efficiencies and data-driven decision-making processes. Among the key developments brought about by IIoT are the higher production efficiency, quality control, and plant safety, all of which answer the need of the industry to perform better and be answerable to customer needs, as written in Pilloni et al. (2018). The transition towards IIoT was also driven by the inefficiencies of previous industrial frameworks, necessitating innovative means to manufacturing processes. Historical production processes tended to depend on manual interventions, which were inefficient and time-consuming. With the coming of digital technologies and automated systems, processes changed, making them more efficient. This was summarized within the grand narrative of industrial development; for example, innovation in new materials and processes of manufacturing has been central to changing paradigms. The integration of additive and subtractive manufacturing technologies, as depicted in existing research efforts on low-cost molding inserts, demonstrates the way new technological paradigms are revolutionizing production capability. Such technologies place high priority on a common platform that encompasses legacy systems and emerging technologies so as to provide a seamless transition into an efficient manufacturing paradigm as suggested by Ewart et al. (2019). With the development in technology comes a history as well that specifies IIoT, which consists of shifting expectations of businesses and consumers. With globalization catching up, industries had to be adaptable to rapidly evolving needs and consumer preferences. This need led to innovation and the development of new business models centered around flexibility, customization, and efficiency. Furthermore, the ability to leverage vast amounts of data generated by networked devices is now critical for organizations aiming to match the level of competition. The data collection and analysis functionality lies at the center of the IIoT topic because appropriate application of said data can enhance performance in many areas of operation. By accomplishing the benefits of smart automation and real-time analysis, the sectors are not only maximizing their operational efficiencies but also reconstructing their strategic goals, thus showing the intensive penetration of IIoT in shaping the future of industrial activities as submitted in Pilloni et al. (2018).

1.1.1. Evolution of Industrial Automation

The evolution of industrial automation has been marked by the appearance of major technologies that have led to the current convergence of the Industrial Internet of Things (IIoT). Industrial control systems were initially segmented from the rest of the environments, with devices such as Programmable Logic Controllers (PLCs) and sensors being physically segregated from external networks. This isolation offered a certain level of security because an attacker would have to access these systems physically to get around it. Nevertheless, as the need for real-time information and scalability of operations became apparent to industries, these air gaps narrowed.

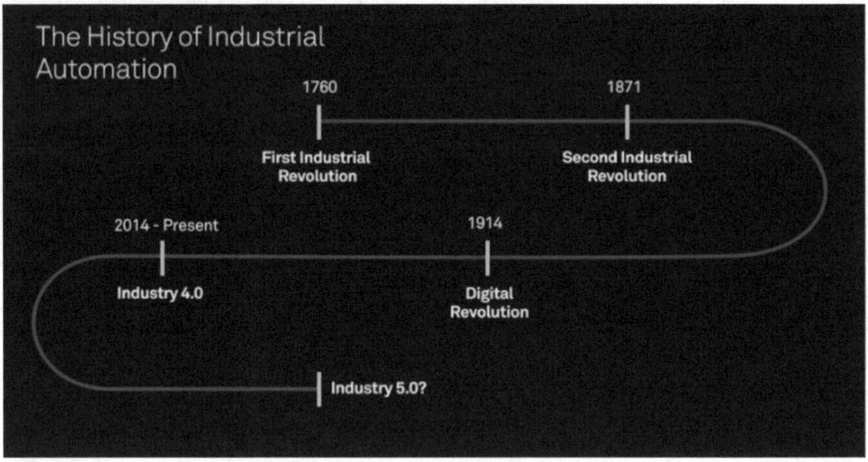

Figure 1.3. The history of industrial automation.

Source: https://external-content.duckduckgo.com/iu/?u=https%3A%2F%2Fglobal-uploads.webflow.com%2F5e81e9c9dad44d11ba330074%2F61c05a0454012b75b1438a7b_history-industrial-automation.png&f=1&nofb=1&ipt=cd20cdcf006a16a5bfe6269905e07f48aaeb9856ae17cb9a5f1bbe7a6140228e.

The use of network switches and gateways allowed industrial protocols to be bridged, laying the groundwork for more sophisticated control of production processes. This movement is a shift of nature, as the management can now utilize this data in broader strategic planning, thus enhancing productivity and efficiency in different manufacturing spaces (Evangelopoulou et al., 2017). With the industrial automation sphere further progressing, the integration of Industrial Wireless Sensor and Actuator Networks (IWSAN) is a significant step forward. These networks facilitate a higher degree of connectivity in industrial environments that supports monitoring and actuation, as well as coordination among various production stages. The increased connectivity facilitates autonomous vehicle and mobile robot integration using automation, enhancing responsiveness and agility of operations. While different wireless technologies have emerged to provide these capabilities, they differ significantly in performance and capability. Thus, engineers will have to consider the specific requirements of their applications when selecting suitable technologies for IWSAN deployment. Determining trade-offs and capabilities is required in order to optimize industrial connectivity and achieve successful implementation of Industry 4.0 projects, which rely heavily on integration of this kind (Poorter et al., 2020) (Figure 1.3). The incorporation of IIoT into industry automation brings revolutionary possibilities alongside new risks. Networked systems bring transparency to operations and facilitate data-driven decision-making yet open up channels of vulnerability that need to be addressed. The move toward increased connectivity has brought to the forefront major security threats, as recent cyber incidents have demonstrated by capitalizing on exploits within control systems. The lessons gleaned from such events highlight the importance of effective security protocols, especially for systems that are becoming more integrated. This evolution makes it necessary for industries to change the way they consider cybersecurity, which places greater emphasis on active action that prevents threats prior to occurrence. By neutralizing such threats, businesses can ensure the benefits of IIoT—such as operational efficiency and scalability enhancements—are achieved without compromising system integrity and safety (Evangelopoulou et al., 2017).

1.1.2. The Role of the Internet in Industrial Settings

In the modern world of industry, the integration of the Internet has played a key role in shaping significant advancements, mostly achieved through the emergence of the Industrial Internet of Things (IIoT). Industrial Automation and Control Systems (IACS) were long isolated from conventional traditional digital networks on the basis of security and efficiency. But with the shifting patterns of connectivity, the terrain has been laid upon which IACS are compelled to transform themselves to accommodate IoT technologies. This new design promotes greater interconnectivity, propelling communication between devices and equipment at the shop floor. The reinterpretation of such networks makes real-time data sharing and analysis possible, which can enhance decision-making processes, increase efficiency, and optimize the management of resources in industrial settings, where every second's downtime could mean substantial economic loss as noted in the IIoT research studies (Boyes et al., 2018). Further, the use of the Internet in industrial settings is not just about connectivity; it is a deciding factor that contributes to the improvement of working strategies. Through IIoT, organizations are capable of gathering loads of data regarding processes of production as well as environmental conditions, which also supports developing advanced analytical models for performance enhancement. For instance, utilization of a multi-objective optimization model has proved useful in cost minimization in different directions such as energy consumption and delays in production.

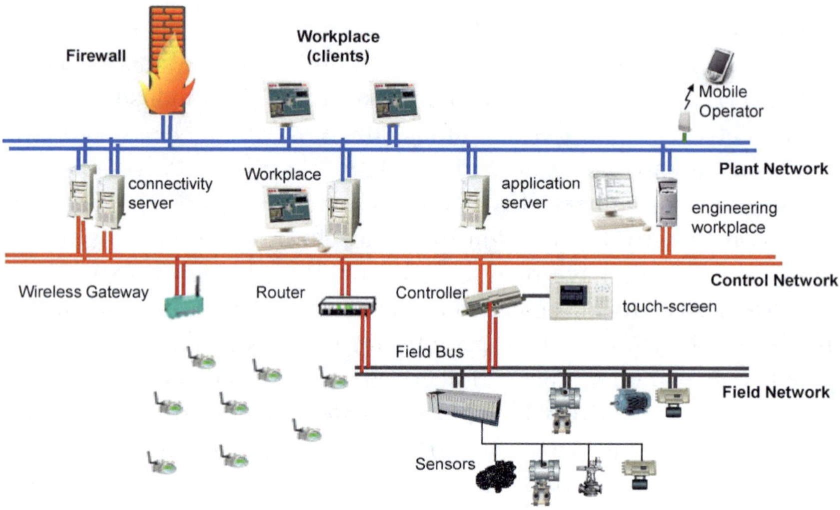

Figure 1.4. Industrial automation and control systems.

Source: https://www.researchgate.net/figure/Industrial-automation-and-control-systems_fig1_333639056.

Such IIoT applications can assist in the achievement of more cost-effective scheduling of production. In an applied context, in one research, it was demonstrated that how a genetic algorithm enhanced the time management of a pasta factory plant, indicating the ability to gain substantial economic advantages because of IIoT-based production planning (David et al., 2019). Also, the importance of cybersecurity cannot be denied amid increasing Internet reliance for industrial operations. As IIoT continues to advance, vulnerabilities created by increased connectivity introduce new threats. Transferring from being physically distinct industrial networks to more connected systems demands robust security measures against likely cyber-attacks compromising operational integrity. It is necessary to understand the interdependence of IIoT and other concepts such as cyber-physical systems and Industry 4.0 to establish a secure environment. By acknowledging and addressing security threats and vulnerabilities inherent in this new model, companies are able to not just safeguard operations but also foster innovation, ensuring they remain competitive within an increasingly digitalized business landscape, as suggested through ongoing research (Boyes et al., 2018) (Figure 1.4).

1.1.3. Milestones in the Development of IIoT Technologies

The evolution of Industrial Internet of Things (IIoT) technologies has been shaped by a series of milestone events that have revolutionized industrial operations. The initial one was the integration of wireless sensor networks (WSNs) as the core for IIoT, and this paved the way for real-time monitoring and data collection across various industries. Industrial Wireless Sensor Networks (IWSNs) have further enhanced these trends, making operational spaces more flexible, scalable, and affordable.

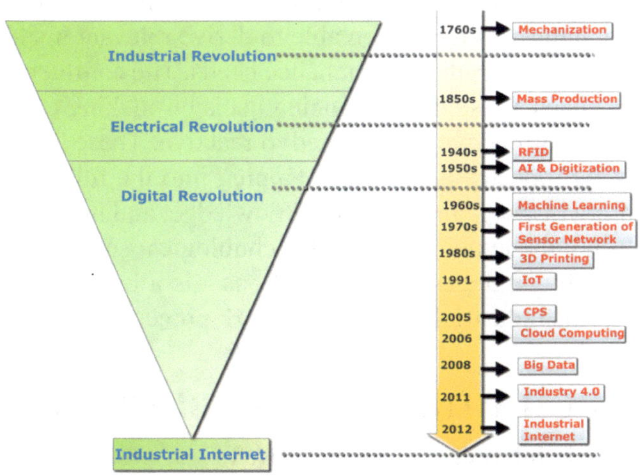

Figure 1.5. Timeline of key milestones of the industrial internet.

Source:https://www.researchgate.net/profile/Shashank-Gupta-34/publication/354825915/figure/fig5/AS:1143128146267574 3@1748203463249/Timeline-of-key-milestones-of-the-Industrial-Internet.png.

As seen in literature, accelerated development in IWSNs applications is experienced across numerous industries, ranging from small manufacturing plants to complex oil and gas fields. Such elasticity has made abundant research easier, focusing on the importance of IWSNs in improving automation and control of industrial processes as well as the design challenges that must be overcome in a bid to deploy it (Aslam et al., 2018). As a sequel to the early breakthroughs in WSNs, the majority of focus has since been turned towards addressing the security concerns within IIoT systems. The widespread use of IIoT technologies has resulted in security breaches being increasingly challenging, undermining the integrity of critical industrial data as well as production processes. With a counteractive measure to this, innovative solutions like blockchain technology have appeared with enhanced security tools specifically tailored for IIoT systems. Blockchain integration with IIoT has introduced a decentralized approach to data transaction protection, providing transparency and trust in heterogeneous devices across industry networks. Research indicates that the application of a structured asynchronous blockchain architecture can not only provide robust security but also enhanced transaction efficiency, hence making industries conduct operations in a more secure and trusted manner (Badikyan et al., 2022) (Figure 1.5). Concurrently with all these advancements in sensor networks and security, data analytics and machine learning algorithms have revolutionized IIoT's landscape. Leveraging the vast amounts of data generated by IIoT devices, industries have been able to derive relevant insights, optimize processes, and precisely predict maintenance needs. The confluence of IIoT and big data analytics has assisted in enhancing decision-making capacities in that it makes companies proactive, as opposed to reactive. These kind of analytical capabilities render industries capable of tapping into the full potential of their data, transforming raw data into valuable knowledge, and innovation as well as efficiency. In total, the evolution of IIoT technologies—coupled with wireless networking, security, and analytics innovations—is a breakthrough track that radically transforms industrial settings and work processes.

1.2. KEY TECHNOLOGIES ENABLING IIOT

As the Industrial Internet of Things (IIoT) is poised to revolutionize manufacturing and industrial processes, there are certain technologies that are pioneer technologies leading the charge. The nucleus of this revolution is bringing advanced sensors and actuators into factory environments. These sensors collect a wide range of data from machines and assembly lines, enabling real-time monitoring and control. The processing and analysis of such data are enhanced by cloud computing solutions, enabling storage, processing, and analysis of large data sets. The marriage of edge computing with cloud enables timely decision-making by localizing the processing of information nearer to the source and leveraging centralized systems' analytical functions. The fusion of technologies enables improved smart operations by means of predictive maintenance, increased efficiency, and reduced downtime. Networking technologies form the other cornerstone of IIoT adoption, facilitating simple communication among devices and systems. Industrial Automation and Control Systems (IACS) have evolved from operating in a standalone basis to open networks utilizing networking technologies, transforming operating structures in industrial settings. Safety-related systems previously operated on an air-gap basis with an added protection layer through isolation from external networks. And as ubiquity arrives, protocols such as TCP/IP are employed to connect industrial devices and enterprise information systems. Along with this follows far-reaching implications for management control and business effectiveness as senior management relies increasingly on access to real-time information in making strategic decisions. But increased connectivity is accompanied by threats that must be met with strong cybersecurity defenses to protect important systems from potential attack, as suggested by reports of recent industry breaches (Evangelopoulou et al., 2017) (Figure 1.6).

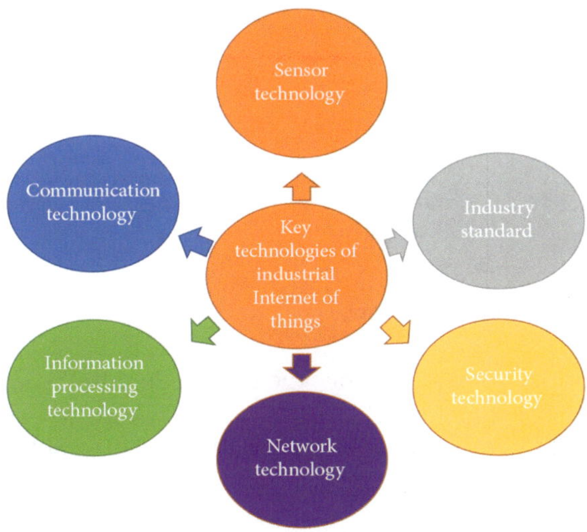

Figure 1.6. Key technologies of industrial IoT.

Source: https://www.researchgate.net/publication/350933376/figure/fig4/AS:1080295319183362@1634573883174/Key-technologies-of-industrial-IoT.jpg.

Also, the IIoT environment is characterized by the integration of IoT technologies with other concepts like Industry 4.0 and cyber-physical systems. The integration is applied in order to generate more interactive and smart production processes.

Also, it generates a need for holistic frameworks that are capable of describing and analyzing IIoT devices in an organized manner. Current work emphasizes the necessity of understanding these interdependencies to cope with security threats and vulnerabilities in IIoT ecosystems (Boyes et al., 2018). By creating effective analytical frameworks, organizations will be able to tally and examine their IIoT deployments, highlighting information that provides anticipation of probable risks while enhancing operational resilience. This integrated approach not only facilitates upgraded security provisions but also fosters an innovation and responsiveness culture in industrial operations.

1.2.1. Sensors and Actuators in Industrial Environments

The addition of sensors and actuators to the industrial environment is a giant step in the realm of operational efficiency and safety. Historically relegated to being kept away from common networks, industrial control systems were usually founded upon custom protocols such as Modbus, which were hugely different from the ubiquitous TCP/IP standards.

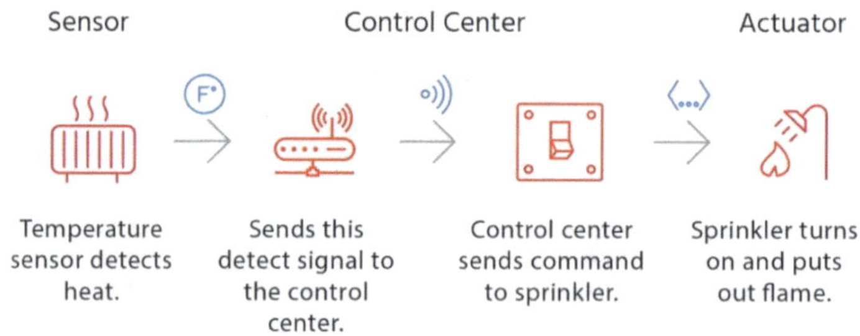

Figure 1.7. Sensors to actuators flow.

Source: https://external-content.duckduckgo.com/iu/?u=https%3A%2F%2Fbridgera.com%2Fwp-content%2Fuploads%2F2017%2F06%2Fsensor_actuator_graphics-sec1_pg16-1024x512.jpg&f=1&nofb=1&ipt=a9e66cdb408d800af62187152d3993015b32310e77d81900651621def345a483.

Isolation helped to provide some amount of security but limited the flexibility and responsiveness of the systems. But with industries embracing the Industrial Internet of Things (IIoT), a great emphasis exists on more connectivity, which allows higher-level enterprise management systems to communicate seamlessly with each other. The connectivity facilitates the fine-tuning of production processes with opportunities and challenges in terms of cybersecurity and operational integrity that have been highlighted in Johnson et al. (2016). Sensors are employed to feed real-time information in aid of decision-making in industrial processes. They monitor several parameters, such as temperature, pressure, and humidity, pumping essential data back to central systems for analysis. On misconfiguration or failure, actuators enable corrective response, varying processes to minimize risk. These components are particularly crucial for applications dealing with hazardous substances, such as refineries, where sensor feedback initiates immediate safety responses (Figure 1.7). Integration of these sensors and actuators to low-power wireless networks gives more monitoring and operation flexibility. Nevertheless, the cross-connecting nature of such devices poses safety and security protocol issues for safeguarding key industrial components, as outlined in Frey et al. (2018). Secondly, the transition to the IIoT involves consideration of the operational challenges entailed with sensing and actuating sensors and actuators in the unforgiving industrial environments. These kinds of environments can potentially introduce variables that impact the functionality and reliability of such devices, hence making it challenging to integrate rugged monitoring systems. Emerging technologies such as Information Centric Networking offer promising solutions to provide enhancements in coping with such challenges, particularly regarding security and effective data transmission. Leverage of such technologies emphasizes enhancements in DoS resistance and general industrial safety, emphasizing the importance of a secure infrastructure. By investigating diverse networking strategies and their corresponding security implications, industries can be better poised to address the issues of a more digitized interconnected world, resulting in a more secure and efficient operating context, as demonstrated in Frey et al. (2018).

1.2.2. Cloud Computing and Data Analytics

The intersection of cloud computing and data analytics is at the heart of the Industrial Internet of Things (IIoT) realization. Cloud computing provides an elastic platform that allows businesses to process and analyze enormous volumes of data collected by networked devices. This ability is essential to industries that are set on accessing real-time insights into their operations. Through a shift to cloud-based solutions, companies can reduce costs of having on-premises data centers while also driving collaboration across different aspects of their operations. Real-time manufacturing data visualization and analysis are paramount to revealing insights that have the potential to lead to further competitive advantage, as emphasized in recent presentations about In-Transit Analytics. This shift is the foundation for the development of productive IIoT solutions based on accessible and more manageable data streams (Ali et al., 2017). Moreover, the position of data analytics in cloud computing is fortified as industries slice through the complexities of next-generation manufacturing. Data analytics enables businesses to extract actionable insights from the immense volumes of data generated by devices and sensors. Using predictive analytics and machine learning capabilities, businesses can forecast equipment failures, plan maintenance, and optimize operational efficiencies. All these analytical possibilities not only aid in enhanced productivity but also help bring about more efficient decision-making across the supply chain. Further, industries such as maritime manufacturing are becoming more and more integrated with smart design and operating models to gain energy efficiency as well as environmental friendliness. With cloud platforms integrating analytics, the organizations get to build an intuitive feeling of their working environments, instilling innovation and responsiveness needed for an Industry 4.0 landscape (Ang et al., 2017) (Figure 1.8).

Figure 1.8. Big data and cloud computing.

Source: https://www.whizlabs.com/blog/wp-content/uploads/2018/07/big-data-cloud-computing.png.

By their definition, data analytics and cloud computing form the backbone of the Industrial IoT ecosystem, the two enabling a transformative leap towards smarter manufacturing approaches. Through these technologies, companies can benefit from enhanced data interoperability across several disparate systems to communicate with each other. This interconnection is paramount in real-time monitoring and control, which are hallmarks of IIoT implementations. Besides, as data becomes increasingly centralized and actionable within cloud environments, businesses can develop a holistic view of their operations, which promotes continuous improvement initiatives. Ultimately, the interdependence between data analytics and cloud computing not only drives operational efficiencies but also positions firms to thrive amidst the challenges of accelerated market conditions and technology shifts (Ali et al., 2017).

1.2.3. Communication Protocols and Standards

The building of communication standards and protocols has been at the heart of Industrial IoT evolution. Industrial networks used to be constructed around isolated systems, with Programmable Logic Controllers (PLCs) and smart sensors operating in isolation without external connectivity. This air-gapped approach provided a veil of security because physical access was required for attackers to breach operations. But with new advancements in network technology, protocols like Profibus and Modbus have emerged, enabling integration of operational technology and enterprise information systems. As noted in recent research, this integration has enabled senior management to see production processes in real-time, enabling strategic planning to improve. But such trends also carry such immense security threats, particularly regarding vulnerabilities that may arise when combining safety-critical systems with broader networks (Evangelopoulou et al., 2017). Moreover, the onset of Industry 4.0 underscores the need for common communication protocols to enable innovation in manufacturing environments. At the heart of this plan is the ability to visualize manufacturing data for better decision-making and innovation. To harness the potential of IIoT, organizations must deploy enabling technologies that facilitate smooth data interconnectivity and exchange among devices. The technologies facilitate In-Transit Analytics, which is imperative for producing real-time insights into production. Communication protocols and standards form the backbone of such an analytical ability, and they contribute to the development of necessary infrastructure to enable data to be gathered, shared, and acted upon effectively (Ali et al., 2017). Therefore, the standardization of communication processes is more critical to maintaining competitive advantage in the rapidly evolving industrial landscape (Figure 1.9).

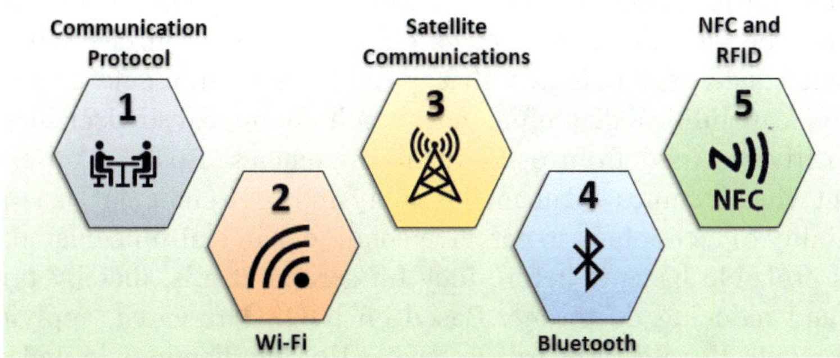

Figure 1.9. IoT communication protocol.

Source: https://cdn.educba.com/academy/wp-content/uploads/2019/11/iot-communication-protocol-1.png.

With the growing complexity of IIoT ecosystems, the development of robust communication protocols and standards becomes more necessary. The networked nature of IIoT means devices will have to exchange information with one another across various networks and systems, necessitating protocols with the capability for interoperability. Not only does this require standards in place but also the development of new protocols that can sustain the specific requirements of IIoT applications. The convergence of such communication models must be done in a way that focuses on scaling up security protection in order to achieve operational effectiveness. Lessons learned from previous security breaches, including those seen within Ukrainian critical infrastructures, are that security must be incorporated into the communication architecture itself. As companies commence the scaling of their IIoT projects, having effective protocols and compliance with them will be what makes them resilient and capable of handling the complexities of contemporary industrial settings (Evangelopoulou et al., 2017).

1.3. BENEFITS OF IMPLEMENTING IIOT

The application of Industrial Internet of Things (IIoT) systems is highly advantageous and can increase the efficiency of operation of various industries. By adopting the use of intelligent devices and sensors incorporated into existing infrastructure, organizations can make the processes better, with less cost of operation and quicker response times. For instance, for the mining sector, there was a study done by the U.S. National Institute for Occupational Safety and Health (NIOSH) demonstrated that the majority of existing post-accident communication systems require little upgrade to support IIoT applications, thereby making it feasible to embrace without an enormous overhaul (N/A). This allows organizations to expand on their current infrastructure while incorporating new technologies that provide real-time data analysis and automation capabilities that ultimately result in improved decision-making and productivity. Apart from operational efficiencies, IIoT is also extremely significant when it comes to enhancing safety and environmental sustainability. The capability of technology to perceive conditions in real-time guarantees that it detects probable hazards before they hit serious levels, thereby protecting workers and reducing downtime. Based on NIOSH research, applying low-cost microcontroller Wi-Fi boards to enable IIoT applications in underground coal mines enhances system safety through monitoring and control. The intervention not only enhances safety aspects in high-risk work environments but also promotes more sustainable practices by maximizing the exploitation of resources and minimizing environmental footprints (N/A). The ability for predictive failure anticipation and proactive maintenance further extends the environmental benefit by minimizing waste and energy consumption associated with unplanned downtime. From a strategic perspective, the convergence of IIoT technologies is in conformity with the principles of the Triple Bottom Line

(TBL) where business decisions involve economic, environmental, and social aspects. As more businesses place priority on corporate social responsibility, IIoT systems become a tool in monitoring and reporting sustainability metrics. Evidence has emerged recently indicating that convergence of IIoT can strengthen the economic aspect of a firm while significantly influencing its environment and society aspects. Specifically, research from Italian manufacturing companies revealed the existence of a positive relationship between IIoT implementation and TBL indicators, which shows that improved environmental performance is more likely to promote value creation by IIoT projects than economic performance alone. The findings encourage organizations to accept an integrative perspective in IIoT implementation, combining technological innovation and overarching sustainability goals (Figure 1.10).

Figure 1.10. The benefits of industrial IoT.

Source: https://www.kaaiot.com/img/ikb/06022024-1.jpg.

1.3.1. Enhanced Operational Efficiency

Evolution of Industrial Internet of Things (IIoT) technology has served as an impetus for enhanced operating effectiveness across various sectors. Traditional industrial processes are based on labor-intensive activities, which are susceptible to human mistakes and inefficiency. With the incorporation of intelligent sensors and IoT devices, companies now stand to take advantage of real-time analytics, offering decision-making insights, and process optimization. For instance, predictive maintenance using IIoT lowers downtime as equipment failure is anticipated in advance, allowing interventions and minimizing disruption of operations. With conventional industries adopting such technologies, maximizing operational efficiency is no longer an aspiration but a groundbreaking standard that redefines productivity measures. Moreover, combining IIoT with communication technologies brings about a paradigm change in operating paradigms. This coming together is particularly apparent in sectors such as the rail industry, where innovation in broadband communication networks including LTE and 5G has become critical to operational effectiveness. Such networks optimize connectivity between trained fleets and their centers of command, improving asset tracking and safety assurances. According to a recent study, implementation of Wireless Sensor Networks (WSNs) in railroads is a reflection not just of more efficient logistics but also of enhanced energy efficiency and reduced operational expenses. This strategic step enables industries to take advantage of the potential offered by IIoT for a smarter infrastructure in accordance with today's operational requirements in the best possible way (Castedo et al., 2017). Investments in IIoT are essential for businesses looking to remain relevant in the face of a more data-driven economy. Greater operational efficiency is not a stand-alone benefit; it is symbiotically paired with greater goals of profitability and sustainability. The exploration of fog computing in IoT settings is emblematic of this trend, as localized processing of data cuts down on bandwidth constraints and improves response times. Despite challenges, especially around security and data integrity, the convergence of these cutting-edge technologies brings more visibility into operations, allowing businesses to make savvy decisions. Notably, the move toward increased operational optimization through IIoT also promotes a culture of ongoing improvement, inviting organizations to innovate and adjust in anticipation of changing market needs and technology advancements (Butun et al., 2018).

1.3.2. Predictive Maintenance and Reduced Downtime

The evolution of Industrial Internet of Things (IIoT) has changed the nature of manufacturing and maintenance operations drastically. Predictive maintenance is one key application emerging from this evolution, founded on actual-time data generated by networked devices to forecast potential future equipment failures. With the aid of sophisticated sensing technology and machine learning, companies can align historical performance data with current operating conditions to forecast when machines require maintenance. This proactive approach is worlds apart from traditional reactive maintenance, which generally equates to costly downtime and unplanned failures. As a result of this, predictive maintenance plays a key role in optimizing operational efficiency and extending the life of critical assets, thus resulting in reduced costs and increased productivity in industrial settings. As predictive maintenance further gains ground, its direct correlation with reduced downtime becomes increasingly evident. Scheduled or unplanned downtime causes significant financial loss to manufacturers in the form of lost production and inefficient utilization of resources. Predictive maintenance methodologies using IIoT enable organizations to anticipate and rectify machinery issues prior to these turning into catastrophic failures that involve long repair hours. As an example, with the monitoring of equipment health through continuous data analysis and the employment of advanced analytics, organizations can automate their regular maintenance processes during low-demand periods in a bid to reduce the disruption of process workflows. Not only does this preserve process manufacturing schedules' continuity but also encourages a stronger operating position.

Figure 1.11. Predictive maintenance with IoT.

Source: https://www.rejigdigital.com/wp-content/uploads/2024/08/benefits-predictive-maintenance-iot.png.

Therefore, the application of predictive maintenance in manufacturing systems is an impetus for the encouragement of efficiency and competitiveness in the new manufacturing environment. Furthermore, predictive maintenance implications extend beyond efficiency gains and cost savings. The shift towards a more services-oriented industrial production model is part of a broader trend in which companies are looking to maximize their competitive advantage and profitability potential via innovative service models. As Chew et al. (2015) has outlined in the findings, embracing a service design with predictive maintenance concepts can result in sophisticated product-service systems (PSS) that capture the evolving needs of customers. In transforming maintenance into a value-added service rather than an obligatory process, manufacturers become differentiated in increasingly competitive markets. By this, strategic predictive maintenance enabled by IIoT technologies not only minimizes downtime but also encourages a responsive, customer-focused strategy that resonates with modern industrial models (Figure 1.11).

1.3.3. Improved Safety and Risk Management

The implementation of IIoT technologies in industrial environments greatly enhances safety and risk management protocols. With the use of intelligent sensors and real-time monitoring systems, companies are in a position to detect potential hazards before their outbreak as catastrophic occurrences. For instance, predictive maintenance through IIoT makes it possible to monitor equipment health continuously, hence the likelihood of failures is greatly reduced. This proactive approach not only minimizes accidents but also fosters a safety culture in the workplace since employees are equipped with timely data that informs their operating decisions. The strategic adoption of such technologies forms the basis for safer operating conditions, consistent with contemporary safety standards and regulations. Ultimately, this shift is a fundamental transformation in how industries prioritize safety with technology to become more robust and operationally effective in a world that is becoming increasingly digitally interconnected. Additionally, risk management in industry contexts is fundamentally transformed by the capacity of IIoT in aggregating large data sets and scrutinizing them. Enhanced data analysis allows organizations to access identifying trends and breakdown points to make risk factor decisions with better understanding. This shift from reactive to predictive risk management offers a robust platform for industries to address vulnerabilities before they emerge. For example, IIoT-integrated systems can handle huge amounts of data regarding operational processes, recognizing anomalous trends that can indicate security threats or operation vulnerabilities. As Boyes et al. (2018) observes, progressing from isolated control systems to interlinked scenarios requires more sophisticated risk management, hence driving industries into scalable architectures that value safety and security measures. Under such a scenario, IIoT becomes a critical driver for integrating multi-faceted risk management strategies in an all-encompassing way that addresses both operational and cyber risks. In addition, safety warranty processes greatly boost the application of IIoT in industrial environments. Upon application of high-end video monitoring systems with remote observation, companies can maintain a twenty-four-seven watch over their operations, ensuring safety measures are upheld round-the-clock. Real-time alerts and notifications through IIoT about unsafe situations or unauthorized access go a long way in immediate corrective action, effectively averting threats. In accordance, businesses not only protect their assets but also their workers, establishing a framework in which safety and operational integrity are attainable. The railroad industry is a case in point; as explained in

Castedo et al. (2017), emerging communication technologies not only enhance the efficacy of operations but also safety procedures by combining systems monitoring railroad infrastructure and passenger interactions. Thus, the creation of safety assurance using IIoT is a major advancement in the direction of safer and more trustworthy industrial processes with a focus on the importance of continuous improvements in risk management processes.

1.4. CHALLENGES AND RISKS ASSOCIATED WITH IIOT

The advantages that the Industrial Internet of Things (IIoT) brings with it are accompanied by inherent and very severe challenges, particularly on the matter of cybersecurity. The highly networked nature of the industrial systems exposes them to the risk of malicious attacks. For instance, the type of incidents such as distributed denial of service (DDoS) attacks of this kind of critical infrastructure such as electricity grids is only indicative of IIoT system vulnerabilities. According to Technology A et al. (2018), the move from offline to online infrastructure escalates threats against industrial activities, and thus it is critical that sound security controls are implemented. Companies have to navigate through issues of securing their networks, implementing best practices, and counteracting vulnerabilities arising from legacy security frameworks. The challenge does not lie solely in the protection of such systems but also in fostering a culture of security among employees, which is critical to risk management associated with IIoT deployments. Another critical domain of the challenges faced by IIoT is data integrity and intellectual property (IP) control. With companies increasingly engaged in interconnected networks, the threat of data theft or misuse increases. Transfer of confidential technical information among firms is bound to inadvertently expose IP assets to misuse or unauthorized access. The intricate nature of collaborative settings demands effective legislation and robust protection mechanisms through governance systems for sensitive information. UK manufacturing companies, as reported in Kauffman et al. (2018), are employing formal contract mechanisms for dealing with these IP management problems. However, it is required that these initiatives be coordinated with overall business goals, in order that companies can exploit interconnectivity while protecting their core assets at the same time. Thus, finding a balance between cooperation and security requires a continuous level of effort and adaptation within the corporate framework. Moreover, the complexity of operation of IIoT systems compounds the risks of adopting them. The integration of various technologies and platforms has a network of interdependencies, which if not handled appropriately could cause operations to come to a complete standstill. This makes it difficult in the nature of comprehending what makes all the pieces work in the IIoT system. According to Technology A et al. (2018), addressing infrastructural complexity and temporal concerns for security will be essential in establishing an enduring IIoT system. Firms must invest in building visibility across their systems, optimizing processes so that all the components function harmoniously together. Fundamental too is the establishment of avenues for ongoing training and adaptation to maintain alignment with shifting technological ecosystems and security threats. As firms strive to access the benefits of IIoT, embracing new practices and a culture of cooperation and safety are essential for overcoming the inherent issues and risks (Figure 1.12).

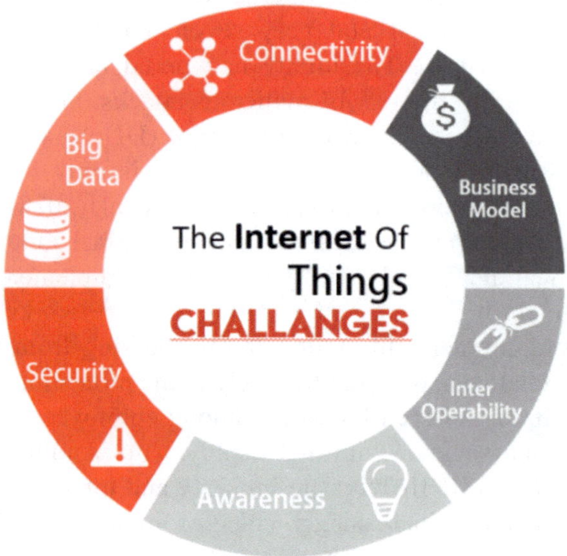

Figure 1.12. Challenges of IoT.

Source: https://external-content.duckduckgo.com/iu/?u=https%3A%2F%2Fcdn-images-1.medium.com%2Fmax%2F1200%2F1*4yNDQEpdw_Dlsv644O9UiQ.png&f=1&nofb=1&ipt=98cacd7a5412f97b2582159160802535 0df28880822d0b958f2737e3af1a27bc.

1.4.1. Cybersecurity Threats and Vulnerabilities

The rapid growth of the Industrial Internet of Things (IIoT) has ushered in a new era of connectivity and productivity, but it has also introduced extreme vulnerabilities that pose critical cybersecurity threats. The integration of numerous devices, sensors, and systems into industrial applications creates intricate networks that are typically susceptible to cyberattacks. These cyberattacks may come in various forms, including malware attacks, denial-of-service attacks, and data intrusion. As more organizations depend on interdependent technologies, the threat to cybersecurity has never been more pronounced, necessitating an active method of protecting sensitive data and ensuring business resilience.

Figure 1.13. Cybersecurity in IIoT.

Source: https://external-content.duckduckgo.com/iu/?u=https%3A%2F%2Fawbi.org%2Fwp-content%2Fuploads%2F2025%2F02%2F1736489594255.jpeg&f=1&nofb=1&ipt=04132e0dd5f1d03c78788aab6f4143719487db7e138674e4476556d0dbbbf651.

Implementing strong cybersecurity measures is essential not only to avoid information breach but also for guaranteeing confidence in the technology driving the industrial economy. Additionally, the IIoT cybersecurity environment necessitates ongoing research and development in the direction of implementing good defense systems. According to recent literature, the industries must identify potential loopholes in their infrastructures and develop a subset of technologies that attack such vulnerabilities. Security practices must catch up with the evolving landscape of threats by continuously revising employee training and awareness within organizations. Organizations must invest in securing devices and networks, applying encryption, and keeping systems updated. As elaborated in current research, such an integrated understanding of cybersecurity not only mitigates threats but improves the resilience of the organization towards potential cyberattacks, and the security culture encompasses the whole industrial ecosystem (Anglano et al., 2018). Despite general fear of potential cyberattacks, experts remain hopeful about the future of IIoT integration, citing that innovation will persist even amidst risks associated with it. The interconnectivity facilitated by IIoT continues to generate valuable insights, making industries more efficient and productive. However, the optimism does not eliminate the need for strong cybersecurity measures. Secure systems of dealing with vulnerabilities must be established to prevent outages and privacy attacks that could drain the confidence of stakeholders. Trends are that as IIoT infrastructure becomes larger, cybersecurity will be a critical issue that needs constant attention and enhancement. By giving priority to protecting connected industrial devices and networks, industries can realize the benefits of IIoT while efficiently mitigating its associated cybersecurity threats (Anderson et al., 2017) (Figure 1.13).

1.4.2. Integration with Legacy Systems

The integration of legacy systems with Industrial Internet of Things (IIoT) technologies is a significant challenge for industries implementing smart manufacturing processes. Legacy systems, although stable and reliable in nature, pose an impediment to the implementation of new IIoT solutions because the interoperability is low and the architectures are backward-oriented. Organizations must now deal with the complexity of bringing new IoT devices into these legacy systems, which were not designed to host real-time data exchange or advanced analytics. With businesses now relying increasingly on real-time insight from IIoT applications to inform operations, the need to create an unbroken link between these heterogeneous technologies has become critical to maintaining operating efficiency as well as competitiveness. To ease the integration, companies are leveraging several strategies to modernize their infrastructure without much disruption. Upgrading piece by piece or phased replacement of older elements can reduce risks that accompany revolutionizing entire systems simultaneously. For instance, in mining, NIOSH researchers reported that existing installed communications systems in U.S. underground coal mines require little modification to support IIoT applications, indicating one potential path for integration (N/A). Such a phased integration allows organizations to introduce IIoT technology without the tremendous up-front capital investment needed to replace an entire system, a viable option for several industries. In addition, industries like railways are seriously exploring how IIoT can enhance operations with their existing systems. Departing from legacy communications technologies like GSM-R to modern-day solutions such as LTE and 5G is the pinnacle of an adept migration strategy that is backward-compatible. Technological innovations of wireless sensor networks and predictive maintenance create opportunities not only to raise the operational efficiency but also to ensure safety and reliability within established paradigms (Castedo et al., 2017). This end-to-end integration, caring for new and existing systems, shows how companies can become modernized without discarding existing technology investments. With such accommodations, industries can effectively overcome the hurdles offered by legacy systems and gain access to the transformative potential of IIoT.

1.4.3. Data Privacy Concerns

In IIoT contexts, data privacy has become a pressing concern with the growing interconnected nature of contemporary industrial systems. Traditionally, safety-focused industrial control systems were housed within isolated environments, called air gaps, that afforded some degree of security from unauthorized access. Advances in technology have diminished this division, with industrial systems now linking to enterprise networks for optimizing operations and facilitating improved decision-making. Therefore, the risk of cyberattacks against such interconnected systems has increased massively, creating deep data privacy concerns for organizations that are reliant on IIoT technology. The recent vulnerabilities targeted in critical infrastructures indicate the significance of good security standards in order to guard against malicious exploitation of sensitive operational data (Evangelopoulou et al., 2017).

Furthermore, the complexity underlying data privacy in IIoT systems is compounded by the decentralized and dynamic characteristics of IIoT networks. Achieving Security, Privacy, Dependability, and Interoperability (SPDI) is key to realizing the highest performance of IIoT applications, yet one that is far from easily attainable. Such requirements need to be delineated not only during the systems design process but also sustained throughout its operational life. Throughout IIoT orchestrations, security mechanisms are built-in to counter those vulnerabilities that can arise post-deployment. This is complexity that needs SPDI issues to be addressed methodically by frameworks so that organizations are able to monitor and respond to threats against privacy on a continuous basis (Fysarakis et al., 2019). Moreover, data privacy problems in IIoT are not only technical but also ethical as well as regulatory. Companies must navigate a labyrinth of compliance requirements, often set by local and international laws on data protection and privacy. With businesses collecting massive amounts of data from factory processes, they also have to protect personal data against intrusions. Failure to comply with such regulations not only subjects them to financial loss but can also lead to depletion of reputation capital. Therefore, it is important for companies to adopt overall data governance strategies, considering privacy concerns in the design and operation of IIoT systems. Properly addressing these matters will not only increase the stakeholders' trust but also secure the future of IIoT technologies in industrial applications (Figure 1.14).

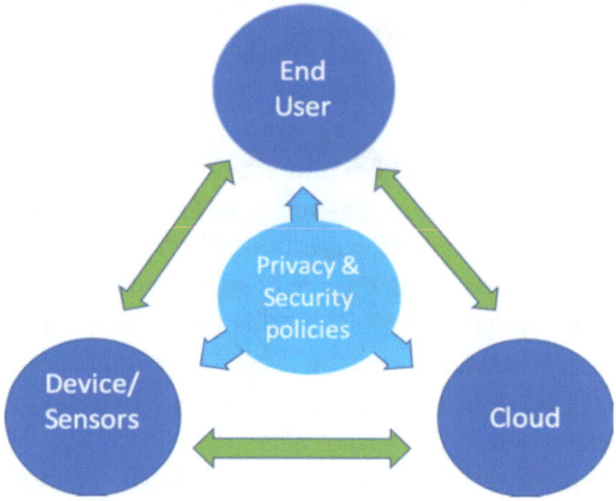

Figure 1.14. IoT privacy and security.

Source: https://www.mdpi.com/applsci/applsci-10-04102/article_deploy/html/images/applsci-10-04102-g001.png.

1.5. APPLICATIONS OF IIOT ACROSS INDUSTRIES

Industrial Internet of Things (IIoT) has introduced revolutionary use cases across industry verticals, transforming the landscape of traditional manufacturing environments. Perhaps the largest aspect of IIoT is that it makes possible smart factories with interconnected machines and systems that enable real-time data sharing. This integration makes possible higher monitoring and automation of the manufacturing process, and this factor directly influences efficiency and productivity. For instance, companies can make use of predictive maintenance procedures that involve data analytics in order to foresee equipment breakdown and hence minimize downtime, as well as reduce operational costs. Such applications tie in with the larger concepts of the Fourth Industrial Revolution in which concepts such as Cyber-Physical Systems significantly redefine manufacturing processes and logistic activities, promoting environments that reflect higher flexibility and sensitivity to shifts in market needs (Ahmad et al., 2017). Aside from manufacturing, the IIoT also inherently has applications in the healthcare sector, where it places on the limelight the intersection of technology and patient care. IoT sensor-imbedded devices can monitor vital signs, offer real-time observation of patient conditions, and allow remote consultations, thereby enhancing healthcare delivery. This aspect not only enhances patient outcomes but also facilitates the use of resources in hospitals. The data collected can make the healthcare professionals aware of the trends and improve the working efficiency without compromising the quality. Further, the shared platforms facilitated by IIoT allow easy data exchange among various stakeholders, thus facilitating more patient-oriented healthcare systems that adapt to the demands of the users. Lastly, the use of these IIoT applications reflects commitment to healthcare innovation, generating service delivery and patient engagement enhancements with the guarantee that vulnerabilities in data security are adequately responded to Kauffman et al. (2018). Similarly, logistics are benefitted by these IIoT applications, enhancing supply chain management as well as operations through better visibility and control. Intelligent systems now allow businesses to track shipments in real-time, getting critical data on inventory levels, transportation status, and customer patterns. With analytics drawn from IIoT technologies, logistics companies can forecast disruptions, route-optimize, and automate procedures, generating significant cost savings. Advanced smart warehousing systems using automation and IoT sensors can also further streamline inventory management, enabling efficient storage and retrieval of products. With an increasing number of industries adopting IIoT, the ability to enable networked systems that trigger interfirm collaboration and knowledge sharing will be heightened, thus driving an era in which logistics is becoming increasingly efficient and responsive to changing market conditions, aligning operational habits with the demands of a fast-paced global economy (Ahmad et al., 2017) (Figure 1.15).

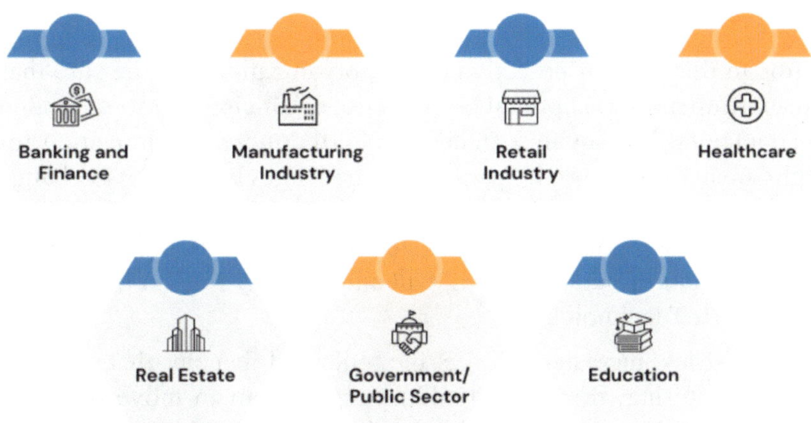

Figure 1.15. IoT application across Industries.

Source: https://prakashinfotech.com/wp-content/uploads/2024/03/iot-applications-across-industries.png.

1.5.1. Manufacturing and Production Optimization

Manufacturing operations over the recent past are significantly influenced by advancements in Industrial Internet of Things (IIoT) technologies. The objective of attaining greater efficiency is facilitated through convergence of IIoT with manufacturing operations, enabling real-time monitoring and control of manufacturing systems. This data-driven approach not only provides insights into areas of inefficiency but also motivates implementation of new strategies to enhance overall capacity for production. As sustainability becomes a focal point, manufacturers are being increasingly pushed by the imperative to implement energy-conserving technologies and maximize the utilization of resources.

Companies can achieve energy-saving potential using IIoT, as stated in available literature that explores methods of enhancing energy efficiency in manufacturing systems (Casta et al., 2019). Greater production efficiency is essential for companies to compete while maintaining pace with environmental governance. Moreover, the application of IIoT technologies within industrial settings allows for greater flexibility and adaptability to customer requirements. As customer preferences evolve, manufacturers with the capabilities of IIoT solutions are able to adjust production schedules easily using real-time demand data, thus reducing downtime and minimizing waste. The ability to collect and analyze vast amounts of data translates to a more elastic manufacturing process by which preventive maintenance can be accomplished to avoid equipment failures.

Through this kind of proactive action, organizations can be sure that their machines are operating at optimal levels, hence enhancing the rate of productivity and guaranteeing high-quality standards. Furthermore, the transition towards the deployment of Industry 4.0 paradigms challenges businesses to change their business models, bringing them in line with the potentiality of IIoT, further allowing for a more sustainable production approach (Cuevas et al., 2017). Finally, the future of manufacturing will significantly rely on the optimization potentials of IIoT technologies.

As industries increasingly see the potential benefit that accompanies smart manufacturing, there is a building momentum to move towards more sophisticated wireless communications such as 5G that will enhance connectivity and enable ultra-low latency services. This is going to unlock new avenues for innovation and efficiency since manufacturers will be able to communicate smoothly with various components of their supply chain and production lines. The support infrastructures for these emerging technologies will need to be heavily invested in, but the potential for the creation of low-cost and innovative models of delivery is substantial. Not only does this transition hold the promise of optimizing traditional means of production, but it also opens a new era of manufacturing that is responsive, energy efficient, and paired with sustainable industrial practices (Casta et al., 2019; Cuevas et al., 2017).

1.5.2. Supply Chain Management and Logistics

The use of Industrial Internet of Things (IIoT) technologies in supply chain management (SCM) and logistics is a paradigm shift in operational efficiency and effectiveness. IIoT facilitates real-time data collection and analysis, using which companies can monitor supply chain activity in real time. Real-time access to information allows organizations to make informed decisions, optimize inventory levels, and better forecast demand. Since businesses have been seeking means to enhance their competitive edge, the application of IIoT can make operations easier through coordination between manufacturers, suppliers, and distributors. Through linked devices and sensors, businesses not only reduce operation costs but also enhance customer satisfaction through timely delivery and improved product quality. Additionally, the integration of IIoT in SCM and logistics systems offers substantial insights into the complexities of supply chain analytics. According to recent research, logistics as a discipline has historically been a leader in the use of analytics techniques but lags behind on certain relative rates if other industries are used for comparison. The domain-specific supply chain analytics characteristics must be understood since they can have the influence to affect the application of analytics projects for supply chain functions in a wider manner. Literatures identify that there are certain success drivers and hurdles in supply chain analytics that need to be tackled to facilitate effective resource optimization as well as process improvements (Herden et al., 2020). Hence, it is critical for a thorough comprehension of such domain-specific characteristics to facilitate organizations to capture the full potential of IIoT technologies in optimizing their SCM operations. Moreover, the influence of IIoT on supply chain logistics extends beyond the costs of operations; it also facilitates creating resilient supply chains that are capable of dealing with sudden disturbances. For instance, interruptions such as natural disasters or global pandemics have enormous effects on supply chains, rendering traditional methodologies insufficient to manage. Implementing IIoT technologies equips firms with the resistance necessary to handle such uncertainty through more predictive analytics and risk management capabilities. The ability to trace shipments in real time and monitor equipment health minimizes lag times and minimizes risks associated with supply chain risks. As industries adapt through the complexities of international manufacturing and distribution, adoption of IIoT can facilitate greater flexibility and responsiveness of supply chain logistics to make organizations competitive and agile within an ever-changing market landscape (Chiew et al., 2017) (Figure 1.16).

Figure 1.16. IoT in supply chain management and logistics.

Source: https://www.scnsoft.com/blog-pictures/internet-of-things/iot-supply-chain-management-and-logistics.png.

1.5.3. Energy Management and Smart Grids

The evolution from traditional power grids to smart grids is a paradigm shift in energy management. Traditional grids operate primarily based on a uni-directional flow of electricity and information, decelerating efficiency and flexibility to changing consumer needs. Smart grids provide a bi-directional flow, where not just is there the supply of energy, but also real-time exchange of usage data between service providers and consumers. This innovation addresses such daunting challenges as energy wastage, reliability, and security, prompted by increasing demand for electricity. Smart grids apply devices to monitor and control energy flow through IoT integration, supporting greater energy management functionalities required for modern industrial processes (Copeland et al., 2019). The integration of IoT devices into the smart grid enables the creation of energy management systems through enhanced monitoring and predictive analytics. Smart meters, sensors, and actuators are deployed throughout the grid infrastructure to provide real-time data on energy usage and grid performance. Consumers and utility companies can optimize energy usage, reduce costs, and react to fluctuating energy needs dynamically based on data collection. Furthermore, analysis of data obtained from the collected devices offers better decision-making through forecasting the energy needs and offering electric mobility, battery storage, and use of renewable energy more efficiently. Integration of IoT systems with energy management hence supports a sustainable and energetic energy system that satisfies the requirements of the current environmental and economic demands (Afonso et al., 2023). With the changing energy management landscape, challenge-related issues and ensuring the long-term robustness of smart grids take precedence of importance. The incorporation of renewable energy sources into smart grids brings with it opportunities alongside challenges, primarily of consistency and reliability of energy supply. Other issues of cybersecurity, data privacy, and device interoperability between different grid systems have to be researched meticulously. The ongoing R&D in the field of IoT plays an important role in overcoming these challenges and enhancing the efficiency of smart grids. While industries evolve, it becomes imperative that they implement forward-thinking strategies employing IoT technologies to further simplify energy management principles. This collaborative effort will ultimately help develop more sustainable business processes and a more resilient energy infrastructure that can support future development and environmental objectives (Copeland et al., 2019; Afonso et al., 2023) (Figure 1.17).

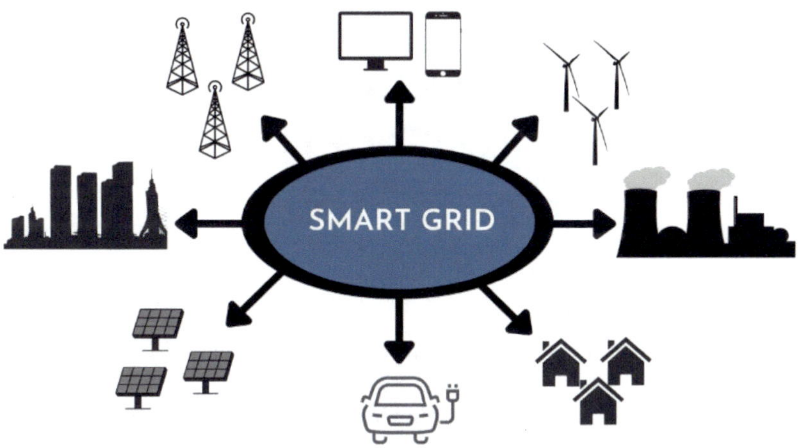

Figure 1.17. Smart grid in IoT.

Source: https://media.licdn.com/dms/image/v2/D5612AQFL8y1l1iW0dA/article-cover_image-shrink_720_1280/article-cover_image-shrink_720_1280/0/1711789260925?e=2147483647&v=beta&t=hVhtHcMf2fmxwTNybf3tBVcoZBoTcM-veOHzsnZZ8Ds.

1.6. FUTURE TRENDS IN IIOT

The future of Industrial Internet of Things (IIoT) will be determined significantly by the integration of big data analytics (BDA) with IIoT infrastructures. As industries continue installing dozens of sensors and IoT devices, industrial data created will be at record proportions. Such a flood of data presents opportunities alongside challenges; whereas BDA has the potential to transform raw data into useful insights on the operational and customer levels, integrating these analytics into current IIoT frameworks is not easy. Prospective research will probable focus on creating new algorithms and techniques that allow intelligent decision-making and timely responses in the context of IIoT. These advancements not only will enhance operational efficiencies but also will provide a competitive advantage to companies that can leverage BDA to enhance their IIoT systems (Imran et al., 2019).

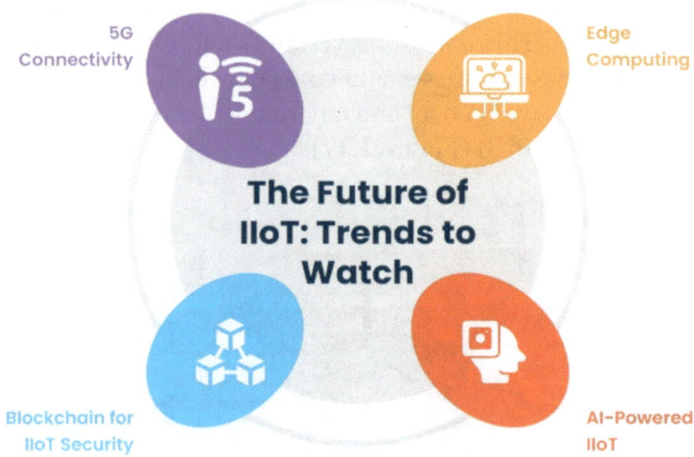

Figure 1.18. The future of the industrial internet of things (IIoT).

Source: https://www.hashstudioz.com/blog/wp-content/uploads/2024/09/future-of-iiot-1060x816.webp.

In addition to BDA, increased application of other innovative technologies such as artificial intelligence (AI) and machine learning (ML) in IIoT structures is likely to transform industrial processes. AI and ML can enable the processing and interpretation of large amounts of data more efficiently, making predictive maintenance, quality assurance, and supply chain optimization possible. AI and ML will make automation intelligent, where machines not only execute tasks but also learn from the surroundings and improve with time. With the industrial arena transitioning towards these latest technologies, businesses will be required to deal with the consequences of technology implementation, such as employee development, cybersecurity challenges, and ethical concerns surrounding autonomous decision-making. Collaborative work between interdisciplinary fields of networking, computing, and industrial automation will become essential for ensuring proper implementation of these technologies in IIoT (Conti et al., 2019). Also, new trends in IIoT will likely emphasize data management and inter-operability among industrial systems. As more devices become connected, the data volume, variety, and criticality will gain prominence. Addressing these challenges will require robust architectural designs that enable efficient coordination and computation of data for the entire industrial ecosystem. Industry must prioritize the creation of protocols and standards that allow seamless communication between heterogeneous platforms and devices to enhance the overall functionality of the IIoT system. Research efforts must also extend beyond to investigate new data-centric services that provide higher scalability and flexibility in industrial setups. Through overcoming these challenges and raising the level of interoperability among interdependent systems, IIoT shall be capable of fulfilling its full potential to create transformative change in manufacturing and industrial automation (Conti et al., 2019) (Figure 1.18).

1.6.1. Advancements in Artificial Intelligence and Machine Learning

The application of artificial intelligence (AI) and machine learning (ML) in the Industrial Internet of Things (IIoT) has enabled significant advances in industrial processes. These technologies enable enormous amounts of data generated by connected devices to be processed, and organizations to provide real-time actionable insights. AI algorithms can recognize patterns and anomalies in operational data to inform predictive maintenance that minimizes downtime and maximizes asset performance. By applying these technologies, businesses can enhance the efficiency of their decision-making and maximize the efficiency of operations. The combination of AI, ML, and IIoT harmoniously together not only induces productivity but also facilitates the development of new production practices that are critical in terms of meeting increasing requirements for high-quality products, as indicated in recent research on precision machining (Benardos et al., 2017). Besides, the smart factory concept is a direct reflection of the way advancements in AI and ML are transforming traditional manufacturing paradigms. Such environments are increasingly being automated to facilitate the smart control of production lines and logistics systems. It is done by embedding Cyber-Physical Systems (CPS) that continuously monitor and analyze operations. With Industry 4.0, the convergence of IIoT technologies and AI becomes the key to the development of knowledge-based environments that generate customized products efficiently. The revolutionary character of these technologies is highlighted by their capabilities to aggregate big data analytics and cloud services, hence making the organizations responsive to the new demands of the marketplace and maintaining high productivity rates (Ahmad et al., 2017). Furthermore, these advancements signal a period of novel industrial labor in which human employees will collaborate with smart technologies to power facility performance. AI and ML are not only automating routine tasks but support human choice by using intellectual systems that predict outcomes from past data. This interoperation between man and machine signifies a movement towards an improved and more productive labor force capable of grappling with complex challenges. As IIoT ecosystems continue to evolve, the contributions of AI and ML will be at the forefront of shaping industrial practice in the future. Lastly, the cumulative effect of the technology guarantees supply chains to be optimized, operational expenditures lowered, and industrial productivity as a whole enhanced, reasserting their pivotal position in today's industrial revolution.

1.6.2. The Impact of 5G Technology on IIoT

The arrival of 5G technology is going to change the landscape of Industrial Internet of Things (IIoT) significantly. With its guarantee of very high speeds, low latency, and the ability to connect a great number of devices simultaneously, 5G overcomes some of the inherent challenges that have typically bedeviled the realization of IIoT systems. For instance, 5G's enhanced data transmission rate facilitates real-time decision-making and analytics, a necessity in industrial applications where timely response has an impact on operational safety and efficiency. Furthermore, 5G's enhanced connectivity enables greater sensor and device integration into the industrial environment, therefore boosting the amount of data that can be collected and analyzed, which is essential in gaining end-to-end insights into manufacturing processes. The impact of 5G on IIoT also comprises improved IIoT industrial communication security and reliability. As IIoT systems become more complex, defending sensitive data becomes more critical. 5G facilitates support for advanced security protocols and procedures needed to safeguard information at various layers of the IIoT stack. By satisfying the essential requirements such as Security, Privacy, Dependability, and Interoperability (SPDI), 5G can enable IIoT infrastructures to be more secure against cyber-attacks. The framework envisioned in research studies has been centered on emphasizing the necessity of optimally orchestrating these characteristics within IIoT systems so that not only security controls are established but also actively monitored throughout the running of the systems (Fysarakis et al., 2019). This security-focused strategic focus is essential to the future growth and acceptance of IIoT technology. Furthermore, the advent of 5G technology opens the door to innovative applications long hindered by network capability. For instance, the reduced latency factor of 5G enables high-end features such as remote control of robotics and autonomous equipment, which can be a necessity in risky settings like manufacturing or logistics. The ability to control operations remotely with minimal latency means there is increased productivity and flexibility in industrial processes. Additionally, with the increased focus on edge and fog computing models converging, the interaction with 5G can be used to facilitate the processing of high amounts of data generated by IIoT devices locally in order to ease the load on central servers and enhance real-time analytical capabilities (Butun et al., 2018). Thus, the intersection of IIoT and 5G not just increases operational effectiveness but also provokes the pursuit of cutting-edge applications among various industry domains (Figure 1.19).

Figure 1.19. 5G technology on IIoT.

Source: https://assets-160c6.kxcdn.com/wp-content/uploads/2023/08/2023-08-22-en-de-1.jpg.

1.6.3. Sustainability and Environmental Considerations

Growing use of Industrial Internet of Things (IIoT) technologies has been a key driver of enhancing sustainability within the manufacturing environment. With industries transforming into effective and sustainable operations, IIoT facilitates the identification of energy-saving possibilities crucial for reducing environmental footprint. The transformation is fueled by the depletion of fossil fuels, increasing energy costs, and stringent regulatory policies aimed at reducing carbon footprints. Here, IIoT enables manufacturers to optimize energy use and resource management through the utilization of data analysis and real-time monitoring that supports more cognitive decision-making. By optimizing energy efficiency strategy in manufacturing systems, IIoT not only leads to cost reductions but also stimulates a sustainable operating paradigm that helps realize the world's environmental agendas (Casta et al., 2019). Furthermore, additive manufacturing (AM) technology is also emerging as a game changer in enabling sustainability within the IIoT ecosystem. With the capability to support intricate, highly personalized designs, AM processes facilitate efficient production with minimal waste, hence keeping significant environmental costs of the traditional manufacturing process at an absolute minimum. This is in compliance with the Industry 4.0 standards where information technologies and smart manufacturing systems are integrated to promote sustainability. The AM processes also contribute to sustainability because they accommodate decentralized manufacturing methods that reduce transportation emissions and the expense. As such, AM's role within the paradigm of the IIoT is pivotal inasmuch as it signifies how advanced manufacturing strategy can play a huge role in addressing environmental issues (Dehghanghadikolaei et al., 2019). What the integration of IIoT with sustainable practices does is goes far beyond immediate energy efficiency and waste reduction; they establish a broader organizational culture centered on the environment. As the industries adopt these new technologies, they are also compelled to redefine their entire mode of functioning, from supply chain management to end-product lifecycle. The sustainability focus pushes organizations to keep innovating, ensuring environmental considerations become an integral part of each business decision. This holistic perspective not only increases the company's competitive edge but also drives the world towards a low-carbon economy. Hence, identifying sustainability and ecological aspects in the IIoT protocol is not a matter of choice; it is crucial to the future of the industry, and adherence to these standards ensures long-term sustainability and societal benefit.

SUMMARY

Industrial Internet of Things or IIoT is a revolutionary force in the realm of industrial operations, literally revolutionizing how organizations collect, analyze, and act on data. The proliferation of IoT sensors and devices has spurred the exponential growth of data creation, thus furthering the depth of complexity in controlling the information henceforth. As noted in recent research, while the integration of fog computing with IoT has immense potential for enhancing operational efficiency, it also raises intricate security concerns that require to be addressed (Butun et al., 2018). Organizations must embrace such a shift responsibly by developing robust frameworks that ensure the security of sensitive data while maximizing the benefits accrued through IIoT technologies. Secondly, IIoT implications extend beyond mere process optimization; they also encompass far-reaching security concerns that industry stakeholders must deal with. The growing adoption of focused distributed denial of service attacks and unauthorized access to industrial control systems is a function of the need for strong security measures. Researchers have listed four primary security concerns prevalent in the IIoT ecosystem, which must be solved: offline-to-online infrastructures, temporal dimensions of security, best practice gaps in implementation, and the complexities associated with modern infrastructural systems (Technology et al., 2018). Overcoming these problems is not just important for asset protection but creating trust among customers and stakeholders in this networked world too. Eventually, the cumulative advances in IIoT technology provide an array of opportunities and challenges that need proactive and integrative efforts. As sectors navigate through this challenging landscape, regulatory frameworks such as the EU Network and Information Security (NIS) Directive and the General Data Protection Regulation (GDPR) will play a critical role in defining best practice and compliance. There needs to be substantial dialogue between technologists, policymakers, and industry stakeholders in order for securing and advancing IIoT. Through a common vision of the risks and responsibilities, organizations can convert the challenges into drivers of innovation and resilience in an ever-evolving industrial environment.

With the evolving Industrial IoT (IIoT) landscape, several important observations emerge that emphasize its transformative impact on business processes. At the core of this transformation are essentially the converging IoT technologies, which have proven pivotal in enhancing operational efficiencies and decision-making within businesses. The ability of IoT to manage vast amounts of data virtually redraws traditional paradigms, with businesses being forced to adopt sophisticated IT architectures capable of supporting the burdens of constantly expanding streams of data. It is important to understand such combinations because they fuel economic sustainability and overall productivity in different sectors of the economy, with a resulting constant debate about reforms in operations. This transformation is concurrent with contemporary trends, as companies are encouraged to re-evaluate their functions to embrace the potential provided by IoT technologies, leading to the reorientation of their market strategies and resource management practices (Allioui et al., 2023). Furthermore, the role of Industry 4.0 within the framework of IIoT cannot be exaggerated, as the fourth industrial revolution represents a revolutionary change in various sectors. Industry 4.0 is mostly based on IoT and wireless sensor networks (WSN) to drive automated processes that keep human involvement at a minimum and increase efficiency in production lines. Applications of IIoT vary from environmental monitoring to home automation, which shows the technology's utility in addressing modern issues. A literature systematic review illustrates that great attempts have been made to scrutinize how such technologies impact industries, highlighting opportunities and existing gaps. Most notably, the relationship between WSN and IoT is employed as a foundation for building advanced control systems, hence necessitating the need to investigate security protocols and framework limitations in such networks as new challenges arise when industries evolve (Majid et al., 2022). Finally, overcoming difficulties associated with IIoT implementations is crucial for effective transformation to smart, autonomous industries. Principal research issues are IoT and WSN contributions toward Industry 4.0, along with network security and intrusion issues. With the discipline evolving, such identification allows researchers and experts to proceed with steps that enhance capability in operations while mitigating vulnerability. The gaps in the research identified above point towards areas to be studied further, offering the possibility of innovation in IoT system design, deployment, and security. Synthesizing existing knowledge with an analysis of the current challenges therefore presents a template for future research and development that will ultimately result in sustainable IIoT ecosystem growth (Allioui et al., 2023; Majid et al., 2022).

REFERENCES

1. Adams, R., Alexander, J., Alperovitch, D., Anastasi, G., Anderson, R., Bilge, L., et al. (2018). Avoiding the internet of insecure industrial things. https://core.ac.uk/download/141198917.pdf (accessed on 16th September 2025).
2. Afonso, J. A., Afonso, J. L., & Monteiro, V. D. F. (2023). Internet of things systems and applications for smart buildings. https://core.ac.uk/download/588865618.pdf (accessed on 16th September 2025).
3. Ahmad, I., Alexopoulos, K., Aly, E., Atzori, L., Augusto, O., Bencsáth, B., Botón-Fernández, V., et al. (2017). The intelligent industry of the future: A survey on emerging trends, research challenges and opportunities in Industry 4.0. https://core.ac.uk/download/145192912.pdf (accessed on 16th September 2025).
4. Ali, M., Anjum, A., Devitt, J., et al. (2017). Towards in-transit analytics for Industry 4.0. http://arxiv.org/abs/1710.04121 (accessed on 16th September 2025).
5. Allioui, H., & Mourdi, Y. (2023). Exploring the full potentials of IoT for better financial growth and stability: A comprehensive survey. *Sensors, 23*, 8015. https://doi.org/10.3390/s23198015 (accessed on 16th September 2025).
6. Anderson, J., & Rainie, L. (2017). The Internet of Things connectivity binge: What are the implications? https://core.ac.uk/download/89472988.pdf (accessed on 16th September 2025).
7. Ang, J. H., Flores Saldivar, A. A., Goh, C., et al. (2017). Energy-efficient through-life smart design, manufacturing and operation of ships in an Industry 4.0 environment. https://core.ac.uk/download/82893542.pdf (accessed on 16th September 2025).
8. Anglano, C., Aniello, L., Antinori, A., et al. (2018). The future of cybersecurity in Italy: Strategic focus area. https://core.ac.uk/download/188830442.pdf (accessed on 16th September 2025).
9. Aslam, N., Cao, Y., Hussain, S., et al. (2018). A critical analysis of research potential, challenges and future directives in industrial wireless sensor networks. https://core.ac.uk/download/96885354.pdf (accessed on 16th September 2025).
10. Baaziz, A., Kleiner, A., Feigelson, E. D., Waller, M. A., Boyd, S., Vandermerwe, S., & Zhou, Z. (2015). Big data and the Internet of Things. http://arxiv.org/abs/1503.07092 (accessed on 16th September 2025).

11. Badikyan, H., Leitão, P., Pedrosa, T., et al. (2022). Secure data exchange in Industrial Internet of Things. https://core.ac.uk/download/512050319.pdf (accessed on 16th September 2025).
12. Benardos, P., & Vosniakos, G. C. (2017). Internet of things and industrial applications for precision machining. https://core.ac.uk/download/82925591.pdf (accessed on 16th September 2025).
13. Boyes, H., Cunningham, J., Hallaq, B., et al. (2018). The industrial internet of things (IIoT): An analysis framework. https://core.ac.uk/download/158139219.pdf (accessed on 16th September 2025).
14. Butun, I., Sari, A., & Österberg, P. (2018). Security implications of fog computing on the Internet of Things. http://arxiv.org/abs/1809.10492 (accessed on 16th September 2025).
15. Castedo, L., Fernández-Caramés, T. M., & Fraga-Lamas, P. (2017). Towards the Internet of Smart Trains: A review on Industrial IoT-connected railways. https://core.ac.uk/download/95054341.pdf (accessed on 16th September 2025).
16. Chen, Y., Crespi, N., Lee, G. M., et al. (2025). Industrial Internet of Things based collaborative sensing intelligence: Framework and research challenges. https://core.ac.uk/download/42478188.pdf (accessed on 16th September 2025).
17. Chew, E. K., Gitzel, R., Krueger, M. W., et al. (2015). Integrative service innovation: An industrial use case. https://opus.lib.uts.edu.au/bitstream/10453/41042/4/ABB%2biSIM%2b2015.pdf (accessed on 16th September 2025).
18. Chiew, K. L., Ong, C. T., Tay, K. G., et al. (2017). Simulation of undular bores evolution with damping. https://core.ac.uk/download/17297499.pdf (accessed on 16th September 2025).
19. Conti, M., Passarella, A., & Raptis, T. P. (2019). Data management in Industry 4.0: State of the art and open challenges. http://arxiv.org/abs/1902.06141 (accessed on 16th September 2025).
20. Copeland, R., Crespi, N., Rehmani, M. H., et al. (2019). Internet of Things-aided smart grid: Technologies, architectures, applications, prototypes, and future research directions. http://arxiv.org/abs/1704.08977 (accessed on 16th September 2025).
21. Cuevas, M., Dohler, M., Laya, A., et al. (2017). Business case and technology analysis for 5G low latency applications. https://core.ac.uk/download/96762095.pdf (accessed on 16th September 2025).

22. David, J., De Pessemier, T., Joseph, W., et al. (2019). An efficient genetic method for multi-objective continuous production scheduling in industrial Internet of Things. https://core.ac.uk/download/275703192.pdf (accessed on 16th September 2025).
23. De Poorter, E., Famaey, J., Hoebeke, J., et al. (2020). Survey on wireless technology trade-offs for the industrial Internet of Things. https://core.ac.uk/download/299792107.pdf (accessed on 16th September 2025).
24. Dehghanghadikolaei, A., Emamian, S. S., Fotovvati, B., et al. (2019). The potential of additive manufacturing in the smart factory Industrial 4.0: A review. https://core.ac.uk/download/231748826.pdf (accessed on 16th September 2025).
25. Díaz Castañeda, J. L., & Ocampo-Martínez, C. (2019). Energy efficiency in discrete-manufacturing systems: Insights, trends, and control strategies. https://core.ac.uk/download/288625543.pdf (accessed on 16th September 2025).
26. Evangelopoulou, M., Johnson, C. W., & Pavlova, T. (2017). Applying lessons from cyber-attacks on Ukrainian infrastructures to secure gateways onto the industrial Internet of Things. https://core.ac.uk/download/111557942.pdf (accessed on 16th September 2025).
27. Ewart, P. (2019). A comparison of processing techniques for producing prototype injection molding inserts. https://core.ac.uk/download/322841895.pdf (accessed on 16th September 2025).
28. Frey, M., Gündoğan, C., Kietzmann, P., et al. (2018). Security for the industrial IoT: The case for information-centric networking. http://arxiv.org/abs/1810.04645 (accessed on 16th September 2025).
29. Fysarakis, K., Hatzivasilis, G., Ioannidis, S., et al. (2019). Pattern-driven security, privacy, dependability and interoperability management of IoT environments. https://core.ac.uk/download/322492567.pdf (accessed on 16th September 2025).
30. Guo, Z., Liu, Y., Lv, J., et al. (2018). A framework for smart production-logistics systems based on CPS and industrial IoT. https://core.ac.uk/download/161514346.pdf (accessed on 16th September 2025).
31. Herden, T. T. (2020). Mapping domain characteristics influencing analytics initiatives: The example of supply chain analytics. https://core.ac.uk/download/287885257.pdf (accessed on 16th September 2025).
32. Imran, M., Jayaraman, P. P., Perera, C., et al. (2019). The role of big data analytics in industrial Internet of Things. http://arxiv.org/abs/1904.05556 (accessed on 16th September 2025).

33. Johnson, C. (2016). Securing the participation of safety-critical SCADA systems in the industrial Internet of Things. https://core.ac.uk/download/46664188.pdf (accessed on 16th September 2025).
34. Kauffman, M. E., & Soares, M. N. (2018). Industry 4.0: Horizontal integration and intellectual property law strategies in England. https://core.ac.uk/download/323060346.pdf (accessed on 16th September 2025).
35. Majid, M., Habib, S., Javed, A. R., Rizwan, M., Srivastava, G., Gadekallu, T. R., & Lin, J. C. W. (2022). Applications of wireless sensor networks and Internet of Things frameworks in the Industry Revolution 4.0: A systematic literature review. *Sensors, 22*, 2087. https://doi.org/10.3390/s22062087 (accessed on 16th September 2025).
36. Nguyen, D. C., Ding, M., Pathirana, P. N., Seneviratne, A., Li, J., & Poor, H. V. (2021). Federated learning for Internet of Things: A comprehensive survey. *IEEE Communications Surveys & Tutorials, 23*, 1622–1658. https://doi.org/10.1109/comst.2021.3075439 (accessed on 16th September 2025).
37. Pilloni, V. (2018). How data will transform industrial processes: Crowdsensing, crowdsourcing and big data as pillars of Industry 4.0. https://core.ac.uk/download/pdf/153541025.pdf (accessed on 16th September 2025).
38. Sima, V., Gheorghe, I. G., Subić, J., & Nancu, D. (2020). Influences of the Industry 4.0 revolution on the human capital development and consumer behavior: A systematic review. *Sustainability, 12*, 4035. https://doi.org/10.3390/su12104035 (accessed on 16th September 2025).
39. Tumino, A., Scarpino, C., & Vadruccio, R. (2024). Unveiling Industrial Internet of Things potential for sustainable manufacturing: A Triple Bottom Line approach. https://core.ac.uk/download/657234337.pdf (accessed on 16th September 2025).

CHAPTER 2

FUNDAMENTALS OF EDGE COMPUTING

Contents

INTRODUCTION

The speed of technological growth has brought about the requirement for more powerful computing solutions, and thus Edge Computing was born as a central framework within the general perimeter of cloud architecture. Unlike conventional cloud computing that focuses on centralized data processing in far-off data centers, Edge Computing prioritizes localized processing power near the source of the data. This shift in paradigm addresses latency issues, since data generated by IoT devices can be calculated in real time, significantly improving response time and system performance. Thus, Edge Computing is essential in applications requiring rapid decision-making, such as smart cities and autonomous cars. To that end, Edge Computing technologies have been adopted not just as a process innovation but as a crucial system effectiveness driver that renders previous models unsuitable for modern computing requirements. Underpinning all of this is the Edge Computing architecture that has several layers including edge devices, edge gateways, and cloud services. Edge devices are typically microcontrollers or sensors inserted within various environments, collecting and initially processing data. The edge gateway acts as an in-between and aggregates data from several devices and performs communication with cloud services. This multi-layer approach enables selective data transport, reducing bandwidth usage and enhancing data quality. Consequently, enterprises can attain performance gain as well as cost savings resulting from minimized cloud resource usage. Besides, the use of Edge Computing solutions can enhance security features by limiting the volume of data transmitted to the cloud, thereby reducing potential attack surfaces and augmenting user privacy. Moreover, the effects of Edge Computing go beyond the efficiencies of technology to address some of the most significant social issues. As there is increasing concern about data sovereignty, privacy, and the carbon footprint of enormous data centers, Edge Computing provides real-world solutions. For instance, on-site processing reduces the energy consumed in transmitting vast amounts of information to far-off servers, hence lowering the carbon footprint. This green aspect is particularly pertinent to today's climate-conscious society. Secondly, through offering control of data at the local level, Edge Computing supports adherence to local data privacy regulations, hence keeping companies free from legal liabilities. Its sum total of advantages reveals the revolutionary potential of Edge Computing as an agent of change in the future of computing that combines technical strengths, social needs, and legal contexts.

Definition and Overview of Edge Computing

Edge computing is a paradigm shift for the deployment of computing resources away from the typical heavy reliance on centralized data centers. With edge computing, processing of data takes place near or at the location where data is generated, reducing latency and speeding up the exchange of data, which is particularly beneficial in applications like the Internet of Things (IoT). At the center of this revolution is the fog computing premise, or bringing cloud capacity to the edge of the network. The architecture limits resource waste while cutting down on bandwidth constraints, which means critical information can be processed in real-time. As enterprises continue to integrate IoT solutions into business operations, the effectiveness of edge computing enables the development of sophisticated applications, such as intelligent healthcare monitoring systems. This convergence of technologies is fundamentally reshaping the consumption and processing of information industry by industry. One of the key mantras of edge computing is that it can enable heterogeneous environments composed of numerous distributed devices, each generating enormous amounts of information. This heterogeneity makes it challenging to keep pace with effective data management and processing techniques. As noted in contemporary studies, edge computing allows effective task processing that would otherwise overwhelm centralized systems. Through offering processing power distributed throughout the network, organizations achieve localized insights, hence enhancing decision-making processes. An example is in the use of self-automated health monitoring platforms that utilize this functionality through the utilization of devices that track important health information while also acting as gateways for transmitting data. One such trailblazing approach not only empowers patients but also bridges patient-physician communication gaps, pointing to the potential of edge computing to transform doctor-patient relationships (Akrivopoulos et al., 2017).

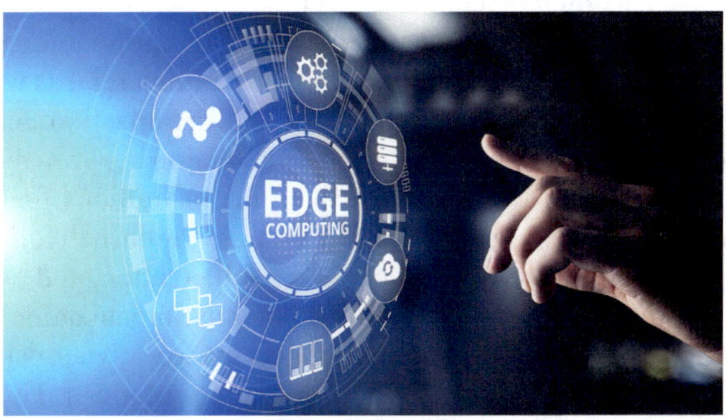

Figure 2.1. Edge computing.

Source: https://innovationatwork.ieee.org/wp-content/uploads/2019/09/bigstock-Edge-Computing-Modern-It-Techn-280957174_1024X684.png.

Beyond the extension of existing applications, the implications of edge computing extend to a new world of innovation for industries. Edge computing technology unlocks a universe of potential, from real-time production analytics to reactive retail customer support. The ability to aggregate and analyze data locally enables an organization's preemptive decision-making culture, improving operational efficiencies. As evident from recent research, harmonious convergence of IoT and edge computing can lead to wiser predictions and responses in various contexts, ranging from supply chains to emergency responders. In the provision of more responsive and agile infrastructures, edge computing not only serves immediate needs but also lays the foundation for future advancements in technology, creating a landscape for exploration and development (Chu et al., 2015) (Figure 2.1).

Historical Context and Evolution

The history of edge computing is intrinsically entangled with the history of data processing and networking technology development. It started in the late 20th century with the fast evolution of the internet and advancements in server capabilities that resulted in a conventional client-server paradigm with computation occurring at centralized data centers. But with the data explosion caused by devices, this model fell under heavy constraints when it involved latency, bandwidth, and real-time processing. With the increasing necessity to overcome these challenges, the idea of edge computing emerged, enabling data processing at places nearer to where data is being generated. This transition emphasized an imperative need to re-engineer the topology of networks and compute resources, leading to a re-designed framework where data centers exist within a multi-layered decentralized architecture. As edge computing evolved, it was clear that its evolution was being propelled by commercial as well as public agendas, suggesting a rich interplay between self-organization and structured methods. Triple Helix model that involves the interaction between the university, industry, and government describes how the three institutions fuel the growth of edge computing technologies. Historical co-operation networks fashioned innovation by allowing novelty production, wealth creation, and even political power in the technology space. Within this dynamic, organization versus self-organization then emerges as a foundation stone, creating a synergistic effect that supports the healthy development of edge computing solutions. This contextual understanding, as it is, not only captures the adaptive nature of technology, which is required, but also illustrates how stakeholders' interests can shape its course to neutralize newly emerging issues and opportunities (Giddens et al., 2012). The latest wave of technological change, and particularly the advent of 5G networks, has further catalyzed the importance of edge computing in digital infrastructure today. Integration of Multi-Access Edge Computing (MEC) will seek to decentralize computation from the traditional cloud to the edge clouds, thereby enhancing the responsiveness and reliability of services. This paradigm shift requires a redefinition of security architectures for mobile networks in the direction of decentralized environments to facilitate more adaptive authentication operations. As technology advancement keeps unfolding, the deployment of a new decentralized authentication framework can facilitate an adaptive manner of managing network components, which is essential to maintaining quality service. The research on these frameworks, based on historical precedent and technical evolution, highlights the ongoing requirement for tailored technology solutions as data traffic increases and low-latency service demand increases (Crippa et al., 2019).

Importance in Modern Computing

In the rapidly evolving paradigm of modern computing, edge computing has emerged as a pivotal enabler of efficient data handling and processing. By decentralizing processing power and moving it closer to data sources, such as IoT devices, edge computing significantly mitigates latency issues typically faced by conventional cloud computing. This architectural change becomes more significant as the spread of IoT devices creates enormous amounts of data that require timely processing. The applications can vary from smart manufacturing to automated health monitoring systems, demonstrating the way real-time data analysis can improve the efficiency of operations and decision-making processes. Most particularly in such instances where real-time responses are most critical, such as in healthcare scenarios where saved ECG information could be analyzed for instant diagnoses, edge computing represents an enormous step forward from current models (Akrivopoulos et al., 2017). The importance of edge computing cannot therefore be overstated, given the fact that it is the foundation stone for future designs. Furthermore, emergence of edge computing provides a means for more scalable and resilient application development within the boundaries of modern computing needs. Convergence of edge and fog paradigms introduces flexibility and redundancy via workload division across multiple nodes in a network, reducing the likelihood of centralized processing risks. This architecture is especially applicable to heterogeneous device environments with variable data processing demands, since it offers adaptive responses to altering conditions. The shift toward distributed processing not only enhances the capacity to process extensive amounts of data but also sustains the heightened need for energy-efficient methods. As there's an increase in demand for organizations to minimize their carbon impact, the potential of edge computing to enhance the utilization of resources without making any sacrifice in terms of performance is exceptional and helps in promoting sustainability in tech practices (Borgo et al., 2006). The implications extend beyond efficiency to the broader societal benefits that address environmental responsibility. With evolving computation architectures, the role of visualization as an inherent component of edge computing is even more prominent. The incorporation of advanced visualization techniques plays an important role in comprehending voluminous data generated by IoT devices in real-time for making informed decisions across various industries. The evolution of functional programming languages provides additional potential for the design and implementation of visualization systems, enhancing their performance with robust type-checking and modularity. These advances not only increase the depiction of data but also optimize cognitive processes that are involved in data interpretation, resulting in quicker insights and enhanced analysis. As data complexities increase, especially where rapid decision-making is essential, efficient visualization along with edge computing methods allows industries to harness their data actively (Borgo et al., 2006). Thus, the continuous interplay between visualization methods and edge computing methods underscores their combined importance in modern computing spaces.

2.1. ARCHITECTURE OF EDGE COMPUTING

The edge computing structure is designed to address the processing demands of the exponential rise in data generated at networks' edges. By placing computing capabilities close to sources of data—such as Internet-of-Things devices—edge computing does away with latency, boosts speed, and improves overall system performance. This decentralization offloads some of the workload of processing to be done away from the cloud servers that are centralized to edge nodes that may range from IoT gateways to dedicated edge servers in proximate environments. This kind of model allows organizations to manage massive amounts of real-time data more effectively, facilitating rapid decision-making processes that are critical in applications such as automated medical surveillance and smart city initiatives. As network demands grow, the need for high-availability edge architecture becomes ever more critical to ensuring that key services operate efficiently and with the smoothness they require. And the overall edge computing architecture raises significant security, reliability, and scale concerns. In their spread of the processing data across multiple nodes, the architecture can avoid potential single points of failure that generally bombard conventional cloud infrastructures. Nevertheless, this deployment brings forth new security concerns, since every edge device can be a point of attack. Therefore, robust security features need to be integrated into the design to protect sensitive data as it traverses devices and centralized infrastructures. There also needs to be scalability requirement, especially with increased Internet of Things (IoT) usage. The architecture must be adaptable to accommodate a variety of applications and services that evolve with hardware and software technological advancement to cope with growing complexity in data analysis and management in edge environments. Apart from coping with real-time data processing and security requirements, the edge computing architecture also has a basic relationship with the science of complex systems. With the dynamic nature characteristic of edge environments, it is important to understand how systems of this nature operate, particularly when the potential for uncertainty and heterogeneity in such configurations is maintained in mind. As emphasized in recent controversy over complex systems, a multidisciplinary approach is essential in designing advanced architectures that optimize seamless communication and efficiency in operations across diverse nodes. Researchers favor new models integrating state-of-the-art mathematical and computational methods, an indication of a developing trend towards inter-disciplinary research to address issues in edge computing environments. Through making architectural design based on the theory of complex systems, the edge computing architecture can transition toward providing smarter, adaptive, and resilient systems that are sensitive to a hyper-connected world (Akrivopoulos et al., 2017; Bourgine et al., 2009) (Figure 2.2).

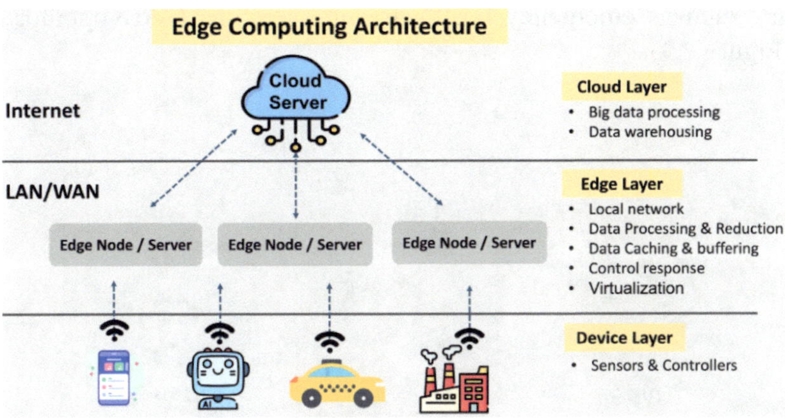

Figure 2.2. Edge computing architecture.

Source: https://www.fsp-group.com/upload/230221-63F436389ECE4.png.

2.1.1. Components of Edge Computing Systems

In the case of edge computing infrastructure, one of the main components is the amalgamation of various devices that support data processing from the source point. This framework significantly enhances the efficiency of handling data by minimizing latency and avoiding heavy volumes of data being passed to core cloud infrastructure. Edge devices like sensors, gateways, and actuators preprocess and collect data locally, maximizing operation, particularly in environments with a high density of Internet of Things (IoT) applications. For instance, real-time monitoring can be managed with the use of wearable devices that track vital signs in the field of healthcare. These setups not only conserve bandwidth but also render systems more secure since confidential data can be processed locally prior to potentially being dispatched out for further processing or storage. Another integral part of edge computing solutions is the role of fog computing as a further extension of cloud characteristics towards the network edge. Fog computing offers a middleman between the edge devices and the cloud, allowing for added computation and storage at the distributed level. This can be beneficial to alleviate the issue of the large number of IoT devices leading to massive volumes of data, an issue that creates immense operational inefficiencies. Greater power of edge processing allows for applications such as automated health monitoring systems, which can utilize data from wearable ECG units to deliver real-time information about patients health condition. The delivery of fog computing allows for real-time data processing, and consequently, this leads to faster responsiveness, particularly where timely responses are necessary such as emergency healthcare interventions (Akrivopoulos et al., 2017) (Figure 2.3).

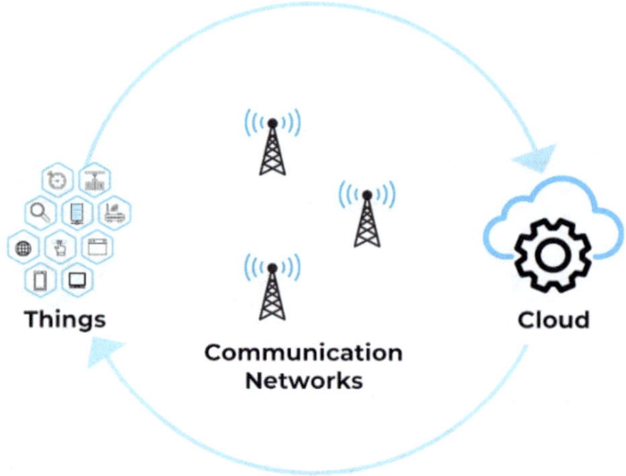

Figure 2.3. Components of edge computing.

Source: https://zd-brightspot.s3.us-east-1.amazonaws.com/wp-content/uploads/2022/01/05125849/Components-of-Edge-Computing-1.jpg.

Apart from that, edge computing platforms have advanced software frameworks to orchestrate and manage data exchanges between disparate devices. These frameworks are key to providing the seamless run of decentralized applications and services. They offer operations such as resource management, data analysis, and access control, which are necessary for ensuring edge devices run harmoniously. For example, algorithms can be developed for an ECG monitoring system that would scan heart activity in real-time, reducing the need for huge cloud resources and prolonging battery life in wearable devices (Akrivopoulos et al., 2017). As edge computing advances, synchronizing hardware capabilities with cutting-edge software solutions will be the key to unleashing the full potential of this technology, paving the way for even more robust and efficient systems in healthcare and beyond.

2.1.2. Comparison with Cloud Computing Architecture

In the case of emerging technologies, the distinction between edge computing and traditional cloud computing framework is gaining increasing prominence. While cloud computing routes data for storage and processing to distant datacenters, edge computing is all about decentralized processing close to the end user. This shift is necessitated by the need for reduced latency and improved response time, particularly in use cases that call for real-time interaction, such as virtual reality and autonomous driving. As per (Anagnostopoulos et al., 2018), placing vNFs at the edge of networks has the effect of significantly lowering end-to-end latency, which is extremely crucial in situations where real-time processing of data is required. In this way, edge computing not only enhances user experience but also takes a portion of traffic off the core networks, leading to efficient utilization of resources across the whole infrastructure. Moreover, the edge computing paradigm better accommodates the changing nature of new Internet of Things (IoT) applications. Traditional cloud computing designs struggle to cope with the sheer amount of data generated by numerous connected devices. Edge computing, on the other hand, facilitates local processing and analysis of data, reducing its dependence on central cloud facilities. This is a critical aspect for real-time decision-making, especially where connectivity may be unpredictable. As has been cited in Akrivopoulos et al. (2017), fog computing, which is a type of edge computing, facilitates this through the aggregation of computational resources from various layers, thereby creating a more responsive system that is built around real-time needs. This form of architecture boosts cross-industry collaborative applications while increasing the functionality and dependability of IoT environments overall. Further, the relative strengths offered by edge computing architectures in maintaining quality of service under shifting network conditions are apparent through their ability to realign vNF scheduling along the edge, as discussed in Anagnostopoulos et al. (2018). This way, an adaptive response to fluctuating latency and user mobility is achieved. By placing computing power close to the user, edge computing can handle latency and bandwidth limitations in a cost-effective way. This real-time responsiveness nature of edge computing is diametrically opposite to the static nature of the conventional cloud models that might not fit as dynamically into real-time requirements. Apart from this, the use of fog computing in

Akrivopoulos et al. (2017) is meant to further enhance the capabilities of edge solutions in terms of delivering a best-in-class distributed platform that fully leverages the Internets large infrastructure for storage and processing of data. This advancement towards edge computing is finally a paradigm shift towards facilitating increased connectivity, usability, and responsiveness in todays increasingly digital world (Figure 2.4).

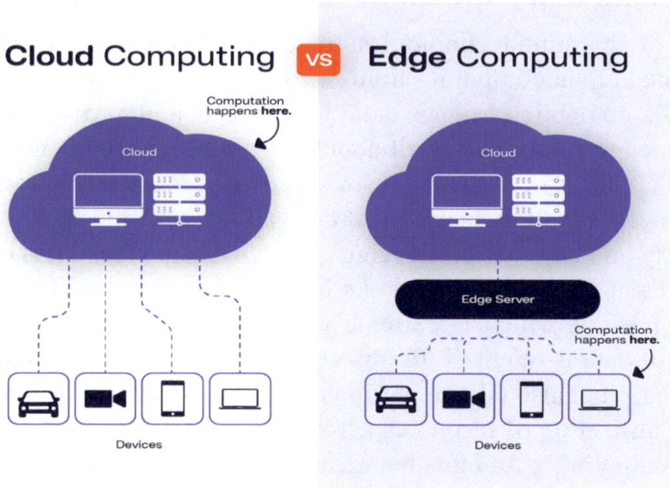

Figure 2.4. The distinction between edge computing and traditional cloud computing architecture.

Source: https://unable-loud-cherry.media.strapiapp.com/Cloud_Computing_vs_Edge_Computing_d6033c7892.jpg.

2.1.3. Role of IoT Devices in Edge Computing

The placement of Internet of Things (IoT) devices in edge computing infrastructure is the driving factor behind making data processing quicker and more responsive. By locating IoT devices close to the edge of a network, data gets processed closer to where it was created, decreasing latency and the burden on core cloud systems. This proximity in the physical sense supports real-time processing, making it particularly beneficial for applications requiring immediate insight, such as autonomous vehicle and industrial automation scenarios. Finally, the offloading of processing operations away from central data centers encourages more fault-tolerant infrastructure since regional decision-making can be performed irrespective of cloud connectivity failures, significantly enhancing operation reliability for mission-critical use cases. One of the vital advancements that have been facilitated by IoT devices in edge computing is the evolution of Smart Grids (SGs). Traditional energy infrastructure is being gradually re-designed into dynamic networks, where IoT devices such as sensors and smart meters form the backbone of monitoring and controlling the distribution of energy. These devices enable two-way communication between energy producers and consumers to provide effective energy distribution and utilization. By incorporating IoT into SGs, utilities can respond promptly to changes in supply and demand, thereby enhancing grid security and reliability. The intermingling of IoT and edge computing not only facilitates expansive data gathering and analysis but also supports rapid reactions to alterations in energy consumption patterns, thereby enhancing the transition towards cleaner energy systems (Copeland et al., 2019) (Figure 2.5).

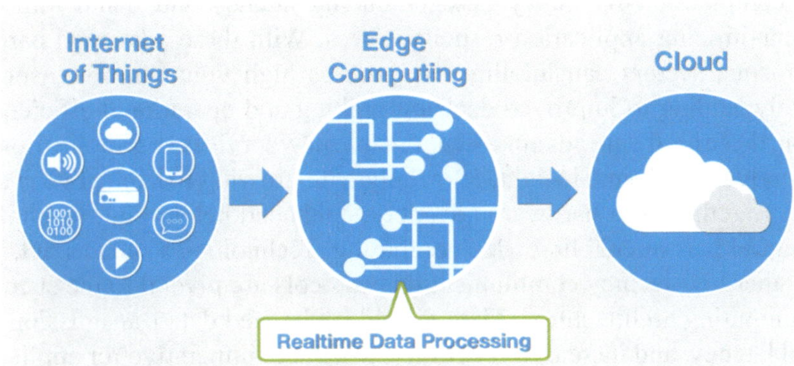

Figure 2.5. The integration of internet of things (IoT) devices within edge computing.

Source: https://www.hiotron.com/wp-content/uploads/2020/01/Edge-Computing.png.

Moreover, the operational usability of an IoT device extends beyond energy systems to cross over into various others like healthcare, transportation, and agriculture. In healthcare, for instance, patient information may be collected at the edge by IoT devices for instant diagnostics and tailored treatment without waiting for cloud processing. In transportation, real-time information about vehicles enhances traffic management systems to make them more efficient and safe. It is supported by precision farming practices propelled by IoT devices, monitoring environmental conditions and thereby enabling efficient use of resources. This co-reliant impact brings the transformative capability of IoT devices into perspective in terms of enhancing the capabilities and implications of edge computing platforms to solidify them in terms of applicability across industries (School of Engineering, 2019).

2.2. KEY TECHNOLOGIES ENABLING EDGE COMPUTING

One of the most significant technologies making it possible to develop edge computing is the low-power hardware development specifically designed for data computations and communications. These advancements imply that devices at the edge of networks can execute calculations that were performed by the cloud-based centralized servers before. The advancements in smaller, more powerful processing devices, such as Field Programmable Gate Arrays (FPGAs) and Application-Specific Integrated Circuits (ASICs), make real-time data analysis at the data generation edge possible. The edge nodes are able to run computationally heavy tasks, reducing latency and bandwidth usage while maximizing application responsiveness. With these advanced hardware deployments, sectors can intelligently process high volumes of sensor data, ultimately leading to improved decision-making and operational efficiency. In addition, these hardware advancements enable new services and applications that heavily rely on real-time insight, especially with growing IoT integration across sectors. Together with hardware advances, enhanced networking technologies are a central part of enabling edge computing. Technologies such as 5G, Wi-Fi 6, and other low-latency communication protocols are pivotal to the success of edge computing architectures. They provide enhanced data transmission rates, reduced latency, and increased reliability, which are imperative for applications such as autonomous driving, remote medicine, and industrial manufacturing. The ongoing growth of 5G networks is particularly remarkable; such technology has the potential to connect hundreds of devices simultaneously, leading to a more connected world. As noted in recent studies, the addition of such networking capability makes information exchange among edge devices more efficient, thus bypassing the bandwidth bottleneck challenges and facilitating real-time analysis and processing. This interconnectedness is vital for achieving the full potential of edge computing applications. Furthermore, context-aware computing is becoming a standard component in taking advantage of the potential of edge computing when it comes to the Internet of Things (IoT). Context-aware systems interpret the gargantuan amount of data generated by sensors into meaningful actions based on the environment that surrounds them. With increasingly widespread use of sensors, similarly there is the demand for efficient data processing that takes many contextual factors into account. To derive value from raw sensor information and make it usable knowledge, context awareness is important. Studies illustrate that context-aware computing can lead to improved accuracy and productivity, especially in automated and real-time decision support systems. This approach points to the nexus of edge computing and IoT, validating the level at which they are integrated in addressing the complexity of the data environments of today and allowing businesses to leverage insights that are brought through holistic data analytics (Zaslavsky et al., 2013).

2.2.1. Edge Devices and Gateways

The convergence of edge devices and gateways is a groundbreaking development in edge computing architecture that makes it possible to process and analyze data in a seamless manner at the source. Edge devices comprising various sensors and IoT devices consume real-time data, thereby avoiding latency and enhancing performance. They process data upfront, reducing the volume of data transmitted to central servers. Gateways are the key to this ecosystem with their positioning as intermediaries between cloud platforms and edge devices, making communication possible.

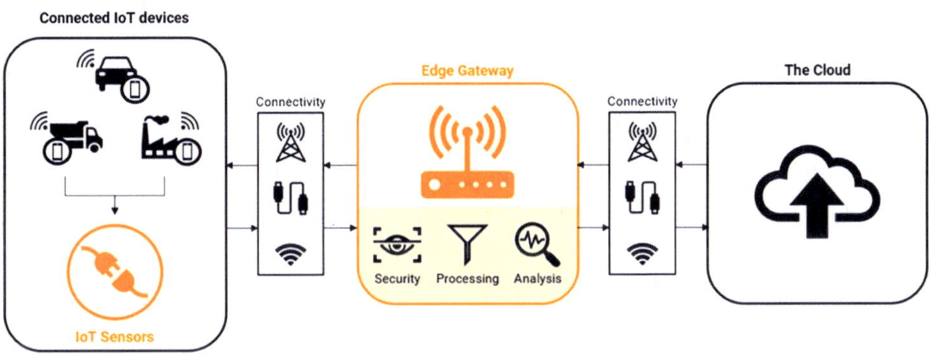

Figure 2.6. Edge gateways.

Source: https://stlpartners.com/articles/edge-computing/edge-gateways-their-role-and-importance/

With their capacity for handling multiple protocols and types of data, gateways offer interoperability support among several devices, which is required for streamlined operation of edge computing systems. As applications demand higher responsiveness, strategic utilization of gateways and edge devices becomes more crucial in achieving high utilization of network resources as well as high service availability. Microservices' architectural pattern also accentuates the significance of gateways in managing complex edge computing-related tasks. Microservices allow developers to create systems that foster software components' independence and decoupling to enable more flexible deployment. Single microservices can execute independent tasks with gateways, which are employed as proxies, encapsulating functionalities such as API management and authentication so that no single service is burdened with it. Modularization, therefore, not only makes a system stronger but also makes services scalable across varying environments. The inclusion of a service proxy framework facilitates the construction of reusable components, like building blocks, that allow for flexibility in assembling services. However, while this architecture pattern has undeniable advantages, it also introduces problems that must be addressed, most notably how to handle the communication between such decoupled components in a networked environment (Gajek et al., 2018) (Figure 2.6). In fast-developing sectors like smart grids, the co-operative functioning of gateways and edge devices becomes evident through the illustration of their vital roles in existing energy infrastructures. Smart grids make extensive use of IoT devices to monitor, analyze, and manage the flow of energy, and therefore need high-speed connectivity for data sharing among remote sources. Gateways function as the key nodes in the network by bi-directional communication between consumers and service providers. It not only enhances energy management reliability but also supports real-time decision-making with data analysis at the network edge. Having the ability to support a number of IoT devices, gateways enable the smart grid to address matters of wastage and energy demand. This alignment of edge computing technologies with smart grids highlights the imperative of endless research and innovation to provide maximum efficiency and security in energy systems (Copeland et al., 2019).

2.2.2. Networking Technologies (5G, Wi-Fi 6)

On the edge computing side, networking technologies such as 5G and Wi-Fi 6 are essential in enhancing the capability of data processing and reducing latency. 5G, with its ultra-reliable low latency communication (URLLC) capability, can revolutionize the way devices communicate with each other in real-time. Such a feature is particularly significant to be utilized in use cases that have instant feedback, such as autonomous vehicles and intelligent manufacturing lines. However, the conventional cellular wireless networks have conventionally been bogged down by inefficiencies, in particular with regard to energy consumption, to the extent of a substantial carbon footprint. As has been seen, improvements in energy utilization, and indeed even at the base stations, can potentially lead to reductions of two orders of magnitude or more. This energy efficiency is not only crucial for environmental sustainability but also to facilitate the increasing demand for mobile traffic projected in the coming years (Ayanoglu et al., 2014) (Figure 2.7).

Similarly, Wi-Fi 6, the latest technology for wireless local area networks, offers superior features that are essential for unobtrusive use cases for edge computing. It has more throughput, higher capacity, and improved performance in dense environments and is therefore ideal for areas with numerous devices connected.

It utilizes various boosts such as Orthogonal Frequency Division Multiple Access (OFDMA) and Multi-User Multiple Input Multiple Output (MU-MIMO) to facilitate enhanced data sharing in crowded places. As businesses continue to integrate edge computing applications in an effort to process information closer to the point where it is generated, Wi-Fi 6 plays an even more vital role. Feature of multi-connection handling is guaranteed to allow edge devices to execute at their best, thus raising the overall performance of the computing platform (Hanzo et al., 2016).

Figure 2.7. 5G and Wi-Fi 6.

Source: https://www.tatacommunications-ts.com/wp-content/uploads/2024/01/5g-wireless-together-1.jpg.

Furthermore, the integration of sophisticated security aspects in these networking technologies is vital in securing the rising number of connected devices. As the very nature of wireless communications is open in nature, the 5G as well as the Wi-Fi 6 are exposed to various security threats and thus necessitate advanced defense mechanisms. It is important that these technologies not only focus on improving speed and capacity but also maintain authenticity, confidentiality, and integrity of data transmissions. Physical-layer security techniques are a strong direction towards the additional protection of data transmissions against possible eavesdropping and jamming attacks. With these networking technologies continuing to evolve, it is essential that their innovation be harmonized with top-down security controls and standards to efficiently safeguard edge computing environments and seal off sensitive data in the more integrated digital environment (Hanzo et al., 2016).

2.2.3. Data Processing and Storage Solutions

Data processing and storage solutions transform at the center of edge computing. Cloud platforms face tremendous issues in handling the massive volume of data introduced by the Internet of Things (IoT). Edge computing addresses such issues by shifting data processing closer to data origination sources. This decentralized approach not only reduces latency but also conserves bandwidth and facilitates on-time data examination and decision-making. That is why this approach enhances the overall performance of applications, especially real-time processing applications such as autonomous vehicles and smart cities. With the proliferation of IoT devices, it is more crucial than ever to provide real-time communication and data handling capabilities at the edge, thereby enabling innovative applications in industrial automation and healthcare, among other sectors. Data sharing and device collaboration are one of the major benefits that edge computing can provide. With the implementation of network edge resources such as processing capacity and memory space, devices can be made to work in partnership. This would be particularly beneficial for health monitoring systems, where devices would be able to collect and analyze vital signs locally before the information needed is relayed to authorized personnel for further review. For instance, a proof-of-concept with a smartphone being used as a Fog gateway illustrates the sharing of health data securely by patients in real time and ensures optimization of communication between patients and doctors. Access to more historical data fosters a better understanding of health patterns, which eventually can lead to improved medical diagnoses and patient care (Akrivopoulos et al., 2017). The integration of Fog computing in data processing and storage solutions provides a more adaptive and fault-tolerant platform for leveraging the benefits of IoT technologies. Unlike traditional cloud-centric solutions, Fog computing provides a distributed architecture where edge devices can perform considerable computations. This model is crucial for industries that want to leverage data-driven insights without compromising latency or performance. For instance, pilot adoption in various fields has illustrated how this hybrid architecture facilitates better resource management and enables efficient data processing. With real-time analytical capabilities at the edge, organizations can react to varying environmental conditions promptly, enhancing operational efficiency. The findings point out the potential of Fog computing in addressing the growing challenges of volume and complexity of data within an increasingly interconnected world (Akrivopoulos et al., 2017).

2.3. APPLICATIONS OF EDGE COMPUTING

The applications of edge computing are rapidly transforming various industries, particularly in environments where real-time processing of data is critical. One instance is how manufacturing can gain real-time analysis of the data that is generated by machines on the shop floor through the application of edge computing, resulting in reduced latency and increased operational efficiency. With edge computation, organizations can directly detect anomalies and handle issues before they are a problem, thus optimizing production lines and reducing downtime. Edge computing also simplifies predictive maintenance, where devices can forecast failures using real-time analysis, ultimately reducing costs and enhancing productivity. The seamless transmission of data increases responsiveness, pointing to the fact that edge computing is a visionary for industrial innovation. In smart healthcare, edge computing plays an important role in revolutionizing patient monitoring as well as data management.

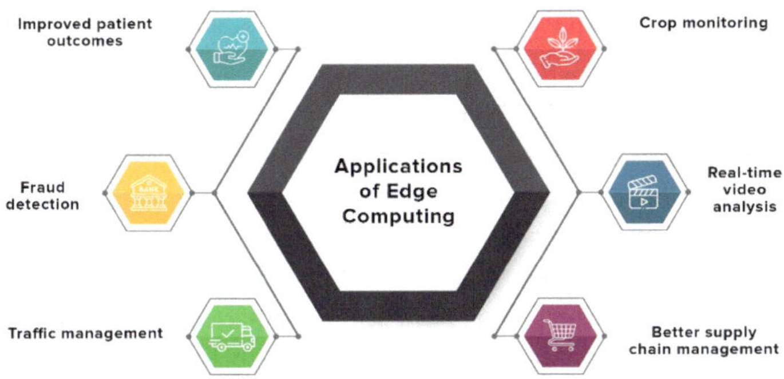

Figure 2.8. Applications of edge computing.

Source: https://insights.daffodilsw.com/hs-fs/hubfs/Applications%20of%20Edge%20Computing.jpg?width=3229&height=1667&name=Applications%20of%20Edge%20Computing.jpg.

Through the deployment of Internet of Things (IoT) devices, healthcare systems are in a position to gain vast volumes of data from sensors and wearables and provide valuable information concerning the health of patients. With edge computing, critical health information can be processed locally in real-time, enabling healthcare professionals to take rapid, informed decisions. An example of such a prototype healthcare monitoring platform captures ECG traces through a device connected to a patient's phone as a Fog gateway and forwards it securely to concerned stakeholders. This paradigm of distribution not just optimizes the immediacy of healthcare monitoring but also empowers patients to take charge of their health, revealing the transformative potential of edge computing in healthcare (Akrivopoulos et al., 2017). The impact of edge computing on smart cities is also tremendous, particularly in the context of optimizing urban infrastructure and facilities. By enabling real-time processing of data from various IoT devices deployed in urban environments, edge computing supports better traffic management, waste management, and public safety initiatives. For instance, on the basis of real-time analytics, cities can redistribute traffic lights based on prevailing conditions to reduce traffic or monitor environmental data to identify hotspots of pollution. These applications will help achieve a more sustainable city by optimizing resource utilization and enhancing citizens' quality of life. Additionally, this technology also spurs innovation in automated technologies, allowing faster emergency response time and more responsive cities to citizens' needs. The more digital-intensive cities become, edge computing will surely be an essential in achieving smarter and more efficient living spaces (Figure 2.8).

2.3.1. Smart Cities and Infrastructure

In the new paradigm of urban development, the emergence of smart cities has profoundly reshaped the management of infrastructure. Beneath the new paradigm is the application of edge computing, which increases the responsiveness and efficiency of urban services through localized processing. By positioning computing resources close to the sources of data generation, edge computing addresses the major challenges of latency, bandwidth use, and reliability. In smart cities, this is particularly critical since services have to respond in real time to the varied demands of urban lifestyles. Traffic systems and public transport information in real time, for instance, are based on data that are locally computed, minimizing delays and enhancing the user experience. The incorporation of edge computing into city infrastructures thus forms a solid foundation for addressing complexities related to urban lifestyles today. Furthermore, Internet of Things (IoT) application in smart cities cannot be overstated. IoT devices are at the center of gathering and reporting data for a wide range of applications, ranging from environmental monitoring to energy management. The value of such applications relies on how well unprecedented amounts of sensor data are synthesized. Edge computing enables this sensor fusion through source-side data processing, independent of centralized cloud infrastructure. This new model is particularly apparent in the scenario of smart city projects, where heterogeneous data streams have to be processed for efficient decision-making and resource management. Research indicates that a good sensor data fusion testbed framework can significantly enhance the performance of these applications. Thus, edge computing not only improves IoT capabilities but also reinforces the infrastructure behind smart city projects (Perera et al., 2015). The transition to edge computing in smart cities is not, however, smooth. The heterogeneity of edge devices creates resource management and system compatibility complexities. The same devices may have differing computational capacities and operational requirements, necessitating an elastic approach in infrastructure design. Also, while the benefits of improved Quality of Service (QoS) are substantial, the inherent complexity of handling edge environments can pose insurmountable barriers. An end-to-end process model for edge-native application development is necessary to ensure a seamless integration into smart city frameworks. These models can provide suggestions that mitigate the issues of heterogeneous structures and resource constraints, hence leading to enhanced performance and smart urban infrastructure sustainability (Bub et al., 2025) (Figure 2.9).

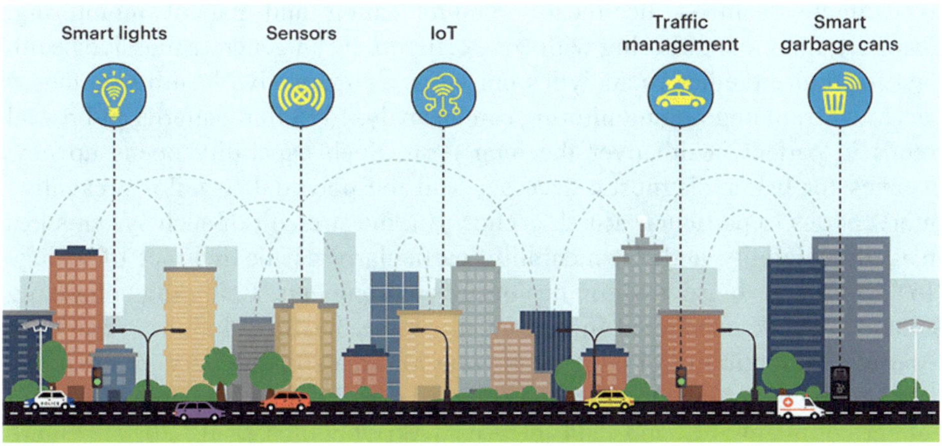

Figure 2.9. Edge computing the key to developing smart cities.

Source: https://stormagic.com/wp-content/uploads/2023/03/IoT_smart_city.png.

2.3.2. Healthcare and Remote Monitoring

The use of remote monitoring in medicine, in the form of edge computing, represents a significant revolution in the way patients are cared for. The technology enables real-time collection and analysis of information from home-based patients without the need for visits to hospitals. Through sensors and wearable devices, physicians can keep track of patients' vital signs continuously and respond promptly to emerging health issues. This preventive measure not only enhances patient outcomes by facilitating timely interventions but also decongests hospitals, resulting in up to minimizing healthcare system burdens. Edge computing application in such systems does this, with the processing occurring locally near the information source, allowing for effective and faster health monitoring. Remote monitoring application has been primarily observed in cardiology, whereby portable electrocardiography (ECG) devices have gained traction. These gadgets, while traditional in design, have evolved with advances in computation technology. They are now able to not only transmit data but process the data locally, identify abnormal heart beats in real time. This reduced dependence on external systems for processing data minimizes transmission needs and enhances overall system performance (Akrivopoulos et al., 2017). These innovations not only empower patients by placing health monitoring within their control but also provide physicians with more accurate, timely information to guide their clinical judgment. The HEART platform demonstrates this shift, combining wearable technology with cloud services to facilitate seamless healthcare communication and patient monitoring. Secondly, remote monitoring with edge computing can generate massive health data for future predictive analytics purposes. Retrospective health data that is harvested from ongoing monitoring can be analyzed to find patterns and reveal trends in patient health over the long term. Such capability opens up new avenues for better diagnostic accuracy and the potential to tailor preventive interventions to particular at-risk groups. But the strength of such systems lies in their scalability and dependability, particularly as the Internet of Things (IoT) continues to grow within healthcare environments. Using fog computing strategies, as demonstrated in current discourse, health solutions are able to leverage the flexibility of edge computing in order to render secure, effective data-sharing operations that facilitate clinical decision-making while upholding patient confidentiality and data integrity (Akrivopoulos et al., 2017) (Figure 2.10).

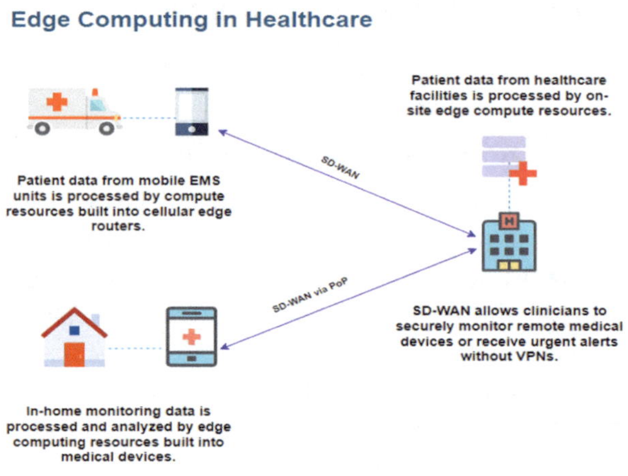

Figure 2.10. Edge computing in healthcare.

Source: https://zpesystems.com/wp-content/uploads/2023/03/Edge-Computing-in-Healthcare.png.

2.3.3. Industrial Automation and IoT

In the current industrial landscape, the convergence of Industrial Automation and Internet of Things (IoT) has emerged as a transformative force. This convergence enables the collection of vast volumes of data from sensors and devices dispersed across manufacturing operations. With the addition of real-time data analysis, organizations are capable of optimizing the effectiveness of operations, reducing downtime, and optimizing product quality. Nonetheless, handling this amount of data involves a lot of challenges, mainly related to latency and bandwidth. Edge computing handles these problems well by processing the data near where it is created, thus reducing the latency of transferring data to central cloud servers for analysis. Such local processing ability not only assists in making timely decisions but also helps to alleviate the burden on network resources, directly influencing productivity and operational efficiency within industrial environments. The role of edge computing is also evoked in intelligent grid infrastructures where IoT technology integrates monitor and control functions in various operating domains. Smart grids substitute the traditional power delivery mechanism with bi-directional communication between power producers and consumers, primarily through IoT devices like smart meters and sensors.

These machines collect and analyze data about energy usage patterns in real time to allow for effective resource allocation and load management. Significantly, the integration ensures seamless and secure energy transmission, which is crucial in an era marked by growing needs for energy and greater demands for sustainable processes. In the mitigation of challenges in uni-directional flow of information as well as energy wastage, smart grids are a classic example of harmony between industrial automation and IoT under the broad umbrella of edge computing in which efficiency is of final concern. Moreover, personalization and automation provided by IoT applications have profound implications for industries like healthcare that can be observed in the development of advanced monitoring systems. These systems are based on edge computing to process and analyze critical health data locally prior to sharing with concerned healthcare providers securely. Patient smartphone-based fog gateway prototypes for ECG data transfer, for instance, are an emerging technology for real-time health monitoring, leading to rapid response systems in case of emergencies. This approach not only empowers the patient by giving him more control of his medical information but also enhances diagnostic accuracy by evaluating past performances so that healthcare professionals can identify patterns relevant to patient care. As mentioned in Akrivopoulos et al. (2017), the importance of these applications in transforming healthcare is a testament to the vast potential for the integration of industrial automation with IoT technologies, and the importance of edge computing in enabling such advancements to be realized.

2.4. BENEFITS OF EDGE COMPUTING

The emergence of edge computing has introduced a transformative shift in the processing and handling of data in a rapidly interconnected world. By physically moving computational resources closer to the data origin, edge computing significantly reduces latency, making it vastly important in real-time analytics and responsiveness-based applications. For instance, in the scenario of self-driving vehicles or healthcare devices based on IoT, any delay in processing data can lead to devastating effects. Edge computing automatically prevents these risks by processing data locally before it is sent to cloud servers, leading to faster decision-making and enhanced user experience. Moreover, this local processing also reduces data transmission bandwidth needs drastically, which is especially helpful in regions with slow connectivity or high-bandwidth data. Another key advantage of edge computing is how it enhances data privacy and security.

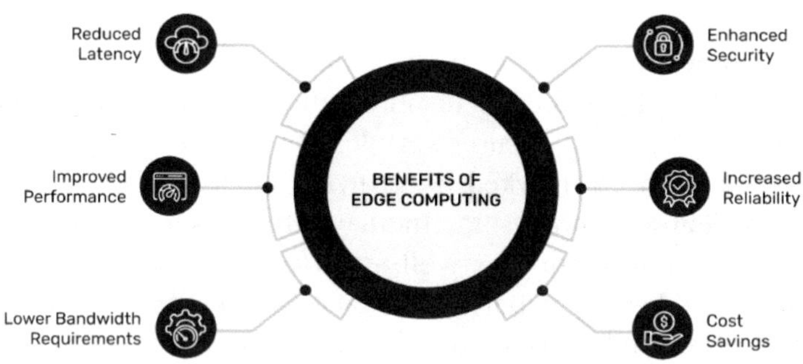

Figure 2.11. Benefits of edge computing.

Source: https://ewzduhvhjkj.exactdn.com/wp-content/uploads/2023/05/05182121/Benefits-of-Edge-Computing.png?strip=all&lossy=1&ssl=1.

Because data will be processed closer to where it is being generated, sensitive information may not need to go through the lengthy networks that are typically the case with traditional cloud computing. This localization reduces the exposure to data breach during transit and enables sensitive user data to be processed potentially more securely at the edge. For example, in automated healthcare systems, patient-sensitive data can be processed and stored within the patients premise, subjecting them to fewer probable cyber threats. Furthermore, edge computing can assist in keeping an organization compliant with data protection regulations by enabling organizations to have control over where and how data is processed, therefore enabling them to guard users privacy more effectively (Akrivopoulos et al., 2017). In addition to increased security and reduced latency, edge computing is crucial in operational efficiency and resource optimization. By using edge data processing, organizations are able to reduce the burden on central cloud servers, i.e., lower operating expenses and increased resource efficiency. This form of distributed computing can leverage cutting-edge technology, such as Massive MIMO, to enhance connectivity and data throughput and maximize energy consumption at network nodes (Larsson et al., 2018). With the deployment of localized computing resources, organizations can automate procedures, reduce cost of data transfer, and free up bandwidth for other essential procedures. As more organizations adopt edge computing paradigms, benefits will find their way into developing smarter, more efficient systems that can hold a huge volume of applications across numerous industries (Figure 2.11).

2.4.1. Reduced Latency and Improved Performance

Edge computing concepts revolve around dynamic management of data processing at the edge of information creation, which subsequently leads to a drastic reduction in latency. Organizations can optimize data analysis and decision making by leveraging the potential of local data centers or edge devices. This shift from centrally located systems to localized computing environments minimizes the physical distance data needs to travel, and hence network latency is lowered, whereas responsiveness is increased. This is evident in the incorporation of technology such as Massive MIMO, which is one of the main components of 5G New Radio. With its power to serve numerous concurrent connections without demanding high power consumption, Massive MIMO enhances effective data transmission and processing, leading to improved operational efficacy and user experience (Larsson et al., 2018). The impact of low latency is particularly evident in real-time data-driven applications, such as autonomous transport, smart cities, and remote medicine. In these environments, milliseconds count; latency can have dramatic effects on performance and service integrity. By the application of edge computing methods, information is processed in real time at or near the source, minimizing delays and enabling instant response times. Also, the use of self-organizing peer-to-peer social networks (SoPPSoNs) enhances distributed system performance by maximizing sharing of resources and connectivity between peers. By using intelligent network design, SoPPSoNs can leverage device social relationships in order to enhance search speed and success rates, two critical elements for application in edge computing (Sun et al., 2008). As businesses are increasingly relying on edge computing for enhanced performance, the ongoing development of technology is of the utmost significance in aiding in scalability and efficiency. Hardware and software advances allow businesses to deploy edge solutions that are both powerful and energy-efficient. For example, today's Massive MIMO deployments achieve significant energy efficiencies in processing vast data streams from a large number of antennas in parallel. This merge of performance and sustainability is most vital during the management of amplified demand for data connectivity without compromising energy consumption. Therefore, edge computing can potentially revolutionize different sectors by improving system responsiveness without compromising efficiency, mirroring its extensive impact on the future of technology and data utilization (Larsson et al., 2018).

2.4.2. Enhanced Data Privacy and Security

The breakthrough of edge computing is a revolution in where, when, and how data is processed, sent, and stored. Decentralizing data processing, edge computing enhances data privacy and security in several significant ways. Data is processed closer to where it is generated, so the risk of exposing personal or sensitive data to traditional centralized data hubs is much lower. This locality principle not only reduces the latency associated with data transfer but also facilitates stringent control over data handling practices.

Figure 2.12. Enhanced data security and privacy.

Source: https://blog.darwinbox.com/hubfs/Blog_Post_Empowering_CIOs_compressed-1.png.

More robust privacy controls can be imposed at the edge, facilitating data protection laws while retaining users in possession of and with control of their own personal data. Consequently, organizations are able to bolster their security positions, securing data breaches and unauthorized access typical of legacy cloud environments. Migration to edge computing is not, however, without challenges, particularly with the security risks inherent in the paradigm shift of cellular networks. As 5G technology is increasingly used in edge computing implementations, threats and opportunities arise. Although 5G is poised to facilitate higher data throughput and lower latency, it also comes with new security risks that must be diligently handled. The nature of 5G networks based on Software Defined Networking (SDN) and Network Functions Virtualization (NFV) requires new approaches to securing data communications efficiently. Current Long-Term Evolution (LTE) networks are not conducive to handling these emerging threats efficiently. To address these shortcomings, organizations must implement cutting-edge proactive security solutions tailor-made for the next generation of cellular networks with emphasis on a robust framework for managing potential points of attack and securing critical data flows (Alzahrani et al., 2016) (Figure 2.12). Moreover, in vehicle communication, Cellular-Vehicle to Everything (C-V2X) technology represents the epitome of embracing security in the context of edge computing. Not only does it facilitate ease of vehicle-to-infrastructure as well as infrastructure-to-vehicle communication but also incorporates cellular security mechanisms to address threats in typical Vehicle to Infrastructure (V2I) and Vehicle to Vehicle (V2V) systems. While LTE-V2X has come a long way in enhancing vehicular communication, it has not yet met the demands of high throughput and ultra-low latency with robust security initiatives. In the 5G-V2X architecture presented here, all these requirements are to be fulfilled by embracing a function-based network setup that is able to cope with the complex security demands of today's vehicular networks. As a focus on ultra-secure transmission support, it raises critical research challenges that must be overcome in order to confirm the performance of security features in preserving the privacy and integrity of data being communicated under such circumstances (Guizani et al., 2019) (Figure 2.13).

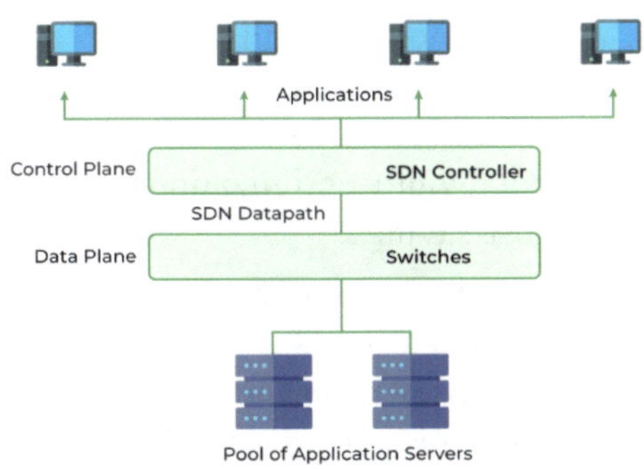

Figure 2.13. Software defined networking (SDN).

Source: https://media.geeksforgeeks.org/wp-content/uploads/20230405132159/Software-Defined-Networking.png.

2.4.3. Bandwidth Optimization and Cost Efficiency

The emergence of edge computing as the primary architecture for today's digital environments emphasizes bandwidth optimization and cost reduction. Traditional cloud-centric solutions fall short with latency-sensitive applications, particularly IoT use cases. By creating data processing at or near the source, edge computing mitigates congestion by bandwidth, an asset given the multitude of IoT devices that generate data. This proximity allows for quick processing and analysis of information, eliminating the need to transmit massive volumes of data to central servers. Additionally, according to recent research, integration of advanced algorithms can enhance resource optimization and task scheduling, thus enhancing overall system performance. The transition to edge-based frameworks is not only a technological shift but also a strategic move towards cost optimization and resource optimization in operation across different industries (Ramadhan et al., 2025).

Another application of the advantages of edge computing, the application of deep reinforcement learning (DRL) also gained prominence in network resource optimization for efficient task allocation. For instance, in vehicular networks with the aid of UAVs, where computation and bandwidth requirements are high, DRL can facilitate optimization of offloading processes such that computation is performed with minimal latency. Real-time adaptability on various computation requirements and network states is facilitated through this method, which optimizes bandwidth directly. With the application of model architectures, i.e., long short-term memory (LSTM) networks, there is even greater predictive capability leading to a system that not only is stable but also dynamically adjusts according to both traffic flow and availability of resources (Yan et al., 2024). Therefore, utilization of such techniques not only curbs latency but achieves significant decreases in operational costs pertaining to wastage of bandwidth. As more companies embed edge computing into their operational frameworks, bandwidth optimization will play a decisive role in determining their overall cost-savings.

With the ability to process large volumes of data at the edge, businesses can significantly minimize their reliance on cloud services, which comes in the form of enormous savings in data transmission and storage fees. Secondly, bandwidth optimization through the application of advanced techniques supports a greener digital world by reducing energy consumption for extended data transfers. Edge computing and modern algorithms' integration encourages a paradigm shift wherein preventive measures can be put in place for resource management prior to congestion. The dynamic optimization manifests as higher customer satisfaction directly because lower latencies and more optimized operations become the new norm rather than rare occasions. Hence, the integration of bandwidth optimization techniques into the edge computing platform not only supports cost-beneficialness but also orients companies towards future developments (Ramadhan et al., 2025).

2.5. CHALLENGES AND LIMITATIONS

The new field of edge computing is connected with numerous challenges and limitations which are to be overcome for its successful implementation. First and foremost, the basic design of today's cellular networks, particularly Long-Term Evolution (LTE) networks, is considered to be inadequate in dealing with challenges brought by future technologies such as the Internet of Things (IoT) and Mobile Cloud Computing (MCC). These technologies lay down challenges that current LTE frameworks struggle to support in a scalable and efficient manner. For instance, as the requirements for distributed content routing and heterogeneous networks increase, the rigidity of current cellular architectures is a big bottleneck. This limitation not only undermines the capacity of networks to perform real-time data processing at the edge, but it also undermines the feasibility of current infrastructures amidst rapid technology evolution (Alzahrani et al., 2016). Interoperability and managing heterogeneous edge devices as well as cloud computing is another major challenge. The coordination and adaptation of edge devices with fog computing—where computation occurs at the network's edge rather than centralized cloud infrastructure—is necessary. As the trend progresses with these edge devices becoming smarter and feature-rich, having the capability to perform computation and make decisions locally, the necessary coordination for best operation becomes increasingly complex. The lack of a one-size-fits-all architecture that can effectively manage such enormous networks of devices in an integrated way is a barrier to realizing smart scenarios such as smart cities and transport systems. Edge service operation on a seamless basis calls for innovative solutions that combat the dynamic state of resource availability and functionality at the edge, thus coordination becomes a priority issue in the field (Jukan et al., 2016). Finally, security and data privacy emerge as primary constraints in the adoption of edge computing solutions. The proliferation of devices that record, store, and process information near user environments increases the vulnerability of sensitive information to attacks and exposure. Since data is processed at numerous local points, it is essential to establish robust security features that ensure data integrity while facilitating real-time processing. In addition, the decentralized nature of edge computing can potentially create issues with uniformity among security protocols across devices and platforms, creating potential vulnerabilities. Placing these security concerns in perspective requires comprehensive frameworks that incorporate hardware as well as software solutions, eventually making deployment strategies complicated and raising further questions about users' trust in edge computing environments (Alzahrani et al., 2016) (Figure 2.14).

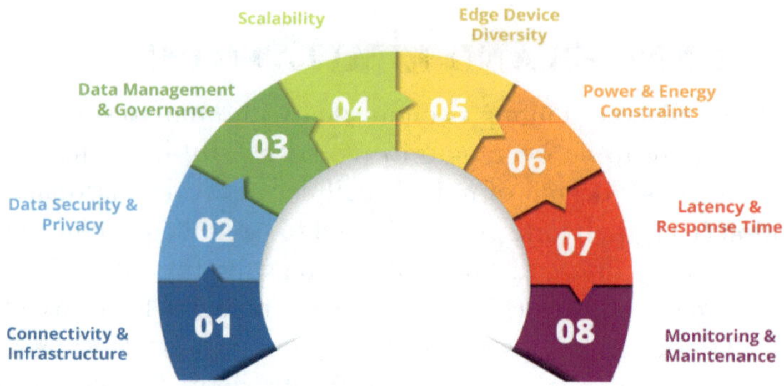

Figure 2.14. Challenges of edge computing.

Source: https://enterprisetalk.com/uploads/2024/05/1715692338256-Challenges-of-Edge-Computing.jpg.

2.5.1. Security Vulnerabilities and Risks

Security vulnerabilities in the context of edge computing are a critical threat that must be tackled by organizations in order to protect sensitive data and maintain system integrity. As edge devices proliferate and become increasingly networked, the attack surface broadens, and thus there are more instances of breach occurring. The unique edge computing architecture, in which data is processed close to the source rather than merely in centralized data centers, poses advanced security issues. For instance, the intimate proximity of devices in edge environments could facilitate unauthorized access and hence necessitate organizations to adopt full-scale methods involving secure encryption, robust access controls, and frequent vulnerability testing. The need for an organized approach to sensing and mitigating security threats is highlighted by current research, indicating that cloud services security vulnerabilities become progressively more vulnerable to exploitation, calling for a consideration of how edge computing security can be treated in an extended cloud computing scenario (Sodiya et al., 2015). In addition, security weaknesses could reach beyond data thievery or system unavailability to impact users trust and operation of newly developed technologies. For example, in Social Virtual Reality based Learning Environments (VRLEs), SPS threats would seriously undermine the learning experiences intended for users, particularly learning impediment sufferers. In order to effectively address these challenges, it is necessary to create and implement systematic models that quantify and measure risks associated with technology deployment in edge environments. Such a model can employ methods like attack trees, allowing organizations to assess probable vulnerabilities and calculate effective risk scores. Comparing different approaches to attack trees, organizations can study the trade-off between managing security frameworks and guaranteeing user protection and data integrity (Calyam et al., 2018). Lastly, the context of security threats and vulnerabilities in edge computing indicates the requirement for proactive and knowledge-based risk management techniques. Organizations must regularly scan their infrastructures with the help of enhanced tools and techniques for combating emerging threats. Also significant is the necessity to formulate robust incident response plans that define roles and responsibilities when there are security breaches. Employee training and education need to be ongoing in a way that enables them to recognize potential weaknesses and take strong action in the event of a breach. Threat handling knowledge whilst ensuring edge computing environments integrity is essential for long-term sustainability and trustworthiness of technology infrastructures. With the development of edge computing infrastructure, investment in security setup must account for the imminence of security problems that come hand-in-hand with technological advancement (Sodiya et al., 2015) (Figure 2.15).

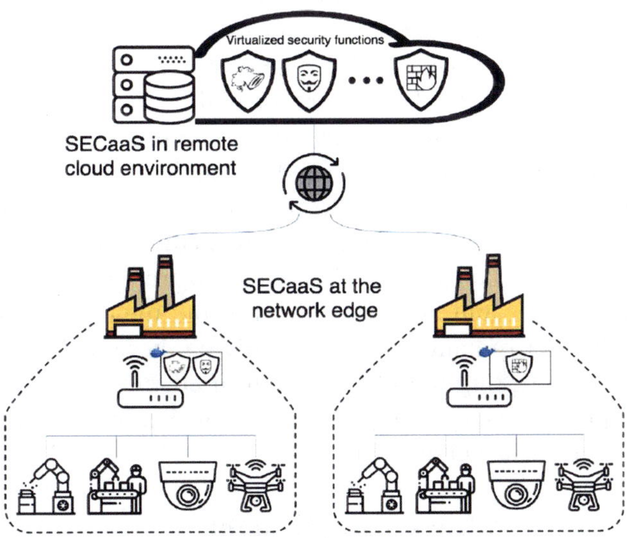

Figure 2.15. Edge computing security risks.

Source: https://in.element14.com/wcsstore/ExtendedSitesCatalogAssetStore/cms/asset/images/common/technology/blogs/2601045/2601045-security-industrial-edge.jpg.

2.5.2. Scalability Issues

Scalability issues are of paramount significance in the context of edge computing as the data produced by IoT devices and sensors is variable in nature. With increasingly more volume, veracity, variability, and velocity of data, traditional cloud frameworks cannot manage and process this quantity effectively. Edge computing provides a promising answer through facilitating closer-to-source processing of data, which helps reduce some of the challenges posed by centralized cloud infrastructures. The issue remains with enhancing the processing capacity of edge devices without escalating power consumption to unwarranted levels. The integration of neuromorphic CMOS-memristive architecture in edge computing devices is one of the avenues that has been suggested for addressing some of these scalability challenges, as in relevant research (Chua et al., 2018). In addition, the architecture of edge networks also brings with it another complexity around monitoring and managing services, a success factor to their scalability. Unlike traditional cloud infrastructures, edge computing is executed inside a distributed setting where data dissemination and data aggregation must be tightly coordinated. This renders the issue to be addressed with innovative solutions for information exchange and service discovery among the edge nodes. One viable solution lies in adopting a gossip-enabled network that supports community networks for edge cloud computing. This method not only enhances the ability to handle computational services at an efficient scale but also alleviates convergence and consistency issues of data that would normally be present in high-latency settings (Freitag et al., 2017). Despite such advancements, edge computing scalability remains a multifaceted issue that requires continued research and development. As the network edge expands to accommodate an increasingly wide range of devices, the need for efficient resource management grows more imperative. The search for best architectures—such as those fusing gossip protocols and neuromorphic computing—gives us a hint at the solutions of the future that will scale well and remain highly performant. Ultimately, solving these scalability issues will be the enabler of unlocking the full potential of edge computing in supplying real-time data processing and support for new technologies across industries (Freitag et al., 2017; Chua et al., 2018).

2.5.3. Integration with Existing Systems

The integration of edge computing with existing systems is a pivotal move towards processing and handling data in cities and complex infrastructures. In line with the expansion of smart cities, the alignment among various technologies, including Internet of Things (IoT) devices, is essential. Using edge computing, local data processing can be achieved closer to the source, enhancing the responsiveness and effectiveness of technology infrastructures in a city. Such paradigm shift not only facilitates real-time analysis but also reduces latency significantly, a significant aspect for application in autonomous vehicles and power management systems. However, to replicate these technologies on a large scale successfully, an unobtrusive integration plan comes into action that integrates various systems under one platform without compromising data accuracy and security. The architecture for such integration should accommodate the tremendous volume of data generated and how it affects interoperability and system management (Almutairi et al., 2017). The issues that edge computing integration presents to existing systems are intricate, particularly those involving security and data management. The more interconnected systems are, the more it is necessary to protect them from potential vulnerabilities. Each new device or application introduced into a prevailing infrastructure can introduce risks that can compromise data integrity as well as system performance. Effective integration must, therefore, include robust security controls and real-time monitoring systems to offset these risks. Moreover, organizations must ensure an overall integration strategy that prioritizes not just connectivity but also the capacity to process vast amounts of data. Solutions must be flexible, with regards to the multiple cloud providers and infrastructures available and having varying capacities. This involves surmounting challenges of central versus distributed computing and how data-intensive applications can benefit from a unified strategy in cloud services (Buyya et al., 2017). In summary, the future of edge computing in modernizing existing systems depends on the potential to bring about a more dynamic and responsive digital environment. With edge computing making possible real-time processing and analytics for data, it is a crucial move toward building modernization in smart cities and other sectors. As city infrastructures continue to evolve, integration approaches that are laid out today will shape the future of technological environments. Cooperation with and the integration of existing systems will not only make urban governance more effective but also stimulate innovation in services and responsiveness. But this integration must be complemented by a commitment to solving security concerns and ensuring that the data generated is utilized properly to create smarter, more efficient places. The future roadmap is very promising with great challenges that will be tackled with utmost vigilance and strategic foresight (Almutairi et al., 2017).

2.6. FUTURE TRENDS IN EDGE COMPUTING

As an increasing number of organizations are turning to edge computing to enhance operation effectiveness, several new trends are poised to redefine this technology landscape. One of these trends is the growing role of artificial intelligence (AI) on the edge. By enabling AI algorithms to process locally, organizations can lower latency and better utilize bandwidth, providing real-time decision-making capabilities. This trend is especially important for applications that require real-time feedback, such as autonomous vehicles and intelligent manufacturing systems. Beyond that, embedding AI at the edge not only enhances the ability of devices but also enables more sophisticated analytics, making way for predictive maintenance and richer user experiences. With continued investment in edge computing by enterprises, the role of AI will become even more central and will need continuous updates in data management functions and infrastructure in order to harness its fullest potential. The second great breakthrough is taking virtualized network functions (vNFs) closer to the end-user, significantly enhancing network speeds and reducing latency. These vNFs will be deployed in future networks and will play a critical part in applications like virtual reality and in-network image processing, achieving highest flexibility and efficiency at the edge.

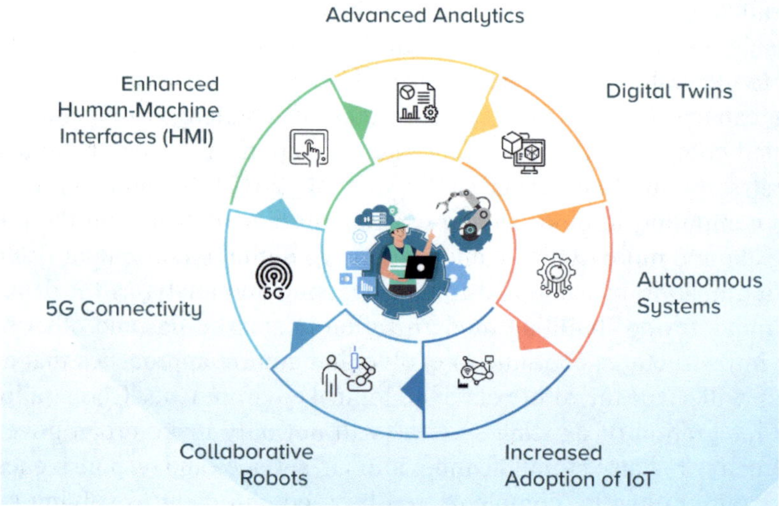

Figure 2.16. Future trends in edge computing.

Source: https://d1krbhyfejrtpz.cloudfront.net/blog/wp-content/uploads/2024/06/25175037/Future-Trends-in-Edge-Computing.jpg.

The focus will likely be on dynamic placement of the vNFs looking not only at the server resource utilization but also at real network conditions, user mobility, and end-to-end latency requirements. Integrating an architecture that is capable of dynamically rescheduling vNFs depending on fluctuating network parameters is the key to achieving Quality of Service assurance. This dynamic scheduler can offer optimized allocation of resources with less latency, thus improving user experience for a variety of applications and solidifying the role of edge computings in next-generation networking (Anagnostopoulos et al., 2018). Furthermore, more security layers on the edge will be required with an increasing number of connected devices. As IoT is growing, edge computing environments will be exposed to increased levels of vulnerability that need robust security systems. Future trends will be placed upon implementing advanced encryption methods, decentralized security schemes, and machine learning-based threat detection systems to make confidential information secure. The challenge lies in balancing performance versus security trade-offs, particularly given the increased attack surface edge computing introduces. As organizations seek new means to secure their edge infrastructure, successful methods will be important to maintain trust with stakeholders and users. This focus on security not only influences the technological paradigms adopted but also fosters a culture of vigilance within the ever-evolving landscape of edge computing (N/A, 2016) (Figure 2.16).

2.6.1. Advancements in AI and Machine Learning

Artificial intelligence (AI) and machine learning capabilities have become integral pillars of the edge computing system, with unmatched data processing and decision-making capabilities. Previously, data gathered across various devices used to be processed centrally within cloud setups, and that would lead to latency and bandwidth constraints. But by shifting AI and machine learning capabilities towards the device holding the data through edge computing, businesses are capable of improving performance and responsiveness. This shift paves the way for real-time data analysis, which, in turn, enables applications such as autonomous vehicles and smart manufacturing systems to react to changing conditions instantly. Moreover, on-device incorporation of AI algorithms optimizes the utilization of resources, thereby reducing the cost of overall system performance and data transmission and storage. Moreover, the relationship between edge computing and advancements in AI has far-reaching potential across various sectors, particularly the healthcare sector. As explained in recent literature, the confluence of 5G technology and AI, coupled with machine learning, has the potential to transform healthcare delivery by making immediate information access possible for patients and enabling remote monitoring of health status (Farooq et al., 2017). With such technology, medical professionals are able to rely on real-time analysis in making timely decisions, improving patient care, and minimizing response time when reacting to critical events. This is particularly crucial when developing telemedicine software, where physicians rely on fast speeds as well as immediate analysis of data for them to provide quality services to patients irrespective of their geographical locations. Therefore, the employment of edge computing along with AI-driven models is poised to revolutionize the landscape of healthcare systems globally. Another prominent area that is benefiting due to AI and machine learning development, as facilitated by edge computing, is the Internet of Things (IoT). The prevalence of IoT devices generates a vast volume of data that should be processed in real time for actionable insight. Edge computing allows data to be processed and gathered at the device or proximal to the device, significantly reducing latency (School of Engineering, 2019). Integrating AI algorithms, devices are capable of identifying patterns and anomalies in real-time, enhancing operational efficiencies across a host of industries, from agriculture to smart cities. The ability to compute at the edge not only takes the load off of centralized cloud servers but also allows organizations to realize the full potential of IoT deployments. As technologies continue to evolve, the convergence of AI, machine learning, and edge computing will be vital in shaping an increasingly connected and intelligent world.

2.6.2. Growth of Edge Analytics

The outbreak of edge analytics is a paradigm shift in the entire topography of edge computing, which radically transforms how data comes to be processed and utilized across various sectors. In contrast to traditional cloud-based models relying on centralized data centers, edge analytics enables data to be examined close to the origin. The switch aids to prevent latency, offers better real-time decision-making capabilities, and minimizes the bandwidth of data transmission significantly. With organizations calling for more agility and responsiveness, the advent of edge analytics is a strategic advantage in manufacturing, healthcare, and smart cities. The integration of edge analytics not only enhances efficiency but also allows organizations to leverage the complete potential of Internet of Things (IoT) devices, hence accelerating the pace of innovation and operational excellence in an increasingly data-driven world. Moreover, the evolution of edge analytics is closely related to compute innovations, which have empowered the deployment of sophisticated data processing capabilities on distributed and smaller devices. The strength of edge analytics is particularly great in environments that generate a lot of data, which need real-time processing to provide actionable insights. For instance, in the field of industrial automation, edge analysis of real-time information enables predictive maintenance, and as a result, it optimizes downtime and reduces operational costs. The intersection of artificial intelligence with machine learning and edge analytics helps to further strengthen its relevance by enabling more beneficial and adaptive interpretation of data at the edges of the networks. The significance of this movement is illustrated in the literature, as it indicates how computational innovation is revolutionizing industries by making more responsive and adaptive systems (Biros et al., 2016). As more organizations deploy edge analytics, the data security and privacy implications must be addressed as well. With data being processed across different edge locations rather than on centralized servers, new threats are being established, and hence more stringent security controls are necessary. This environment calls for a comprehensive approach towards data governance that not only offers compliance with the regulation but also builds trust among the stake-holders. Edge analytics development therefore not only points towards technological and operational innovations but also calls for a revamp of existing security paradigms for protecting sensitive information. Thus, the intersection of expanded security features with edge analytics is one example of more universal responsible innovation in the digital world where the advantages of edge computing must be balanced against the ethical considerations of ensuring data integrity and privacy (N/A, 2017).

2.6.3. Potential Impact on Various Industries

Edge computing is about to change many sectors with the improvement of processing speed and efficiency of data. This solution allows for data generated by devices located at the edge of networks to be processed locally closer to where it's generated, which reduces latency and bandwidth consumption. Sectors such as the health sector would particularly enjoy the real-time processing aspect as it would enable faster decision-making in the event of emergencies. For instance, wearables are capable of monitoring patient vital signs and, in real-time, informing healthcare professionals to facilitate early interventions. Additionally, in sectors such as manufacturing, edge computing integration allows for predictive maintenance via real-time processing of equipment performance data, thereby reducing downtime and operational costs. With increasing enterprises recognizing the value proposition of edge computing, its applications have the potential to usher in transformative changes across sectors, enabling increased operating efficiencies and innovation in approaches to problem-solving. The retail industry also stands to gain immensely with the implementation of edge computing technology. With localized processing of consumer data, retailers can gain valuable insights into customer behavior, tastes, and shopping patterns without the central cloud-based processing latency. This makes it easier for targeted marketing campaigns and enhanced customer experience, leading to higher sales and loyalty in the long term. Edge computing also allows smart inventory management systems with automatic tracking of stock and effective optimization of supply chains. Real-time analysis of transaction data also enables retailers to quickly respond to changing demands.

With a more competitive market climate, the proactive nature enabled by edge computing not only maximizes operations but also builds the foundation for long-term success and stability in the retail industry as organizations are more responsive and nimble to marketplace drivers. In sectors like agriculture, edge computing is forcing a paradigm shift towards precision farming, transforming productivity and sustainability. Farmers are able to monitor soil health, crop health, and weather conditions in real time with the help of sensors and IoT devices placed in fields. Localized data processing allows for real-time feedback and action such as adjustment of irrigation or fertilizers used only in areas where they are required, thereby minimizing wastage of resources. According to research, deployment of edge computing in agriculture leads to reduced environmental impacts and improved yields, validating the technology as an effective means of guaranteeing food security. Data-intensive sectors such as logistics and transport also leverage edge computing to real-time optimize routes and fleet management. The synergistic advancements in these diverse sectors point to edge computings capability to revolutionize traditional methods for innovating and achieving sustainability in todays industry practices.

SUMMARY

In synthesizing the key points discussed in this essay, one can observe that edge computing is paradigm-shifting in the data processing and analysis paradigm. Through distribution of computational power close to end-users, edge computing enables tremendous reductions in latency and bandwidth utilization, enabling real-time decision-making for applications ranging from IoT devices to smart cities. The implications of this paradigm shift extend beyond technological innovation; they extend also to economic efficiencies and enhanced user experiences, as cited in many case studies. These developments point towards the future where bringing together computing power and data creation at the edge has the potential to carry us into new realms of operational efficiency and innovation. Moreover, the evolution of edge computing is not without pitfalls. Security concerns rank highest given the fact that the additional points of entry for data processing amplify native vulnerabilities in the decentralized ecosystem. Mitigating these concerns relies on robust protocols and solutions to ensure data integrity and confidentiality in transit through edge networks. Developments in decentralized identity management and enhanced encryption methods are crucial to protecting edge computing environments against threats. Thus, while the potential benefits of edge computing are significant, the importance of cybersecurity cannot be overemphasized since vulnerabilities could undo the very efficiencies edge architecture promises to bring. Finally, the future of edge computing will most likely involve increased convergence with other cutting-edge technologies, such as artificial intelligence and sophisticated analytics. When businesses leverage edge computings capability, they must consider interoperability with such complementary technologies to be able to leverage new levels of performance and insight. The synergy between real-time data processing on the edge and machine learning methods will provide opportunities for predictive analytics and autonomous reaction to changing user needs. With these advancements, businesses are able to access data-driven strategies that drive agility and responsiveness in todays fast-evolving world. The synergistic development potential between the technologies implies that the future of edge computing is only just beginning and that the virtual space will keep changing and becoming richer (Fuster et al., 2015; Kasai et al., 2011).

The proliferation of edge computing has broad implications for networked infrastructures' architecture and management. As devices and applications increasingly require greater amounts of real-time data processing, effective management frameworks take center stage. Knowledge of the basics of programmable networking is one of the main components of healthy management since dynamic configuration manipulation of networks allows for dealing with diverse application requirements. Research identifies that despite numerous attempts being focused on router architecture in programmable networks, there is definitely a gap in addressing heterogeneous system management. The gap directs to the requirement for high-level middleware solutions that are secure, fault-tolerant, and user-friendly, which are essential in fueling widespread industry support (Hughes et al., 2002). Therefore, with ongoing developments in edge computing, strategic focus on developing robust management frameworks goes a long way in realizing its full potential. As regards edge computing, network slicing is at the forefront that allows operators to define personalized, resource-efficient environments for various applications. This approach not only optimizes bandwidth usage but also allows service providers to monetize their services through differentiated pricing models. Although network slicing is beneficial, it is a resource management challenge that needs innovative solutions. Recent research on deep reinforcement learning (DRL) presents potential directions towards handling the challenges. Using DRL, networks can adjust resources dynamically based on real-time users' activities and demands and thus achieve the best delivery of service for various slices. Such programmability is essential to ensuring edge computing's promise of low latency and optimized data processing, illustrating the way advanced algorithms can transform resource planning in a diversifying digital age (Chen et al., 2018). Ultimately, the intersection of programmable networking ideas and novel resource management strategies is the foundation upon which the future of edge computing rests. As the landscape becomes increasingly sophisticated, the deployment of middleware that is capable of supporting scalability and efficient delivery of configurations is critical. In addition, the research into technologies like DRL not only addresses the operational challenges posed by network slicing but also offers a pattern for continuous improvement in the model of service delivery. In a bid to attain the potential of edge computing, stakeholders must concentrate on developing resilient systems that would be simple to integrate with existing infrastructures as well as support innovative applications. In summary, to enable that, collaboration between industry and academia in these areas will be fundamental in dealing with the evolving requirements of edge computing to enable it to thrive in next-generation networks.

REFERENCES

1. Akrivopoulos, O., Amaxilatis, D., Antoniou, A., et al. (2017). Design and evaluation of a person-centric heart monitoring system over fog computing infrastructure. https://core.ac.uk/download/158328002.pdf (accessed on 16th September 2025).
2. Akrivopoulos, O., Amaxilatis, D., Chatzigiannakis, I., et al. (2017). Enabling stream processing for people-centric IoT based on the fog computing paradigm. https://core.ac.uk/download/158328004.pdf (accessed on 16th September 2025).
3. Almutairi, J., Clement, S. J., McKee, D. W., et al. (2017). Massive-scale automation in cyber-physical systems: Vision & challenges. https://core.ac.uk/download/77514390.pdf (accessed on 16th September 2025).
4. Alzahrani, B., Logothetis, M., Moscholios, I., et al. (2016). A software-defined architecture for next-generation cellular networks. https://core.ac.uk/download/46598280.pdf (accessed on 16th September 2025).
5. Alzahrani, B., Logothetis, M., Moscholios, I., et al. (2016). On the security of software-defined next-generation cellular networks. https://core.ac.uk/download/46598397.pdf (accessed on 16th September 2025).
6. Anagnostopoulos, C., Cziva, R., & Pezaros, D. P. (2018). Dynamic, latency-optimal vNF placement at the network edge. https://core.ac.uk/download/141886296.pdf (accessed on 16th September 2025).
7. Ayanoglu, E., & Davaslioglu, K. (2014). Quantifying potential energy efficiency gain in green cellular wireless networks. http://arxiv.org/abs/1501.06099 (accessed on 16th September 2025).
8. Baucells Fuster, X. (2015). Study of alternative geometries for fluidic oscillators by means of computational fluid mechanics. https://core.ac.uk/download/81579235.pdf (accessed on 16th September 2025).
9. Biros, G., Bungartz, H., Corones, J., et al. (2016). Research and education in computational science and engineering. https://core.ac.uk/download/148025463.pdf (accessed on 16th September 2025).
10. Borgo, R., Duke, D., Runciman, C., et al. (2006). Multi-cultural visualization: How functional programming can enrich visualization (and vice versa). https://core.ac.uk/download/55486.pdf (accessed on 16th September 2025).
11. Bourgine, P., Hales, D., & Johnson, J. (2009). Complex systems science: Expert consultation report. https://core.ac.uk/download/285844.pdf (accessed on 16th September 2025).

12. Bub, U., Huseynli, M., Ogbuachi, M. C., et al. (2025). A process model for the development of microservice-based applications in 5G edge computing. https://core.ac.uk/download/658474911.pdf (accessed on 16th September 2025).
13. Bushnell, D. M., & Wygnanski, I. (2025). Flow control applications. https://core.ac.uk/download/pdf/288485741.pdf (accessed on 16th September 2025).
14. Buyya, R., & Varghese, B. (2017). Next generation cloud computing: New trends and research directions. https://core.ac.uk/download/96664300.pdf (accessed on 16th September 2025).
15. Calyam, P., Gulhane, A., Hoefer, G., et al. (2018). Security, privacy and safety risk assessment for virtual reality learning environment applications. http://arxiv.org/abs/1811.12476 (accessed on 16th September 2025).
16. Chen, X., I, C. L., Li, R., et al. (2018). Deep reinforcement learning for resource management in network slicing. http://arxiv.org/abs/1805.06591 (accessed on 16th September 2025).
17. Chu, A., Preim, B., Hansen, C., DeCarlo, D., Eberly, D., Marr, D., Hameiri, E., et al. (2015). Feature lines for illustrating medical surface models: Mathematical background and survey. http://arxiv.org/abs/1501.03605 (accessed on 16th September 2025).
18. Chua, L. O., James, A. P., & Krestinskaya, O. (2018). Neuro-memristive circuits for edge computing: A review. http://arxiv.org/abs/1807.00962 (accessed on 16th September 2025).
19. Copeland, R., Crespi, N., Rehmani, M. H., et al. (2019). Internet of Things-aided smart grid: Technologies, architectures, applications, prototypes, and future research directions. http://arxiv.org/abs/1704.08977 (accessed on 16th September 2025).
20. Crippa, M. R., Han, B., Mannweiler, C., et al. (2019). Context-awareness enhances 5G multi-access edge computing reliability. https://core.ac.uk/download/245883230.pdf (accessed on 16th September 2025).
21. Farooq, S., Imran, M. A., Latif, S., et al. (2017). How 5G wireless (and concomitant technologies) will revolutionize healthcare? https://core.ac.uk/download/143476480.pdf (accessed on 16th September 2025).
22. Freitag, F., Girdzijauskas, S., Navarro Moldes, L., et al. (2017). Gossip-based service monitoring platform for wireless edge cloud computing. https://core.ac.uk/download/157810796.pdf (accessed on 16th September 2025).

23. Gajek, F. (2018). API diversity for microservices in the domain of connected vehicles. https://core.ac.uk/download/159514492.pdf(accessed on 16th September 2025).
24. Giddens, A., Giddens, A., Godin, B., Latour, B., Latour, B., Lengyel, B., Freeman, C., et al. (2012). Sociological and communication-theoretical perspectives on the commercialization of the sciences. https://core.ac.uk/download/191515756.pdf (accessed on 16th September 2025).
25. Guizani, N., Sharma, V., & You, I. (2019). Security of 5G-V2X: Technologies, standardization and research directions. http://arxiv.org/abs/1905.09555 (accessed on 16th September 2025).
26. Hanzo, L., Wang, X., Zhu, J., et al. (2016). A survey on wireless security: Technical challenges, recent advances and future trends. http://arxiv.org/abs/1505.07919 (accessed on 16th September 2025).
27. Hughes, A. (2002). Requirements of a middleware for managing a large, heterogeneous programmable network. https://core.ac.uk/download/1669444.pdf (accessed on 16th September 2025).
28. Jukan, A., Marín Tordera, E., Masip Bruin, X., et al. (2016). Foggy clouds and cloudy fogs: A real need for coordinated management of fog-to-cloud computing systems. https://core.ac.uk/download/81582274.pdf (accessed on 16th September 2025).
29. Kasai, K., & Sakaniwa, K. (2011). Spatially-coupled MacKay-Neal codes and Hsu-Anastasopoulos codes. http://arxiv.org/abs/1102.4612 (accessed on 16th September 2025).
30. Larsson, E. G., Liu, L., & Van der Perre, L. (2018). Efficient DSP and circuit architectures for massive MIMO: State-of-the-art and future directions. http://arxiv.org/abs/1807.05882 (accessed on 16th September 2025).
31. N/A. (2019). *Engineering News, Fall 2019.* https://core.ac.uk/download/232208551.pdf (accessed on 16th September 2025).
32. Perera, C., Wang, M., Zhang, M., Strazdins, P., Jayaraman, P. P., Shyamsundar, R. K., & Ranjan, R. (2015). City data fusion: Sensor data fusion in the Internet of Things. http://arxiv.org/abs/1506.09118 (accessed on 16th September 2025).
33. Ramadhan, G., Rahmatullah, S., & Ruskardi, O. (2025). Deep learning-driven *Onthophagus* efficiency optimization in IoT-edge computing environments. *International Journal for Science Review*. https://www.semanticscholar.org/paper/49deebb3cda3ceaafb19af0ccfab804f925018d1 (accessed on 16th September 2025).

34. Sodiya, A. S., Carrier, B. D., Zissis, D., Swiderski, F., Dykstra, J., James, J. I., Ruan, K., et al. (2015). Determining training needs for cloud infrastructure investigations using I-STRIDE. http://arxiv.org/abs/1502.05191 (accessed on 16th September 2025).
35. Sun, Y., & Wang, F. (2008). Self-organizing peer-to-peer social networks. https://core.ac.uk/download/20665835.pdf (accessed on 16th September 2025).
36. Sykulski, J. K., & Trowbridge, C. W. (2006). Some key developments in computational electromagnetics and their attribution.
37. Yan, M., Xiong, R., Wang, Y., & Li, C. (2024). Edge computing task offloading optimization for a UAV-assisted Internet of Vehicles via deep reinforcement learning. *IEEE Transactions on Vehicular Technology, 73*, 5647–5658. https://www.semanticscholar.org/paper/729c79c7f208b7ffb1c9bfba17172189ce42f6bd (accessed on 16th September 2025).
38. Zaslavsky, A., Perera, C., Georgakopoulos, D., Christen, P., & Lin, J. C. W. (2013). Context aware computing for the Internet of Things: A survey. https://core.ac.uk/download/327950084.pdf (accessed on 16th September 2025).
39. Zhang, Z. (2019). Advanced design and optimization of wind turbines based on turbine theories. https://core.ac.uk/download/286703685.pdf (accessed on 16th September 2025).

CHAPTER 3

EDGE DEVICES AND HARDWARE PLATFORMS

Contents

INTRODUCTION

The rapid evolution of technology has significantly transformed the world of computing, particularly with the introduction of edge devices and hardware platforms. These innovations are changing paradigms in data processing and service delivery, with computing functions growing more proximate to data sources relative to reliance on centralized data centers. The change is bringing numerous advantages in terms of lower latency, greater bandwidth efficiency, and better user experiences. With these edge solutions gaining widespread adoption among organizations and industries, they are compelled to rethink current infrastructure, and the revival of cloud computing strategies ensues. The mention of edge devices necessitates an exploration of how these technologies will be integrated into existing systems and facilitate new forms of people and device connection, ultimately transforming traditional operational paradigms. Moreover, the integration of edge devices is significantly influenced by the changing dynamics of cloud computing infrastructure. As suggested, traditional cloud services are now being more decentralized, and businesses are depending on multiple different providers of services to become stronger in their computing activities. This advancement not only enables greater scalability and flexibility, but it also enables growing needs for data-intensive computing and auto-learning systems driving today's application development. With a multi-provider platform, organizations are able to circumvent risks and gain more control over their computing environments. Thus, organizations are prompted to modify their frameworks and operating models to fully leverage such technological advancements. With this convergence of cloud services and edge devices continuing, an understanding of these trends is crucial for stakeholders seeking to realize their complete potential (Buyya et al., 2017). Furthermore, pushing computing resources to the network edge opens up immense opportunities for service providers, especially in telecommunications. Network function virtualization (NFV) deployment allows providers to decouple services from hardware, thus streamlining operations and reducing costs. This paradigm is required to support the needs of modern mobile devices and Internet of Things (IoT) services with reduced latency and enhanced dependability. The advent of light, container-based platforms such as Glasgow Network Functions is proof of this trend toward edge virtualization. These platforms not only enhance core network utilization, but also enable innovative applications, such as IoT DDoS protection and telecommunications dynamic troubleshooting. The research of these advancements is important in understanding the means edge devices can transform network effectiveness and unlock the way to next-generation computational solutions (Cziva et al., 2017).

Definition of Edge Devices

The edge device idea has become the central feature in modern network models, particularly with the rampant expansion of IoT applications' data. Edge devices act as transit points between centralized data centers and the end points responsible for processing data close to its origin rather than through the remote servers. This edge processing of data minimizes bandwidth and latency, allowing for quicker response and improved resource utilization.

These aspects are particularly important in real-time analytics or decision-making environments where lag can result in failure of critical operations. In brief, edge devices not only enhance operational effectiveness but also develop a more responsive computing environment that facilitates digital innovation. At the heart of edge computing is the integration of hardware and software platforms that would conduct some or all of the computational tasks locally. These gadgets can be as simple as sensors or sophisticated enough to perform advanced processing and analytics. Their versatility is underscored by the ability to do various things, ranging from filtering data, real-time analysis, to even machine learning operations. By utilizing heterogeneous hardware platforms, edge devices can handle different workloads and processing demands. Such flexibility is imperative in fields such as industrial automation, environmental monitoring, and smart cities, where data processing demands are significantly diverse. With increasing complexities in applications, the role of edge devices becomes more significant in facilitating sophisticated technologies that demand agility and responsiveness (Figure 3.1).

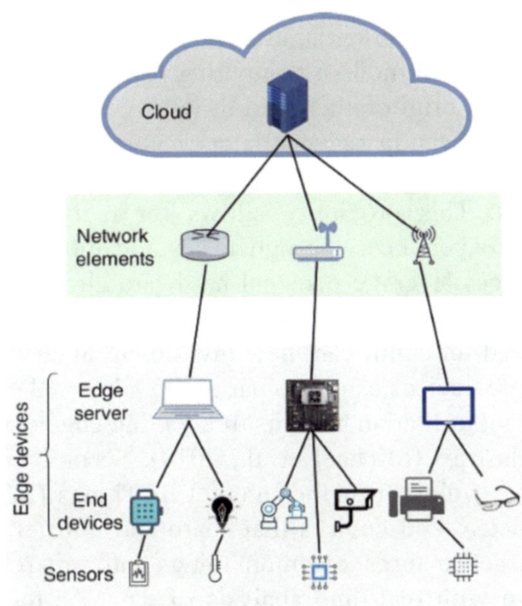

Figure 3.1. Edge devices are connected over networks.

Source: https://external-content.duckduckgo.com/iu/?u=https%3A%2F%2Fviso.ai%2Fwp-content%2Fuploads%2F2021%2F04%2Fgeneral-overview-of-the-edge-computing-architecture.jpg&f=1&nofb=1&ipt=2006975acbc21223f0dfd208b78bb5ace89e1130be5f453748be8b972e63eb0c.

Future edge device technology innovations are anticipated under Mobile-Fog-Cloud ecosystems that will be the decisive factor for enhancing the efficiency of computations in mobile and resource-constrained environments. Multi-level 5G-supported technology will be able to maximize the interaction between edge devices and cloud platforms in such a manner that applications will execute in real time with reduced power drain. But optimization and performance evaluation of such interconnected systems are ridden with tremendous challenges, particularly operational expense and field trial replicability. Research like VirtFogSim, a MATLAB-supportive software package, tends to enhance the simulation and optimization of energy and latency performance for such paradigms. This highlights a key development in understanding how edge devices are able to exist alongside next-generation technologies and enable the wider context of smart product creation, as reflected in recent debates within associated academic fields (Kantorovitch et al., 2009; Baccarelli et al., 2019).

Importance of Edge Computing

The evolution of edge computing is, in a way, overhauling how information is processed and managed in modern computing paradigms. By facilitating data processing close to its origin rather than through centralized cloud platforms, edge computing significantly reduces latency issues that can hinder timing-sensitive applications, such as autonomous vehicle applications or medical monitoring devices. This proximity allows for real-time decision-making and enhances user experiences through faster and more efficient results. In addition, edge devices leverage personal hardware already available, such as smartphones and laptops, that not only maximizes the use of resources but also lessens the need for significant new investment in custom hardware. The fact that these single devices can keep pace with advanced computing devices indicates the inherent utilitarian benefits of adopting edge computing solutions across various industries (Michael et al., 2019). Second, edge computing is a key driver in the evolution of the Internet of Things (IoT), wherein there are large sets of networked devices that share and transfer information with ease. Such convergence turns common things into smart devices that can reply on their own with real-time analysis of data. As the demand for IoT solutions grows, edge computing becomes a necessity; it delivers the right middleware solutions that enable sensor-to-sensor, actuator-to-actuator, and sensor-to-Internet connectivity, addressing the diverse requirements of multiple stakeholders such as device vendors, app developers, and end-users. The ability of edge computing to customize these platforms is making it more desirable for mass market adoption, fostering innovation and competition among multiple stakeholders in the IoT ecosystem (Mazhelis et al., 2016). Furthermore, the impacts of edge computing extend beyond pure technological advancement; they impart significant benefits as far as privacy and security are concerned. By locally processing sensitive information, edge computing prevents the amount of data sent to central servers from being as voluminous, hence minimizing the chances of data breaches and maximizing the privacy of users. This localized processing is particularly important in industries such as healthcare and finance, where proprietary and personally identifiable information is involved. Additionally, edge computing facilitates a more solid architecture less susceptible to centralized points of failure, thus ensuring system integrity even during adverse circumstances, such as network failures. Overall, the place of edge computing in promoting security, facilitating efficiency, and enabling the IoT infrastructure cannot be overemphasized, and it is a key innovation in contemporary digital infrastructure (Figure 3.2).

Figure 3.2. Importance of edge computing.

Source: https://rapidise.co/wp-content/uploads/2025/02/Importance-of-Edge-Computing.webp.

Overview of Hardware Platforms

Hardware platform innovation is at the heart of edge computing development, particularly where it intersects with the Internet of Things (IoT). Centralized server-based computer systems are becoming obsolete as distributed systems of edge devices become the norm. Hardware platforms, which are designed to compute nearer to the location where data is created and thus reduce latency and maximize data transmission efficiency, facilitate this. It is this paradigm shift that addresses the intrinsic limitations in power-constrained environments, where real-time data processing and power usage are most prominent. Furthermore, the addition of light-weight communication protocols plays a crucial role in facilitating transparent interactions between heterogeneous devices, thereby providing new IoT applications based on edge computing capabilities. While scientists continue to study how to improve these hardware platforms, it is increasingly evident that their innovation is essential to meet the complex requirements of modern applications, as highlighted in recent studies (Leung et al., 2018). With the proliferation of edge devices, the hardware platforms to cater to them must develop to address the challenges posed by their respective operating natures. These deployments are more focused on processing, power efficiency, and scalability, making hardware design even more significant. Hardware platforms have begun to incorporate more sophisticated components such as sophisticated microcontrollers and application-specific sensors to enable certain processes.

These developments are significant, remembering that edge devices operate under stringent resource constraints and must enable critical functions in real-time contexts. Furthermore, while cloud computing resources are decentralized, there is a need for hardware platforms to accommodate distributed architectures that are readily applicable across various services and providers.

Not only does this innovation enhance performance but also constructs a stronger infrastructure that can be capable of supporting various types of applications, as researched in literature reviews on trends in cloud infrastructure (Buyya et al., 2017). The intersection of application needs and hardware platforms brings emphasis to a future-oriented mindset within the paradigm of edge devices. R&D activities are increasingly directed toward enabling smart systems to access advanced computing designs for applications ranging from intense data processing to self-healing algorithms.

These hardware platforms must not only enable current technologies but also be adaptable enough to enable emerging innovations in computing. Embracing this dynamic landscape requires a deep understanding of the strengths and limitations of existing hardware realizations. As the growing demands for quicker and more adaptive systems, the coordination between the software developers and the hardware engineers is essential in an attempt to make future hardware platforms ready for meeting the evolving demands of complex applications. Such collaboration may unlock new potential in edge computing, ultimately resulting in a more harmonious and seamless technological framework (Leung et al., 2018).

3.1. TYPES OF EDGE DEVICES

There are numerous edge device types in edge computing that function to enhance data processing, reduce latency, and improve system efficiency. The devices range from straightforward sensors to more complex gateways that are each designed for use in specific applications and environments. For instance, IoT sensors can be used to collect real-time environmental information such as temperature and humidity, which is critical for smart agriculture and environmental observation purposes. Further, gateways are mid-level devices that collect data from various sensors and then transmit the data to the cloud or other data centers. This architecture not only makes data handling simpler but also ensures that useful information is handled at the edge, significantly reducing the bandwidth needed for cloud communication and enabling quicker decision-making in time-sensitive applications. An essential category of edge devices is the edge servers, which possess advanced computing capabilities to manage huge amounts of data locally. Unlike simple IoT devices, edge servers can handle complex algorithms and machine learning frameworks, enabling real-time analytics and intelligence without disproportionately depending on cloud resources. They are particularly valuable when immediate processing of data is paramount, for example, for autonomous cars or industrial automation. In addition, the inclusion of edge servers in IoT systems is complementing the increasing need for real-time data-driven decision-making, which serves as a prime example of how edge devices will mature to address the needs of various stakeholders in the IoT ecosystem. Mazhelis et al. (2016) highlights the need for smooth connectivity and compatibility between various types of platforms to maximize efficacy in such systems, pointing out that solid edge servers can go a long way toward addressing these user requirements. During the exploration of the evolving edge device horizon, it is essential that the contribution made by innovation in cloud infrastructure be considered. As elucidated by Buyya et al. (2017), the shift towards a decentralized mode in cloud computing has paved the way for revolutionary edge device architectures that eschew traditional data center dependence. This paradigm makes it possible for devices not only to satisfy local processing needs but also to facilitate access to other computing resources as and when needed. Consequently, edge devices are increasingly designed to integrate seamlessly with local and cloud resources, providing a hybrid computing model greater flexibility and scalability. This convergence of cloud services and edge devices is crucial in the realization of the full potential of the Internet of Things, in the optimal processing of data, and in driving the use of self-improving systems that learn to adapt based on changing operational needs.

3.1.1. IoT Devices

Internet of Things (IoT) is an extensive variety of devices communicating and exchanging data with one another through the internet, thereby creating an irreparable and uniform ecosystem. Actuators and sensors are the core of IoT devices, which receive real-time data and perform specified actions in accordance with user input and sensory information. IoT devices have revolutionized numerous industries from healthcare to agriculture by enhancing connectivity and automation.

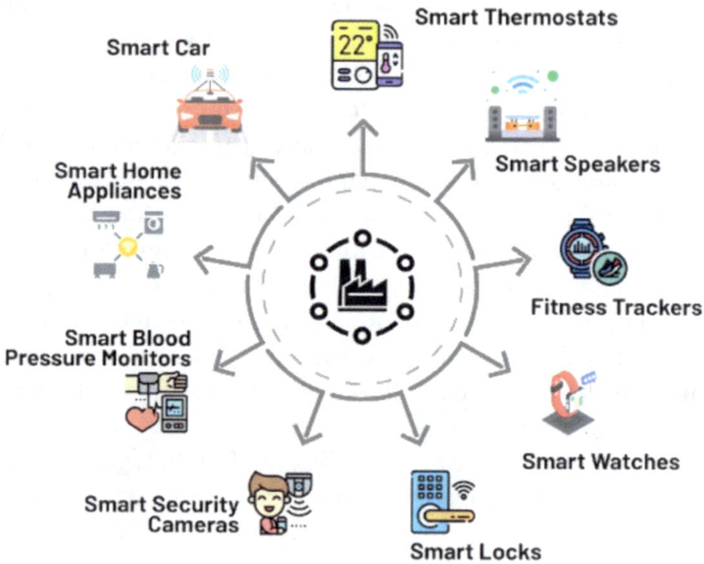

Figure 3.3. Common IoT devices.

Source: https://www.infosectrain.com/wp-content/uploads/2024/05/Common-IoT-devices-.webp.

The ability to remotely monitor and control equipment encourages operational effectiveness, while the analytics extracted from real-time information guides primary decision-making processes. With the overall spillover of IoT technology, the need for robust edge devices and hardware platforms is rapidly becoming a prerequisite in order to support quick data processing and low latency (Buyya et al., 2017). The effectiveness of IoT applications hinges on the architecture of such platforms, which must be able to handle the enormous volumes of data being generated without burdening centralized cloud infrastructures. The interfacing of IoT devices with current systems necessitates new modes of data and energy efficiency management. For instance, optimization of such devices' performance without undermining sustainability in energy is one such challenge. Interestingly, recent research indicates initiatives aimed at inculcating energy efficiency awareness, particularly in younger generations, to drive enhanced energy-saving habits (Akrivopoulos et al., 2017) (Figure 3.3). By establishing an innovative ICT environment that is specifically tailored for schools, stakeholders can come up with a model that balances technology incorporation with energy-saving initiatives. This is the approach that is significant because it not only shows the potential of IoT devices in terms of tracking and monitoring but also as agents for improving larger environmental sustainability. The common architecture of these IoT platforms makes them adaptable to various uses, ranging from monitoring energy usage in schools to smart grids, illustrating the broad range of their applications. With the continued evolution of IoT devices, there are several important issues to address in order to have them effective and sustainable in their applications. The shift towards decentralization of cloud infrastructure has the potential to improve performance by distributing computing power over a group of providers. This evolution mirrors the growing sophistication of IoT systems, which need scalable and adaptable hardware platforms capable of supporting varied applications as well as diverse environments (Buyya et al., 2017). One illustration of how IoT hardware with an open-source technology base is being deployed in learning environments is a pointer to the capacity of such systems to be environment-specific while being adaptable (Akrivopoulos et al., 2017). Through the use of both proprietary and open-source platforms, organizations are able to enhance their operational abilities while driving innovation. The future is likely to see further pushes towards developing edge devices that not only interact well with existing systems but also anticipate the particular needs of future technologies.

3.1.2. Gateways

The roles of gateways in the context of hardware platform and edge device are increasingly taking center stage with rising network service need. Gateways serve as strong mediaries between end-user devices and cloud services, enabling end-to-end communication between different networks effortlessly. By placing computation resources closer to data sources, gateways enable reduced latency, enhanced performance, and improved data processing capabilities. With the age of the Internet of Things (IoT) where there are numerous devices that all speak simultaneously, the function of such gateways gains immense importance. They not only perform the important processing and aggregating of data but also enhance operational effectiveness by using virtualization with Network Functions Virtualization (NFV) methodologies. According to recent research, such virtualization progress enables container-based virtual network functions (VNFs) to be utilized at the network edge with impressive preservation of core network resource utilization and increase in overall system performance (Cziva et al., 2017). Besides their application in traditional networking, gateways increasingly deploy edge computing strategies that cater to emerging applications and services. The modularity of current edge computing platforms allows gateways to host third-party services on them, with open development environments for enterprises and developers. This shift is required, particularly in ambient intelligence and IoT-dominant areas where user engagement and device connectivity drive next-generation service delivery models. The migration toward open architecture in gateway development lessens entry barriers as well as facilitates interoperability across disparate hardware and software technologies. As articulated in recent research, creating gateways that facilitate open settings and the implementation of local services not only optimizes use of resources but also enhances response capability for the unique needs of an increasingly dynamic technological setting (Freitag et al., 2017) (Figure 3.4).

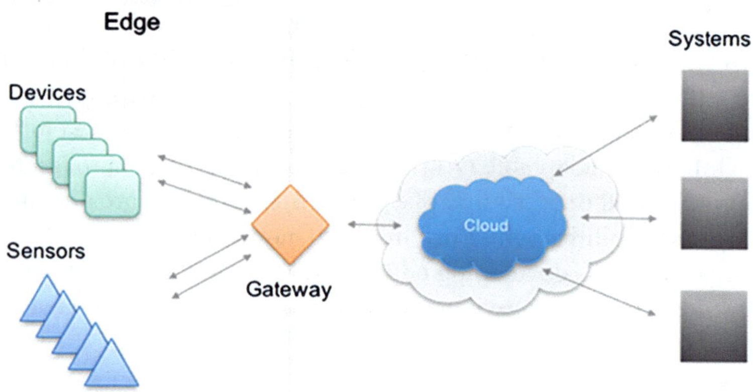

Figure 3.4. The role of gateways within the context of edge devices.

Source: https://external-content.duckduckgo.com/iu/?u=https%3A%2F%2Fcdn.tt-gtmedia.com%2Frms%2Feditorial%2FIoTA_gateway_model_figA_mobile.png&f=1&nofb=1&ipt=b7c643098b376c949c20440c331132a9a71662724bf7368b8ca263dbc92ccc8c.

In addition, the goal of using agile and powerful gateways facilitates a broad variety of applications based on edge data processing. Real-time consumer interaction analytics, dynamic resource management, and support for local services are some applications that will greatly benefit from advances in gateway technology. The light footprint here of new gateways, and particularly containerized NFV-based ones, allows them to function smoothly without the lighter footprint legacy systems bear. This ability is essential for telcos and service providers to face increasing demands on performance-oriented services. By these advanced gateway configurations, organizations can enhance the service delivery, minimize the cost of operations, and build a stronger network infrastructure—critical factors toward sustaining competitiveness in an ever-evolving digital economy (Cziva et al., 2017; Freitag et al., 2017).

3.1.3. Edge Servers

In today's computing environments, edge servers are now essential components that facilitate decentralization of data processing and storage. Located close to end-users, they reduce latency, accelerate delivery of data, and optimize networks as a whole. With processing of data done closer to where it originated, edge servers take the load off central data centers, which are clogged by data traffic and experience performance degradation due to the excess load of data generated by various applications. This transition is the expression of the evolving landscape of cloud computing, with more flexible infrastructure using multiple vendors and adopting new models of computing appropriate to address changing needs of mobiles and IoT use cases. As settled in recent discussion of cloud infrastructure, the move towards edge servers is one expression of this decentralizing direction, which allows for more reliable and interactive computing solutions in many applications, foremost among them real-time analysis of data and service delivery (Buyya et al., 2017) (Figure 3.5).

Figure 3.5. Edge servers.

Source: https://external-content.duckduckgo.com/iu/?u=https%3A%2F%2Fwww.whiteboxsolution.com%2Fwp-content%2Fuploads%2F2022%2F04%2FWhat-is-an-Edge-Server-1.jpg&f=1&nofb=1&ipt=9853fe5f4eb69be9e6c1383f5b6113eb7c71ef9be5203137aec68397be4cf7f4.

Moreover, NFV and edge servers have created new opportunities for telecommunication service providers. With their efforts to address growing bandwidth requirements and higher-order services, NFV allows for virtualization of traditional network services such that they can be executed on light-weight, containerized platforms. This is a novel technology in the network edge where conventional NFV strategies are hobbled with heavy resource requirements. By using edge servers capable of orchestrating virtual network functions (VNFs), service providers can use core networks more efficiently while offering services with lower latency. Glasgow Network Functions is a good example of such a principle, demonstrating how edge orchestration can bring various applications such as IoT security and on-demand network diagnostics, enhancing the operational efficiency of telecommunications considerably (Cziva et al., 2017). The implication of deploying edge servers extends beyond improved performance; it also facilitates breakthroughs in scalability and service innovation. Decentralizing compute resources makes it easier for organizations to scale quickly, meeting fluctuating levels of demand without the need to make significant hardware investments within centralized data centers. This flexibility is becoming increasingly important across sectors where real-time processing and analysis are critical, such as finance, health, and smart cities. Edge servers thus play a vital role in utilizing data generated by different sources, facilitating timely action and insight. In addition, with new edge computing infrastructures emerging, they will have a greater influence on how companies plan and roll out their infrastructure, revealing challenges and opportunities inherent to future developments in the edge devices and hardware landscape (Buyya et al., 2017).

3.2. KEY FEATURES OF EDGE DEVICES

Edgy device architecture is characterized by local processing of data, which reduces latency associated with cloud computing. This is a central aspect that allows edge devices to carry out analytics in real-time, a prerequisite that makes them central in applications where response times are critical, for instance, autonomous vehicles or industrial automation. Because edge devices process information close to the source, they decrease network bandwidth overhead and lower data to be sent to central cloud databases. Furthermore, edge processing enhances operation efficiency and enables real-time decision-making response, which is crucial in cases requiring quick response. The utilization of several sensors and actuators is also crucial in the functionality of these devices in providing greater flexibility in other IoT settings as well as enhancing overall usability by different stakeholders in the IoT ecosystem (Mazhelis et al., 2016). The other major aspect of edge devices is the fact that they are capable of empowering greater security and privacy functionalities. Since edge devices handle sensitive data, it is essential to integrate robust security measures. Adopting technologies like ARM TrustZone, which keeps sensitive tasks isolated within a secure execution context, ensures that important data does not become a victim of potential attacks (Baumann et al., 2017). Significantly, edge devices essentially reduce the threat of data breaches by reducing the volume of sensitive data that must traverse the network. Through local encryption techniques and pre-transmission data processing and analysis, edge devices are able to maintain compliance with privacy regulations. Last but not least, through solving security problems at the local end, edge devices enhance trustworthiness and integrity in IoT applications and make them appealing to both users and developers. Lastly, the scalability and flexibility of edge devices contribute significantly toward making them applicable in the fast-evolving context of the IoT ecosystem. As the demand for intelligent, connected systems grows, the edge devices are made such that they are able to support multiple applications across different industries. Supporting multiple operating systems and with middleware options provided, integration is seamless into current infrastructures, with support of multiple users' requirements (Mazhelis et al., 2016). Moreover, some edge devices are built on modular designs, allowing for easy maintenance and upgrade. This agility not only extends the life of the devices but also enhances their ability to embrace new technologies and standards. Thus, with businesses set to tap the full potential of IoT, the inherent characteristics of edge devices become critical in driving innovation and operational excellence in a competitive environment.

3.2.1. Low Latency

The coming of age of low latency as an important performance parameter has made a significant contribution to edge device design and deployment in modern computing systems. As applications have been demanding more real-time computation, reducing latency has been crucial in ensuring seamless user experiences. This has necessitated more focus on the optimization of hardware platforms that enable low-latency operations. With deep neural networks (DNNs) at the forefront of artificial intelligence, the resultant computational intensity is a serious challenge, particularly for mobile and pervasive devices. To assist in mitigating these issues, the integration of specialized processors into commodity devices has become prevalent. Knowledge about the compatibility between varying DNN architectures and their targeted hardware platforms is important since this may lead to greater gains in performance as well as a more efficient use of resources within the boundaries defined by the constraint of low latency requirements (Almeida et al., 2019). Furthermore, the deployment of edge computing solutions has been a strategic step in response to the latency challenge of cloud-based architectures. Data transmission to cloud-based datacenters incurs significant communication latency, particularly causing damage to applications that need rapid response. Researching cloudlets and in-network computing is revealing promising alternatives that bring processing closer to the point of origin of the data, minimizing network saturation. Recent trends show an increasing reliance on edge nodes consisting of powerful hardware, such as Field Programmable Gate Arrays (FPGAs), that have been demonstrated to reduce computation latency by a significant amount. This shift towards localized computing not only addresses low latency concerns but also enhances network efficiency overall, making the application of such novel models of computing an appealing option (Putnam et al., 2020) (Figure 3.6).

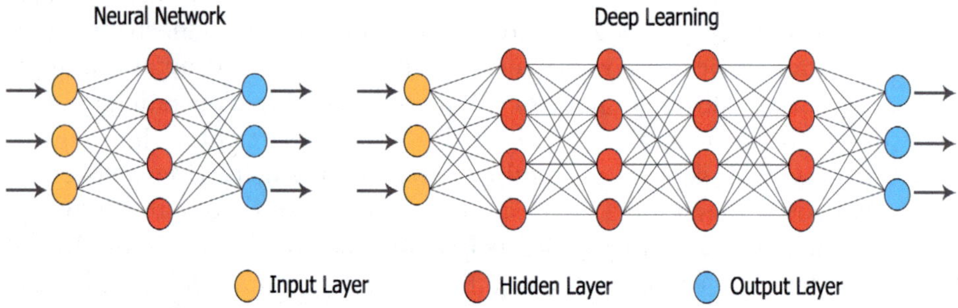

Figure 3.6. Deep neural networks (DNNs).

Source: https://miro.medium.com/v2/resize:fit:1400/0*zIxxBVIXy0l4tXP3.jpeg.

Furthermore, experiments with various edge devices and their performance in latency-critical environments also underscore the importance of end-to-end approaches to hardware optimization.

Comparison of various platforms reaffirms that there are numerous variables affecting latency, including hardware design and application demands. Careful comparison of cutting-edge DNNs on a large variety of edge devices has helped researchers assess primary bottlenecks that could inform the design of future devices. Hardware acceleration design to cater to the particular requirements of applications in domains such as IoT and real-time analytics can enhance system responsiveness and scalability. The requirement for co-design strategies between DNNs and hardware platforms becomes increasingly clear, as low-latency optimization across the entire computing stack is essential to enabling advanced, responsive applications in the digital world of today (Almeida et al., 2019).

3.2.2. Data Processing Capabilities

The development of data processing capability in edge devices has become increasingly pertinent in the application of the Internet of Things (IoT). As devices are more and more interconnected, effective processing of data is needed to cope with the large volumes of data generated by actuators and sensors. At the core of this effectiveness is the development of middleware solutions that not only collect and enable connectivity but also augment data processing capabilities. An examination of existing proprietary and open-source platforms reveals varied levels of performance in respect to their ability to accommodate heterogeneous actuating and sensing technologies. Gap analysis emphasizes the need for platforms that are able to simply plug into the IoT ecosystem while being augmented with good data processing and data sharing capabilities, which are essential to facilitate innovation and drive widespread adoption throughout the market (Mazhelis et al., 2016). In exploring the processing capacity of data at the edge, the computational capability of personal devices such as smartphones and laptops can be said to be underestimated. Models such as personal volunteer computing showcase how the easy-to-possess devices can be utilized to perform extensive computational tasks such as animation rendering and image processing without the need for additional hardware investment.

This approach not only capitalizes on available resources but also emphasizes accessibility and ease of implementation in developing effective data processing systems. Because it is demonstrated that current personal devices are able to provide performance on par with high-end laptops of older generations, their use for data processing can lead to higher efficiency and facilitate innovative applications taking advantage of the edge computings benefit (Michael et al., 2019). Moreover, the effects of increased data processing ability extend beyond measuring performance; they also encompass essential matters of security and confidentiality. With organizations integrating more sophisticated edge devices into their processes, data ownership and security management progressively become a matter of concern.

Having the ability to process and share information securely while safeguarding the privacy of users is fundamental in building trust across the IoT ecosystem. By addressing these challenges through the development of integrated platforms supporting data processing and sharing capabilities, stakeholders can enhance the resilience of overall ecosystems. In the end, the convergence of effective data processing capabilities, privacy concerns, and facilitating infrastructure creates the opportunity for new innovations in edge computing and IoT solutions (Mazhelis et al., 2016).

3.2.3. Connectivity Options

For the domain of edge computing, connectivity option selection is critical for optimizing the performance of edge devices and hardware platforms. Connectivity options dictate the behavior of how devices communicate with one another and with cloud services central to them, eventually influencing the speed of data transmission, reliability, and scalability. Ethernet and Wi-Fi are conventional connectivity options despite their disadvantages due to the invested infrastructure and relatively better data transfer rates. But with the spread of IoT devices, new technologies such as low-power wide-area networks (LPWAN) and cellular technologies such as 5G have entered the mix as prime contenders. Such new methods of connectivity have the ability to reduce latency and improve energy efficiency, both of which are essential in edge environments where real-time analysis of data is needed. These advancements highlight the need for a balanced approach for the selection of connectivity solutions that meet specific use-case needs and leverage available technology. Connectivity solutions at the edge are confronted with numerous challenges, particularly as environments become more heterogeneous. In past discussions on the IoT, ubiquitous proliferation of the connected device introduces complicating factors in terms of management, aggregation, and storage of data. Along with simply selecting an adequate technology for connectivity, interoperability among different devices and platforms is an urgent need. Middleware technologies have been seen as the way to overcome them, effectively acting as intermediaries that foster ease of communication between disparate systems. Enabling effortless integration of devices with different interfaces and operating systems, middleware solutions are essential to the construction of healthy networks. Hence, the function of middleware can be considered as pivotal in facilitating effective communication, hence enhancing overall connectivity in edge computing platforms, as noted in Farahbakhsh et al. (2017) and Farahbakhsh et al. (2017). Apart from technology solutions, analyzing the security aspects of connectivity alternatives is most important in current data-centric environments. The proliferation of edge devices and their networked state also makes them attractive targets for malicious actors, and there is a need for a robust system of data protection and device integrity. There are a number of protocols that can be utilized to secure the connections, ranging from encryption protocols like TLS to secure authentication like OAuth. Incorporating these security protocols into the connectivity capabilities not only protects edge environments but also establishes trust with users within edge-based solutions. Furthermore, because each connectivity option carries associated security implications, it is important to use a risk-based approach when selecting and implementing these technologies. Overall, complete understanding of the available connectivity options, coupled with rigid focus on security, can significantly enhance the performance of edge devices and applications (Figure 3.7).

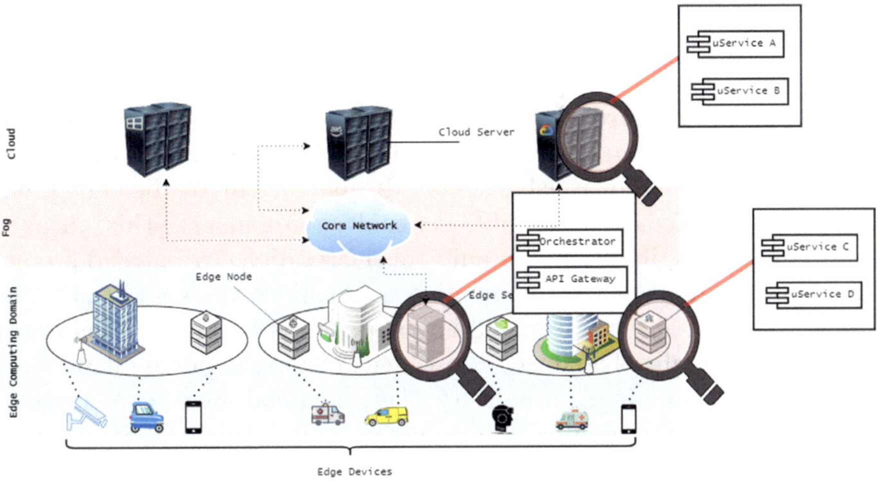

Figure 3.7. Computational domain of cloud, fog, and edge computing.

Source: https://www.researchgate.net/profile/Lucas-Souza-De-Castro/publication/367241301/figure/fig1/AS:11431281113777774@1674080764605/Computational-domain-of-Cloud-Fog-and-Edge-Computing-employing-Microservices.png.

3.3. HARDWARE PLATFORMS FOR EDGE COMPUTING

Evolution of hardware platforms in edge computing is one of the most important driving factors in optimizing data processing within the Internet of Things (IoT). As applications requiring low latency continue to increase, historical cloud computing models are being undermined by localized processing requirements. Edge devices, powered by robust computing capabilities, can perform necessary functions closer to where the data is coming from, thereby doing away with the latency that typically accompanies sending data to distant cloud data centers. This shift not only enhances the response rate but also encompasses bandwidth concerns, thereby making edge computing an integral component of today's digital infrastructure. With the injection of sophisticated hardware such as Graphics Processing Units (GPUs) and application-specific processors, the platforms lay the ground for wide-ranging applications, such as industrial automation and smart cities, as a matter of transforming data management and use at the edge. In examining the several hardware platforms for edge computing, the following approaches emerge that are imperative to bypassing the latencies in computation and communication. Emerging technologies, such as Field Programmable Gate Arrays (FPGAs), have significant advantages in terms of the capability to alter processing tasks en route. Such flexibility is particularly useful in time-varying environments, where types and rate of data require support for real-time processing. Besides, vehicles like cloudlets and in-network computing describe how compute resources can be strategically placed to achieve optimal performance. By spreading processing away from traditional data centers, such solutions enable a more flexible system to efficiently process several streams of data in variable-demand environments. This change in hardware platforms, in return, not only enhances efficiency but also promotes innovation in deploying edge computing applications (Putnam et al., 2020). Also, the current trajectory of cloud infrastructure is heavily shifting towards hybrid and decentralized architectures, which are more important than ever for effective edge computing. As industry players extend their service delivery, integrating disparate computing architectures is key to realizing the full potential of edge devices. The trend parallels a broader shift away from monolithic cloud architecture toward a more integrated, flexible, and interdependent landscape. By using the services of multiple cloud providers, organizations can optimize utilization of resources, using localized computing to meet specific operating requirements with the assurance of scalability. The implications of such shifts are widespread and impact everything from data-intensive computing to the development of self-learning systems, calling for a detailed examination of hardware platforms that will fuel next-generation edge computing innovations (Buyya et al., 2017).

3.3.1. Raspberry Pi

Raspberry Pi has emerged as a central component in the edge device and hardware platform market due to its cost-effectiveness, versatility, and miniaturization. The small single-board computer provides users with the ability to execute complex computational processes that can have both pedagogical and practical applications. With a complementary build environment to programming and hardware hacking, Raspberry Pi enables learning of embedded systems by hand for students, hobbyists, and researchers. Support from a robust community also encourages innovative projects ranging from smart home devices to green monitoring, making its immense application in varied fields like Internet of Things (IoT) applications evident. Since it is open source, it provides a model for collaboration and sharing of knowledge collectively and, therefore, is a good candidate for pedagogic settings and research in controlled environments (Brander et al., 2017) (Figure 3.8).

Figure 3.8. Raspberry Pi.

Source:https://lh7-us.googleusercontent.com/zFifouPOw-XZ_v_Xxf-cVmXyhHPltagTKPBu3Jg2fFMbK7xmnmqQ99Jueka3Y2JZ-VuCgCrcC-M3YmGju8YwAafulzhRLmC7BLwCTkG6GAuLhqI-ZCrwqigb7XxQQkNWyJi-9wUics9WIyQT-Ud2xYDHw.

The modularity of Raspberry Pi makes it easier to develop advanced edge solutions, as users can customize applications according to their requirements. As a part of the larger trend of democratization of digital technology, Raspberry Pi not only reduces the entry point for electronics and programming but also lets novices work on advanced research. This system is particularly relevant in agriculture technology, where it can be utilized to engineer controlled-environment devices that monitor and measure plant growth. Such an application is a paradigm of how Raspberry Pi can bridge specialization and usability, transforming scientific inquiry into actionable activity. The ability to utilize platforms like the OpenAg Personal Food Computer also identifies the use of Raspberry Pi as a building block in the creation of interactive learning experiences and making significant contributions to the discipline (Brander et al., 2017). Raspberry Pi also plays a critical role in edge computing through facilitating required processing capacity for data harvesting and analysis at the point of source. This can be particularly utilized in cases where traditional cloud processing would be latency- or bandwidth-intensive. With Raspberry Pi employed in edge devices, real-time data processing requiring services can be deployed, such as smart monitoring systems or real-time analytics applications. For example, by combining with data compression techniques such as Principal Component Analysis (PCA), Raspberry Pi-based solutions can significantly streamline data processing, providing memory-limited and high-speed computing. These strategies are critical for performance optimization on low-capacity embedded devices, illustrating that even low-cost devices like Raspberry Pi can meet the demands of sophisticated applications in structural health monitoring and otherwise.

3.3.2. NVIDIA Jetson

The NVIDIA Jetson platform is a significant improvement on edge devices, particularly for intense computing power in compact form factors, in uses that require additional computational power at the edge. It incorporates GPU-accelerated processing, which is necessary for the execution of deep learning algorithms at the edge.

Figure 3.9. NVIDIA jetson.

Source: https://d29g4g2dyqv443.cloudfront.net/sites/default/files/akamai/embedded%2Fimages%2FjetsonNano%2Fjetson_orin_nano-devkit-front_top-right-trimmed.jpg.

This aspect is particularly helpful as AI workloads require significant computational capabilities to deliver real-time processing needed in uses such as image recognition and autonomous navigation. As DNNs grow more complex, the edge device like the Jetson must not only be high-performance but also low-power, as combining specialized processors becomes of prime concern in achieving optimal performance without excess energy consumption (Almeida et al., 2019). Specifically, researchers have explored the Jetson platforms capacity to run computationally intensive calculations compared to other future hardware options. For instance, comparisons of NVIDIA Jetson TX2 against CPU-based systems like the Intel NUC7i7BNH indicate the advantages of employing GPU design in real-time inference operations. Those comparisons highlighted that although both systems were capable of standing their ground, the Jetsons design is well suited to efficiency and speed in DNN operations, particularly in mobile and robotics use. This performance advantage emphasizes the shift to GPU-oriented computing for specific edge applications where fast decision-making is critical and power consumption must be minimized (Jabbar et al., 2019) (Figure 3.9). Also, with the increased need for edge computing solutions, the NVIDIA Jetson platform is set to be at the forefront of upcoming portable AI applications. The continuous enhancement of Jetson's performance, including improved thermal management and processing capabilities, allows more demanding models that are becoming increasingly prevalent across various industries to be processed. Effective performance analysis and benchmarking against competing hardware options is essential for application developers and researchers to optimize applications specifically for use cases at the edge. This paradigm shift calls for a deep understanding of the interplay between DNN architectures and hardware realization so that one uses the properties of platforms like the Jetson to their fullest extent (Almeida et al., 2019).

3.3.3. Intel NUC

The Intel NUC is a compact computing platform that is a robust edge device solution with small size and varied applications. Well designed to be efficient and perform, its tiny size makes it easy to integrate in environments with limited space, such as in industries, retail, and in schools. The ability to customize the NUC according to specific processing needs makes it a premier choice among developers in terms of deploying edge computing applications. Its compatibility with various operating systems as well as applications makes it even more useful, making it capable of being easily integrated into existing infrastructures, thus becoming a vital component of modern hardware systems. Analyses of the Intel NUCs potential, especially in machine and deep learning applications, show its dualistic behavior as a CPU-focused and versatile computing platform. Comparisons between the Intel NUC7i7BNH and GPU-centric environments such as the NVIDIA Jetson TX2 illustrate the subtle performance behavior that comes with varying architectural designs. The NUC architecture, while optimized for CPU operations, has shown both strengths and weaknesses in benchmark scenarios such as pedestrian detection in autonomous systems, indicating its efficacy in applications that call for intensive computational resources. Performance indicators such as processing speed and power efficiency are important to developers when comparing hardware platforms for edge applications, thus influencing deployment decisions in varied scenarios, according to empirical studies (Jabbar et al., 2019) (Figure 3.10).

Figure 3.10. Intel NUC.

Source: https://images-cdn.ubuy.co.in/63aa6bbd82d0a652986235c3-intel-nuc-11-with-core-i7-1165g7.jpg.

Besides being required to perform, the Intel NUC is also built to be easily integrated into various network protocols, hence well suited to complex applications in which secure data handling and communication are required. For instance, its architecture supports standards such as PROFINET for industrial Ethernet, where security is very crucial. Developers are guided by hardware suitability tests for specific tasks, such as tests of cryptographic algorithms that are paramount for secure data exchange in automated environments (Leßmann et al., 2025). As edge computing becomes more widespread, the demand for reliable and adaptable platforms like the Intel NUC will continue to increase, emphasizing its role not merely as a processor device but also as a part of the edge hardware platforms and devices ecosystem.

3.4. CHALLENGES IN EDGE COMPUTING

With the advent of edge computing, there has come a shift in paradigm regarding the processing and analysis of data, but along with it, numerous challenges are there to be addressed to fully exploit its prowess. Among the most important of these challenges lies connected with the inherent resource constraints of edge devices, which are typically endowed with limited computation and available power. This limitation hinders the execution of complex algorithms data-intensive applications demand, particularly in the realm of the Internet of Things (IoT). With various applications vying for the use of these edge systems, it becomes essential to learn how to maximize resource usage without sacrificing performance. Indeed, as pointed out in the current work, exploring smart devices and networks, particularly wireless sensor networks (WSNs), represents a significant prospect for meeting these challenges in edge computing and leveraging the new chances in the IoT ecosystem (Leung et al., 2018). Furthermore, the integration of edge computing into current infrastructures is another degree of complication. In indigenous cloud infrastructures, the central processing nodes are the data centers, but with edge computing, a decentralized approach is needed that can actually lead to uneven data management and processing qualities. As the future of cloud computing is heading towards a decentralized system, with multiple vendors and decentralized resources, the interoperability of heterogeneous hardware platforms and standards is a challenge for edge computing. This fragmentation can lead to inefficiencies and excess latency, particularly for applications that must be processed in real time. Researchers have called for the need for new computer architecture that, in addition to supporting data-heavy processes, improves service delivery to various edge devices, and it is thus important that these issues are addressed in future advancements (Buyya et al., 2017). Lastly, issues related to security and privacy are significant challenges that must be met during edge computing solution implementation. Because the data is being processed close to where it originates, oftentimes within untrusted settings, there is a heavy risk of unauthorized access and data leakage. Offering robust security features that can protect sensitive information without sacrificing system performance is imperative. In addition, with edge devices accumulating increasing volumes of data, privacy laws must be adhered to, necessitating adequate data governance processes. Security-based issues, along with the need for adequate data handling, necessitate a holistic approach with a combination of technical innovation and compliance. Resolution of these concerns is essential not only for the sake of establishing user trust but also for establishing a functional and secure edge computing platform (Figure 3.11).

Figure 3.11. Challenges in edge computing.

Source: https://external-content.duckduckgo.com/iu/?u=https%3A%2F%2Fcdn.sketchbubble.com%2Fpub%2Fmedia%2Fcatalog%2Fproduct%2Foptimized1%2F6%2Fa%2F6a91065787d4544329ebb0118d62e959a483a287d30e5c62706ab21bf49e1d44%2Fedge-computing-challenges-slide3.png&f=1&nofb=1&ipt=a44c594f8e84e3dc748941554978848 1bbb24c65ec5ecf66df6e62c99ab37fa7.

3.4.1. Security Concerns

The expansion in edge devices and hardware platforms has resulted in a new wave of technological advancements, but simultaneously, greater security threats that must be addressed on an urgent basis. With these devices penetrating into multiple applications—smart homes to industrial automation—their susceptibility to cyberattacks is more apparent. The decentralized nature of edge computing offers hundreds of access points, each susceptible to exploitation. It is possible for malicious users to take advantage of these loopholes to gain unauthorized access, undermining not only the devices but the vital data they collect and pass on as well. As cited in recent studies, the shift from traditional data centers to edge computing requires the development of sufficient security mechanisms that are strong enough to safeguard both the hardware and the data processed therein (Buyya et al., 2017). Failing to close these vulnerabilities can lead to catastrophic breaches, breaching user privacy and corporate integrity. Further, integrating edge devices into larger networks, such as the Internet of Things (IoT), further complicates the security dilemma. With so many devices linked to each other, cascading vulnerabilities are a certainty; if one device is compromised, it unwittingly becomes an open door for others in the network. The difficulties introduced by such heterogeneity are compounded by the varying operating systems and protocols utilized across different devices. Therefore, the development and deployment of middleware solutions become essential for the creation of a secure footing. Effective middleware can help ensure secure communication between different devices, countering security threats by creating an environment that is controlled for the exchange of data as well as device interaction (Farahbakhsh et al., 2017). Thus, maintenance of this middleware is a priority in bolstering the overall security structure of edge computing systems. Apart from technical vulnerability management, regulatory and ethical standards are required to govern the deployment of edge devices. Such standards must prioritize not only cybersecurity matters but even the responsibility of organizations in protecting user data and compliance with privacy law. While edge devices take enormous amounts of personal information, practices must be established to provide data security as well as end-user approval. A combined approach where technology measures and ethical principles complement each other will enhance trust among users as well as stakeholders. The path to take is through a combined effort by manufacturers, software houses, policymakers, and users in an endeavor to provide an ecosystem that prioritizes security and integrates it from the ground up, bolstering the immunity of edge devices and hardware platforms to potential future threats.

3.4.2. Scalability Issues

Scalability is a significant concern for edge hardware and device platforms with the rapid advancements in cloud computing and Internet of Things (IoT) applications. With increased devices getting connected and generating vast amounts of data, scalability is unavoidable. Legacy systems tend to get bogged down with increased demands and produce bottlenecks that decrease performance and responsiveness. Scalability issues call for adjusting cloud architecture to fit in a position to support decentralized models of computing, consistent with evolving cloud environments and services. Transitioning towards multi-provider cloud solutions improves flexibility and enables developers to more easily navigate potential points of failure. Therefore, utilization of innovative architectures that facilitate these end-to-end service models is essential to ensuring that edge devices work as optimally as possible within large networks and handle increased data traffic generated by IoT systems, demonstrating the need for scalable solutions in heterogeneous technology landscapes (Buyya et al., 2017). Device heterogeneity also complicates the task of solving the scalability problem in edge computing environments. As IoT expands, device and data type heterogeneity creates a significant management, aggregation, and storage problem for data. Devices are capable of being accessed using different interfaces and communication protocols, and this will create friction in data exchange and processing. In response to these challenges, the deployment of middleware has increased. Middleware acts as an integrating layer that simplifies communication between different devices, making interoperability and a more scalable design feasible. The value of this layer cannot be exaggerated, as it decreases complexity while making disparate systems easier to integrate. By focusing on middleware solutions, the developers can address the issues created by rapidly growing functionalities and connectivity, ultimately increasing the potential of the edge device in scalable IoT applications (Farahbakhsh et al., 2017). Unless scalability issues are addressed early, organizations risk losing significant potential, which can translate to inefficiency and resource misallocation. The ever-increasing demand for real-time processing and analysis of data necessitates robust infrastructure that can scale to keep pace with user and application requirements in real-time. Future deployments must consider the rate at which connected devices are growing as well as the nature of use cases to which they might be exposed. With a maturing ecosystem of edge computing, adopting a comprehensive roadmap of issues and solutions will be essential. By addressing scalability in this step first, organizations are able to keep their edge devices and hardware platforms up-to-date and beneficial in a constantly developing technology landscape, ultimately acquiring a more enduring and efficient integration of IoT solutions (Buyya et al., 2017).

3.4.3. Data Management

Data management is of prime importance to the operational efficiency of edge hardware and hardware platforms, particularly with the evolving technology landscape still in motion. More applications of IoT devices and the far greater volumes of data they generate have created the need for more capable management systems that are optimized for real-time processing, data integrity, and security. Edge computing significantly reduces latency by enabling data processing closer to the source, thereby allowing timely insights and decision-making. Such an arrangement lowers the burden on centralized data centers, optimizes bandwidth, and lessens latency. Consequently, sound data management strategies not only lead to improved operational efficiency but also allow organizations to harness the full potential of edge devices, transforming them from mere data sampling points into operational analytical agents that learn and adapt in their ecosystems, ultimately improving overall system responsiveness. In addition to real-time data processing, effective data management also includes the imposition of vast storage and recovery mechanisms. As edge devices generate large amounts of data, organizations require scalable storage technologies that are capable of adapting to fluctuating data levels while enabling fast access. A hybrid storage model that includes local and cloud storage is poised to enhance availability and resilience for edge deployments. Furthermore, attention must be placed on data governance to assure adherence to regulatory climates and industrial standards. Organizations must establish policies for the management of the data lifecycle detailing the manner in which data is collected, stored, accessed, and erased. This includes taking into account privacy considerations, particularly with regard to personal data, further highlighting the need for careful data management methods in accordance with compliance with law as well as moral standards. The intersection of data management and emerging technologies such as artificial intelligence and machine learning creates new opportunities for innovation in edge computing environments. Organizations can train machine learning models more effectively and precisely with the proper management of data, which makes it possible to build sophisticated algorithms with predictive analytics and decision-making automation. This makes not only efficient operation but also enhances the potential for proactive maintenance and other intelligent systems. Moreover, it offers prospects to explore the use of data-driven information in a number of domains, such as education and social integration, where strategic applications have the capability to trigger significant developments. As delineated in certain research, the impact of such technologies, combined with combined data management strategies, has the potential to drive transformative developments across industries, eventually leading to better outputs and user experiences in a data-oriented society (Evans et al., 2005; Misuraca et al., 2013).

3.5. FUTURE TRENDS IN EDGE DEVICES

The fate of edge devices will probably be shaped significantly by trends in information and communication technologies. While sophisticated urban management systems become more prevalent, they also become increasingly reliant on overall solutions that take into account economic, socio-cultural, and urban development aspects. This is enabled by the outstanding progress in telecommunication infrastructure, which enhances data transmission capabilities via wired and wireless networks. The integration of edge devices into such systems supports real-time monitoring and management of urban environments, therefore improving the general quality of life. The shift towards applying multifunctional devices, such as smartphones, not only increases access to numerous services but also acts as a motivator for successful urban management. Consequently, the future of edge devices will not merely rely on technological sophistication but also on how effectively they can integrate with the greater city plans, as briefly explored in Yigitcanlar et al. (2009). Fog computing thus emerges as another breakthrough phenomenon, particularly suited for edge devices that adhere to data processing at the network's edge. Such a paradigm plays a key role in reducing latency and total throughput, which is precisely why it is so valuable in applications requiring instant access to geospatial information. The Fog-based architecture, explored by initiatives like Fog GIS, demonstrates the way in which edge devices can serve as double-duty infrastructure for analytics and decision-making. The implementation of microprocessors such as Intel Edison within these platforms demonstrates the practicality of edge computing in real application, permitting real-time analysis and reaction.

As more organizations adopt fog computing principles, the capacity of edge devices to derive sound insights from massive sets of data will become increasingly strong, demonstrating considerable potential for most industries and applications, as demonstrated by Barik et al. (2016). Further, there is interoperability between edge devices when coming up with a harmonized ecosystem that promotes functionality and experience. With edge devices being networked, they not only facilitate data sharing but synchronization of diverse technologies across different platforms. Interoperability allows for the development of smart environments where devices will communicate and collaborate to simplify processes. The capability of these devices to be connected to cloud services increases their potential even further, allowing them to offer users accurate analytics and insights. As more industries begin to research the effects of edge and fog computing, the need for more interoperability will increase, forcing manufacturers to be innovative. Thus, the fate of edge devices is not just defined by technological innovations, but also by ever-growing varied requirements for collaboration between hardware platforms, bringing into action the efficiency and effectiveness in applications (Figure 3.12).

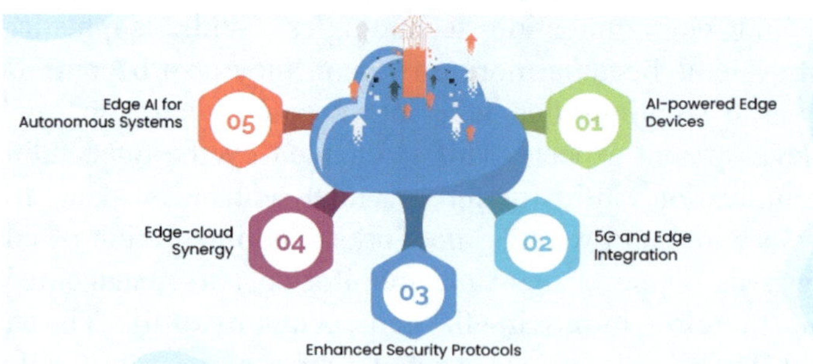

Figure 3.12. Future trends in edge devices.

Source: https://www.veritis.com/wp-content/uploads/2024/10/Future-Trends-in-The-Edge-Computing.webp.

3.5.1. AI Integration

The incorporation of artificial intelligence (AI) into edge devices is a paradigm-shifting revolution in the computing landscape where data processing occurs closer to the source of information. The paradigm not only improves the process but also reduces latency, an aspect of crucial significance in real-time applications in IoT-like systems. With platform evolution in hardware, computational loads of sophisticated AI algorithms, particularly convolutional neural networks (CNNs), are bridging typical limitations. Though integration of deep learning methods into edge devices promises spectacular capabilities such as real-time visual tracking, it is difficult to balance power consumption and processing capacity. As argued, AI performance on platforms such as NVIDIA Jetson TX2 has successfully addressed such issues in a satisfactory manner and also demonstrated promise without compromising energy efficiency, reflecting a significant movement towards deployment in mobile scenarios (Blanco-Filgueira et al., 2018) (Figure 3.13).

Figure 3.13. Artificial intelligence (AI) into edge devices.

Source: https://syoft.com/blogs/uploads/post_images/20230215010214Picture1_8.png.

As researchers examine the convergence of AI and semantic technologies, smart products emerge as one of the most important concepts in edge computing. Smart products employ AI to understand and react to information they have sensed in their surroundings and offer a more user-friendly interface. The use of semantic technologies makes devices communicate with each other and exchange insights in a better way, making them improve their performance in interconnected environments. Yet, this emerging area is fraught with challenges, such as the demands for strong frameworks that will enable unproblematic integration between hardware and software systems. The distinction between smart products and semantic sensor networks explains how knowledge technologies are able to augment operational capacity. Therefore, a concerted examination of such interactions is warranted for purposes of compensating for prevailing limitations and propelling innovation in the area of AI integration (Kantorovitch et al., 2009). Furthermore, a successful edge AI adoption has significant implications for a range of industries, from medicine to manufacturing. By doing local processing, edge devices can provide rapid feedback to real-time scenarios, which is particularly useful in high-stakes environments. For instance, in telemedicine, edge devices with AI capabilities can analyze data from patients and provide instant feedback to healthcare professionals, enhancing decision support. However, the technological challenge of developing AI algorithms that will perform optimally on constrained hardware is one significant obstacle to larger-scale rollout. Continued research and collaboration between AI researchers and hardware designers are necessary to optimize systems and algorithms to execute well on edge platforms so that AI integration not only enhances capability but is also viable for resource-constrained environments (Blanco-Filgueira et al., 2018).

3.5.2 5G Connectivity

The advent of 5G connectivity is a watershed moment for data transmission, data processing, and utilization of data across various sectors. This technology enables much higher data rates, low latency, and guaranteed communication, which are critical to drive the next wave of innovation on the topic of edge computing.

Figure 3.14. 5G connectivity into edge devices.

Source:https://external-content.duckduckgo.com/iu/?u=https%3A%2F%2Fthinkrf.com%2Fwp-content%2Fuploads%2F2019%2F02%2FAdobeStock_210310514-e1549988752563.jpeg&f=1&nofb=1&ipt=d19b641befd28d94406a869977442e6d5986c830826872cdab27a34553837b1e.

As networks evolve, devices and edge hardware platforms must coordinate with one another in order to avail themselves of the benefits brought about by 5G. These advancements pave the way for greater throughput and reduced response times, essential for application in autonomous vehicles, smart cities, and telemedicine. Subsequently, stakeholders must consider how to best position edge devices to maximize the full potential of 5G in ways that drive service delivery and operational efficiency improvements across sectors (Figure 3.14). 5G deployment is accompanied by new network architecture paradigms, mainly concerning the deployment of the network functions virtualization (NFV) at the edge. Separating the network services from the traditional hardware enables operators to deploy virtualized services that correspond to better utilization of resources and costs. The Glasgow Network Functions (GNF) platform, for instance, offers a container-based NFV solution that is effective at the network edge, thus addressing scalability and latency issues inherent in conventional NFV platforms. Through this approach, operators can take advantage of 5Gs capabilities while keeping operational expenditure (OPEX) to a minimum and creating new business opportunities. Besides, the light weight of such platforms makes it possible to have enormous cuts in core network consumption, a condition pivotal in facilitating uninterrupted connectivity across various environments (Cziva et al., 2017). Furthermore, the variety of services that 5G supports offers an abundance of opportunities for operators and users alike. With the ultra-low latency requirements propelling demand in areas such as augmented reality and the Internet of Things (IoT), cost-savings of such investments come into play. Operators will need to navigate through the challenges embedded in these technologies and factor their feasibility of return on investment with changing business models. Planned deployment of edge devices capable of supporting these new applications can ensure that operators remain ahead of the game. With creative application of the advantages of 5G, including lower latency and better coverage, the operators can position themselves to better serve an increasingly dynamic market and ultimately thrive in this new digital era (Cuevas et al., 2017).

3.5.3. Enhanced Energy Efficiency

The evolution of edge devices and hardware platforms is basically motivated by the quest for additional energy efficiency, a key parameter in the design of green computing systems. Given the additional emphasis on moving away from centralized cloud infrastructure towards decentralized platforms in handling data, the energy squeeze on computing resources further tightens. This change is not a trend, but rather an inevitability to the rising volumes of data generated continuously by IoT and other technologies. There is greater energy efficiency to be achieved through heterogeneous computer architectures that optimize resource usage, thereby reducing total energy consumption while guaranteeing performance. These advances interfere with present paradigms of cloud computing by splitting workloads among multiple providers and edge devices, which can operate more efficiently in their local environments (Buyya et al., 2017). Moreover, edge computing presents opportunities for reducing latency and optimizing performance while simultaneously reducing energy consumption. By performing calculations closer to where they occur, edge devices cut down on the need for remote data transmission to cloud data centers, something that typically comes at a high energy cost. Cloudlets and in-network computing are some of the new things that further embody this trend, making it possible to compute data closer, not only to make responses quicker but also to power cost reduction. As exemplified by the subject of hardware acceleration, the application of technologies like Field Programmable Gate Arrays (FPGAs) has been shown to enable decreased computation latency and higher efficiency, which makes users better able to tap the potential of edge computing (Putnam et al., 2020). This movement towards energy-efficient measures not only benefits individual companies but also to the larger environmental benefit through the reduction of the carbon footprint inherently embedded in high computing demands. The emphasis on more energy efficiency is also underscored by calls for sustainable practice in deployment and hardware design. Energy-efficient components, such as low-power processing elements and effective coolants, are increasingly of priority importance to manufacturers to design into edge devices, centrally contributing to overall energy consumption in edge devices. Bringing these energy-conscious components into edge computing platforms equals massive resource savings, correlating with global sustainability goals. Apart from this, the symbiotic relationship between performance and energy efficiency justifies a strong case for organizations to invest in upcoming edge technologies. In implementing energy-efficient hardware technologies, companies not only enhance their working capacities but also contribute towards reducing environmental impacts, developing organizational culture that recognizes the importance of sustainable development of technology (Buyya et al., 2017).

SUMMARY

The emergence of edge devices and hardware platforms represents a revolutionary change to the computing environment, particularly in regards to the Internet of Things (IoT). As processing demands rise, the limitations of traditional cloud computing designs fall into marked relief, including higher communication latency and inefficiencies. This realization has initiated significant advancements in edge computing frameworks to carry out data processing close to the source and bypass latency issues inherent in sending data all the way to centralized cloud datacenters. By studying innovative approaches such as in-network computing and cloudlets, we can enhance responsiveness and dependability in networked systems, ultimately achieving more efficient applications across different sectors, from smart cities to industrial automation, reasserting hardware choices as a key determinant of system performance and scalability (Putnam et al., 2020). Interestingly, the idea of personal volunteer computing reflects another aspect of the edge computing revolution, calling on people to utilize their existing hardware for computational workloads that were previously the preserve of high-performance machines. The paradigm not only democratizes computational power but also enables important processing capabilities without requiring additional hardware investment. Through the use of personal devices such as smartphones and laptops, we are able to achieve stunning performance gains on par with leading-edge laptops of recent years. Not only is this approach optimized for resource utilization, but it is also fostering community-based collaboration in problem-solving activity, bringing out the power of using personal devices as part of a broader edge computing approach (Michael et al., 2019). Lastly, continued innovation surrounding edge devices and new hardware platforms can redefine our understanding of the edges of computation and capabilities. Combining advanced technologies like Field Programmable Gate Arrays (FPGAs) and other in-network acceleration methods is crucial in mitigating computation delay and improving processing efficacies. As the world continues to evolve into more interconnected and data-driven ecosystems, investing in these edge solutions will be crucial in addressing challenges of tomorrow with scalable and responsive infrastructures that cater to the growing demands of modern applications. Through the development of these advancements, we not only enhance the computational effectiveness but also open up new avenues for research and development in edge computing, justifying its core place in the future of technology (Putnam et al., 2020).

The growing demand for network services and performance assurance has prompted telecom companies to implement virtualization in their infrastructure. This shift, which is known as Network Functions Virtualization (NFV), decouples network services from hardware devices, improving operations while reducing operational costs (OPEX) and opening up new business models. However, the problem is that existing NFV platforms are clunky and struggle to function at their best at the network edge, where latency is of the essence. To address this issue, novel solutions like the Glasgow Network Functions (GNF) platform have emerged for facilitating lightweight container-based Virtual Network Functions. By employing this method, the providers can optimize the utilization of the network, thereby improving overall performance as well as minimizing latency for end-users in applications such as IoT and mobile enterprise networks (Cziva et al., 2017). Alongside NFV breakthroughs, the concept of personal volunteer computing is gaining more popularity as an excellent use-case to leverage the processing capabilities of common devices. This paradigm leverages people's personal smartphones, laptops, and other devices that they already own, so that computationally intensive tasks such as animation rendering and image processing can be done without additional hardware investment. Users' access to their own personal computing resources ensures public engagement in technical solutions, providing an environment through which volunteers can contribute during their spare time. Interestingly, technology has evolved such that contemporary personal devices are as capable as top-of-the-line computers a few years ago, indicative of potential utilization of such platforms (Michael et al., 2019). The ability of edge devices to converge with hardware platforms is a real paradigm shift in telecommunications and computing strategies. By moving computational resources nearer to the user, network latency can be significantly reduced, enhancing the experience for applications that rely on real-time processing. By the combination of NFV and personal volunteer computing, not only is resource utilization optimized but also an environment for collaborative innovation is encouraged. As service providers and consumers move towards these emerging technologies, the potential of creating more responsive and efficient networks becomes increasingly probable. This context also emphasizes the imperative for ongoing research and development in edge computing, as communications of the future will likely be founded on the intelligent integration of hardware platforms and emerging computing methods (Cziva et al., 2017; Michael et al., 2019).

REFERENCES

1. Abdelgawad, A., Allen-Zhu, Z., Hardt, M., Li, J., Mitliagkas, I., Reyer, M., Rooshenas, A., et al. (2019). Embedding principal component analysis for data reduction in structural health monitoring on low-cost IoT gateways. https://core.ac.uk/download/578214124.pdf (accessed on 16th September 2025).
2. Abdul Jabbar, D., Speck, D., Pierson, H. A., Levine, S., Chalup, S. K., Houliston, T., Lee, V. W., et al. (2019). Comparing computing platforms for deep learning on a humanoid robot. http://arxiv.org/abs/1809.03668 (accessed on 16th September 2025).
3. Akrivopoulos, O., Amaxilatis, D., Chatzigiannakis, I., et al. (2017). An IoT-based solution for monitoring a fleet of educational buildings focusing on energy efficiency. https://core.ac.uk/download/158327961.pdf (accessed on 16th September 2025).
4. Almeida, M., Lane, N. D., Laskaridis, S., et al. (2019). EmBench: Quantifying performance variations of deep neural networks across modern commodity devices. http://arxiv.org/abs/1905.07346 (accessed on 16th September 2025).
5. Alvarez, C., Bautista, L., Becker, T., et al. (2018). LEGaTO: First steps towards energy-efficient toolset for heterogeneous computing. https://core.ac.uk/download/224976296.pdf (accessed on 16th September 2025).
6. Armbrust, M., Balouek, D., Nakamoto, S., & Pan, Y. (2019). Personal volunteer computing. http://arxiv.org/abs/1804.01482 (accessed on 16th September 2025).
7. Baccarelli, E., Momenzadeh, A., & Scarpiniti, M. (2019). VirtFogSim: A parallel toolbox for dynamic energy-delay performance testing and optimization of 5G mobile-fog-cloud virtualized platforms. https://core.ac.uk/download/196295551.pdf (accessed on 16th September 2025).
8. Barik, R. K., Dubey, H., Gupta, R. D., et al. (2016). FogGIS: Fog computing for geospatial big data analytics. http://arxiv.org/abs/1701.02601 (accessed on 16th September 2025).
9. Baumann, A., Becher, M., Bonomi, F., Guanciale, R., Halderman, J., Hulton, D., Lipp, M., et al. (2017). TrustShadow: Secure execution of unmodified applications with ARM TrustZone. http://arxiv.org/abs/1704.05600 (accessed on 16th September 2025).
10. Blanco-Filgueira, B., Brea, V. M., Fernández-Sanjurjo, M., et al. (2018). Deep learning-based multiple object visual tracking on embedded system for IoT and mobile edge computing applications. https://core.ac.uk/download/599627049.pdf (accessed on 16th September 2025).

11. Brander, G., Chambers, D., England, H., Hildreth, F., et al. (2017). Personal food computer: A new device for controlled-environment agriculture. https://core.ac.uk/download/85123494.pdf (accessed on 16th September 2025).
12. Buyya, R., & Varghese, B. (2017). Next generation cloud computing: New trends and research directions. https://core.ac.uk/download/96664300.pdf (accessed on 16th September 2025).
13. Cuevas, M., Dohler, M., Laya, A., et al. (2017). Business case and technology analysis for 5G low latency applications. https://core.ac.uk/download/96762095.pdf (accessed on 16th September 2025).
14. Cziva, R., & Pezaros, D. P. (2017). Container network functions: Bringing NFV to the network edge. https://core.ac.uk/download/80697015.pdf (accessed on 16th September 2025).
15. Delgado Prieto, M., Fernández Sobrino, Á., Fibla Biosca, P., et al. (2019). Active learning-based laboratory towards engineering education 4.0. https://core.ac.uk/download/294830056.pdf (accessed on 16th September 2025).
16. Evans, D., Kukulska-Hulme, A., & Traxler, J. (2005). Landscape study in wireless and mobile learning in the post-16 sector. https://core.ac.uk/download/30275708.pdf (accessed on 16th September 2025).
17. Farahbakhsh, R., Farahzadia, A., Rezazadeh, J., et al. (2017). Middleware technologies for Cloud of Things–A survey. http://arxiv.org/abs/1705.00387 (accessed on 16th September 2025).
18. Farahbakhsh, R., Farahzadia, A., Rezazadeh, J., et al. (2017). Middleware technologies for Cloud of Things: A survey. https://core.ac.uk/download/333623071.pdf (accessed on 16th September 2025).
19. Fischer, M., Meiling, S., Purnomo, D., et al. (2018). MONICA in Hamburg: Towards large-scale IoT deployments in a smart city. http://arxiv.org/abs/1803.06854 (accessed on 16th September 2025).
20. Freitag, F., & Khan, A. M. (2017). On participatory service provision at the network edge with community home gateways. https://core.ac.uk/download/294830456.pdf (accessed on 16th September 2025).
21. Goldberg, D. E., Alba, F., MacWilliams, F. J., Dantzig, G. B., Curnow, H. J., Morell, J., Dongarra, J. J., et al. (2018). Running genetic algorithms in the edge: A first analysis. https://core.ac.uk/download/214834320.pdf (accessed on 16th September 2025).
22. Kantorovitch, J., Motta, E., Nikolov, A., et al. (2009). Position paper on realizing smart products: Challenges for Semantic Web technologies.

https://core.ac.uk/download/81998.pdf (accessed on 16th September 2025).

23. Leßmann, G., Niemann, K. H., Otto, J., et al. (2025). Hardware and lifecycle requirements for secure PROFINET devices. https://core.ac.uk/download/661066186.pdf (accessed on 16th September 2025).
24. Leung, V., Sheng, Z., & Tian, D. (2018). Toward energy and resource efficient Internet-of-Things: A design principle combining computation, communications and protocols. https://core.ac.uk/download/111629233.pdf (accessed on 16th September 2025).
25. Mazhelis, O., Mineraud, J., Su, X., et al. (2016). A gap analysis of Internet-of-Things platforms. http://arxiv.org/abs/1502.01181 (accessed on 16th September 2025).
26. Misuraca, G., & Stewart, J. (2013). The industry and policy context for digital games for empowerment and inclusion: Market analysis, future prospects and key challenges in videogames, serious games and gamification. https://core.ac.uk/download/28977794.pdf (accessed on 16th September 2025).
27. Putnam, A., Fahmy, S. A., Kwon, H., Neugebauer, R., Noa, S., Shanker, S. S., Kizheppatt, V., et al. (2020). Quantifying the latency benefits of near-edge and in-network FPGA acceleration. https://core.ac.uk/download/305119902.pdf (accessed on 16th September 2025).
28. Sklar, M., & Wegerif, D. (2025). An advanced telerobotic system for shuttle payload changeout room processing applications. https://core.ac.uk/download/pdf/42821796.pdf (accessed on 16th September 2025).
29. Yigitcanlar, T. (2009). Managing ubiquitous eco cities: The role of urban telecommunication infrastructure networks and convergence technologies. https://core.ac.uk/download/10895362.pdf (accessed on 16th September 2025).

CHAPTER 4

EDGE NETWORK ARCHITECTURE AND COMMUNICATION PROTOCOLS

Contents

INTRODUCTION

The rapid development of technology in the 21st century has brought numerous paradigms of communication, among which is Edge Network Architecture due to its efficiency in addressing the challenges of cities today. Urban dwellers keep increasing, and cities are under increased pressure of infrastructure and service demands. Innovative solutions through ICT can address these challenges. An Edge Network Architecture functions as a pivotal framework, facilitating the seamless interconnection of devices and systems with localized computing resource implementation. The architecture proves essential to the functioning of Smart Cities, where efficient processing of city information at the network edge optimizes city governance by eliminating latency and enhancing capabilities of data management. The function of communication protocols in this architecture aims at ensuring efficiency and reliability in transmitting data, making them necessary to the achievement of smart urban ecosystems. The usage of Edge Network Architecture shows great potential in enhancing the operational effectiveness of Smart Cities through the integration of Internet of Things (IoT) technologies. Such technologies have a central role in facilitating real-time data collection and analysis, which are vital in ensuring decision-making. The network communication dependency of the architecture fosters collaboration between public institutions and the numerous IoT devices installed throughout urban regions. For instance, as outlined in the EU project MONICA, this integration can facilitate the large-scale deployment of sensors to observe city conditions in real-time, thus supporting effective urban planning and resource management. The ability to handle vast amounts of data that such sensors generate is dependent upon good communication protocols that can provide connectivity among heterogeneous systems, thus assuring a well-integrated urban environment that is sensitive to citizens' needs and climatic conditions, as promoted by Fischer et al. (2018). Besides, research on communication protocols in Edge Network Architecture provokes crucial aspects related to mobility and network efficiency. As more and more cities implement advanced mobile computing solutions, understanding the architectures enabling smooth handovers and communication continuity becomes vital. Handover method classification for various mobility architectures describes how various systems can be controlled and managed efficiently to enable vertical and horizontal connectivity. The detailed literature review emphasizes the need for flexibility in designing mobility architectures with legacy systems as their focus points, providing end-to-end support in various layers of communications. The communication between Edge Network Architecture and structured communication protocols thus becomes an important area of research. Not only does it address short-term urban issues, but it also produces a flexible and resilient digital infrastructure, which is vital in the future of Smart Cities, as posited by Ferretti et al. (2015).

Definition of Edge Network Architecture

The Edge Network Architecture definition is based on its ability to maximize performance and efficiency in data processing by moving services and applications closer to the end-user. This architecture model arises as a result of the exponential growth of data consumption, driven by the innovation of

IoT devices, increases in streaming media, and need for latency-sensitive applications. By shortening the distance information needs to travel, Edge Network Architecture eases bandwidth strain on centralized data centers and reduces latency, which is crucial for apps that rely on real-time processing. It also facilitates improved reliability and availability, as services are able to operate even when they lose contact with the central network, ensuring a more reliable user experience in different scenarios. Central to Edge Network Architecture is the convergence of high-level communication protocols that enable high-performance data transmission and resource management. Such protocols need to support the specific nature of edge computing environments, where devices and applications tend to display dynamic patterns calling for real-time adjustments.

One of the primary breakthroughs here is the Segment Routing (SR) architecture, which addresses bandwidth handling issues as well as state information across the network. By reducing the overhead typically associated with routing, SR architecture enables efficient flow of data, which specifically proves useful in edge networks handling complex, multiparty services. With increasingly more organizations embracing this architecture, it is crucial to understand how edge computing coexists with the communication protocol in a bid to maximize performance and scalability across heterogeneous applications (Abdelsalam et al., 2020) (Figure 4.1).

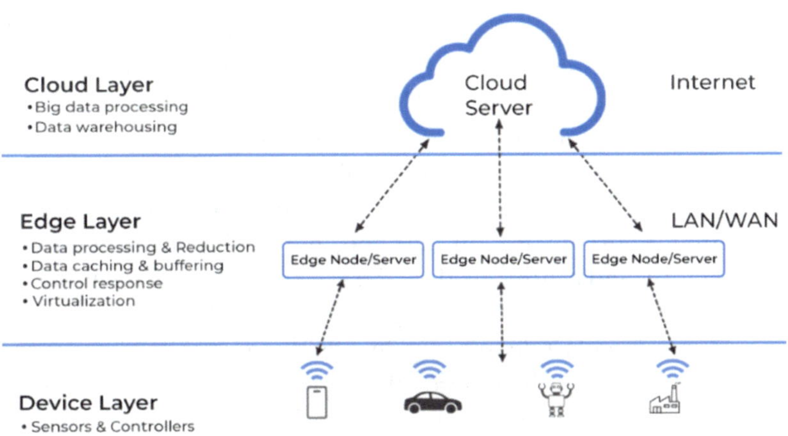

Figure 4.1. Edge network architecture.

Source: https://external-content.duckduckgo.com/iu/?u=https%3A%2F %2Fimages.spiceworks.com%2Fwp-content%2Fuploads%2F2022%2F01%2F06142823 %2F21.png&f=1&nofb=1&ipt=b7d145d94a2a6b342450a398d6dc7a9e116e3627e 011bd9be15bc03987758610.

Furthermore, Edge Network Architecture design also considers actively performance bottlenecks that may decelerate the efficacy of deployed communication protocols. Complex signaling protocols are required in managing varying service requests arising at the edge due to applications. These protocols must react promptly to changing user activity and service requirements in a bid to offer seamless connectivity and interactivity. For example, a performance model constructed under different signaling parameters can be used to determine possible interference in network efficiency, which can direct the optimization of edge deployments. With progress in Edge Network Architecture, rigorous approaches need to be employed in assessing these protocols to find out if they possess the mettle to manage the intricate networks of tomorrow and hence take edge systems to a higher level of what can be achieved on their behalf of next-generation communication services (Hou et al., 1994).

Importance of Communication Protocols

Reference is made to edge network topology, and communication protocols play a critical role in facilitating information transmission and reception within and among disparate network entities. Protocols establish the conventions and rules that determine how information is transmitted, received, and interpreted, thus facilitating structured interaction among devices in the network. With increasing levels of network complexity, there is a need to understand and handle these communication protocols. Inadequate compliance with established standards can lead to communication failures and subsequently impaired performance or system crashes. Thus, robust communication protocols not only enable efficient data exchange but also ensure system resilience, offering a safeguard against probable vulnerabilities that may be brought about by technological interdependencies, which are typically unavoidable in edge computing environments. In addition, the evolution of communication protocols is significantly influenced by the novel challenges resulting from the needs of current technology. With programmable wireless networks, there is a requirement for protocols able to navigate quickly through evolving conditions. As is stated in recent research, traditional Internet architecture has expanded into static designs that hinder innovation and operational efficiency. Programmable networks designed for enhancing flexibility and controllability best capture the imperative of dynamic communication standards that can accommodate a wide range of applications, such as software-defined networks and cognitive radio networks. The formulation of these new protocols is critical; they allow in-time modification to allow networks to dynamically respond to user demand and regulatory conditions and to maximize resource utilization, hence ensuring enhanced connectivity in edge network infrastructure (Ahad et al., 2014). Also, the intrinsic complexity that arises with edge network architectures demands a highly evolved communication protocol that can balance the capacity to be robust with fragility that is a natural aspect of such networks. While complicated networks are able to deliver maximum functionality and resilience gains, they present challenges too that have to be handled sensitively. The addition of newer mathematical models and techniques highlights the ongoing need for unifying and consistent communication mechanisms to manage the underlying system architectures complexity. Under poorly controlled situations, robustness-induced complexity can paradoxically lead to vulnerabilities and generate a robust but fragile state in the network architecture. Therefore, constant refinement of communication protocols is crucial not just to maximize performance but also to keep pace with technological progress without compromising security and stability in increasingly complex network environments (Alderson et al., 2010).

4.1. FUNDAMENTALS OF EDGE NETWORK ARCHITECTURE

The emergence of edge network architecture is induced by the increasing demands of the Internet of Things (IoT) and the need for more data processing capability. With the integration of more devices, the traditional centralized models of computing face challenges in terms of latency, bandwidth, and data security. Edge network architecture addresses such challenges through data processing decentralization, thereby moving computation and storage closer to the source of data. It not only reduces the amount of time involved in copying data to and from a cloud at the center but also relieves the network infrastructure load. Organizations can take advantage of the power of local processing to enhance responsiveness and develop real-time applications that are indispensable in industries like healthcare and smart cities, as explained in terms of IoTs revolutionizing capability (Akrivopoulos et al., 2017). Communication protocol integration with edge network architecture is necessary for enabling the smooth interaction between devices. Edge computing protocols must be capable of handling the particular operational needs that occur because of distributed settings. For instance, typical service discovery protocols would experience low performance as far as message loss and network inconsistency are concerned. New protocols like FRODO, however, have shown superior performance in maintaining operational consistency without focusing too much on lower network layers. By incorporating a light protocol stack, FRODO and others of its kind allow quick recovery from failure, hence allowing devices to communicate effectively even during poor network conditions. This resiliency feature is relevant in real applications where reliability is concerned because it facilitates the overall integrity of edge network operation (Glind et al.,

2005). Furthermore, edge network design promotes not just efficiency, but also security and privacy as a result of localized data management. Having sensitive data in close proximity to its location means there is less data traveling through large networks, reducing the opportunity for interception and unauthorized access. This applies very much to industries that require patient data privacy, such as healthcare. By implementing edge computing solutions, medical professionals are in a position to use solutions such as automated monitoring solutions, which allow individuals to simply transfer important health data safely to their physicians without revealing personal details. Moreover, the historical data aggregated at the edge can be locally analyzed to offer real-time insights that will improve medical diagnosis and patient treatment. Thus, the edge network architecture fundamentals extend beyond simple efficiency and encompass essential aspects of security and real-world use in fast-evolving sectors (Akrivopoulos et al., 2017).

4.1.1. Key Components of Edge Networks

Edge network design is specifically geared towards increasing data processing capacity by distributing computing power closer to where the data originates. Decentralization cuts down on latency, which is a high priority for applications that need real-time processing, such as autonomous vehicles and manufacturing automation. Key components typically include local computing nodes that are integrated with high-performance processing power and storage facilities, so that the data gets processed near the place where it is being created rather than depending on distant cloud servers. Such an arrangement not only improves response times but reduces loads on bandwidth within central networks. As highlighted in existing talk, this form of architecture plays an essential role in facilitating Industrial Internet of Things (IIoT) effectiveness by acknowledging its potential to facilitate advanced analytics and process enhancement within hierarchical data processing environments (Ali et al., 2017). Apart from local nodes, the role of communication protocols in edge networks is required to facilitate seamless data exchange and system integratability. They establish how devices communicate within the network, with secure and trustworthy connections between unlike components. MQTT and CoAP are examples of protocols that have emerged as enablers of choice, specifically designed for low-bandwidth, high-latency conditions found in edge environments. Their lean nature does not compromise on high-security levels when data is transmitted, an important feature in maintaining sensitive data securely. Successful communication procedures not only enhance data integrity but also facilitate edge network scaling at high speeds. Developments like these are significant, particularly in the context of edge computing's involvement with larger infrastructures like smart grids, where highly secure and reliable communications systems need to be operational to prevent vulnerabilities and service disruption (Qian et al., 2012) (Figure 4.2).

Figure 4.2. Components of edge commuting architecture.

Source: https://external-content.duckduckgo.com/iu/?u=https%3A%2F%2Fin tel-lipaat.com%2Fblog%2Fwp-content%2Fuploads%2F2023%2F05%2FComponents-of-Edge-Computing-Architecture.jpg&f=1&nofb=1&ipt=cacaa5fa5181aff5a14a3178c71c75b43cfd3dc98c9a175ac332eaf20f9d8f16.

Moreover, the integration of edge networks into existing infrastructures also has its own set of challenges and possibilities, particularly in sectors such as manufacturing and energy. By facilitating instant data access and computation through on-site computing facilities, edge networks can significantly enhance operational efficiencies. For instance, in manufacturing, edge computing-led technologies can provide real-time monitoring and predictive maintenance, making it possible for organizations to make decisions based on immediate insights. Moreover, the creation of edge networks directly supports the transition to smarter, more resilient utilities, where interconnectivity of devices leads to better energy management and sustainability practices. As more sectors increasingly rely on these technologies, an understanding of the foundation of edge networks becomes vital to realizing their full potential in next-generation applications and alignment with strategic security practices (Ali et al., 2017; Qian et al., 2012).

4.1.2. Differences Between Edge and Cloud Computing

The variations between edge computing and cloud computing are mainly based on the models of operation and data processing. Edge computing minimizes latency and response time by processing data close to its source. It is particularly crucial for applications requiring real-time analysis. Through dissemination of computation closer to the end user, edge networks are able to efficiently manage the increasing amount of data generated by the devices in the Internet of Things (IoT) connectivity. Decentralization decreases the requirement of large data transfers to the centralized cloud servers, thereby relaxing bandwidth constraints and enhancing overall system performance. Compared to centralized processing of data typical of cloud computing, edge solutions provide localized processing necessary for applications demanding instant access and responsiveness, as explicated in the recent advent of IoT paradigms (Akrivopoulos et al., 2017).

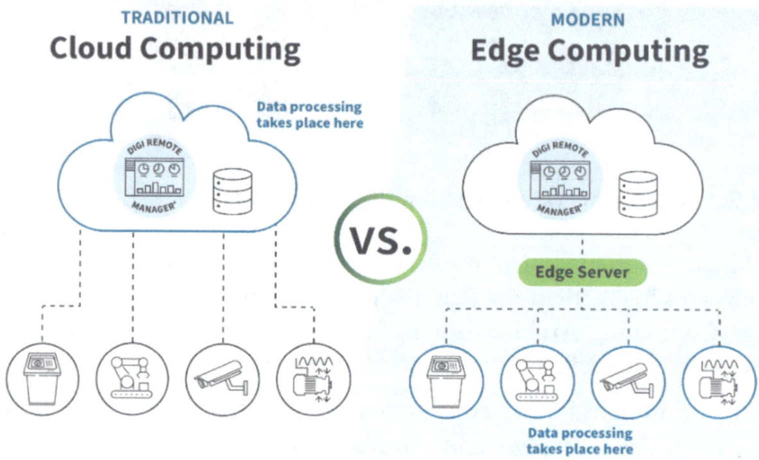

Figure 4.3. Differences between edge and cloud computing.

Source:https://www.digi.com/getattachment/Blog/post/Edge-Computing-vs-Cloud-Computing-Differences-and/a3-graphic-1-cloud-vs-edge-computing.png?lang=en-US.

Further, management and operational intricacies specific to edge networks vary significantly from those in the cloud. With cloud computing, services are kept centrally, where dissemination of data and allocation of resources can be done effortlessly. However, edge computing architecture raises complicated challenges related to data synchronization, compatibility, and supervision between distributed nodes. With a more dynamic edge scenario, management of services has to incorporate new methods in achieving consistency while ensuring effective data handling. The intricacy in such a situation highlights the advantage of using edge computing in very latency-prone setups where decisions have to be done in real-time. By means of distributed resources, edge networks can converge data in real-time even in challenging conditions, predicating the architectural strengths of such emerging technologies (Freitag et al., 2017). Moreover, the implications spill over to technical parameters, affecting other fields that make use of these paradigms of computing. The healthcare, transportation, and manufacturing industries are some of those which benefit extensively from the real-time data analysis ability of edge computings, enhancing operational efficiency and decision-making. For instance, in smart healthcare systems, processing patient data in real-time at the point of origin can lead to quick diagnosis and improved outcomes for the patient. In contrast, cloud computing remains useful for applications requiring high computational capabilities and storage capacities, forming a robust base for high-scale data analysis and storage. Lastly, the understanding of the difference between edge and cloud computing is vital for organizations seeking to optimize their technological building blocks and match them with their operational requirements (Akrivopoulos et al., 2017; Freitag et al., 2017) (Figure 4.3).

4.1.3. Benefits of Edge Network Architecture

The advantages of edge network architecture are increasingly evident, particularly in enhancing data processing efficiency. By decentralizing computing resources closer to data sources, edge networks significantly reduce latency, facilitating real-time data analysis and decision-making. This is pivotal in various applications, especially those requiring immediate responses, such as autonomous vehicles and industrial automation. Traditional cloud computing architectures, despite functioning smoothly, get bogged down by the volume of data being generated at the edge, leading to bottlenecks. Organizations are able to utilize edge computing in order to facilitate efficient bandwidth utilization as well as decrease latency involved in moving data across long distances to central servers. This architecture is not merely an additive but increasingly a central part that underpins the requirements of contemporary digital networks, enabling innovation based on real-time processing capabilities. Another significant benefit of edge network architecture is its ability to enhance security and privacy. With traditional cloud setups, sensitive data is transmitted over large networks to one place, making it very easy for interception and cyberattacks. By contrast, edge networks move processing nearer to data, so sensitive data can be processed and reacted to at or near the source without being transported over potentially insecure channels. This localization can significantly minimize the attack surface, enabling organizations to apply proprietary security controls that address specific dangers in localized data. Furthermore, as more organizations make use of regulations over data privacy, like GDPR and HIPAA, edge networks offer an alternative that is compliant by locating data on-premises and limiting exposure to vulnerabilities off-premises. In general, the elasticity of edge architecture not only guarantees maximum performance but also guarantees maximum data integrity and security. In addition, edge network architecture plays a major part in making new technologies such as the Internet of Things (IoT) possible. As IoT technology devices expand, the volume of data created is more and more substantial, with processing and handling that data requiring innovative solutions. Edge computing enables the devices to perform localized processing, thus eliminating the challenges of bandwidth and latency. For instance, as discussed in recent studies, electronic noses (e-noses) used in IoT applications require best practices in data transmission for them to achieve optimized performance (Husam, 2024). With the adoption of edge networks, e-noses are better able to manage odor-specific information and perform at a more efficient level, adding depth to applications from environmental monitoring to health diagnostics. Thus, the synergy between edge architecture and IoT offers a more dynamic and responsive network environment, enabling cutting-edge technologies to operate at their full potential while remaining responsive to user demand.

4.2. TYPES OF EDGE NETWORK ARCHITECTURES

Among edge network topologies, there are several variant models that cater to varying operational requirements and resource deployment. One such prevalent model is the hierarchical edge model, which implements multiple levels of processing capability that are placed strategically in proximity to the end user. The architecture facilitates localized processing of data to reduce latency and enhance performance for applications with real-time needs. It also facilitates more efficient resource management through workload spreading across multiple nodes in the edge. Hierarchical design also facilitates scalability as new resources can be added without necessarily modifying the basic architecture. In general, hierarchical edge networks have a significant contribution to efficient management of data, hence it is highly sought in sectors like finance and telecommunications where performance and high-speed processing capability are of high importance. Peer-to-peer (P2P) structure is another cutting-edge approach under edge network architectures. Such architecture allows devices to communicate directly with each other, forming a decentralized architecture that facilitates collaboration and sharing of resources between the nodes. An example includes the Juxtapose (JXTA)-Overlay, a P2P system that capitalizes on the strength of Java and JXTA technologies. Such platforms are applied to distributed computing while providing robust collaborative environments for operations such as social networking and online learning. By leveraging the inherent decentralized paradigm of P2P topology, they empower users to maximize the utilization of resources and deliver access to computing capacity that is transparent, global, and secure. This property is particularly beneficial in industries requiring flexible networking possibilities under changing loads and needs, covering loopholes of traditional centralized structures (Barolli et al., 2011). Lastly, edge computing infrastructure for Internet of Things (IoT) security provides an essential element in edge network planning. With the proliferation of IoT devices, there has also been increasing demand for a secure communications standard that manages several specialized standards, resource constraints, and running applications. One emerging trend in this regard is the reconfigurable security framework, which leverages near-user edge devices as security agents. This new strategy streamlines key management and lowers the computational burdens of IoT devices running complex security protocols. Through extensible key management and facilitation of instantiation of advanced cryptography techniques with ease, this system significantly improves IoT security without compromising usability and performance (Chen et al., 2017). Such innovations highlight the importance of integrating security solutions in edge network design in a way that they are positioned to effectively serve the heterogeneous, dynamic environments common to modern digital communication.

4.2.1. Centralized vs. Decentralized Edge Networks

The ongoing evolution of edge network topology brings inherent issues related to the decentralized versus centralized models that govern their operation. Centralized edge networks usually have a single point of control that centralizes data processing, storage, and management capacities.

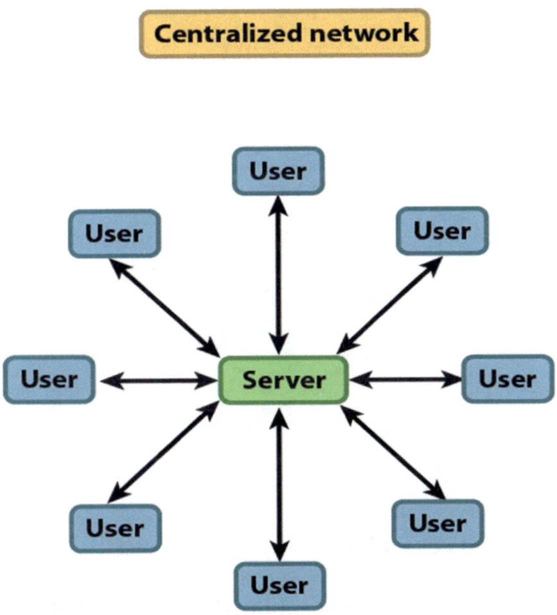

Figure 4.4. Centralized networks.

Source: https://www.researchgate.net/publication/354905755/figure/fig4/AS:1143 1281389818173@1745238446976/Centralized-vs-decentralized-networks.tif.

This facilitates simpler deployment and faster response times because data processing is being performed at the center. Nevertheless, the shortcomings of this centralized approach come to the forefront concerning scalability and fault tolerance, particularly for scenarios demanding real-time processing from various geographical locations. As user demand grows, central hubs' workload can become a cause of performance bottlenecks as well as latency growth, particularly in situations where rapid data access is paramount for applications like smart cities and autonomous vehicles. In contrast, decentralized edge networks offer a tempting alternative, dispersing processing efforts across multiple nodes instead of relying on a central point. The dispersal enhances scalability and resilience, as the network remains operable even when a node is lost. It also allows for enhanced data security and privacy because local processing minimizes data to be transmitted across vast networks. When technologies like Blockchain are being integrated into decentralized systems, new sets of challenges exist, specifically related to computational load and bandwidth overhead. It is critical to overcome these challenges effectively to provide support for decentralized architectures in terms of being able to process the expansive demands of future Internet of Things (IoT) applications (Abdolee et al., 2019) (Figures 4.4 and 4.5).

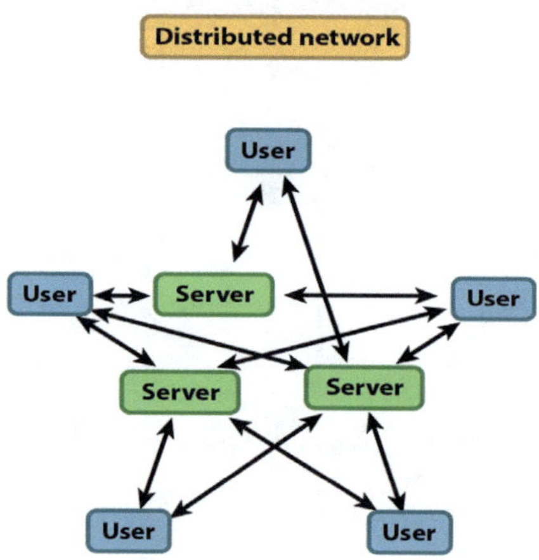

Figure 4.5. Decentralized networks.

Source: https://www.researchgate.net/publication/354905755/figure/fig4/AS:1143 1281389818173@1745238446976/Centralized-vs-decentralized-networks.tif.

Performance implications from the adoption of decentralized edge networks are nuanced, particularly when benchmarked against cloud applications. Field research has reported on the trade-offs that underlie the applications of blockchain technology within decentralized systems, including their impact on response time and transaction throughput. While decentralized networks can make cooperation and service quality more reliable, the computational resource burden stemming from blockchain protocols can be very onerous, and it affects overall performance metrics (Beck et al., 2019). Keeping the relevant resource requirements in check while leveraging the advantages of decentralization is hence crucial. Through understanding these dynamics, stakeholders can develop strategies to maximize edge network functionality and communication protocols and to encourage innovation in multiple applications.

4.2.2. Fog Computing as an Extension of Edge Networks

As the demands for real-time processing and low-latency communications in Internet of Things (IoT) applications continue to rise, fog computing is a realistic expansion of edge networks. It merely bridges the gap between centralized cloud setup and the scattered nature of edge devices by situating computational capabilities close to data sources.

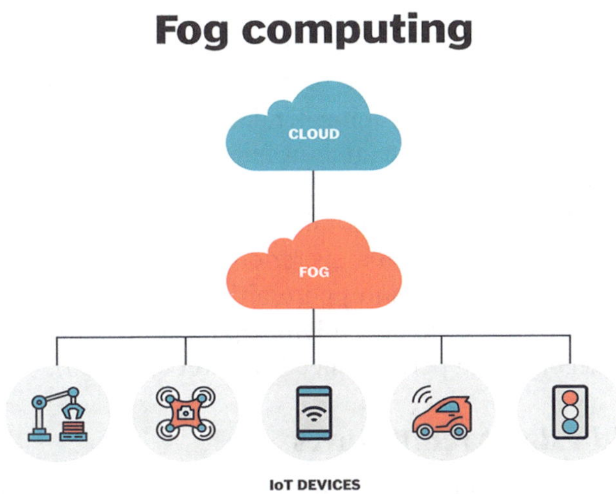

Figure 4.6. Fog computing.

Source: https://www.techtarget.com/rms/onlineimages/storage-fog_computing_mobile.png.

This location makes latency requirements for use cases such as autonomous transport and real-time surveillance smaller. By enabling data processing at network edges, fog computing lightens bandwidth stress on core networks, making it possible to have efficient resource sharing and more interactive interaction with IoT devices. In addition, it enhances overall network performance through minimal data transportation of only necessary data to the cloud to conserve bandwidth and optimize data transfer efficiency in edge networks. Besides performance benefits, fog computing addresses some of the security and privacy concerns of edge computing and cloud services. The traditional fog computing paradigm often does not facilitate key functions like device-to-device (D2D) communications, which can enhance the functions of various IoT applications. For instance, poor security solutions may expose data to vulnerabilities in large-scale networks. To counter such challenges, emerging security architectures focus on privacy in fog computing environments utilizing lightweight cryptographic methods to reduce overhead on resource-limited edge devices. They are important since they can provide a foundation upon which secure communication among IoT devices can be established and the security issues inherited from traditional cloud computing systems mitigated (Gope et al., 2019) (Figure 4.6). Enhancing resource management in fog computing systems also necessitates efficient deployment of monitoring mechanisms, whose role is pivotal to maintaining the efficiency of the fog architecture. Dynamic resource provisioning in the fog nodes requires real-time visibility of the network state, enabling the network administrator to respond proactively to performance demands. The utilization of programmable data planes, as seen in technologies such as P4, enables effortless detection of telemetry data within fog networks. Incorporating programmable elements such as these, fog computing is able to utilize gathered telemetry data to optimize resource management mechanisms. This aspect not only maximizes the operation of fog nodes but also paves the way for future traffic engineering opportunities based on telemetry, enabling networks to be scaled up based on evolving application demands and maintain extremely high security and performance levels (et al., 2020).

4.2.3. Hybrid Edge Architectures

The hybrid edge architecture idea seems to be an imperative paradigm in the evolving time of edge network architecture and communication protocols. In bringing together centralized as well as decentralized processing powers, hybrid architectures actually reduce latency and enhance responsiveness for real-time use cases. The approach is quickly gaining relevance as the need for immediacy in data processing is escalating with the increasing dependence on IoT devices and intelligent applications. Basically, hybrid structures leverage the processing power of cloud infrastructure and local processing at the network edge to create an effective balanced system that can deal with fluctuating workloads with ease. Consequently, this framework not only optimizes utilization of available resources but also facilitates better control over data and analytics, which play critical roles in deploying the latest applications. Furthermore, hybrid edge architectures are also flexible in the sense that they can support different communication protocols and networks. This flexibility allows such architectures to support multiple mobility scenarios and multiple technologies and services. For instance, hybrid frameworks are able to support both IPv4 and IPv6 networks, as can be seen in the overarching taxonomy of mobility frameworks that categorizes handover operations based on their efficiency and compatibility in different systems (Ferretti et al., 2015) (Figure 4.7).

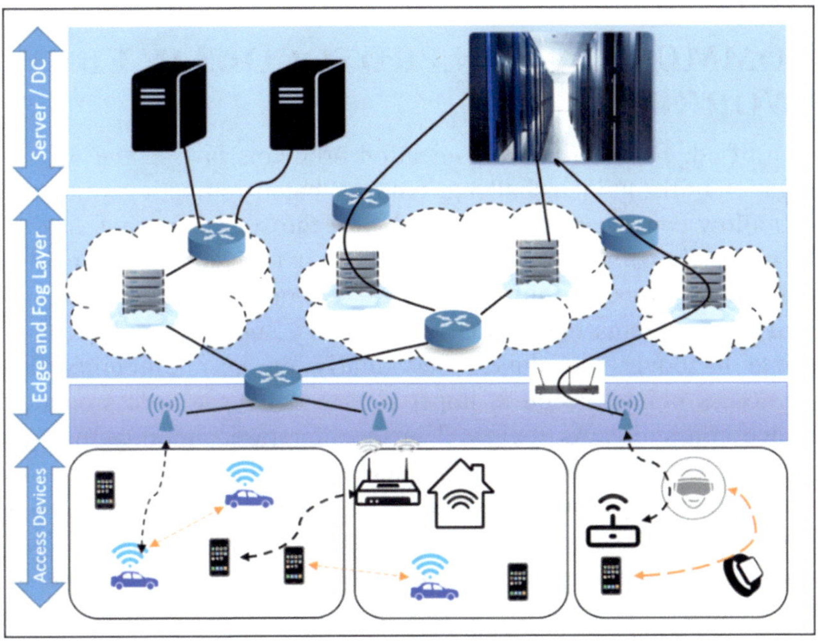

Figure 4.7. Hybrid edge cloud architecture.

Source: https://www.researchgate.net/figure/Hybrid-Edge-Cloud-Architecture_fig1_328198753.

This adaptability makes it possible for hybrid designs to provide seamless service in the presence of the diverse set of devices and standards encountered in modern networks. Consequently, the usability of hybrid architectures expands with increasing network environment complexities and the demand for seamless integration across heterogeneous platforms. Finally, operational efficiency in hybrid edge designs hinges on effective switching techniques capable of providing integrated services without compromise. Defined in presentations of edge networks' integrated strategies, burst and high-speed packet switching are essential techniques to provide high data rates with application-independent provisioning of services (Bradley et al., 1989). These techniques support the maximum bandwidth usage and fast response to dynamic traffic changes, which are essential for hybrid systems carrying multiple applications at the same time. By using these new-generation switching mechanisms, hybrid edge architectures can not only enhance the overall network service performance but also provide a robust platform for next-generation innovations in communications protocols. Thus, ongoing innovation of these architectures will be instrumental to addressing an increasingly interconnected world's need.

4.3. COMMUNICATION PROTOCOLS IN EDGE NETWORKS

Evolution of edge network communication protocols is essential to facilitate the mitigation of the unique challenges in distributed computing systems. Edge networks allow computation near the edge of the source of data, minimizing latency and optimizing the effective utilization of bandwidth. In this case, communication protocols must not only support the resource constraints typical of edge systems but also ensure mobility support. Implementation of appropriate handover techniques, particularly on users' mobility between multiple access points, becomes imperative to deliver seamless connectivity and service continuity. As reviewed in the literature, mobility management techniques development and categorization enable significant enhancement in offering stable and dynamic communication capable of supporting horizontal and vertical handovers and multihoming (Ferretti et al., 2015). Therefore, a thorough understanding of these protocols is necessary to enhance user experience and operational efficiency in edge networks. Resource management is another critical domain of communication protocols in edge networks, particularly radio access and Internet Protocol (IP) functionality integration. IP-based networking in Radio Access Networks (RANs) has complexities in terms of requiring protocol support for wireless communication's high mobility and dynamic nature. Traditional modeling approaches are also incapable of fulfilling the requirements of low-bandwidth and low-latency common in edge domains. The emergence of resource management frameworks such as Resource Management in DiffServ (RMD) introduces a systematic solution that extends mainstream architectures with new schemes for admission control and resource reservation. This paradigm emphasizes an efficient model of resource management appropriate for the high-speed demands of IP-based RANs, thus ensuring secure communication in edge networks (Heijenk et al., 2001). Such a characteristic points toward building protocols able to accommodate the unique demands of edge computing. Communication protocol success in edge networks also relies on scalability and implementation efficiency. As edge environments scale to encompass a vast array of devices and services, protocols must be able to efficiently process increasing amounts of data with minimal overhead in operations. Techniques such as the Per Hop Reservation (PHR) and Per Domain Reservation (PDR) defined in the RMD framework are great examples of techniques that streamline reservation processes in DiffServ domains. With a focus on having one reservation state per behavior aggregate, these protocols support increased scalability and simpler resource management (Heijenk et al., 2001). Furthermore, the development of light protocols is essential to accommodate the different computationally intensive demands of edge applications, keeping communication responsive as well as agile to shifting network demand. This equilibrium of efficiency and flexibility is central to enhancing edge network architecture.

4.3.1. Overview of Common Communication Protocols

The large body of communication protocols is the basis of edge network architecture, and they provide the means to forward data and devices communicate effectively.

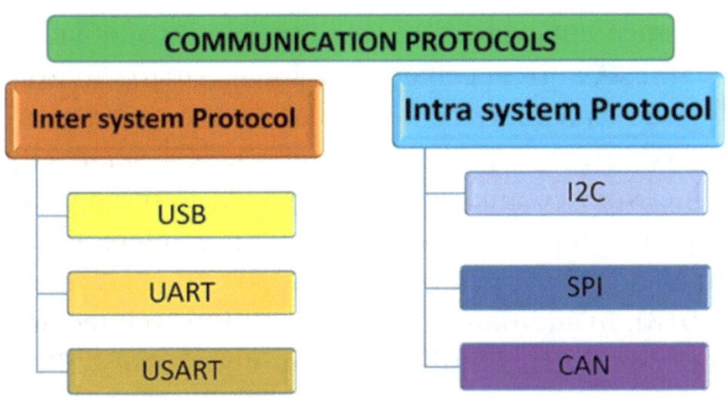

Figure 4.8. Communication network protocols.

Source: https://external-content.duckduckgo.com/iu/?u=https%3A%2F%2Fmy.element14.com%2Fwcsstore%2FExtendedSitesCatalogAssetStore%2Fcms%2Fasset%2Fimages%2Fcommon%2Ftechnology%2Farticles%2F2924710%2F2924710-communication-protocol-types.jpg&f=1&nofb=1&ipt=c6215e244486f932b84f1b4e47ed909f88ec85a58cfcd49cc402b34e900dbeab.

Transmission control protocol (TCP) and user datagram protocol (UDP) are the most prevalent protocols that both operate at the transport layer of the Internet Protocol Suite. TCP is identified with its connection-oriented, reliable service that ensures data integrity through mechanisms of error checking and retransmitting. Conversely, UDP offers a connectionless service that is faster but excludes the reliability aspects of TCP and is hence useful for applications where speed is more valuable than reliability, such as online gaming or real-time video streaming. It is often a matter of using one of these protocols or the other depending on the specific needs of the application in question, involving knowledge of the features of each protocol in edge networks (Figure 4.8). Another set of highly critical protocols are those that operate at the application layer, e.g., Hypertext Transfer Protocol (HTTP), File Transfer Protocol (FTP), and Simple Mail Transfer Protocol (SMTP). HTTP is the foundation for World Wide Web data communication that carries hypertext documents. Its newer incarnation, HTTP/2, improves performance through the capability to multiplex multiple requests and responses within a single connection. FTP, on the other hand, is designed especially for file transfer between client and server and can handle both binary and text types of data. SMTP is an essential component of email delivery, with the sending, receiving, and relaying of email messages between email servers and email clients. These protocols all contribute to the fundamental aspect of the user experience and operational performance of edge networks, where there has to be seamless data transmission between dozens of applications and devices. The intersection of the Internet of Things (IoT) with traditional communication protocols is an opportunity and a challenge in edge network architecture. As urban centers develop as smart environments, access to IoT technologies has a central role to play in governance, urban planning, and municipal services. According to recent studies, smart city applications require a robust network communication system with these protocols for them to function properly—these protocols permit the interconnection of many sensors and actuators in city infrastructure to obtain real-time data and process it (Fischer et al., 2018). In addition, designing mobility architectures that adapt to changing network conditions is still a must; protocols must allow for seamless handover processes to support user mobility in an effort to maintain service continuity across different environments (Ferretti et al., 2015). Such crossing of paths between IoT and mainstream communication protocols does show their cardinal role towards shaping future urban environments and connectivity.

4.3.2. Role of IoT Protocols in Edge Networks

The discreet embedding of Internet of Things (IoT) protocols within edge networks vastly optimizes data processing efficiency and responsiveness. As IoT devices continue to proliferate unchecked, the past excess dependence on cloud computing is no longer able to keep up with demands as latency and bandwidth are now critical concerns. Edge computing has risen to the call as the essential solution, placing processing closer to the origin of the data. Different communication protocols in IoT, like publish-subscribe systems and request-reply, allow edge networks to effectively manage the flow of data created by numerous devices. The protocols support quick data transfer and resource usage, ensuring applications benefit from improved latency and better throughput that are critical to real-time analytics and decision-making in edge settings. Thus, understanding the strengths and limitations of different protocols is essential in order to optimize edge network structure (Carpio et al., 2019). In addition, security in IoT protocols cannot be overlooked with regards to edge networks since data integrity and confidentiality should be top priorities. Because IoT devices are heterogeneous and each has disparate communications standards, security issues are numerous. A reconfigurable model of security enhances edge computing security by applying solutions for addressing important key management issues and computational burdens typically placed on IoT devices. Offloading of computationally intensive cryptographic processes through leveraging a proximal security agent makes the overall IoT system more efficient. By adopting standards-based security mechanisms such as anonymous authentication and guarded data access control, this model addresses common vulnerabilities found when implementing IoT protocols within edge networks. Given that security is always the pillars of any network model, this model is a giant leap towards having robust defense mechanisms against potential threats (Chen et al., 2017) (Figure 4.9).

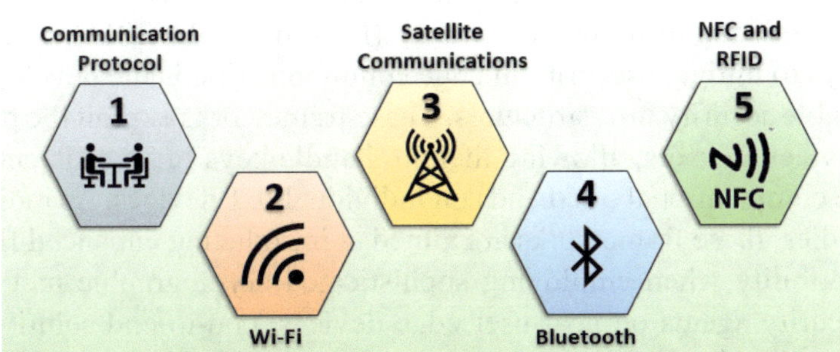

Figure 4.9. IoT communication protocol.

Source: https://cdn.educba.com/academy/wp-content/uploads/2019/11/iot-communication-protocol-1.png.

Finally, the union of IoT protocols and edge networks determines the fate of agile system architectures that not only perform well but are also flexible. As the unique requirements of various applications drive the evolution of communication protocols, research and development work actively in enhancing this domain. Foraying into the synergistic usability of edge computing with IoT protocols can lead to increased performance metrics, such as lower latency and optimized energy efficiency. As cited in persuasive research, the integration of advanced protocols within edge networks functions as innovation drivers, spurring innovation within smart cities, healthcare, and industrial automation. According to these findings, there is a clear need for system architects and protocol designers to prioritize interoperability among protocols, paving the way to end-to-end strong edge network architectures. This can ultimately allow organizations to fully leverage their IoT rollouts (Carpio et al., 2019).

4.3.3. Security Protocols for Edge Communication

The advent of edge computing has brought with it advanced security protocols tailored for edge communication to ensure that sensitive data within decentralized networks is safe. With use extending to varied industries such as healthcare, logistics, and finance, the need for strong security measures becomes more pressing by the day. The edge architecture not only enhances processing capabilities but also comes with unique security challenges due to its distributed nature. A general security infrastructure will be required to recognize the vulnerabilities inherent in edge devices—often characterized as resource-scarce and heterogeneous communication protocols. Multifeatured network application planning and instantiation will be required to support self-organization and decentralization, thereby enabling secure and reliable access to global resources and accommodating different use cases (Barolli et al., 2011). One of the critical ways to mitigate security in edge communication is the development of reconfigurable security infrastructures. These frameworks exploit the proximity of edge devices to users, allowing them to handle keys in an efficient manner and reduce computational overheads on individual IoT devices. As indicated by current studies, these frameworks are aimed at introducing enhanced flexibility and compatibility when employing sophisticated cryptographic methods. By placing security agents on near-user edge devices, end-to-end solutions focus on simplifying authentication operations, cryptographic key management, and secure data access controls in an effective manner. Their execution is crucial in reducing risks that may come with unauthorized access and data breaches, especially in the case of settings where devices can run under different security standards (Chen et al., 2017). Additionally, it is imperative to make security protocols for edge communication not only effective but also user-friendly in order for them to be adopted on a large scale. This user-centric design approach can significantly enhance security feature usability, resulting in higher levels of user compliance. The interface design should enable easy-to-use interactions that allow users to securitize their data without needing special technical expertise. In addition, utilizing collaborative solutions compatible with existing systems can result in an easy user experience while maintaining high standards of security. With devices becoming increasingly interlinked at the edge, it is critical that security features evolve to draw lessons from experience garnered from past failures and nurture a secure digital environment that enables innovation and optimization (Figure 4.10).

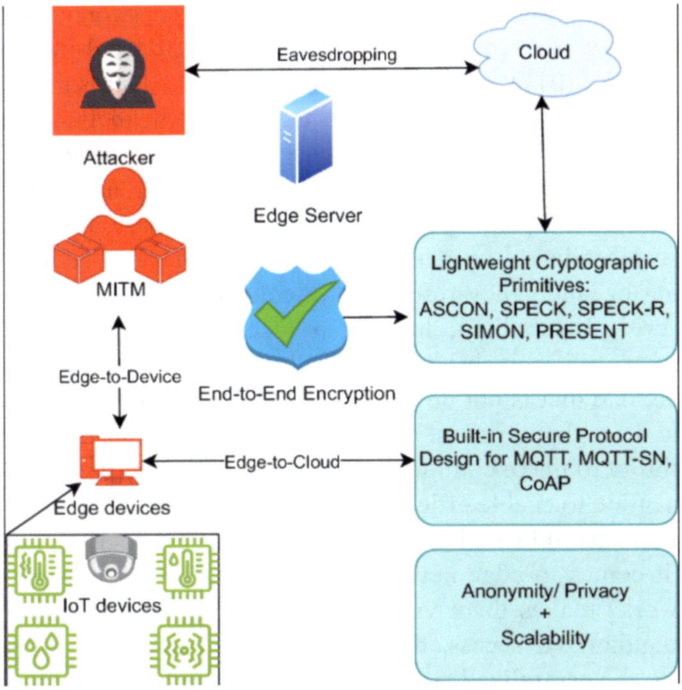

Figure 4.10. Securing IoT edge.

Source: https://media.springernature.com/lw1200/springer-static/image/art%3A10.1007%2Fs10207-025-01071-7/MediaObjects/10207_2025_1071_Fig7_HTML.png.

4.4. CHALLENGES IN EDGE NETWORK COMMUNICATION

The incorporation of edge network communication into modern structures is faced with actual challenges that can limit efficiency and efficacy. The heterogeneity of devices interconnected in an edge network is one significant challenge. The devices, ranging from the most basic sensor to the more advanced machinery, have varied standards and protocols of communication, leading to interoperability problems. Lack of standardization necessitates advanced middleware technology to facilitate proper communication and sharing of information. Such middleware requires regular updates and reiterations to accommodate new devices and protocols, resulting in an exciting but generally unstable picture. Furthermore, the increased latency and bandwidth constraints of remote data processing can exacerbate such situations, reinforcing the importance of robust and dynamic solutions to edge network communication reliability in uses such as remote industrial monitoring and real-time analytics, as argued in Ali et al. (2017). Another most important problem is the management of data traffic over edge networks. Due to the growth in Internet of Things (IoT) devices, there has also been increased data generation, which creates bottlenecks in communication infrastructure. Congestion would negatively impact the network's capability to send timely and accurate information, which is vital for services based on real-time processing of data, such as intelligent manufacturing or emergency response systems. This is where fog computing becomes a critical paradigm, looking to decentralize data processing and management capabilities by bringing them closer to edge devices. By doing this, it lightens the load that is put on centralized cloud services and avoids latency and network throughput issues. Effective implementation of fog computing has the capability to make communication protocols effective, enabling proper resource allocation to enable efficient management of the load on edge network communications, as indicated in Carpio et al. (2019). Security is also a major issue when it comes to edge network communication. The distributed nature of such networks makes them vulnerable to a range of cybersecurity attacks including unauthorized access, data breaches, and denial of service attacks. As opposed to the centralized architectures, which may employ more standard security measures, edge networks require multi-faceted security strategies to protect the large array of endpoints scattered across a large number of sites. Data encryption, secure authentication, and intrusion detection systems become essential but challenging with diverse operating environments and purposes of edge devices. Moreover, compliance with evolving regulation with respect to data protection and privacy adds another level of complication. Thus, security aspects not only enhance edge network communication trust but also ensure successful implementation of applications based on handling and processing of sensitive data, rendering them resilient towards anticipated threats.

4.4.1. Latency and Bandwidth Limitations

Latency and bandwidth limits are critical problems in edge network design and communication protocols. Latency has a negative impact on the performance of applications with real-time requirements, such as video conferencing and online gaming, where minor delays can result in poor user experience. Network design, in this respect, needs to emphasize low-latency solutions in order to support modern applications. With the more extensive application of edge computing, latency reduction mechanisms like localized processing and routing can significantly improve communication efficiency. Good architecture should also consider the impact of network congestion, which can exacerbate the latency problem and diminish the aggregate bandwidth. The relentless pursuit of low latency thus requires a great understanding of both network topology and data transmission protocol behavior. Bandwidth limitations are yet another equally important aspect of edge network infrastructure that needs intense examination. Current communications systems, particularly those with traditional protocols such as TCP, lag behind in maximizing bandwidth utilization, especially for high frequency systems such as millimeter waves. While operating with such high-frequency bands, as is the case with the rising deployments of mmWave technology, bandwidth variability can be particularly troublesome, e.g., physical interference sensitivity and drastic line-of-sight vs. non-line-of-sight fluctuations. Such inherent instability can lead to suboptimal bandwidth consumption, therefore further aggravating latency issues. Protocol evolutions have to battle these bandwidth constraints. For instance, employing a TCP proxy architecture to optimize traffic streams illustrates the urgency of matching network layer characteristics with physical medium properties to reduce congestion and amplify throughputs (Figure 4.11).

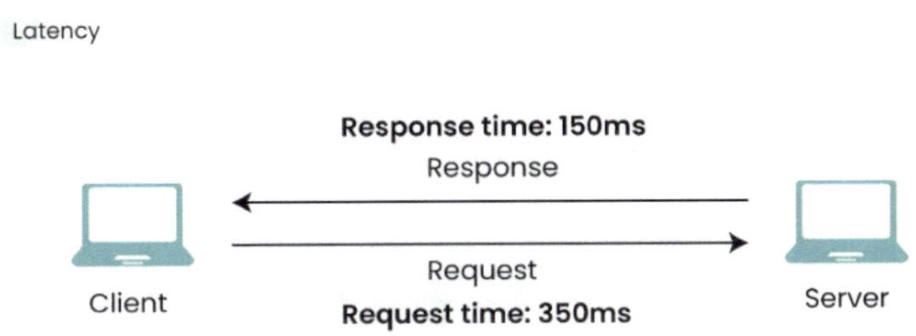

Figure 4.11. Latency in system design.

Source: https://media.geeksforgeeks.org/wp-content/uploads/20240130132455/Latency.jpg.

Further, the technical challenges presented by latency and bandwidth limitations are emphasized by the aggressive technical expectations placed on 5G systems. The IMT 2020 specifications of a peak data rate of 20 Gbps with a latency of just 1 millisecond are a paradigm shift in expectation in wireless technology. Achieving these goals necessitates a rethinking of the overall protocol stack—namely the Medium Access Control (MAC) layer and congestion control mechanisms. As mmWave frequencies offer dense spectrum opportunities, the reliance on these frequencies introduces hurdles in the direction of maintaining reliable, ultra-low latency links. The solutions must address not only the physical layer behavior but also involve complex algorithms and architectural shifts within the network, which shows the intricate interplay between bandwidth and latency. Addressing both dimensions is essential to fulfill the stringent requirements of next-generation communication protocols, thus facilitating stronger and more efficient edge network architectures.

4.4.2. Security Vulnerabilities in Edge Networks

The pervasiveness of edge networks significantly enhances application responsiveness and data processing times through placing computation closer to the source of data. However, this architectural shift is accompanied by a multitude of security threats that can be exploited by attackers. The decentralized nature of edge networks enables a higher attack surface as a result of the different nodes and devices involved, and it is challenging to implement similar security policies across these heterogeneous nodes and devices.

Figure 4.12. Cellular-vehicle to everything (C-V2X).

Source: https://www.emnify.com/hubfs/Title-c-v2x.webp.

These weaknesses have the potential to attack not only the integrity and confidentiality of an individual edge device but also the broader interdependent systems. The employment of more than one communication protocol between these networks makes the security situation even more difficult to defend, as each protocol can have different weaknesses and require special defense strategies. In particular, with the increasing embracement of smart grid infrastructures, effective security frameworks should be established to protect communication channels vigilantly and reduce exploitations that breach basic functionalities and lead to catastrophic incidents (Qian et al., 2012). The emergence of technology-enabled applications, such as Cellular-Vehicle to Everything (C-V2X), also presents the complexity of securing edge networks from sophisticated attacks. While C-V2X attempts to automate vehicle communication, its integration with edge network frameworks has serious security implications. Legacy LTE-V2X systems, for instance, provide inherent weaknesses that jeopardize data integrity and user privacy. The transition to 5G-V2X offers an opportunity to overcome these weaknesses; however, the high-end features of the technology need to be ensured not to also inadvertently instill further security flaws (Figure 4.12). Specifically, while extensive reports have highlighted the security aspects of 5G, the specific weaknesses in 5G-V2X systems necessitate particular research. The need for an efficient Security Reflex Function (SRF)-based architecture is evident, indicating the necessity for ongoing threat contemplation and the establishment of proactive defense mechanisms to safeguard the fast-growing interconnected vehicular networks (Guizani et al., 2019). Moreover, the contrast between edge network weaknesses and conventional centralized frameworks is of highest priority to comprehend. Given that edge computing is prevalent, classical security models that deal with security from a perimeter-first stance no longer suffice. Instead, an evolution to a more holistic security system encompassing local devices, processing data, and communication processes needs to occur. This architecture must adapt to the changing nature of edge networks, which are generally characterized as dynamic and with varying operating conditions. In addition, the consolidation of a huge number of devices with varying security posture demands the utilization of continuous monitoring systems that can detect anomalies in real-time. With an adoption of proactive security as deep monitoring, risk assessment, and response in the face of incidents, stakeholders can better mitigate the built-in vulnerabilities of edge networks and provide a solid infrastructure on which to base the dynamic digital world.

4.4.3. Interoperability Issues Among Protocols

Interoperability of communication protocols plays an important role in designing edge networks, particularly due to the explosive increase in Internet of Things (IoT) devices. As IoT devices are increasingly integrated into the digital ecosystem, interoperability between various protocols through which they can communicate efficiently is paramount to optimizing performance. Request-reply and publish-subscribe strategies have been found to be viable contenders in enabling interoperability in blended IoT-to-fog-to-cloud scenarios. Such models of interaction must cater to both individual network demands and facilitate multi-form services and applications to be integrated across various platforms. Consequently, the use of protocols to communicate has a highly significant influence on the functionality and scalability of edge networks because multiple layers from IoT, fog computing, and cloud services depend upon seamless exchange of data to operate coherently and effectively (Carpio et al., 2019). The challenges of achieving interoperability usually arise from variation in communication protocol characteristics and performance criteria. Energy consumption, latency, and network throughput are some of the most important parameters that have a direct effect on making the protocol integration efficient. With varying protocols being used to cater to the distinct requirements of IoT devices, fog nodes, and cloud environments, the risk of incompatibility. These interoperability issues can lead to bottlenecks, thus resulting in suboptimal performance and reduced user experience. It is therefore critical that challenges are addressed by critically examining the protocols fundamental principles and how they act in the architecture. By understanding how the dynamics of interaction work, architects can ensure better smoothening and enhanced system performance across all levels of edge networks (Carpio et al., 2019). Besides, with the continuous progress of networked media, there has never been a higher demand for robust and adaptive communication protocols. With individuals consuming and sharing multimedia information at historic levels, there are challenges to be overcome in maintaining the quality and integrity of service. The competition to establish new transport protocols and multimedia coding schemes creates additional layers of complexity. Good interoperability is crucial to the functioning of these enhancements with the stipulation that different media types and network types can freely communicate. To this effect, further development in machine-to-machine communication and peer-to-peer networks contributes to the complexity of the environment with successive revisions in protocol standards. As the Internet continues to trend towards more dynamic and user-oriented content sharing, trouble-free protocol interoperability will remain a dominant factor in shaping edge network architecture in the years to come.

4.5. APPLICATIONS OF EDGE NETWORK ARCHITECTURE

The evolution of edge network architecture significantly supports the utilization of sophisticated networking applications within different industries, including smart cities, transportation, and healthcare. With growing demands from industries for more utilization of real-time data processing and efficient usage of resources, edge computing becomes an essential solution. Edge network architecture enables localized processing of data closer to the source, reducing latency and bandwidth consumption by less data being transferred to central servers. In particular, software such as the Juxtapose (JXTA)-Overlay demonstrates the capability of edge networks to provide decentralized, self-healing systems that federate disparate resources from desktop PCs to sensors guaranteeing efficient distributed processing and cooperative functions in trusted environments (Barolli et al., 2011). Edge network design further optimizes processes and provides innovative services that are pivotal to today's digital landscapes. In addition, edge network architecture applies particularly in smart cities, where management relies increasingly on intelligent connectivity and data integration. Urban communities are faced with complex issues such as climate change, pollution, and traffic management, and as such must adopt advanced solutions that leverage information and communication technologies (ICT). With the application of edge computing, cities can utilize numerous sensors and actuators feeding into the Internet of Things (IoT) for smart urban governance and infrastructure (Fischer et al., 2018). This integration allows for a responsive and adaptive city environment as it enables stakeholders to link multiple municipal authorities and activate more citizen engagement via access to data and services in real-time. Thus, edge network design is the key to making the Smart City vision a reality, facilitating efficient governance along with sustainable city living. Finally, one of the most exciting applications of edge network architecture is integrating cooperative processes that can enhance multi-platform user experience. With edge computing, various industries not only facilitate conventional computing needs but also groundbreaking collaborative activities such as social networking and online education. For example, schools are utilizing the capabilities of edge networks to deliver interactive learning experiences that respond to various access points as well as preferences. According to edge application analysis, the integration and cooperative work facilitation capacity are essential in environments with a focus on rapid technology evolution and user high interactivity (Barolli et al., 2011). Hence, as businesses keep exploring the edge network architecture potential, they will find new applications that will facilitate increased interaction and formation of bonds in a more connected society.

4.5.1. Smart Cities and Urban Infrastructure

The Smart City concept is a revolutionary method of managing cities by the widespread adoption of advanced information and communication technologies (ICT) to enhance the quality of urban living. With increasing population numbers and increased pressure for sustainable urban life, the application of smart technologies has become necessary. By connecting public services to a sophisticated matrix of sensors and communications networks, cities have the potential to better manage issues such as traffic congestion, environmental monitoring, and smart energy use. This coordinated framework is the ultimate manifestation of the Internet of Things (IoT), which is a critical component in building a cohesive urban space. The emphasis on data collection and analysis in real time facilitates informed decision-making for urban planners and administrators, creating a more robust infrastructure that effectively responds to contemporary urban issues (Fischer et al., 2018) (Figure 4.13).

Figure 4.13. Smart cities represents a transformative approach to urban management, relying heavily on advanced information and communication technologies (ICT) to enhance the quality of urban life.

Source: https://media.infrastructureinvestor.com/uploads/2022/05/T2_Smart-city-wireless-connected_1200-x-680-1.jpg.

At the core of the Smart City strategy is the incorporation of edge network architecture, which facilitates near-data processing and analysis. Such strategic placement of data processing not only reduces latency but also optimizes bandwidth use on city networks. Edge computing also facilitates a symbiotic partnership between communications infrastructure and urban services, which has been elaborated in the evolving SymbioCity vision. By leveraging real-time data in various city services, including traffic management and public safety, edge architectures can alter and optimize network performance in real-time. Consequently, with urban sensor networks that are dense and communication protocols being utilized in cities, the potential of more urban services increases, and this leads to better citizen engagement as well as coordinated urban planning (Abrougui et al., 2017). Implementation of Smart City initiatives demands a comprehensive understanding of communication protocols that are the basis of these technologies. With increasingly integrated cities, interoperability between various systems becomes the necessity to enable them to function without glitches. Data exchange protocols that facilitate smooth data transfer and security protocols that are robust and adaptive to threats are critical in safeguarding urban infrastructure against attacks. For instance, converging various IoT platforms within cities must incorporate unified communication standards of guidelines to ensure reliability and consistency of performance. A unifying approach for urban infrastructure, which incorporates such developing protocols, allows municipalities to manage high volumes of data without a reduction in the quality of service. Through the advancement of innovation in communication technology, cities not only become efficient in their activities but also create a sustainable city life for citizens' well-being and the environment (Fischer et al., 2018).

4.5.2. Industrial IoT and Manufacturing

The Industrial Internet of Things (IIoT) is actually transforming the manufacturing world by enabling the connectivity of systems, sensors, and machines within a production environment. Through seamless data transfer, manufacturers can boost operational efficiency, supply chain management optimization, and product quality. By integrating next-generation analytics and AI, IIoT enables predictive maintenance wherein equipment can be monitored in real time to predict failure before the event occurs, thus reducing unplanned downtime. The technology is crucial as businesses seek to optimize productivity while reducing expenses. The massive amount of data generated by these connected devices presents, however, where powerful edge network architectures are needed to deal with the flow efficiently. Thus, the optimization of data exchange between the edge and cloud comes to acquire a central role in unleashing the full potential of IIoT in industrial settings, facilitating real-time decision-making and operational agility (Devarasetty, 2023). The application of high-capacity communication protocols takes center stage in the case of IIoT, particularly in terms of avoiding interoperability issues across varied devices and platforms. One-to-one industrial protocols are not necessarily compatible with other one-to-one protocols, and this can hinder fluid information transfer across different manufacturing systems. As a countermeasure, the adoption of open standards and lightweight protocols like MQTT has transformed prominence. MQTT serves as a bridge for communications, allowing real-time data exchange between machines and IoT platforms. This is crucial in smart manufacturing because it can make disparate data streams meaningful operational insight. An implementation of intelligent factory network architecture by protocols such as MQTT is a daunting step toward enhanced connectivity for manufacturing environments. It enhances greater scalability and flexibility, which are required to cater to the high pace of change in production requirements and technological innovation (Yeh et al., 2021) (Figure 4.14).

Figure 4.14. IoT in manufacturing.

Source: https://www.kompanions.com/blog/assets/admin/uploads/Iot-in-manufacturing.jpg.

Moreover, strategically integrated edge computing within IIoT platforms yields enormous advantages in manufacturing. Edge computing reduces latency, alleviates bandwidth constraints, and enhances security protection by local processing of the data close to the origin point. Not only does local processing accelerate the processing of data, but it also allows manufacturers to respond instantly to operational needs and sensor alerts. For example, the combination of edge devices and IIoT can facilitate real-time monitoring of equipment with dynamic user interfaces that provide operators with immediate access to critical information. New applications such as real-time gesture recognition for human-machine interaction are examples of the new innovative possibilities edge computing can support. As the companies race to roll out digital transformation initiatives, the intersection of IIoT and edge computing will play a crucial role in defining intelligent, responsive manufacturing landscapes that are efficient and resilient (Devarasetty, 2023).

4.5.3. Healthcare and Remote Patient Monitoring

The intersection of healthcare and remote patient monitoring (RPM) is a revolutionary shift in the collection and transmission of medical information. With every step forward in technology, strict communication protocols are more and more necessary. Edge network topology allows decentralized processing to become viable, particularly beneficial in health applications where instant data access is imperative. By using local edge nodes, healthcare practitioners are able to offer immediate monitoring and analysis of patient health data, thereby improving responsiveness and reducing latency. The systems accommodate real-time data streaming from devices such as wearable ECG monitors, allowing patients to take a proactive approach to managing their health. Furthermore, the implementation of edge computing in RPM ensures enhanced data privacy and security because patient information can be processed and managed locally rather than being transmitted to far-end cloud servers (Akrivopoulos et al., 2017). Remote patient monitoring systems also address key issues in emergency healthcare response, particularly as healthcare systems come under mounting pressure. This increased demand for services is aggravated by increasing population statistics and resources, leading to increased response times and strained capacities. By employing the use of edge computing architectures, initiatives like the Smart Hospital Emergency System (SHES) aim to streamline communication between emergency responders and patients. This involves processing health information from people's own mobile phones alongside environmental sensors to generate real-time intelligence. These innovations are made to shatter communication bottlenecks previously encountered in the process of transferring information during emergencies, hence enhancing the efficiency of response mechanisms. Therefore, remote monitoring not only empowers patients to be involved in their care but also helps emergency services to make data-informed decisions promptly (Al-Khafajiy et al., 2019). Other than improving healthcare delivery, remote patient monitoring also facilitates longer health data analysis for, in turn, impacting the progress of patient care. By analyzing data collected in RPM systems, one can identify patterns helpful in preventing care and enhance diagnostic processes. With machine learning algorithms used on the large volumes of data collected through RPM, healthcare providers can predict potential health complications before they become critical. This proactive approach not only demarcates the complementarity of edge network architecture and health care but also the promise of transformation of communication protocols in improving patient outcomes. Thus, as health care itself evolves further, the use of state-of-the-art technologies and protocols in remote monitoring will be essential to form more adaptive, cost-efficient, and patient-centric models of care. The implications for future healthcare innovation and system performance are significant, and it is high time research and integration continued (Akrivopoulos et al., 2017).

SUMMARY

Edge network topology and communication protocol development is at the heart of mitigating the problem of a more networked world. As explained in this essay, the traditional Internet topology is wasteful and inadequate in some way, namely in terms of programmability and device capability. Study of programmable wireless networks has been a major step toward the overcoming of these challenges. With emphasis on methods such as software-defined networking, cognitive radio networks, and virtualized networks, there is room for more robust and adaptable network infrastructure that can be synchronized with the needs of diverse applications. These advancements also have the potential to bridge the gap between existing legacy infrastructure and future adaptability required for innovations, ultimately leading to a more sustainable system for communication. Moreover, deployment of fog computing enhances traditional paradigms of clouds, particularly in its application to the Internet of Things (IoT). As noted by the context, heterogeneous environments and extensive spreading of devices in the IoT pose problematic issues that have the potential to endanger underlying functional models. However, with the application of fog computing, intelligent processing and analysis can be executed closer to the edge, facilitating better data management generated by more than one IoT node. This design not only alleviates network overload but also makes next-generation applications across domains such as healthcare more possible, where real-time monitoring and seamless data sharing can be more impactful on patient outcomes. Thus, as the protocol continues to evolve, integrating edge computing with IoT architectures forms a critical bridge that can be used to enhance overall system performance. Lastly, the potential and challenges surrounding next-generation programmable wireless networks cannot be overstated. Although great strides have been made in accommodating the growing demand for connectivity, ongoing research is essential to mitigate the complexities introduced by varied communication protocols. As noted in earlier paragraphs, interoperability and network management concerns remain areas of concern. The convergence of solutions, such as those which are fog computing-based, also supports the evolution of scalable and reactive network topologies that are capable of keeping up with evolving technology paradigms. Therefore, the research agenda for the future needs to revolve around extending programmability, ensuring there is interoperability between diverse technologies and streamlining the process of creating innovative applications that are well-placed to thrive in these new settings, finally designing the future of networking and communication.

Edge network infrastructure and communication protocol investigation reveals a convergence of various technological innovations to maximize data processing and communication efficiency. One of the fundamental aspects of the infrastructure is the convergence of Robotic Wireless Sensor Networks (RWSN), representing a novel intersection point of wireless communication and robotics. RWSNs support adaptive learning and cooperative control, enabling multi-robot systems to achieve some sensing objectives while the communication performance is resilient. Such an interaction dictates several research directions, namely in connectivity, localization, and routing, and articulating the necessity of novel solutions in providing a robust information flow. By organizing existing literature and formulating the gaps in the literature, we are given a motivation for additional research in this hybrid discipline, therefore enriching the discussion around edge network architecture and its proficiency at addressing modern communications issues (Balasubramanian et al., 2018). In addition to the model offered by RWSNs, the introduction of Software Defined Networking (SDN) and Network Function Virtualization (NFV) is responsible for taking edge network architecture forward. These innovations have revolutionized network resource management into a flexible and scalable process. However, with the softwarization of radio access networks (RAN) aided by SDN, the transition process is very tough and has to be addressed to be able to enjoy its full benefits. The current literature is extensive but is meant to show that the solutions are still directed towards solving specific issues and not the complete ecosystem required for SDN-enabled deployment in the RAN. The timeliness of fronthaul, backward compatibility, and security vulnerability is compounded by the latency of general-purpose processors such that means more comprehensive in scope can address these multifaceted hurdles (Aghvami et al., 2018). The demand for consistent communication protocols in edge networks comes to the forefront in satellite applications and far-forward operating environments. In examining the current developments, we understand that there is a pressing need for advanced protocols that can offer reliable connectivity, particularly in areas that require low latency and robust signal integrity. Networks incorporating embedded advanced edge architecture frameworks must prioritize developing communication strategies that allow free interaction among devices, especially under circumstances characterized by varied bandwidth and intermittent connectivity. A review of existing literature involves looking into key gaps in focused research aimed at the challenges and therefore outlining a line of future research to focus on advanced protocols resilient to high-level data exchanges. Investigation of such gaps will not only contribute to the inherent malleability of edge networks but also improve their deployment across sectors, gradually implementing this new architectural landscape.

REFERENCES

1. Abdelsalam, A., Camarillo, P., Cianfrani, A., et al. (2020). Segment routing: A comprehensive survey of research activities, standardization efforts and implementation results. http://arxiv.org/abs/1904.03471 (accessed on 16th September 2025).
2. Abdolee, R., Maroufi, M., & Tazekand, B. M. (2019). On the convergence of blockchain and Internet of Things (IoT) technologies. http://arxiv.org/abs/1904.01936 (accessed on 16th September 2025).
3. Abrougui, A., Aloi, G., Araniti, G., Batty, C., Biral, A., Centenaro, M., Checko, A., et al. (2017). SymbioCity: Smart cities for smarter networks. https://core.ac.uk/download/77066421.pdf (accessed on 16th September 2025).
4. Aggoun, A., Amon, P., Arbel, I., et al. (2008). Multimedia delivery in the future Internet. https://core.ac.uk/download/335423.pdf (accessed on 16th September 2025).
5. Aghvami, H., Dohler, M., Fletcher, S., et al. (2018). Will SDN be part of 5G? https://core.ac.uk/download/157863188.pdf (accessed on 16th September 2025).
6. Ahad, N., Ahmed, N., & Qadir, J. (2014). Building programmable wireless networks: An architectural survey. http://arxiv.org/abs/1310.0251 (accessed on 16th September 2025).
7. Akrivopoulos, O., Amaxilatis, D., Chatzigiannakis, I., et al. (2017). Enabling stream processing for people-centric IoT based on the fog computing paradigm. https://core.ac.uk/download/158328004.pdf (accessed on 16th September 2025).
8. Akrivopoulos, O., Antoniou, A., Chatzigiannakis, I., et al. (2017). On the deployment of healthcare applications over fog computing infrastructure. https://core.ac.uk/download/98343526.pdf (accessed on 16th September 2025).
9. Alderson, D. L., & Doyle, J. C. (2010). Contrasting views of complexity and their implications for network-centric infrastructures. https://core.ac.uk/download/4885216.pdf (accessed on 16th September 2025).
10. Ali, M., Anjum, A., Devitt, J., et al. (2017). Towards in-transit analytics for Industry 4.0. http://arxiv.org/abs/1710.04121 (accessed on 16th September 2025).
11. Al-Khafajiy, M., Baker, T., Kolivand, H., et al. (2019). Smart hospital emergency system via mobile-based requesting services. https://core.ac.uk/download/305108854.pdf (accessed on 16th September 2025).

12. Alsayyed, M. M., Manickam, S., Wulandari, E. R. N., Widia, I. D. M., & Karuppayah, S. (2025). A review of applicable technologies, routing protocols, requirements, and architecture for disaster area networks. *IEEE Access, 13*, 91129–91160. https://www.semanticscholar.org/paper/e41fa4408ec29eb2e64092dbb185d16a64f4ed0e (accessed on 16th September 2025).
13. Balasubramanian, A., Chattopadhyay, A., Fida, A., Gasparri, A., Gasparri, A., Ghaffarkhah, A., Gonzalez-Ruiz, A., et al. (2018). Robotic wireless sensor networks. http://arxiv.org/abs/1705.05415 (accessed on 16th September 2025).
14. Barolli, L., & Xhafa, F. (2011). JXTA-Overlay: A P2P platform for distributed, collaborative, and ubiquitous computing. https://core.ac.uk/download/187265156.pdf (accessed on 16th September 2025).
15. Beck, R., Eklund, P., & Spasovski, J. (2019). How blockchain impacts cloud-based system performance: A case study for a groupware communication application. https://core.ac.uk/download/286340937.pdf (accessed on 16th September 2025).
16. Bradley, T. T., & Suda, T. (1989). Survey of unified approaches to integrated-service networks. https://core.ac.uk/download/287623360.pdf (accessed on 16th September 2025).
17. Buyya, R., & Varghese, B. (2017). Next generation cloud computing: New trends and research directions. https://core.ac.uk/download/96664300.pdf (accessed on 16th September 2025).
18. Carpio, F., Dizdarevic, J., Jukan, A., et al. (2019). A survey of communication protocols for Internet of Things and related challenges of fog and cloud computing integration. https://core.ac.uk/download/187266039.pdf (accessed on 16th September 2025).
19. Chen, J. C., Hsu, R. H., Lee, J., et al. (2017). Reconfigurable security: Edge computing-based framework for IoT. http://arxiv.org/abs/1709.06223 (accessed on 16th September 2025).
20. Delic, S., Khirallah, C., Tassi, A., et al. (2018). Random linear network coding for 5G mobile video delivery. https://core.ac.uk/download/157816966.pdf (accessed on 16th September 2025).
21. Devarasetty, N. (2023). Scalable data engineering approaches for AI-driven industrial IoT applications. *International Journal of Scientific Research and Management (IJSRM)*. https://www.semanticscholar.org/paper/818383aae07983b835143f4a6fec70da1786f715 (accessed on 16th September 2025).
22. Dutta, S., Ford, R., Mezzavilla, M., et al. (2016). Achieving ultra-low latency in 5G millimeter wave cellular networks. http://arxiv.org/

abs/1602.06925 (accessed on 16th September 2025).

23. Ferretti, S., Ghini, V., & Panzieri, F. (2015). A survey on handover management in mobility architectures. http://arxiv.org/abs/1509.01396 (accessed on 16th September 2025).
24. Fischer, M., Meiling, S., Purnomo, D., et al. (2018). MONICA in Hamburg: Towards large-scale IoT deployments in a smart city. http://arxiv.org/abs/1803.06854 (accessed on 16th September 2025).
25. Freitag, F., Girdzijauskas, S., Navarro Moldes, L., et al. (2017). Gossip-based service monitoring platform for wireless edge cloud computing. https://core.ac.uk/download/157810796.pdf (accessed on 16th September 2025).
26. Glind, G. J. van de, Hartel, P. H., Scholten, J., et al. (2005). The performance of a second-generation service discovery protocol in response to message loss. https://core.ac.uk/download/pdf/11469984.pdf (accessed on 16th September 2025).
27. Gope, P. (2019). LAAP: Lightweight anonymous authentication protocol for D2D-aided fog computing paradigm. https://core.ac.uk/download/286316324.pdf (accessed on 16th September 2025).
28. Guizani, N., Sharma, V., & You, I. (2019). Security of 5G-V2X: Technologies, standardization and research directions. http://arxiv.org/abs/1905.09555 (accessed on 16th September 2025).
29. Heijenk, G., Karagiannis, G., Rexhepi, V., et al. (2001). DiffServ resource management in IP-based radio access networks. https://core.ac.uk/download/pdf/11469636.pdf (accessed on 16th September 2025).
30. Hou, X., Kalogeropoulos, N. D., Lekkou, M. E., et al. (1994). A methodological approach to BISDN signaling performance. https://core.ac.uk/download/pdf/11474561.pdf (accessed on 16th September 2025).
31. Ishaya, N., Sulaimon, H. A., & Abdullahi, H. (2025). Optimizing energy efficiency in IoT networks for sustainable smart cities: A focus on energy-efficient communication protocols. *Proceedings of the Nigerian Society of Physical Sciences.* https://www.semanticscholar.org/paper/bf4ee4f3a0d8305e4fc2199e866a67161922bf51 (accessed on 16th September 2025).
32. Malik, M., Kothari, A., & Pandhare, R. (2024). Stand alone or non-standalone 5G tactical edge network architecture for military and use case scenarios. *2024 IEEE International Conference on Intelligent Signal Processing and Effective Communication Technologies (INSPECT).* https://www.semanticscholar.org/paper/6d6725dc789ba4fc9c643daf6929a2ac9552ba64 (accessed on 16th September 2025).

33. Mezzavilla, M., Panwar, S., Polese, M., et al. (2017). milliProxy: A TCP proxy architecture for 5G mmWave cellular systems. http://arxiv.org/abs/1712.02700 (accessed on 16th September 2025).

34. Nyakuri, J. P., Nkundineza, C., Gatera, O., Nkurikiyeyezu, K., & Mwitende, G. (2025). AI and IoT-powered edge device optimized for crop pest and disease detection. *Scientific Reports, 15.* https://www.semanticscholar.org/paper/c64ea50f069f8d96c5f529f64f80b147fb7b477e (accessed on 16th September 2025).

35. Ollora Zaballa, E., Yan, Y., & Zhou, Z. (2020). Detection of fog network data telemetry using data plane programming. https://core.ac.uk/download/296708960.pdf (accessed on 16th September 2025).

36. Qian, Y., Sharif, H., Tipper, D., et al. (2012). A survey on cyber security for smart grid communications. https://core.ac.uk/download/12211131.pdf (accessed on 16th September 2025).

37. Rao, S. M., Adinarayana, B., Vaddikasulu, K., Dontamsetti, S. P., & Ranganadh, P. S. V. (2024). Optimizing cloud IoT applications with machine learning driven hybrid key management protocols for WSN performance. *2024 2nd International Conference on Signal Processing, Communication, Power and Embedded System (SCOPES).* https://www.semanticscholar.org/paper/732c3342756c6ffb368329e9e02b883334a62c71 (accessed on 16th September 2025).

38. Salih, H. K., & Al-Ani, A. A. (2024). Enabling the E-NOSE: Evaluating network technologies for optimized odor data transmission in IoT and edge computing applications. *Journal of Electrical Systems.* https://www.semanticscholar.org/paper/b0f2a97092ce92c3d59a5f3deab4c30b58a4c85d (accessed on 16th September 2025).

39. Yeh, C. S., Chen, S. L., & Li, I. C. (2021). Implementation of MQTT protocol-based network architecture for smart factory. *Proceedings of the Institution of Mechanical Engineers, Part B: Journal of Engineering Manufacture, 235*, 2132–2142. https://www.semanticscholar.org/paper/7ca75236160969569341489bcf26436277b6e4ad (accessed on 16th September 2025).

CHAPTER 5

DATA PROCESSING AT THE EDGE

Contents

INTRODUCTION

Over the last few years, edge computing has come into the spotlight, particularly with the increased need for faster data processing and real-time analytics. Edge data processing is the act of processing the data close to where the data is generated rather than relying on the centrally located cloud servers. This paradigm has been dictated by the imperative of latency reduction and the enhancement of overall data processing and transmission efficiency. As devices have gone into exponential growth in the Internet of Things (IoT) era, data output has grown exponentially as well, necessitating novel frameworks for optimal management. One of the key benefits of edge computing is the ability to utilize local computing resources and thus facilitate quicker decision-making and improved responsiveness in numerous applications, from autonomous vehicles to smart cities and beyond. In addition, utilization of advanced data visualization tools is an important element to improve edge data processing. Data visualization refers to presenting data in graphical or pictorial form, and a data visualization tool is the program used to create this presentation.

Figure 5.1. Data processing.

Source: https://external-content.duckduckgo.com/iu/?u=https%3A%2F%2Fd2ds8yldqp7gxv.cloudfront.net%2FBlog%2BExplanatory%2BImages%2Fdata%2Bprocessing%2B1.webp&f=1&nofb=1&ipt=1cbb00919209a017c67f684d84ed637cca82e82be93b0d67c0b89718aa57d6bb.

Data visualization provides users with intuitive means of interactively exploring and analyzing data, enabling them to quickly identify interesting patterns, infer causality and correlations, and facilitates sense-making activities (Bikakis et al., 2018). With these tools at the periphery, businesses can instantly convert complex data sets in real time, creating more strategic choices. The ability to view and analyze information rapidly produces better situational awareness, allowing businesses and users to respond ahead of dynamic contexts and rapidly changing conditions. Despite the major advantages of edge data processing, there remain areas to be overcome, and in particular data accuracy and depth perception in certain applications. For instance, in time-of-flight range imaging environments, traditional methods might suffer from limitations, including depth ambiguity that can be caused by cyclic phase measurements. Current advancements provide new ways of dealing with such vaguenesses through the post-processing software techniques, enhancing performance and reliability

(Cree et al., 2010). Such synergy between edge computing and sophisticated data processing allows for more robust operation against harsh conditions, which is particularly beneficial in fields like robotics and autonomous navigation. With the rapidly evolving environment of data processing, the intersection of these advanced techniques will be most likely to dictate the path of smart data management at the edge (Figure 5.1).

Importance of Data Processing at the Edge

How crucial edge data processing is cannot be overstated, particularly in light of the exponential increase in data being processed through IoT devices and real-time analytics becoming increasingly essential. Data processing at the edge assists organizations in reducing latency, improving response times, and optimizing bandwidth. This localized solution makes instant decision-making possible, which is necessary for a number of applications, such as autonomous vehicles, smart cities, and industrial automation. For instance, within a smart factory environment, edge computing supports real-time analysis of machines' performance, allowing for fast adjustment to optimize efficiency in operations. As companies seek to unlock the full potential of data, the strategic significance of edge computing becomes clear. Companies that are looking to remain competitive in an evolving digital world can only do so by adopting it. Moreover, the ability to execute advanced data analysis on the edge greatly boosts the performance of applications based on data. Central models get bogged down by data volume and data velocity of data generated, leading to bottlenecks and latency in insights. Edge computing solves this problem by enabling processing of complex algorithms and machine learning models within local devices. This not only enhances data privacy and security because sensitive information is processed away from centralized servers but also enables corporations to react to emerging environmental conditions in real-time. For instance, consider the application of edge computing in healthcare; patients' data can be processed in real-time through wearable sensors, prompting timely alerts to healthcare practitioners in the presence of identified anomalies. Thus, the incorporation of edge data processing methods instills a culture in which companies are placed in a position where they can better leverage opportunities and problems. Finally, combining data processing at the edge facilitates green data management practices. In the face of increasing digital visibility for organizations, the environmental impact of their data centers is rapidly becoming a major issue. Decentralization of data processing and minimizing the volume of data sent to central nodes helps companies significantly cut down energy consumption and its carbon footprint. Projects such as the upcoming Euclid telescope project illustrate how edge processing can facilitate complex cosmic simulations while optimizing resource utilization. This approach not only supports scientific discovery but also supports global sustainability objectives, showing the potential of technology in driving innovation and wise management of environmental resources. For this reason, embracing edge computing is not merely a strategic operational innovation but also a commitment to ecological responsibility in the age of information (Figure 5.2).

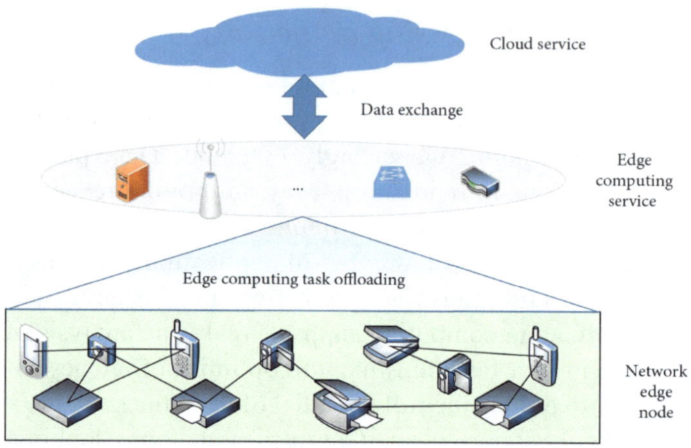

Figure 5.2. Schematic diagram of data processing and calculation using edge computing.

Source: https://www.researchgate.net/publication/347020090/figure/fig1/AS:1083896817033216@1635432547673/Schematic-diagram-of-data-processing-and-calculation-using-edge-computing.jpg.

5.1. THE EVOLUTION OF DATA PROCESSING

The history of data processing has witnessed revolutionary periods, marked with an advancement in technology and procedures that have shaped the processing of information. Data processing began on the foundation of mainframe computers that needed a centralized approach, where enormous amounts of data were consolidated, processed, and stored in large-capacity centers. This paradigm shifted with the coming of personal computers that made data processing more democratized and enabled individuals to process data on their own systems. This trend is now gaining traction with the coming of edge computing, which pushes data processing to the edge where the data is being created. This distributed approach not only encourages speed and efficiency but also lessens the burden on central data centers, enabling real-time data processing that is critical in many applications like IoT and smart city initiatives. With advancing technology, convergence of machine learning and artificial intelligence with data processing frameworks has gained greater importance. Advanced systems, such as drone magnetometer systems, are very fine examples of improving data processing capacity in real-time environments using AI. The drones carry an integration of sensors, including magnetometers and GPS, to monitor environmental data and recognize anomalies. This innovation is indicative of a point of inflection where data processing is no longer restricted to traditional infrastructures but is able to function in changing and varied environments. Apart from this, adoption of IoT in these systems offers open data transmission and analysis at the edge in real time, enhancing decision-making across industries.

These innovations have broadened the scope of data processing to deliver new applications that were impossible to dream about earlier. Amidst all such developments, critical security and privacy-related issues are at the forefront of data processing evolution. With increasing reliance on biometric authentication systems, for instance, there is a pressing need to address the ethical implications and regulatory concerns that come with handling the information. Biometric systems utilizing methods like facial recognition and fingerprint scanning need robust protocols in place to protect sensitive user information from likely compromise. In addition, as these technologies evolve, the convergence of artificial intelligence with biometric authentication also presents challenges as well as opportunities with regard to accuracy, velocity, and ease of use. Therefore, the existing debate on the consequences of such advances serves to further emphasize the need for responsible innovation in data processing practice so that technological progress is harmonized with ethical guidelines and societal demands, paving the way towards a secure digital future (Figure 5.3).

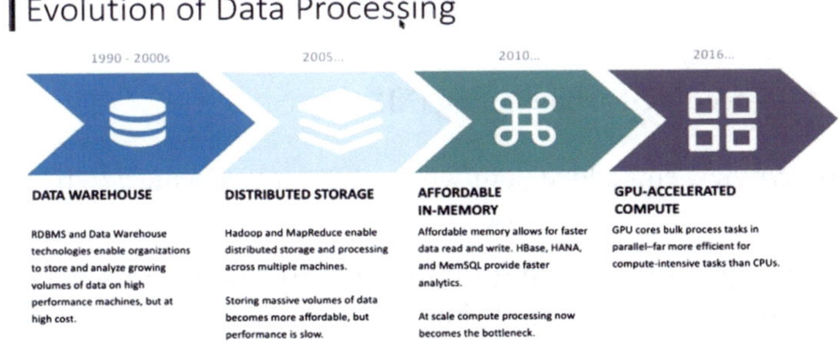

Figure 5.3. The evolution of data processing.

Source: https://i.ytimg.com/vi/kayQBl5zdjk/maxresdefault.jpg.

5.1.1. Historical Context of Data Processing

The historical context in data processing is significant for the analysis of its evolution and usage in today's technology, particularly at the network edge. Data processing began with a focus on mainframes that had a heavy reliance on them dictating the pace and efficiency of processing operations. The trend towards more distributed forms began when personal computing was introduced in the late 20th century, where users could perform data processing close to the data source. The shift opened the door for distributed processing environments, which promoted flexibility and accessibility. As more and more data volumes grew, the necessity for new paradigms arose, and newer paradigms that address efficiency and responsiveness came into the limelight, particularly in environments that have to process in real-time. Energy-aware wired networking technologies are a significant milestone towards optimizing the design and efficiency of data processing systems.

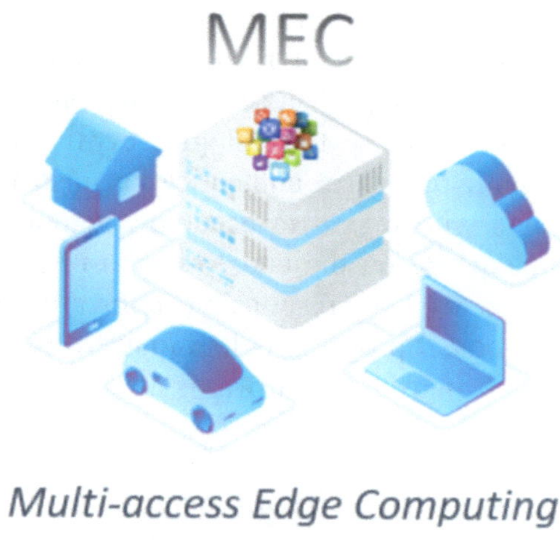

Figure 5.4. Multi-access edge computing (MEC).

Source: https://www.embedded.com/wp-content/uploads/sites/2/2021/06/06etsi_fl_t.png.

As the study on green networking highlights, efforts towards energy savings have gained increasingly pivotal importance on both the economic and environmental fronts (Bianzino et al., 2010). This work identifies significant paradigms that enable energy-efficient networks, e.g., Adaptive Link Rate and energy-aware infrastructure, which have a direct correlation with the efficiency of data processing. With the incorporation of energy-awareness within devices and protocols, data processing not only has offered high performance but also advocated sustainable causes. The capability to develop in such a way reflects on the capability of data processing technologies in addressing shifting values in society and also responding to environmental issues. As we continue looking forward, the unification of such technologies as Multi-Access Edge Computing (MEC) is the future of data processing. The arrival of 5G networks has enabled this through the distribution of computation tasks to edge clouds localized at the edge to ensure enhanced responsiveness and reduced latency in data processing operations (Crippa et al., 2019). With focus on decentralized architecture, the possibility of more efficient and customized processing at the edge takes center stage. This revolutionary configuration not only optimizes procedures but also converges with modern requirements of cheap, flexible solutions that take into account situational information, thus redefining the potential within the domain of data processing. Therefore, learning about this historical development recaptures the significance of recasting data processing methods to cope with existing as well as forthcoming challenges (Figure 5.4).

5.1.2. Transition from Centralized to Decentralized Systems

The transformation from central to distributed systems is a radical departure from the manner in which data processing occurs within modern networks. Central architectures have, in the past, enabled effective control and management with data processing tasks being performed within enormous central data centers. The proliferating demands for real-time processing and low-latency throughput have made decentralized models more viable options. The movement towards edge computing is one such example; by distributing computing functions closer to data sources, organizations can dramatically enhance response times and improve overall operational efficiency. This transformation not only removes bottlenecks that are typically present in centralized systems, but also allows for local nodes to compute in isolation, resulting in a more resilient and versatile network topology. One such technology driving this decentralization is the development of Multi-Access Edge Computing (MEC) that aims to get cloud capabilities nearer to the edge of the networks. Computation in MEC occurs nearer the user and thus avoids latency and reduces bandwidth usage for data processing from the cloud. For successful deployment of MEC, an effective security model is required, considering the fact that decentralized models carry built-in vulnerabilities. A decentralized authentication framework for proposal prioritizes local, context-dependent authentication actions to allow adaptive security policies based on specific network conditions. Such advancements in network structures provide a dramatic cost-efficiency versus reliability trade-off, ultimately enhancing the overall user experience and supporting more complex applications in edge computing installations (Crippa et al., 2019).

Further, integration of Mobile Social Networks (MSNs) in decentralized systems provides an alternative path through which data propagation can be optimized. Utilizing the inherent social connections among users, MSNs facilitate the creation of ad hoc networks that are transient in nature but are specifically designed for content dissemination, thereby avoiding the typical traffic bottlenecks associated with centralized systems. This decentralized approach not only conserves operating costs but also improves network performance by a significant amount. Enabled by the growing availability of mobile terminals, MSN-assisted content distribution can address the growing need for efficient data access in a variety of user populations. As the case of MSNs demonstrates, the operational versatility achieved through decentralization is a key enabler; future challenges will need to be addressed through a combined effort to leverage the full capabilities of these novel network topologies (Hanzo et al., 2013).

5.1.3. Role of IoT in Edge Computing

The integration of Internet of Things (IoT) devices into edge computing platforms has revolutionized data processing at the network edge. Being able to create data at the source, IoT devices enable real-time analytics and immediate application of insights. This is crucial in industries like smart cities, healthcare, and industrial automation, where timely decision-making has the potential to significantly enhance operational effectiveness. Higher reliance on IoT generates an enormous body of data, and this leads not just to higher bandwidth usage but also the necessity for sophisticated systems of data management. A keen exploration of the trend discovers that while problems, particularly with security and integration, are generated with this convergence, the benefits far outweigh the adverse outcomes, putting IoT and edge computing as dual forces in modern data processing environments (Butun et al., 2018). One of the key features of the IoT and edge computing union is the emergence of fog computing, which is an interface level between central cloud infrastructure and IoT nodes. Fog computing enhances real-time responses of IoT applications by processing data closer to the edge and reducing latency. This setup also facilitates not only efficient routing but also optimized resource allocation, significantly reducing the pressure on cloud infrastructure. The potential for real-time analytics and communication allows businesses to access data more meaningfully, promoting proactive measures and reducing downtime. With the adoption of IoT, the compatibility with fog computing offers some opportunities for innovation, particularly in enhancing security solutions guarding sensitive data acquired from diverse sources under this framework (Butun et al., 2018). In addition, the emerging phenomenon of open data markets in the IoT context represents a paradigm shift in how data is valued and traded. Such markets enable data owners and consumers to conduct transactions, promoting data sharing while calling for significant privacy concerns. IoT-generated data has the potential to provide invaluable insights, allowing companies to provide customized services and streamline operations. However, with these data exchanges on the rise, protecting stakeholders' privacy is the utmost importance. The need for robust privacy-preserving mechanisms is stronger with data that could reveal personal information coming into trade negotiations. Thus, eliminating such privacy concerns is paramount to realizing the sustainable development of IoT applications in edge computing platforms designed to foster productivity without compromising security.

5.2. KEY TECHNOLOGIES ENABLING EDGE PROCESSING

The development of edge processing technologies has pushed strongly from the arrival of neuromorphic architectures. These architectures, designed to emulate neural networks within the human brain, present sophisticated data processing functions at the edge. These CMOS-memristive circuit-based systems promise to be more energy efficient and fast, countering the issue of the increasing number and speed of data generated by billions of sensors in the Internet of Things (IoT). The integration of neuromorphic computing in edge devices not only counters latency but also reduces power consumption which is generally associated with centralized cloud processing. As such, the use of such technologies can lead to more environmentally friendly cloud computing options while providing scalable processing for resource-constrained environments and multistatistical applications (Chua et al., 2018). Equally important in edge processing is the use of sophisticated algorithms that enable real-time analysis of data. Machine learning and artificial intelligence techniques can be used directly on the edge devices, allowing for faster decision-making and predictive analytics without relying heavily on the cloud. The application of such algorithms decreases the burden on network bandwidth as the data is filtered and analyzed locally before they are transmitted. This edge processing paradigm not only enhances operational efficiency but also security, as sensitive information is processed close to its source, reducing exposure while in transit. Ultimately, the resilience of edge processing platforms is greatly enhanced by this intricate interplay of these algorithms, which maximize the use of resources while, at the same time, addressing the quality and timeliness of data intelligence required by various applications. The collaborative nature of innovation in edge processing technology also points toward the possibility of revolutionizing traditional data architectures. Projects like the SciDAC Fusion Simulation Project have progressed towards the development of end-to-end simulation platforms that combine cutting-edge computational methodology with penetrating physics-based insights. The integration of kinetic codes and established fluid dynamic models, such as through the development of the End-to-end Framework for Fusion Integrated Simulation (EFFIS), is a demonstration of the potential that cross-disciplinary synergy holds to produce game-changing solutions that make edge processing more efficient and reliable. Such collaborations are essential for the resolution of complex challenges, like edge instability and data volatility. Consequently, the convergence of various disciplines—physics, computer science, and applied mathematics—will continue to drive the path to future advancements in edge processing technologies, complementing their position within the data processing ecosystem at the edge (Khan et al., 2008).

5.2.1. Edge Devices and Their Capabilities

In the data-processing environment today, edge devices are phenomenal building blocks as they possess outstanding capabilities. In contrast to mainstream cloud-based designs whereby data gets streamed to centralized servers to process, edge devices enable localized processing, significantly boosting efficiency and responsiveness. Smart city infrastructure that utilizes video analytics is one example of the drastic impact of edge computing. By pre-processing raw video streams at the point of capture, these devices eliminate bandwidth-related issues and real-time responsiveness, ensuring that critical conclusions can be provided in a timely fashion. All these edge processing technologies not only enhance efficiency but also enhance data privacy, providing an orderly solution to handle sensitive information in real-time systems, as evident from several instances varying from crowd surveillance to traffic governance, ultimately leading towards the path of smart cities (Ballas et al., 2018). Edge device development has been facilitated to a great extent by recent advancements in emerging technologies, particularly in the domain of IoT and fog computing. These have enabled edge devices to process, store, and transfer data in an effective way, thus creating smarter scenarios such as smart transportation and smart homes. As devices at the edge end up being more sophisticated and capable of executing intricate functions like decision-making and data processing, the complementing architectural models that enable these capabilities must enhance as well. Fog-to-cloud (F2C) computing becomes a paradigm that is requisite in a bid to enable coordinated control of spread resources with a mix of edge devices and cloud services. This layered architecture is instrumental in the optimization of cloud and fog computing orchestration, which finally enhances resource use and service delivery for various applications (Jukan et al., 2016) (Figure 5.5).

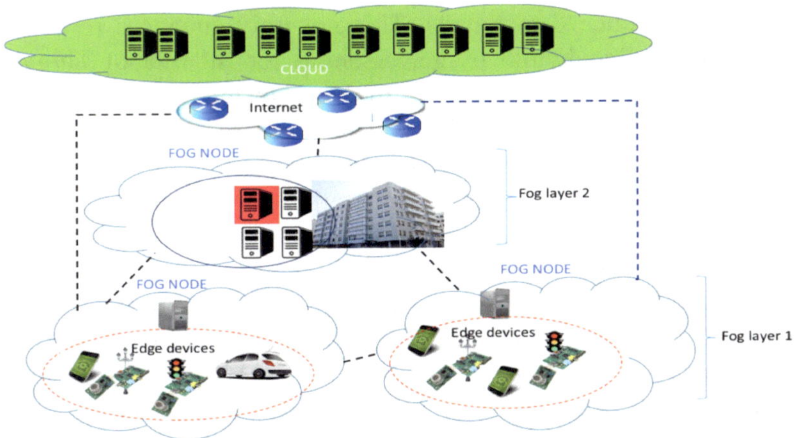

Figure 5.5. Fog-to-cloud architecture (F2C).

Source: https://www.researchgate.net/profile/E-Marin-Tordera/publication/311066913/figure/fig1/AS:433599901114369@1480389680285/Fog-to-cloud-architecture-F2C.png.

The implications of edge device capability development extend beyond the gains in efficiency; they portend a revolutionary transformation in how we conceptualize processing information and offering services in other industries. When edge devices assume more functionality, such as storage and processing capability, the complementarity of the same with cloud-based services can lead to levels of innovation opportunity unseen before. Better edge analytics performance is evidenced through use cases like crowd counting and activity detection, where real-time data processing significantly improves operational performance. Moreover, integration of deep learning capabilities allows the processing of complicated analytics that change based on various conditions, as observed in input size optimization while handling videos. Thus, the ongoing advancement of edge device technology not only empowers organizations to tap into real-time data-driven insights but also forms the basis for future growth, attesting to the cornerstone role of edge computing in the new digital age (Ballas et al., 2018; Jukan et al., 2016).

5.2.2. Networking Technologies Supporting Edge Computing

As the demand for rapid data processing grows, networking technology becomes a catalyst for edge computing. By decentralizing data computation and storage away from the core, edge computing provides a solution to latency issues prevalent in traditional cloud settings. By implementing edge nodes that act as buffers between data sources and central cloud services, organizations can significantly reduce data travels. This not only enhances response time but also minimizes bandwidth usage, essential for Internet of Things (IoT) networks that generate copious amounts of data. The integration of the network technologies is smooth, making the system more dynamic and responsive, ultimately fulfilling the growing need for real-time processing of data for most applications. Green networking is an imperative consideration in the case of edge computing technologies. As companies have realized how environmental implications result from networking energy consumption, mechanisms to prevent energy-wasteful usage have gained prominence. Efforts like Adaptive Link Rate, which adjusts the link rate dynamically based on current traffic loads, and energy-aware infrastructures enhance networking systems' efficiency. Central to these developments is the understanding that an innovative design has the potential to minimize energy wastage in wired networks by significant amounts. By incorporating energy-awareness into protocol and device design, edge computing can be made more sustainable with increased resource usage without compromising performance (Bianzino et al., 2010) (Figure 5.6).

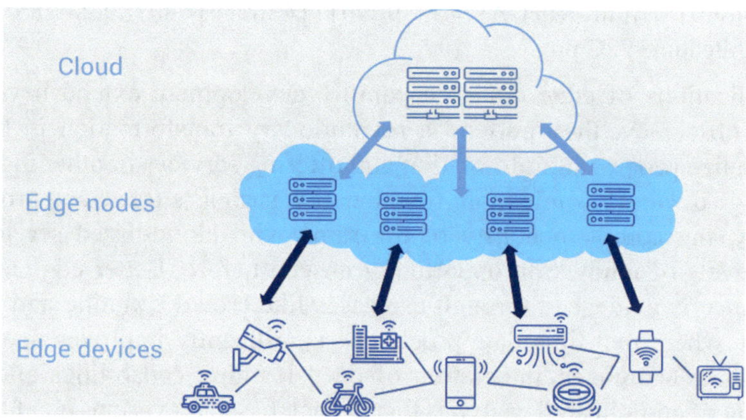

Figure 5.6. Networking technologies play a pivotal role in enabling edge computing.

Source:https://external-content.duckduckgo.com/iu/?u=https%3A%2F%2Fdevopedia.org%2Fimages%2Farticle%2F250%2F2416.1593710342.png&f=1&nofb=1&ipt=750ac7f08ab92c5cf907e17fe0db4ca097e8f3d5dc346979ce46c8667fad2098.

Adding more robustness to networking technologies is the incorporation of fog computing into the model of edge computing. Wider enhancement of cloud computing capabilities closer to the network edge, fog computing meets the particular requirements offered by the widespread set of IoT devices ubiquitously installed. Decentralized in approach, this methodology is paramount to support use cases calling for processing and response of data in real-time, such as autonomous health monitoring. For instance, a smartphone-based fog gateway prototype ensures secure sharing of ECG data, offering real-world health monitoring implementations using fog computing. Furthermore, learning from past data enables ongoing analysis, which advocates for improved medical diagnosis and patient care. This multilateral incorporation of network technologies demonstrates the edge computing potential to revamp data processing with regard for practical and environmental considerations (Akrivopoulos et al., 2017).

5.2.3. Data Analytics Tools for Edge Environments

With the rapidly evolving data processing world, the contribution of edge environments is undoubtedly pivotal. Edge computing makes it possible to process data in real time at or near the point at which it is generated, which not only minimizes latency issues but also maximizes efficiency. Data analytics software specifically designed to be used in edge environments is a vital component in such a situation.

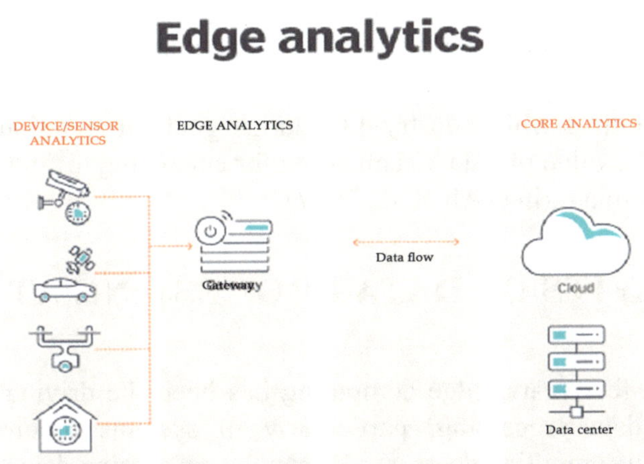

Figure 5.7. Edge analytics.

Source: https://www.techtarget.com/rms/onlineimages/business_analytics-edge_analytics-f_mobile.png.

These tools are characterized by the ability to manage vast amounts of data in real-time, enabling organizations to obtain actionable insights and gain a competitive edge. Utilization of edge analytics in manufacturing is an excellent instance of this approach because visualizing manufacturing data creates space for creative practices that form competitive advantage, eventually leading to a culture of continuous improvement and responsiveness in an ever-changing market environment (Ali et al., 2017). Moreover, the transition from centralized cloud infrastructures to decentralized ones is extremely crucial in the evolution of data analytics solutions for edge environments. As more and more organizations are shifting towards a multi-provider approach of cloud infrastructure, there is an immediate need for robust analytics capabilities that can execute across various platforms. This change allows for computation resource distribution, thereby addressing data-intensive workload and bottleneck issues typically suffered by single-provider data centers. Data analytics solutions are, therefore, evolving to this new thinking by offering elastic structures that facilitate easier device cooperation and unproblematic data integration, which is essential for achieving the maximum value of edge computing (Buyya et al., 2017) (Figure 5.7). The scope of using sophisticated data analytics solutions in edge environments extends beyond rudimentary operational efficiency; they also have the potential to influence groundbreaking business models. With the use of edge analytics functionality, companies are capable of developing real-time data-driven tactics that optimize resource utilization and reduce production intricacies. The solutions also facilitate the adoption of self-improving systems that develop and adapt with time, thus establishing a more intelligent environment. The edge analytics functionality does not just support cutting-edge application scenarios but also harmonizes with Industry 4.0's larger goals of attention to combined services and the value of data visualization for enhancing insight and decision-making in manufacturing (Ali et al., 2017).

5.3. BENEFITS OF DATA PROCESSING AT THE EDGE

Over the past few years, edge computing has been the driving force behind streamlining data processing, particularly in systems requiring real-time analytics. Edge computing decreases latency by processing data close to where it originates, making quicker decision-making that is critical in applications as varied as self-driving automobiles and intelligent cities. This data immediacy not only increases the responsiveness of operations but also reduces the bandwidth demands from centralized data centers significantly since merely critical data is transmitted to be analyzed. Moreover, with local processing being emphasized, resource utilization improves because systems dynamically adapt to data load variations, thereby overall performance is enhanced. As per recent studies, the inclusion of newest telecommunication technologies facilitates such processes and forms an excellent foundation for new urban management systems that optimize the quality of life in Ubiquitous Eco Cities. Such developments show exactly how edge data processing can be revolutionary (Yigitcanlar et al., 2009). Another particular benefit of edge data processing is that it can ensure improved security and privacy. By keeping sensitive data close to the source and reducing data transmission over networks, organizations can lower risks for data breach and interception. The localized approach allows more stringent security controls, optimized for specific environments, to be applied, reducing the attack surface typically presented by centralized stores of data. Additionally, individuals have greater control over their information, as edge computing allows users to make informed decisions about data sharing. With growing emphasis on data protection laws, such as GDPR, the ability to process at the edge facilitates compliance and increases consumer trust. While companies are grappling with the complexities of digitalization, the strategic benefits of enhanced security through edge processing are invaluable in an evolving threat landscape (Dehghanghadikolaei et al., 2019). The green value of data processing at the edge cannot be overlooked as well. By lessening the quantity of data to be processed and then shipped to central servers, edge computing minimizes energy consumption and allows for cleaner operational practices. This reduced energy use is in line with global initiatives for developing more sustainable systems, like in smart city and Internet of Things (IoT) contexts. Furthermore, the philosophy of edge computing encourages decentralized manufacturing techniques that can save on transportation costs as well as material wastage. Such developments are in line with the advantages realized in additive manufacturing technologies that allow for economical design with less environmental impact. As industries adopt these new means, the potential for achieving equilibrium between technological advancement and ecological responsibility will become increasingly feasible, leading to a more sustainable future for city management and industry in general (Dehghanghadikolaei et al., 2019).

5.3.1. Reduced Latency and Improved Performance

Data processing has increasingly focused on minimizing latency and enhancing performance, notably by applying edge computing. Numerous models utilize centralized cloud resources, which results in significant delays due to the time required for data to travel long distances to the servers. Edge computing addresses this issue by bringing processing power closer to where the data originates and streamlining data flow. This decrease in latency is especially crucial in real-time applications, such as the ones utilized in the Industrial Internet of Things (IIoT), where prompt decision-making is a necessity. Emerging technologies such as cloudlets and in-network computing support a more decentralized computing environment, enhancing responsiveness and data processing efficiency of the systems (Putnam et al., 2020). By making use of distributed computing frameworks, edge processing plays a key role in optimizing performance. The ability to do initial data processing near the source also minimizes bandwidth consumption significantly, as only processed data is transmitted to cloud servers. The two-level model not only minimizes communication latency but also reduces operational costs involved in data transportation. Experimental studies have indicated that while central cloud solutions might be able to provide brute computing capacity, they struggle with the latency in network traffic, particularly in applications depending on high video data streams. Edge solutions, on the other hand, provide quicker processing capacity, answering to the needs of industries based on real-time observation and decision (Krook et al., 2025) (Figure 5.8).

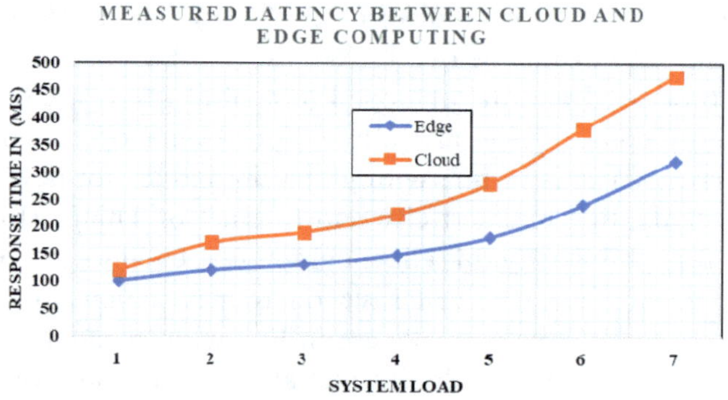

Figure 5.8. Latency of cloud and edge computing of application and database server.

Source: https://www.researchgate.net/figure/Latency-of-Cloud-and-Edge-computing-of-Application-and-database-server_fig3_344218742.

As more and more industries adopt edge computing strategies, the role of hardware design advancements in low latency and improved performance cannot be overemphasized. Innovations such as Field Programmable Gate Arrays (FPGAs) enable fast data processing with minimal overhead of computation, and thus are ideal for real-time applications. These hardware accelerators not only accelerate the processing of data but also provide predictable performance under varying workloads. Through the deployment of tasks at the edge in coordination with cloud resources, organizations can leverage the exclusive strengths of both systems. The combination effectively resolves the issue of intensive bandwidth usage and delivers scalable solutions that can respond to varied sources of data, thereby creating a more agile and efficient data processing environment (Putnam et al., 2020).

5.3.2. Enhanced Data Privacy and Security

Increased use of edge computing has also introduced considerable improvements in the field of data privacy and protection, which are more critical with more devices connecting to the Internet of Things (IoT). Edge computing reduces the transmission of sensitive data across wide networks to central cloud infrastructures by processing data closer to where it is produced, thus avoiding possible data breaches and unauthorized use.

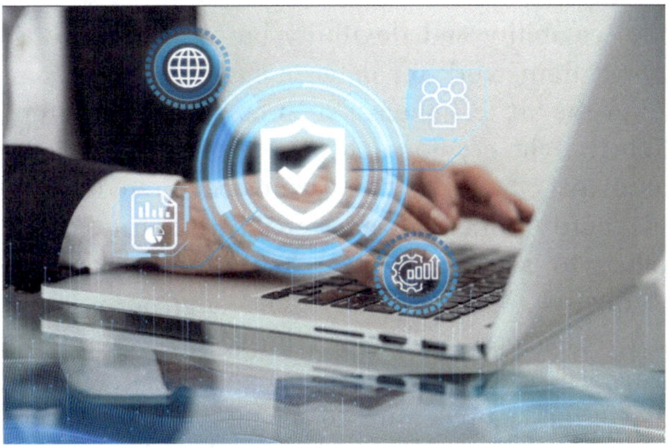

Figure 5.9. Edge computing enhances data security and privacy.

Source: https://www.coherentmarketinsights.com/blogimg/1739360526.jpg.

This closeness allows for rapid response to security issues in the future, allowing organizations to implement effective security solutions at the edge. In addition, shorter distances for data transmission not only increase the efficiency of operations but also significantly lower data transmission expenses. With secure edge servers, companies can still protect sensitive user data while complying with stringent data privacy laws enacted by regulatory agencies. Localized processing is then the utilization of localized processing as a major strategy towards enabling data security within current digital ecosystems, curbing vulnerabilities arising from centralized data processing. Federated Learning (FL) is an inevitable strategy in the context of edge computing, enhancing data privacy even further. FL enables collaborative model training on different edge devices without transferring sensitive user data from its original location. Instead of aggregating raw data to a server, FL allows local models to train on their local data, highly reducing the possibility of attacks on privacy. In practice, practical use of FL has been impeded by high training overheads, rendering its deployment unrealistic for edge environments with limited resources. Through FL's hyper-parameters tuning, as promoted in recent studies, organizations can effectively minimize the training loads of this distributed learning approach while ensuring strong data privacy (Figure 5.9). The blend of FL with edge computing not only enhances the privacy of user data but also redefines the way organizations are able to leverage data to be utilized for machine learning activities while upholding ethical standards in data processing activities. The synergy between cloud and edge computing is also an important aspect that helps in enhancing data privacy and security since it addresses the increasing complexity of connected systems. The integration of these technologies does not only provide scalability and flexibility but also requires a solid security policy management framework for defense against contemporary threats. By employing state-of-the-art techniques, such as machine learning-based threat analysis and light-weight cryptography, organizations can provide effective security policy management in cloud and edge environments. Dynamic enforcement of security policies further enables security controls to become dynamic responses to active threats in real-time, making data protection strategies more effective. As security threats become more complex, addressing identity and access management along with secure communications will be crucial in ensuring a secure infrastructure capable of safeguarding confidential data. Ultimately, further innovation and development in security models for cloud-edge infrastructure will be crucial to establishing trust and confidence among users along with enhancing overall data security and privacy in edge computing environments.

5.3.3. Bandwidth Optimization and Cost Efficiency

In edge data processing, bandwidth optimization is key to minimizing costs with high performance. As the volume of data generated by edge devices increases higher, particularly in real-time processing environments, maximizing utilization of bandwidth is essential. Reducing the amount of data that has to be transferred across networks can significantly lower operating costs because it both reduces pressure on bandwidth and lowers fees related to transfers. With techniques such as compression of data and judicious filtering of data, organizations can make sure that only the most valuable and actionable data gets through to cloud-based systems in the middle. This strategic approach enables improved responsiveness in applications that is critical to use cases for sectors like healthcare, transport, and smart cities, thus enhancing overall operational efficiency. Cost efficiency is an important consideration for bandwidth optimization, particularly in distributed computing environments like Edge-Cloud systems. The relation between cloud providers and edge providers needs a structural process for distributing resources in a manner that tries to maximize each party's utility while increasing systemic efficiency. For addressing this issue, employing revenue-sharing mechanisms can significantly influence the providers' decision-making within the network. This is exemplified in Cao et al. (2018), which illustrates how competitive dynamics are established in a non-cooperative game setting between service providers. With the right establishment of incentives, service providers are able to align their interests with system efficiency as a whole, leading to reduced operational costs while improving service dependability and performance at the same time. Furthermore, the advancement of edge computing technology, particularly in sensor-based use cases, further maximizes bandwidth and cost. For example, novel camera systems designed for specific operations such as face detection or real-time processing of 3D video are based on embedded acceleration techniques that reduce the volume of data to be transferred. As discussed in Alaghi et al. (2017), these systems can operate on low-power resources and outperform traditional processing configurations. By applying initial stages of data reduction on the camera node, organizations can minimize the amount of data that must move across the network, thereby lessening latency and bandwidth consumption. Not only is it making processing of data affordable, but it also provides new avenues for machine learning and real-time analytics use cases at the edge, making an ecosystem that is scalable long term and sustainable.

5.4. CHALLENGES IN EDGE DATA PROCESSING

The assistance of edge data processing is seriously challenged by issues that scale its implementation and scalability. Crucially, the aspect of resource allocation becomes critical in managing the limited capacities of the computing resources of the edge devices. As the devices are likely to be hardware-constrained, they might not handle computationally intensive tasks well. This is further added to by latency and jurisdiction of data, particularly in situations where real-time data processing is required. In such situations, the serverless model has emerged as a potential solution, with benefits including 35% reduced operating costs and a 50% boost in scalability than in conventional cloud models. However, the transition to this architecture involves meticulous planning and execution to address the foundation security risks emerging from distributed environments and thereby provide robust data processing protocols in edge environments (Sudarshan, 2023). In addition, the unprecedented explosion of Internet of Things (IoT) devices has facilitated advancements in collaborative machine-learning exercises posing unique challenges at the edge. The heterogeneity of the connected devices results in high data and device heterogeneity, increasing the complexity and likelihood of bottlenecks in communication processes. In wireless networks, such restrictions provide a complex operating environment further complicated by constrained resources that inhibit the processing of data efficiently. Edge learning, being a newer technology, poses the need for new frameworks like distributed swarm learning (DSL), which aims to merge artificial intelligence with biological concepts to address such complications. Through the assistance of advanced signal processing techniques, DSL can bypass some of these challenges and provide functional solutions for bulk IoT applications. However, the most important issues of security and privacy still loom large, and it is necessary that robust protocols are formulated that can guarantee data integrity and prevent leaks in such complicated ecosystems (Cai et al., 2024). Lastly, the distributed nature of edge data processing makes theoretical and practical problems more prominent to be tackled. Security risks, non-convex optimization problems, and dynamic wireless scenarios must be overcome in order to provide efficient data processing. The nuanced requirements of edge-based datasets, combined with the limitations of devices that handle them, render an iterative process of developing stronger systems unavoidable. Research must focus on enhancing existing frameworks and exploring new methods that optimize edge computing efficiency without compromising security or performance. By addressing these issues, edge computing can potentially emerge as a core component of new paradigms for processing data, supporting a range of applications with speed, reliability, and data protection in increasingly complex operational environments (Sudarshan, 2023; Cai et al., 2024).

5.4.1. Scalability Issues

Growing levels of Internet of Things (IoT) devices have been associated with phenomenal advancements in the capability of edge data processing. With the increasing level of connected devices, scalability has become a significant issue. IoT devices generate humongous network traffic, and they may cause bottlenecks as well as increased communication latency with cloud-based systems. As has been noted in recent literature, fog computing has been a response to these scalability issues by providing the ability to distribute computations close to the source of the data. This distributed approach attempts to eliminate some of the latency and bandwidth problems associated with cloud processing and increase overall system performance. Nonetheless, the fog computing paradigm is still under development, and there are open questions related to scalability that exist, particularly with regards to accommodating new computing nodes as well as effective management of overlapping network environments (Desai et al., 2020) (Figure 5.10).

With increasing advances in fog computing, the most important area of interest must be changing robust methods of dynamic scalability. This means coming up with mechanisms that enable seamless addition of new nodes into existing networks without interrupting in-progress operations. Node discovery is particularly vital because it has a direct bearing on fault tolerance, resource management, and overall system performance. Failure to manage these scalability problems can result in long-term poor performance, rendering edge computing solutions useless. Early studies indicate that solutions applied to optimize node discovery can significantly enhance scalability in fog computing systems to increase their responsiveness and adaptability and better align with the rising expectations of IoT environments (Desai et al., 2020). In addition, to increase scalability, the architecture and implementation of more efficient edge computing could be crucial. Emerging technologies such as neuromorphic CMOS-memristive circuits are promising developments in processing capabilities without straying from low power constraints.

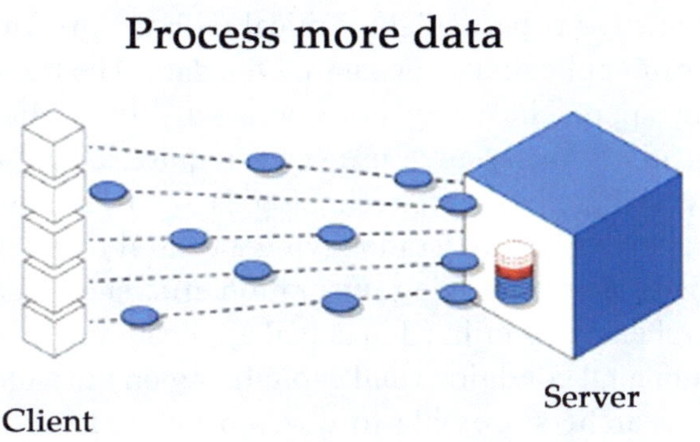

Figure 5.10. Scalability issues in edge data processing.

Source: https://external-content.duckduckgo.com/iu/?u=https%3A%2F%2Ftse2.mm.bing.net%2Fth%2Fid%2FOIP.Za0oG4dZ3uHW2VJTChIkwgHaEp%3F-pid%3DApi&f=1&ipt=1f5d5c3bc545d8433cbb257ba2ea3880e411c244de41ce7ae5b5e314eec949a5.

These advancements can reduce the overhead that otherwise accompanies cloud computing frameworks, hence reducing some of the scalability problems. As argued, the expanding quantity, legitimacy, and heterogeneity of data from networked sensors tax traditional cloud paradigms, necessitating the exploration of novel edge processing methodologies. With the leverage of neuromorphic architectures, edge devices can potentially process data more effectively, leading to improved scalability and sustainability in data processing. Overall, it is addressing these intrinsic scalability issues that is essential for the viable deployment and eventual sustainability of edge computing infrastructure.

5.4.2. Data Management and Integration Difficulties

Data integration and management issues at the edge are a result of the inherent complexities of processing and analyzing data in real-time environments. With the development of edge computing, organizations typically encounter heterogeneous data sources, varying formats, and the need for data integrity across decentralized nodes. The integration of IoT device data, for instance, presents unique challenges because each device may have varying communication protocols and data formats. These integration issues lead to wasteful data use, eventually undermining timely decision-making and analytical value. In addition, the requirement for dynamic data structures necessitates the re-evaluation of proven models in order to seek out innovative solutions that can accommodate the dynamic nature of edge environments. Seamless integration of the data at the edge is particularly critical with the growing amount of data and the number of applications consuming the data. The traditional centralized data processing approaches may not necessarily be sufficient in satisfying the latency sensitivity many edge use cases require. Based on the concept of 'models of everywhere,' current technologies such as cloud computing and advanced data analysis can assist in playing a central role in transforming data handling practices, thus improving integration efficiency. Such approaches are yet to be comprehensively utilized in actual applications. By understanding the various environmental conditions and capitalizing on the strengths of emerging technologies, researchers are able to develop tailored strategies that address specific data management challenges, driving the overall edge computing operations efficiency to its maximum potential (Ahmed et al., 2019) (Figure 5.11).

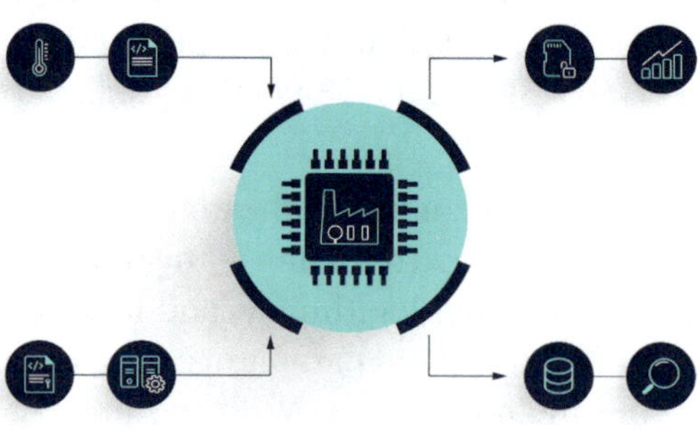

Figure 5.11. Data management on the edge.

Source: https://www.mm-software.com/fileadmin/user_upload/05_more-news-room/blogbeitraege/mm-software-techshorty-data-management-on-edge-zeichnung.jpg.

Furthermore, the exclusive challenge in data routing and management in vehicular networks illustrates the requirement for innovative methods, especially in vehicular networks. The faster mobility of vehicles and rapid topology variations make data transfer challenging, and packet loss and delays are greater. Methods such as Dynamic Fog for Connected Vehicles (DFCV) illustrate how merged fog computing can prevent such issues by dynamically allocating resources based on real-time communication demands. This adaptability not only reduces packet latency but also ensures the transfer of messages under changing network conditions. Such advancements highlight the potential of data handling techniques that can accommodate high-density settings, which may serve as key models in terms of solving integration issues in edge computing (Atiquzzaman et al., 2018).

5.4.3. Security Vulnerabilities and Threats

The evolution of edge data processing brings with it a myriad of security vulnerabilities that can be exploited by malicious agents. While edge computing improves efficiency by decentralizing data processing, in the process, it also expands the attack surface for potential threats. This is also compounded by the convergence of devices that may not have effective security protocols. Equipment that engages with other equipment typically possesses dissimilar security requirements, creating differences that expose networks to unauthorized exploitation. For instance, SCADA system vulnerabilities allow malicious actors to gain legitimate access permissions, manipulating processes such that they disrupt while appearing harmless. These weaknesses need to be dealt with by an active security stance that is as much focused on the perimeter defenses as it is on the risk inherent in the systems themselves, as described in applied threat discovery techniques for essential infrastructure like water treatment facilities (Bolzoni et al., 2012) (Figure 5.12).

In addition to the issues of physical devices at the edge, the shift towards greater reliance on cloud computing services is deeply problematic for data security. The more functions that are shifted to cloud environments, the more potential vulnerabilities at this point may be overlooked. The explosive growth in the use of clouds creates serious technological and political concerns, particularly in the forensic capabilities required to trace and combat breaches. Experts recommend an aggressive method of digital evidence gathering to maintain the integrity of sensitive data coupled with a fast response to security breaches. The use of models like the STRIDE asset-based risk assessment method allows institutions to evaluate their capacity to respond to security vulnerabilities in preparation for cloud-based attacks. The tests can guide institutions to develop strategies that weigh operational efficiency and drastic security precautions

(Sodiya et al., 2015). The union of edge computing and cloud infrastructures requires an unified view of security posture in organizations. Being aware of the specific vulnerabilities of edge data processing is necessary to creating effective countermeasures. In particular, the capability to react in a timely manner to an incident—without affecting the integrity of digital evidence—is of greatest concern for entities that operate in such environments of high dynamism. By evolving existing risk assessment frameworks, organizations can anticipate and prepare for potential breaches more effectively, enabling them to leverage their technological infrastructure without maximally exposing themselves to threats. Not only does this practice enhance incident response strategy but it also makes organizations more resilient against evolving threats on an increasingly interconnected platform. Continuous vigilance by security audits and enhanced training of response incident staff will also help safeguard sensitive data in edge computing situations.

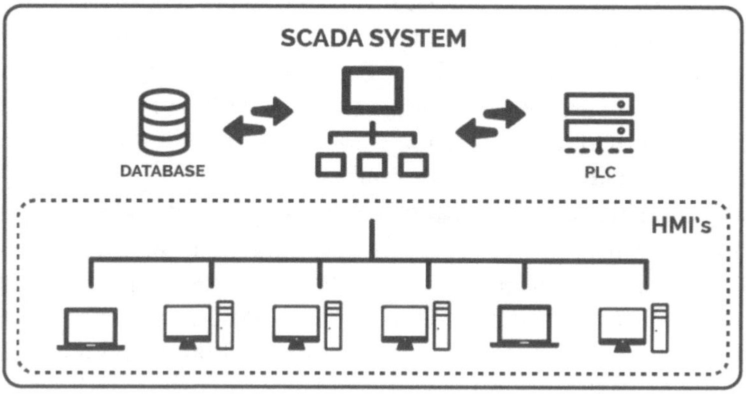

Figure 5.12. SCADA (supervisory control and data acquisition) systems.

Source: https://5.imimg.com/data5/SELLER/Default/2020/11/BO/YB/XX/2563435/supervisory-control-data-acquisition-scada-.png.

5.5. FUTURE TRENDS IN EDGE COMPUTING

As the world sees more demand for accelerated and more efficient processing of data, edge computing trends in the future are likely to change the manner in which businesses operate and innovate. One such trend is decentralization of processing resources in data, facilitating improved latency and bandwidth control. This is particularly significant for operations that require real-time data analysis, such as autonomous cars and smart cities. By distribution processing close to the data source, edge computing eliminates some of the natural shortcomings pertaining to centralized cloud services, such as bottlenecks with data and delay, and builds a more responsive and nimble system. Further, the integration of mobile edge computing (MEC) into fifth-generation (5G) networks provides new opportunities for extended services, enabling service providers to offer applications with minimal delay, thereby enabling the increasing demands of mobile customers in various sectors, including healthcare and entertainment (Belesioti et al., 2016). Edge computing is another groundbreaking aspect in that it shares a symbiotic relationship with the Internet of Things (IoT). With more devices becoming interconnected, the volume of data generated increases exponentially, which calls for robust edge computing solutions to manage this deluge. Future edge computing architecture will employ the concept of a Computing Continuum, integrating cloud, edge, and IoT technologies to create an integrated network platform. The new paradigm facilitates effective processing and analytics across devices of varying capacities, aiding organizations in extracting rich insights in real-time. The Computing Continuum implications are wide-ranging across different industries, from production and logistics to agriculture and energy management (Alvarez et al., 2023). By taking advantage of the strengths of distributed computing, businesses can enhance the efficiency of operations and develop more innovative solutions, resulting in more sustainable businesses and improved service delivery. Moreover, security and data privacy will become increasingly critical considerations as edge computing evolves. With processing closer to the source, exposure to cyber threats can increase without adequate protection. Future trends will probably include more robust encryption methods and robust access controls to ensure data integrity and confidentiality. Edge computing can also usher in a shift in compliance requirements, necessitating the development of new policies that involve dealing with data sovereignty and privacy concerns. When companies implement edge technology, maintaining a culture of security will be essential in order to protect users' trust and maintain secure data. Last but not least, such developments emphasize the importance of having an active security philosophy built into edge computing systems to ensure that innovation is not sold at the expense of data protection (Belesioti et al., 2016; Alvarez et al., 2023).

5.5.1. Advancements in AI and Machine Learning at the Edge

The wave of artificial intelligence (AI) and machine learning (ML) innovation at the edge profoundly transforms the game of data processing. Traditionally, computationally intensive activities such as human activity recognition (HAR) have been significantly reliant on cloud for analysis and training of models. But innovations like MAGNETO show a paradigm shift by making HAR feasible directly on edge devices. This edge computing eliminates the needs for continuous data exchanging with cloud infrastructure and thus significantly enhances data security and minimizes latency. Such advancements not only allow users to have personalized learning experiences but also transform edge devices into critical nodes for real-time decision-making in a diverse set of applications. The ability to execute sophisticated ML algorithms locally on local hardware is the promise of increased efficiency and user interaction in intelligent environments, which means the move towards decentralized models of computation that prioritize both privacy and immediacy. In the agricultural sector, the convergence of AI and ML at the edge is making possible the advent of smart farming trends with the objective of increasing efficiency and sustainability. New developments in autonomous agri-technologies make use of machine learning for applications like navigation and crop monitoring. For example, a study established a low-cost local motion planner based on RGB-D cameras for path planning and localization tasks (Figure 5.13).

Figure 5.13. Edge machine learning (ML).

Source: https://www.veritis.com/wp-content/uploads/2023/01/What-is-Edge-Machine-Learning-Why-You-Should-Use-Edge-ML.jpg.

This technology combines double-layer control algorithms that ensure robust performance even under dynamic and unstructured conditions. Using on-device inference optimized via methods like model pruning and quantization, this technology reduces the utilization of bulky cloud computing power while maximizing efficiency. These innovations highlight how AI is revolutionizing traditional industries through enabling precision agriculture practices that are adaptive to real-time conditions, ultimately towards maximizing resource efficiency and yield in varied agricultural environments. Innovations in AI and ML at the edge are not merely technological breakthroughs; they have profoundly transformative effects on user experience and interaction as well. By supporting incremental learning on edge devices in a step-by-step manner, as demonstrated by platforms like MAGNETO, users benefit from personalized and adaptive uses that are tailored to their own activity patterns without sacrificing privacy. Edge computing also facilitates more technology deployment availability within remote or underprivileged areas where cloud connectivity could be inconsistent. Moreover, the convergence of self-operating systems with machine learning capabilities, as seen in advanced farm machinery, demonstrates the technology's potential to be applied across sectors. With the growth of edge computing, its capability to power smarter, more interactive environments will definitely bring revolutionary modifications not only in the efficiency of data processing but even in the manner individuals and organizations utilize technology for innovation and usability.

5.5.2. Integration with 5G Technology

5G technology adoption is a revolution in the ability of network edge data processing. With the ongoing further development of the infrastructure by operators, it is now clear that 5G deployment will support an enormous range of next-generation applications that demand ultra-low latency. These environments bring about a root-level transformation in business models, enabling service providers to penetrate new markets that were previously beyond reach. However, the roll-out of such new services needs massive investment in upgrading the network and infrastructure. This raises issues about the economics of such a venture, particularly when the stakes are so high. With close scrutiny of the opportunities and market benefit offered with such new business models, it is apparent that there is an excellent chance for operators to build a solid footprint in the expanding 5G economy and raise the value that they offer businesses and consumers alike (Cuevas et al., 2017). In addition, the advent of 5G technology creates the potential for mobile video delivery evolution, a field that demands high data rates and low latency to ensure the optimal user experience. As high-definition and large-scale multicast video services see demand grow exponentially, the integration of 5G is poised to revolutionize content delivery across networks. The key to this evolution is the application of packet-level random linear network coding (RLNC) technology, a new approach enabling enhanced video quality, highest throughput, and highest data loss resilience. Synchronizing RLNC techniques with the new features of the 5G NR standard can enhance video streaming performance by leaps and bounds. These advancements not only underscore the strengths of 5G to transform multimedia applications but also open doors to research and development, strengthening the mutually dependent alliance between edge data processing and future mobile networks (Delic et al., 2018). The implications of 5G technology adoption on edge data processing have wide-ranging impacts, extending to all areas like healthcare, manufacturing, and smart cities. The ultra-low latency and high bandwidth capabilities of 5G allow for real-time decision-making and data analysis capacities crucial in environments where immediate responses are necessary. Telemedicine, for instance, can have rapid data transmission to support remote surgery or real-time monitoring of patients, enhancing efficiency of treatment and operation effectiveness. Similarly, in intelligent manufacturing, the ability to connect hundreds of millions of devices with low latency transforms production lines into smart systems that can quickly respond to changing conditions. As edge computing pressure increases, operators must consider how they will harness 5G prowess in offering tailored services that react to the singular needs of individual industries. This alignment not only ensures enhanced service provision but positions 5G at the forefront of digital transformation across industries on a massive scale.

5.5.3. Potential for Edge Computing in Emerging Markets

There is a large potential for edge computing in emerging markets, driven by the demand to improve local processing capacity in the face of infrastructural constraints. Emerging markets are plagued by poor internet connectivity and an absence of centralized data centers. Edge computing, where data is processed closer to a location rather than being shipped to distant cloud-based servers, automatically addresses such limitations by reducing latency and bandwidth consumption. This local processing of information is most critical in industries such as agriculture, healthcare, and manufacturing, which can leverage real-time analysis to optimize operations even more. This synergetic relationship between emerging technologies and dominant industry paradigms can lead to improved productivity and economic advancement, evocative of strategic interventions towards innovation-led development in domains aspiring technological development (Consulting et al., 2016). Furthermore, the inclusion of edge computing is likely to facilitate financial inclusion between emerging markets. FinTech, or financial services using technology, presents a unique opportunity for paradigm economic development. As the legal and regulatory climate improves, countries are using FinTechs potential to enhance access to financial services. Edge computing has the potential to augment this environment by providing secure and efficient data processing, which is critical in mobile payments and micro-financing scenarios. For instance, real-time processing can facilitate transactions in low-connectivity areas, thus facilitating greater economic activity in under-banked communities. As argued by organizations like the IMF and World Bank, the FinTech-edge computing intersection is pivotal in making financial affordability and inclusion a reality, which aligns with universal efforts for sustainable economic growth (Rupeika-Apoga et al., 2020). Despite such promising prospects, some obstacles need to be crossed in order for edge computing's full potential to be realized in the emerging market. Training of experts and infrastructure investment are paramount for a viable ecosystem that is edge deployment-friendly. Technical expertise and capital may not be present in various regions to develop and maintain edge computing infrastructures, which could stagnate progress and innovation. Accordingly, data privacy issues, security risks, and regulatory matters must be addressed to create trust among users and stakeholders. Specialized government intervention and support mechanisms will be required in overcoming such constraints to enable edge computing technologies to be used to create economic resilience and innovation for emerging markets. With growing evolution in emerging markets, the use of strategic initiatives focused on technological advancement will be most essential in encouraging their growth trajectory in the digital economy (Consulting et al., 2016).

SUMMARY

Conclusion of the essay on edge data processing offers huge insights into the revolution that can be facilitated through the integration of edge computing with emerging technologies such as blockchain and the Internet of Things (IoT). As indicated throughout the discussion, locating data processing close to the point of generation significantly minimizes latency and enhances the efficiency in overall operations. This is especially so in environments based on real-time data analysis, where timely processing can be quite crucial. Synthesis of evidence points to a clear trend towards decentralized models of computation, which optimize the use of available computing resources and boost security measures. The resolution of the issues listed above, such as scalability and the topology of decentralized networks, is of the highest significance to future rollouts in various commercial sectors and applications, and is thus a building block for the next generation of technological advancements (Bentayeb et al., 2025). In addition to that, the implications of offloading data processing tasks on IoT edge devices cannot be emphasized enough. The reduction of latency currently seen in traditional cloud networks becomes a reason to adopt edge solutions even more. Leveraging the advantages of edge computing not only allows for high-speed data generation but also addresses the unique needs of some embedded IoT systems. The research demonstrates a resourceful method of loading computational burdens across networked devices and thereby maximizing response times and enhancing the responsiveness of the systems. As businesses continue to adopt IoT frameworks, encouraging innovative strategies with the focus on the efficiency of edge computing can lower the cost of operations significantly while improving the experience of users (Kuchuk et al., 2024). Overall, the integration of edge computing into data processing methods is an imperative move towards addressing the challenges brought about by conventional cloud-based models. By integrating edge computing with blockchain and IoT devices, organizations can harness decentralized models that circumvent the latency issues of cloud reliance, thus improving overall efficiency. Any future research would not only have to respond to the current operations issues but also accord extra importance to innovative algorithmic solutions that enhance task allocation between computing nodes further. This evolution toward a distributed information system is not merely an improvement in data processing methodologies but also a dramatic change in organizations' use of technology to enhance performance and security (Bentayeb et al., 2025; Kuchuk et al., 2024).

While looking at the critical issues with data processing on the edge, it is increasingly clear with each new day that human mental limitations halt the ability to process large and heterogeneous data sets; with the more sophisticated data analysis, semi-automatic abstraction of complex data in well-structured information spaces becomes ever more crucial. This is particularly the case in skill demand research, where current, multi-faceted data sets are needed in analyzing workforce capabilities within a fast-changing, tech-based economy. The knowledge derived from these analyses not only informs seasoned practitioners in career path mapping but also determines required sets of skills to be imparted for new roles. These findings emphasize the need for systems facilitating intuitive and exploratory discovery in dynamic spaces, consistent with broader trends driving innovations in data processing at the edge (Dadzie et al., 2018). Furthermore, ontology development to structure information spaces is a significant contribution toward discovering and interpreting various skill requirements. This approach allows individuals and organizations to delve into the complexity of heterogeneous and dynamic information in an interactive manner, facilitating individuated insights for specific use. In this case study, the dynamic field of Data Science illustrates how exploratory data analysis and knowledge discovery are essential, where exploratory data analysis and knowledge discovery are critical. By applying context-specific and task-specific scenarios, researchers can guide the iterative construction and evaluation of ontology-based techniques. All these innovations not only add value to the work of the users' analysis but also add to the strength of enhanced decision-making in the context of continued changes in the demand for skills driven by developing technologies (Dadzie et al., 2018). Also, the addition of optical pattern recognition techniques to the processing of data is another interface of complexity and innovation. A vast amount of research carried out in this domain resulted in a rich body of imagery under different conditions like multisensor input, seasonal variability, and ambient conditions. Correlating these images based on state-of-the-art scaling optical correlators has resulted in useful information regarding different classes of data, leading to better knowledge of preprocessing needs and image difference types. The advance in air-based applications with new optical systems showcases how pioneering technology can make data processing operations easier, significantly reducing size and weight while offering better operating performance. This integration of approaches not just propels the advantages of data processing at the edge but also provides a foundation for upcoming advancements in the same.

References

1. Aghi, D., Chiaberge, M., & Mazzia, V. (2020). Local motion planner for autonomous navigation in vineyards with a RGB-D camera-based algorithm and deep learning synergy. https://core.ac.uk/download/pdf/327177639.pdf (accessed on 16th September 2025).
2. Ahmed, F., Atzori, L., Hankin, B., Basco-Carrera, L., Bastin, L., Beven, K., Beven, G., et al. (2019). Models of everywhere revisited: A technological perspective. https://core.ac.uk/download/322489447.pdf (accessed on 16th September 2025).
3. Akrivopoulos, O., Antoniou, A., Chatzigiannakis, I., et al. (2017). On the deployment of healthcare applications over fog computing infrastructure. https://core.ac.uk/download/98343526.pdf (accessed on 16th September 2025).
4. Alaghi, A., Ceze, L., Cowan, M., et al. (2017). Exploring computation-communication tradeoffs in camera systems. http://arxiv.org/abs/1706.03864 (accessed on 16th September 2025).
5. Ali, M., Anjum, A., Devitt, J., et al. (2017). Towards in-transit analytics for Industry 4.0. http://arxiv.org/abs/1710.04121 (accessed on 16th September 2025).
6. Alvarez, J. E., Bellussi, E., de Majo, C., et al. (2023). Mapping cloud-edge-IoT opportunities and challenges in Europe. https://core.ac.uk/download/586795189.pdf (accessed on 16th September 2025).
7. Arvanitakis, G., Hacid, H., Ndhlovu, M., et al. (2024). MAGNETO: Edge AI for human activity recognition–Privacy and personalization. http://arxiv.org/abs/2402.07180 (accessed on 16th September 2025).
8. Atiquzzaman, M., Khan, M. S., & Paranjothi, A. (2018). DFCV: A novel approach for message dissemination in connected vehicles using dynamic fog. http://arxiv.org/abs/1805.07662 (accessed on 16th September 2025).
9. Ballas, C., Little, S., Marsden, M., et al. (2018). Performance of video processing at the edge for crowd-monitoring applications. https://core.ac.uk/download/157781033.pdf (accessed on 16th September 2025).
10. Baraldi, A., Rosenfeld, A., Jardine, C., Mattiussi, C., Ronse, C., Zahn, C., Wishart, D., et al. (2012). On morphological hierarchical representations for image processing and spatial data clustering. http://arxiv.org/abs/1209.3925 (accessed on 16th September 2025).
11. Belesioti, M., Bliznakov, P., Bohnert, T. M., et al. (2016). Introducing mobile edge computing capabilities through distributed 5G cloud enabled small cells. https://core.ac.uk/download/81572469.pdf (accessed on 16th September 2025).

12. Bentayeb, Y., Chaoui, K., & Badir, H. (2025). Integrating blockchain and edge computing: A systematic analysis of security, efficiency, and scalability. *International Journal of Advanced Computer Science and Applications*. https://www.semanticscholar.org/paper/e572039d7a3f4b46901d1838c8bbf69afe6d3992 (accessed on 16th September 2025).
13. Bianzino, A. P., Chaudet, C., Rossi, D., et al. (2010). A survey of green networking research. http://arxiv.org/abs/1010.3880 (accessed on 16th September 2025).
14. Bikakis, N. (2018). Big data visualization tools. http://arxiv.org/abs/1801.08336 (accessed on 16th September 2025).
15. Bolzoni, D., Hadziosmanovic, D., & Hartel, P. (2012). A log mining approach for process monitoring in SCADA. https://core.ac.uk/download/pdf/11483058.pdf (accessed on 16th September 2025).
16. Butun, I., Sari, A., & Österberg, P. (2018). Security implications of fog computing on the Internet of Things. http://arxiv.org/abs/1809.10492 (accessed on 16th September 2025).
17. Buyya, R., & Varghese, B. (2017). Next generation cloud computing: New trends and research directions. https://core.ac.uk/download/96664300.pdf (accessed on 16th September 2025).
18. Cai, Z., Fan, F., Nowzari, C., Tian, Y., et al. (2024). Distributed swarm learning for edge Internet of Things. http://arxiv.org/abs/2403.20188 (accessed on 16th September 2025).
19. Cao, Z., Liu, B., Sheng, B., Zhang, Y., et al. (2018). A game-theoretic framework for revenue sharing in edge-cloud computing system. http://arxiv.org/abs/1711.10102 (accessed on 16th September 2025).
20. Casasent, D., & Luu, T. K. (2025). Optical processing for landmark identification. https://core.ac.uk/download/pdf/42859570.pdf (accessed on 16th September 2025).
21. Chen, L., Wang, M., & Zhang, X. (2012). Efficient multi-way theta-join processing using MapReduce. http://arxiv.org/abs/1208.0081 (accessed on 16th September 2025).
22. Chua, L. O., James, A. P., & Krestinskaya, O. (2018). Neuro-memristive circuits for edge computing: A review. http://arxiv.org/abs/1807.00962 (accessed on 16th September 2025).
23. Cree, M. J., Dorrington, A. A., McClure, S. H., Payne, A., et al. (2010). Resolving depth measurement ambiguity with commercially available range imaging cameras. https://core.ac.uk/download/29197550.pdf (accessed on 16th September 2025).

24. Crippa, M. R., Han, B., Mannweiler, C., Schotten, H. D., et al. (2019). Context-awareness enhances 5G multi-access edge computing reliability. https://core.ac.uk/download/245883230.pdf (accessed on 16th September 2025).

25. Cuevas, M., Dohler, M., Laya, A., Lema, M., et al. (2017). Business case and technology analysis for 5G low latency applications. https://core.ac.uk/download/96762095.pdf (accessed on 16th September 2025).

26. Dadzie, A. S., Brooke, C., Cunningham, E., Davenport, E. M., Sibarani, S., Einsfeld, M., Elia, et al. (2018). Structuring visual exploratory analysis of skill demand.

27. Dehghanghadikolaei, A., Emamian, S. S., Fotovvati, B., Gisario, A., et al. (2019). The potential of additive manufacturing in the smart factory industrial 4.0: A review. https://core.ac.uk/download/231748826.pdf (accessed on 16th September 2025).

28. Delic, S., Khirallah, C., Tassi, A., Vukobratovic, D., et al. (2018). Random linear network coding for 5G mobile video delivery. https://core.ac.uk/download/157816966.pdf (accessed on 16th September 2025).

29. Desai, N., Karagiannis, V., Punnekkat, S., Schulte, S., et al. (2020). Addressing the node discovery problem in fog computing. https://core.ac.uk/download/296708941.pdf (accessed on 16th September 2025).

30. Euclid Collaboration, Humphrey, A., Cunha, P., Bisigello, L., Tortora, C., Bolzonella, M., Pozzetti, L., Baes, M., et al. (2025). Euclid preparation. Estimating galaxy physical properties using CatBoost chained regressors with attention. https://www.semanticscholar.org/paper/58c1a77baf35ad89938e067ed60367cbb5964c84 (accessed on 16th September 2025).

31. Euclid Collaboration, Kashlinsky, A., Arendt, R. G., Ashby, M., Atrio-Barandela, F., Scaramella, R., Strauss, M., Altieri, B., et al. (2024). Euclid preparation XLVI. The Near-IR background dipole experiment with Euclid. https://www.semanticscholar.org/paper/d5796d4f86717a4d2a686ac0db3d4d569fd12730 (accessed on 16th September 2025).

32. Fu, L., Liu, X., Zhang, H., Zhang, Y., et al. (2023). Federated learning hyper-parameter tuning for edge computing. https://core.ac.uk/download/568374086.pdf (accessed on 16th September 2025).

33. Hanzo, L., Hu, J., & Yang, L. L. (2013). Mobile social networking aided content dissemination in heterogeneous networks.

34. Jukan, A., Marín Tordera, E., Masip Bruin, X., Ren, G., et al. (2016). Foggy clouds and cloudy fogs: A real need for coordinated management of fog-to-cloud computing systems. https://core.ac.uk/download/81582274.pdf (accessed on 16th September 2025).

35. Kaiypbergen, D., & Begimbayeva, Y. (2025). Research of innovative authentication: A deep dive into biometric access technologies. *Herald of the Kazakh-British Technical University*. https://www.semanticscholar.org/paper/fec252356229adc6719b28412ec1d6fc5239cb20 (accessed on 16th September 2025).

36. Khan, A., Kritz, A., Pankin, A., Shoshani, A., Sim, A., Aymar, R., Docan, C., et al. (2008). Toward a first-principles integrated simulation of tokamak edge plasmas. https://core.ac.uk/download/4881614.pdf (accessed on 16th September 2025).

37. Krook, T. (2025). *AWS-Based Edge Computing Optimization for Industrial IoT Video Streams*. https://core.ac.uk/download/652048081.pdf (accessed on 16th September 2025).

38. Kuchuk, N., Kashkevich, S., Radchenko, V., Andrusenko, Y., & Kuchuk, H. (2024). Applying edge computing in the execution IoT operative transactions. *Advanced Information Systems*. https://www.semanticscholar.org/paper/76a64d6b1edbabeeab190c05d95f6efb8685ec3c (accessed on 16th September 2025).

39. N/A. (2016). *New Hampshire University Research and Industry Plan: A Roadmap for Collaboration and Innovation*. https://core.ac.uk/download/215517669.pdf (accessed on 16th September 2025).

40. Parihar, B., & Chimmwal, P. (2021). An integrated framework for security policy management in cloud and edge computing environments. https://core.ac.uk/download/666027014.pdf (accessed on 16th September 2025).

41. Perera, C., Ranjan, R., & Wang, L. (2015). End-to-end privacy for open big data markets. https://core.ac.uk/download/327950102.pdf (accessed on 16th September 2025).

42. Putnam, A., Fahmy, S. A., Kwon, H., Neugebauer, R., Noa, S., Shanker, S. S., Kizheppatt, V., et al. (2020). Quantifying the latency benefits of near-edge and in-network FPGA acceleration. https://core.ac.uk/download/305119902.pdf (accessed on 16th September 2025).

43. Rupeika-Apoga, R., & Thalassinos, E. I. (2020). Ideas for a regulatory definition of FinTech. https://core.ac.uk/download/322748662.pdf (accessed on 16th September 2025).

44. Singh, P., Kanna, R., Venkatraman, K., & Sagar, S. (2025). Edge computing and AI-powered drone magnetometers module application. In *2025 3rd International Conference on Communication, Security, and Artificial Intelligence (ICCSAI)* (Vol. 3, pp. 405–410). https://www.semanticscholar.org/paper/ecaee383611e720d679c08a33f3fa16ead08bb44 (accessed on 16th September 2025).

45. Sodiya, A. S., Carrier, B. D., Zissis, D., Swiderski, F., Dykstra, J., James, J. I., Ruan, K., et al. (2015). Determining training needs for cloud infrastructure investigations using I-STRIDE. http://arxiv.org/abs/1502.05191 (accessed on 16th September 2025).
46. Sudarshan, V. (2023). The future of cloud computing: How serverless architectures and edge computing are redefining scalability, efficiency, and innovation. https://core.ac.uk/download/654637484.pdf (accessed on 16th September 2025).
47. Yigitcanlar, T. (2009). Managing ubiquitous eco cities: The role of urban telecommunication infrastructure networks and convergence technologies. https://core.ac.uk/download/10895362.pdf (accessed on 16th September 2025).

CHAPTER 6

EDGE ASSISTED MOBILE VR

Contents

INTRODUCTION

The advent of mobile virtual reality (VR) has transformed the landscape of interactive experience, as users can immerse themselves in digitally constructed environments through the convenience of their mobile devices. With advancing technology, edge computing has emerged as a vital component to enhance the performance and efficiency of mobile VR applications. Through the calculation of data at or close to its source rather than relying on remotely situated centralized cloud servers, edge computing significantly reduces latency, something that is highly critical in real-time applications such as gaming and simulation. Besides raising the satisfaction of the user through smoother experience, this technology also facilitates the growing demand for mobile applications that facilitate spontaneous learning and engagement across various sectors such as education and entertainment. Thus, where edge-enabled technologies come together with mobile VR there are new possibilities of innovation in the shape of enhanced user interaction and learning success. In educational contexts, m Technology coupled with edge assistance has the potential to enhance learning experiences. As evidenced by the study that reveals a 35% boost in students understanding of geometry with interactive games used, edge-assisted mobile VR can enable enhanced visualization and understanding of challenging concepts. The learning technique takes a back seat to students native familiarity with mobile technology in order to allow for teachers to implement immersive strategies that facilitate enhanced engagement and retention of information.

Figure 6.1. Edge assisted mobile virtual reality (VR).

Source: https://hypertec.com/blog/wp-content/uploads/2020/05/MOBILE-EDGE-COMPUTING_blog_header-1200x720.jpg.

Through instant feedback and tailored experiences through localized data processing, edge computing is able to effectively support diverse learner requirements, rendering mobile VR a compelling learning platform. These applications are scalable by design, opening doors for a broader audience, and therefore it becomes increasingly important for educational institutions to seek and adopt these advanced approaches. Edge-enabled mobile VR also holds the promise of transforming the way companies deploy immersive technologies. Since 5G networks will revolutionize connectivity, low latency requirements of mobile VR applications become all the more feasible. Analysis of existing and upcoming use cases indicates that business models might change and operators can innovate in situations where instant data transmission and processing are required. With edge computing, companies are not only able to optimize their operations but also create new revenue streams through personalized mobile VR experiences for both consumers and industries. This adaptability highlights the flexibility of edge-powered mobile VR that transcends gaming and education to eventually map out an increasingly connected and interactive tomorrow where technology is seamlessly woven into everyday life (Figure 6.1).

Definition of Edge Assisted Mobile VR

The introduction of Edge Assisted Mobile Virtual Reality (VR) is a paradigm shift in the manner in which end-users are engaged through virtual worlds. Concepts of edge computing are utilized to deliver richer experiences through lower latency and better computational power. Edge-assisted systems, through processing data in relatively closer proximity to users, are capable of delivering richer VR experiences that otherwise face the inherent limitations of typical mobile devices.

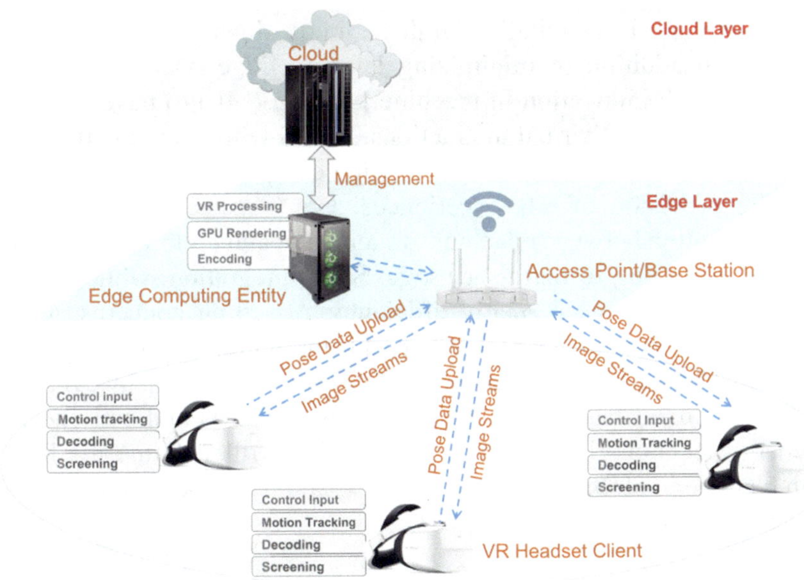

Figure 6.2. Edge VR layered architecture.

Source: https://www.researchgate.net/publication/363680902/figure/fig1/AS:11431281085250846@1663692042024/Edge-VR-layered-architecture.png.

With sustained expansion of uses of VR across sectors, from gaming to learning and industrial training, the use of edge computing becomes increasingly important. Not only does the integration smoothen interactions and deliver lifelike simulations, but it also facilitates the high-speed processing of data necessary for realistic VR applications. Hence, understanding the role played by edge technology in mobile VR is vital to its possible contribution to technological advancement and user experience. The need for ultra-low latency in VR use cases is imperative because minor levels of delays can significantly disrupt the feeling of presence that is fundamental to immersive settings. Edge Assisted Mobile VR effectively addresses this challenge by offloading computing activity away from mobile devices to nearby edge servers. This forward-looking approach enables near-instant data manipulation, which is essential for applications that necessitate immediate feedback loops, such as those with user movement and dynamic content. Existing studies show that making computational power nearer to the end user can significantly reduce response latency and consequently enhance overall user experience. Furthermore, with the advancement of 5G technology, its importance in enabling these edge computing systems will be central. It offers the possibility of new business models and new uses in the VR market concerned with smooth interaction and real-time connection, and with operators poised to capitalize on these innovations (Cuevas et al., 2017) (Figure 6.2). In addition to minimizing latency, Edge Assisted Mobile VR also intersects with innovation in machine learning (ML) to pave the way for even more sophisticated virtual interactions. As 6G wireless networks begin to emerge, integration of ML algorithms in edge computing systems can further optimize the provision of VR experiences. For instance, ML can improve resource distribution between edge nodes such that bandwidth gets dynamically redistributed according to real user usage. Such integration, while enhancing performance, also enhances energy efficiency, offsetting concerns about the resource-hungry nature of VR technology. Furthermore, continued innovation in ML models has the capability to personalize user experiences by dynamically adjusting VR content based on a user's own preferences and activities. With these synergy technologies maturing further, they will redefine the limits of what can be done in mobile VR, ultimately expand its scope of application and market size (Abbas et al., 2020).

Importance of Mobile VR in Today's Technology Landscape

The incorporation of mobile virtual reality (VR) in current technology is significant to the improvement of user experiences across different industries like education, healthcare, and entertainment. The groundbreaking technology enables experiential environments accessible through mobile phones, hence making VR accessible to everyone. In schools, for instance, mobile VR provides interactive learning through simulated environments that can be utilized to visualize and interact with intricate concepts, leading to better retention and understanding. Moreover, in medicine, VR applications assist with therapy and rehabilitation by simulating real-world situations, enabling patients to practice coping mechanisms or body movement in a controlled yet real setting. The simplicity of mobile VR makes it a powerful tool, bridging classroom education with therapy sessions, thereby demonstrating its applicability in the ever-evolving tech landscape. Furthermore, the use of edge computing facilitates the improvement of mobile VR performance through real-time processing of data and improved application performance. Edge-supported mobile VR leverages computing power closer to the user, thereby reducing latency and offering greater interactive experiences in virtual spaces. This is paramount in applications that require instant decision-making, like gaming or remote training simulations, whereby delay would water down the experience. Processing data at the network edge, mobile VR can offer more immersive and richer experiences without overloading users devices. The edges of edge computing not only make users happier but also provide room for developers to create more sophisticated applications that can adapt in real time to the users input and even external conditions, yielding both timely pertinence and long-term growth in the tech field. Finally, while advantages of mobile VR and its supported features are apparent, there are also ethical concerns that must be addressed for the better integration into society. Concerns regarding user privacy, data security, and addiction are becoming prevalent as immersive technologies are brought into the mainstream. They pose challenges, though, that require a balance in the use of mobile VR, such that people's rights are not infringed upon by innovations. As in recent literature has observed, the interface between technology and ethics and, in particular, in platforms like the Metaverse, needs to be examined with care so that social values are protected while technological innovation is enhanced (Yogesh et al., 2023; Allam et al., 2022). Thus, the future of mobile VR is not only about technical competence but also about the frameworks that will decide how it is used ethically in various spheres.

6.1. MOBILE VIRTUAL REALITY TECHNOLOGY

The marriage of Mobile Virtual Reality (VR) technology and edge computing opened new doors for immersive experience. With the help of edge computing, it is possible to significantly reduce latency, accelerating the responsiveness of VR applications. This is crucial for delivering seamless user experience, particularly in real-time interactive scenarios like games and training simulations. As users engage with VR content, the proximity of data processing to the device minimizes the latency associated with data having to travel large networks. This paradigm shift allows developers to build more sophisticated and interactive worlds without compromising performance, thus achieving enhanced user satisfaction and immersion in mobile VR experiences. Further, the intersection of edge-assisted mobile VR and the Internet of Things (IoT) demonstrates the technology's vast potential. Edge computing gives the system the ability to process data from various sources simultaneously, which is a critical functionality when mixing real-time sensor data. Through the use of a content and computation-aware communication control framework, such mobile VR apps can implement efficient multi-streaming, enabling concurrent data processing and rendering. This capability not only provides users with real-time analytics but also enhances the overall experience by inserting the virtual world into the context of an ever-shifting reality of actual-world data. The developments that emerge from edge computing are remaking the design and delivery of mobile VR experiences, positioning them according to the requirements of the user. Finally, the implementation of 5G technology is a significant driver of the future of mobile VR. With its ultra-low latency capability, 5G will open up new realms of interactions in the virtual reality world. It will challenge and revolutionize networks, and these will be testing as well as interesting times for the service providers. As 5G network deployment goes on, the infrastructure will need to manage high-bandwidth applications, which will deliver richer virtual experiences without buckling under the load. The initial investments in such change will look formidable; however, the potential of unlocking new markets and models of business through immersion-related applications continues to be an even stronger incentive for network operators. Capitalizing on these innovations effectively, the future of mobile VR can be underpinned by a seamless integration of technology that enhances user experience as much as operational efficiency (Figure 6.3).

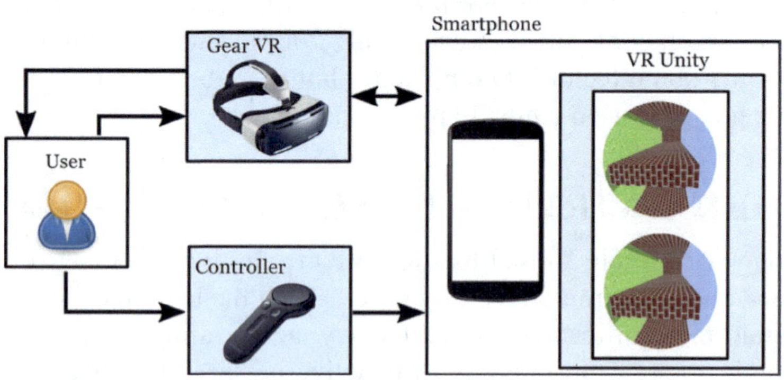

Figure 6.3. Mobile virtual reality system.

Source: https://www.researchgate.net/profile/Jose-Varela-Aldas/publication/335327349/figure/fig1/AS:794711602245632@1566485419208/Mobile-virtual-reality-system.ppm.

6.1.1. Overview of Mobile VR Hardware and Software

Virtual reality (VR) mobile is a serious area of technological development, where the association of cutting-edge hardware and rich software comes together to create a fully immersive experience for the user. Behind the hardware of mobile VR are headsets that employ smartphones, and through this, convenience without sacrificing functionality. The headsets typically incorporate motion tracking sensors as well as high-definition screens for delivering an immersive space for the user. Show technological advances, such as OLED displays and premium lenses, that have significantly enhanced visual realism, allowing users to become immersed in an environment with higher degrees of realism. Greater computational power within mobile hardware has facilitated this advancement, with advanced graphics and interactions once reserved for desktop VR systems now being made possible, thus turning mobile VR into an accessible and interactive choice for the masses. Its programming environment is equally significant, since it facilitates the experience with which the user interacts within the virtual world. Programs range from games to educational simulations, each of which is designed to take advantage of the special capabilities of the mobile VR system. The design of user-friendly interfaces and intuitive controllers facilitates better user interaction, allowing them to navigate complex environments easily. Besides, the advent of 6G wireless networks will further accelerate the performance of mobile VR by facilitating low latency and high bandwidth for real-time communication and large content dissemination, which is essential to applications such as remote collaboration or virtual tourism, where seamless communication is paramount (Abbas et al., 2020) (Figure 6.4).

Figure 6.4. Mobile VR hardware.

Source: https://www.augmented-minds.com/wp-content/uploads/2018/01/Augmented-Reality-AR-devices.jpg.

These technological improvements not only increase the variety of software on the market but also improve the general effectiveness of mobile VR applications. Incorporating edge computing into mobile VR is a major potential for enhanced performance and reduced latency. Processing data close to the end-user, edge computing can assist in reducing the burden on mobile networks, delivering users smooth experience no matter where they are. This technology innovation would enable real-time analysis and adaptive streaming, providing an interactive experience that learns users' requirements in various applications, from gaming to sophisticated training simulation. Moreover, as discussed in future 5G applications, use cases for low latency entail massive investments in infrastructure, challenges and opportunities for mobile VR development and operators (Cuevas et al., 2017). Its merging with edge support and mobile VR has not only the potential to revolutionize the presentation of content but also the redefinition of user expectations within the virtual space.

6.1.2. Key Features of Mobile VR Systems

The evolution of mobile virtual reality (VR) systems has been immensely shaped by emerging wireless technologies, particularly the presence of 5G networks. A primary differentiating characteristic of such mobile VR systems is support for real-time processing and interaction of data, which is quite readily supported through ultra-low latency connectivity. Such a requirement is critical to immersive applications because any form of latency, however minute, has a tendency to disrupt the continuity of interaction and lead to a disjointed user experience. Therefore, the rollout of network infrastructure by operators, as highlighted by the theme of new business models with 5G, is not just about optimizing broadband speeds but also about supporting frictionless, responsive interactions in VR contexts (Cuevas et al., 2017). This combination of mobile VR systems and fast wireless networks provides fertile ground for new application opportunities with a direct effect on user satisfaction and engagement. Another key feature of mobile VR systems is their versatility in interfacing with different user environments, a capability that is required for ensuring maximum usability. The integration of edge computing in mobile VR has been a game-changer in this context. Edge-based mobile VR platforms calculate nearer to the user, reducing latency and making applications more responsive overall. This setup improves user experience by allowing fast calculations within the nearby network rather than frequent interaction with faraway servers. In this manner, users get access to richer and more interactive experiences without the drawbacks of bandwidth limitations and slow feedback. These innovations demonstrate how the utilization of edge computing not only enhances performance but also provides an enhanced intuitive and interactive experience with VR content, highlighting the limitless potential of mobile VR across various applications (Chen et al., 2019) (Figure 6.5).

Figure 6.5. Feature of mobile VR systems.

Source: https://external-content.duckduckgo.com/iu/?u=https%3A%2F%2 Fup-loads-ssl.webflow.com%2F5a9058c8f7462d00014ad4ff%2F5ca78a4504fdce8d3f93f4c2_fTHwqCc1lyzEReDXmM6JEwSIltI4IOeS1Umg36PLheWO-aecsY2s-0riWW8-I--OCGcZAhS9TQ4GgR09scJcfJ8-i9YQrGJQeymaRAn5ASmiQn-QGsmReePMmi4lr98qKWZBKcoTti.png&f=1&nofb=1&ipt=800b7098437b0fbb4a7b1b5e70ab9bc7b9a62ac05661bcb954e9aec2aa950cca.

The final critical feature of mobile VR systems is their availability and democratization of virtual experience. The extensive usage of smartphones equipped with advanced sensors and processor power has progressively popularized VR accessibility among the broader masses. Now with mobile VR devices becoming widespread, they enable inclusive experiences that transcend geography and economics and extend the invitation to virtual worlds to users across multiple spectrums. This democratization is also supported by the influence of 5G networks that enable greater bandwidths and lower latencies, necessary to deliver high-quality VR content on phones. This assembly of these technologies not only supports gaming and entertainment but also cuts across educational and professional applications, thus demonstrating the flexibility and broad scale of mobile VR systems. With these qualities merging, consumers and firms are brought into a new age of promise for innovation and exploration (Cuevas et al., 2017; Chen et al., 2019).

6.1.3. Current Trends in Mobile VR Development

The new mobile virtual reality (VR) development environment is characterized by an increased focus on amplifying the experience of users through innovative technologies that facilitate performance as well as accessibility. The new trends identify the application of edge computing and cloud resources in facilitating the processing of heavy VR data in the user's proximity. This kind of a computational environment minimizes latency issues, which are extremely crucial in offering immersive experiences. Developers are utilizing more light frameworks and bandwidth-optimizing to enhance application responsiveness, rendering mobile VR more adaptable for varied environments. Furthermore, the incorporation of artificial intelligence (AI) and augmented reality (AR) technology in mobile VR software produces a more immersive interactive experience, transforming user interaction and satisfaction to unprecedented levels, in harmony with the pace being set by rolling innovations in the industry. A key trend is the development of gamified and interactive mobile VR experiences designed to involve and retain users. This is evident in the educational category, with gamification-based platforms leading to dramatic increases in student involvement and participation. Interactive elements such as real-time feedback and gamified quizzes not only improve learning engagement but also offer deeper understanding of complex concepts, such as geometric thinking, through the utilization of immersive technologies. The use of mobile VR in combination with learning material, particularly through tools such as interactive worksheets, has been discovered to improve students' geometric thinking capacity. Concurrently, the expanding extension of mobile VR applications into multidisciplinary areas such as training, therapy, and entertainment demonstrates its multidimensional potential and expanded exposure in daily usage, meeting users' multidimensional needs and demands. Moreover, user data confidentiality and ethics are now more frequently debated in the case of mobile VR development. Along with the evolution of technology, so emerges the practice of collecting personal data through immersive technologies, with enormous questions about the consent and safety of users' information. Developers thus have the dual challenge of innovating and ensuring user rights protection. Emerging trends in secure data practices are now being integrated into the design process and provoking developers to create technologies that revolve around transparency and trust with the users. This interdisciplinary strategy not only adheres to the legal and ethical standards but also opens doors for wider consumer adoption of mobile VR technologies. As stakeholders like event planners utilize mobile VR for life-altering experiences, it is imperative that technological advancements catch up with good practices so as to foster beneficial social influences, as indicated by studies studying technologys influence on shaping event experiences in various cultures (Sulaimi et al., 2023).

6.2. INTEGRATION OF EDGE COMPUTING WITH MOBILE VR

By integrating edge computing and mobile virtual reality (VR), there is a paradigm shift in how immersive is introduced into the experience. Traditional models of cloud-based computing are typically plagued by excessive latency and bandwidth limitations that detract from the seamless requirements of VR applications. By implementing edge computing, it becomes feasible to push computational resources closer to the end-user, thereby significantly trimming latency. Such an improvement is critical for uses like mobile VR, where responsiveness and real-time processing are essential to ensure the immersivity of the user experience. Strategically locating edge servers enables faster data transmission and processing, ultimately enhancing the quality and interactivity of VR experiences. Edge-enabled mobile VR can thus transform entertainment activities such as gaming and virtual travel so that users can interact with high-quality, immersive worlds that were previously inaccessible due to infrastructural limitations. Network slicing is also an important factor when it comes to the convergence of edge computing and mobile VR, particularly in 5G networks.

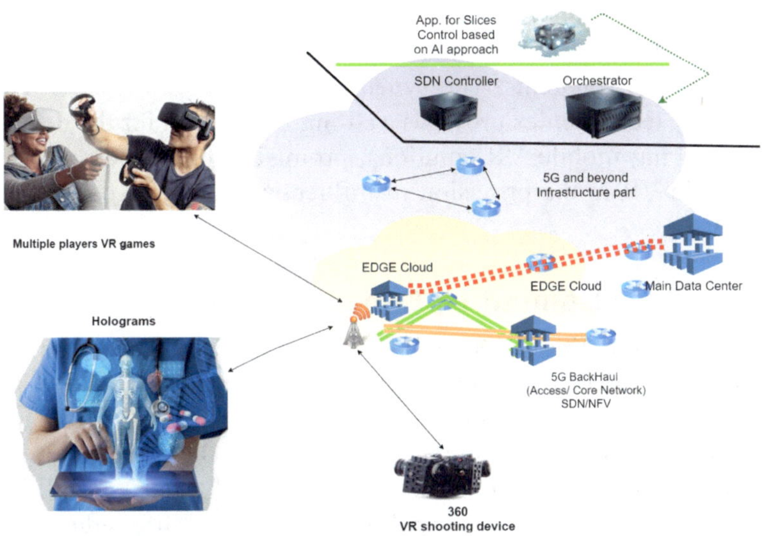

Figure 6.6. Intelligent core network based on mobile edge computing (MEC) servers with multiple users.

Source: https://www.mdpi.com/applsci/applsci-10-05515/article_deploy/html/images/applsci-10-05515-g001.png.

This technology allows multiple virtual networks to be established over a single physical network depending on varying performance requirements for different applications. Network slicing can facilitate the desired conditions of VR applications by allowing dedicated resources that offer better bandwidth and less latency. This dynamic resource approach is required for mobile VR, where changing activity of users makes bandwidth requirements fluctuate. Secondly, the management and orchestration of such network slices are impelled by advanced protocols and frameworks, hence emphasizing the mutual dependency of edge computing technology and network management in offering an improved VR experience. The compatibility of edge computing and network slicing, thus, creates the possibility for realizing an end-to-end integrated mobile VR ecosystem with optimal efficiency and performance. Multi-Access Edge Computing (MEC) also supports the coupling of mobile VR with edge computing by offering low-latency, high-bandwidth access to critical network resources. MEC facilitates mobile VR applications by placing compute power at the network's edge, allowing operators to provide the high demands of immersive applications. One of the most valuable advantages of MEC is that it offers facilities for real-time data processing and analysis, which are imperative in applications where immediate interaction and feedback are paramount. Furthermore, leveraging the potential of MEC along with new technologies such as NFV, SDN, and IoT opens up new avenues for the creation of rich and interactive environments. The synergistic integration of MEC with these complementary technologies provides a strong foundation for the development of groundbreaking mobile VR solutions, promising future potential of edge-assisted mobile VR in the provision of influential, engaging user experiences (Figure 6.6).

6.2.1. How Edge Computing Enhances Mobile VR Experiences

Merging edge computing with mobile virtual reality (VR) experience can revolutionize the manner in which users interact and are satisfied with VR experience. Edge computing eliminates latency and enhances the responsiveness of VR programs by making computing resources available closer to the user, which is critical in providing immersive environments. Because mobile hardware typically has limited processing capability and battery life, edge computing facilitates offloading computationally intensive tasks to nearby servers. This way, it reduces the amount of data that must travel from device to cloud, thereby lessening lag time and creating a more realistic VR experience. As mobile VR continues to evolve, the synergy between edge computing and 5G technologies will support new applications that were not previously possible, perhaps giving rise to more immersive levels of user experience and supporting innovative content delivery models within the VR domain (Cuevas et al., 2017). The future potential for mobile VR is not just limited to entertainment, but it holds promise for educational, training, and cultural heritage applications as well. Edge computing can greatly enhance such applications by facilitating real-time computation on data and low-latency feedback, which is critical for applications such as simulations and interactive learning systems. For instance, via edge computing, teachers can provide great VR content that adapts automatically to user inputs, offering a richer interactive learning experience. The importance of this can be seen in the development of large-scale heritage games that combine entertainment and learning elements, with the use of advanced real-time graphics and interactivity (Lerner et al., 2010). Being able to connect the virtual space to current real-time data not only provides better learning outcomes but also supports increased user interaction and retention with learning content. Furthermore, the monetary viability of adding edge computing infrastructures for catering to mobile VR is of greatest concern. While operators invest in network upgrades to be capable of handling ultra-low latency requirements, they unlock a goldmine of opportunities across industries. While the transition would be costly, the prospective benefits, including enhanced customer satisfaction and new revenue streams, are motivating. The report describes that firms which strategically position themselves in this new marketplace can ride the burgeoning demand for advanced VR applications. By being the leaders in edge computing as a core component of their service capabilities, they can enable a more interactive and responsive VR environment that responds appropriately to business and consumer needs, thereby attaining the maximum technological innovation and economic return (Cuevas et al., 2017) (Figure 6.7).

Figure 6.7. The integration of edge computing into mobile virtual reality (VR) experiences.

Source: https://stlpartners.com/wp-content/uploads/2019/10/Mobile-Edge-Computing.jpg.

6.2.2. Case Studies of Successful Edge-Assisted Mobile VR Applications

The deployment of edge-enabled technology for mobile virtual reality (VR) applications is exemplified best through various successful case studies, which demonstrate its ability to enhance experience and increase accessibility. A case in point for an application is the use of VR in cultural heritage experiences wherein high-definition graphics and real-time interaction are facilitated by edge computing for a deeper appreciation of history. These serious games draw upon development in real-time computer graphics and artificial intelligence to increase historical learning as a more engaging and interactive experience. As recorded, communication and interactivity are the strengths of serious gaming applications, thus establishing how edge-assisted mobile VR can redefine educational models across cultural institutions.

This innovation promises a shift from static learning methodologies to more dynamic paradigms, allowing users to learn and explore heritage sites in an unprecedented manner and allow greater public access to history and culture (Lerner et al., 2010). Edge-assisted mobile VR applications have also emerged in medical training, namely laparoscopic surgical skill acquisition. VR training courses utilize the low-latency processing capability of edge computing to allow real-time comments and analyses of a trainee's psychomotor skills.

Utilization of tracking technology and advanced statistical methods allows assessors to attain a more objective appreciation of a surgeon's skills, as a requirement in accreditation processes. By deflecting focus away from conventional mentorship-focused training toward structured objective curricula, as in top-performing instances, institutions can make surgical education more effective and safer. This paradigm shift shows the dramatic potential of edge-supported mobile VR to revolutionize the way medical competencies are trained and tested, and in the process, raise standards of patient safety (Chmarra et al., 2011). If one looks at the broader implications of mobile VR applications based on the edge, it can be observed that their success lies in the extent to which they are able to scale and enhance user experience across different realms. The intersection between edge computing and mobile VR not only enables more sophisticated content but also works to alleviate challenges such as bandwidth constraints and latency.

The case studies described in this paper demonstrate how education, health, and cultural heritage fields have effectively employed this technology to facilitate participation, productivity, and understanding. It is crucial that while applications of this type continue to evolve, unresolved problems and areas for future research be identified, particularly concerning interaction design and scale-up of VR experiences. Ultimately, further advancement and use of edge-supported mobile-based VR solutions are a good promise to transform the manner in which digital content is used across various industries (Lerner et al., 2010; Chmarra et al., 2011).

6.2.3. Challenges in Integrating Edge Computing with Mobile VR

The symbiosis of edge computing and mobile virtual reality (VR) is impressive in its challenge, according to the very nature of complexity of each. Edge computing, constructed to process information closer to the source rather than relying solely on centralized clouds, strives to enhance responsiveness and reduce latency, which are top priority for an immersive VR experience. However, the disparity in hardware capability in edge computing systems and mobile devices might render deployment challenging. Smartphone users use devices with varying processing power and battery, which might undermine the uniformity of VR experiences. The inconsistency can break the illusion of immersion for users, making developers create adaptive apps that can leverage both edge computing potential and mobile hardware. Without such flexibility, the potential of VR to deliver immersive education or entertainment opportunities may never be actualized, thus limiting user acceptance and satisfaction. In addition, the successful adoption of edge computing in mobile VR platforms is being threatened by network performance and bandwidth limitations. While high-definition content consumption keeps booming, the mobile networks are being driven to their limits more than ever before, laying bare the vulnerabilities of today's architectures. Evolution from 4G LTE to 5G technology is needed in order to accommodate growing traffic, which is bound to consist of diverse applications from 4K video streaming to online multi-player games. Yet, as it has been reported, the technological developments surrounding 5G, particularly those developed by projects like SESAME, are still in their infancy. These advances, including the concept of Small Cells-as-a-Service (SCaaS), aim to exploit small cells and edge computing to facilitate improved performance. Broad-based uptake is required to obtain these improvements in their entirety, though, highlighting the present problem of attempting to keep technology progress ahead of mobile user expectations in VR environments (Albanese et al., 2016). Besides technical constraints, mobile VR's association with edge computing also raises significant data privacy and security concerns. With personal data being produced and processed in large volumes at the edge, such data must be protected from any compromise. Moreover, as mobile devices increasingly emerge as endpoints for VR content consumption, hacking or unauthorized access becomes a growing concern. This vulnerability can deter consumers from utilizing edge computing-based mobile VR apps to their full potential. For mitigating these threats, developers and network operators will have to provide robust encryption methods and privacy mechanisms in position, instilling confidence in users. As the application of mobile technologies in education demonstrates, improved learning experiences can be achieved through VR, and addressing these security issues is important to leveraging the full potential of edge-assisted mobile VR (Leitão et al., 2018).

6.3. USER EXPERIENCE IN EDGE ASSISTED MOBILE VR

The convergence of edge computing and mobile virtual reality (VR) technologies has fundamentally shifted the user experience, enhancing the quality and accessibility of immersive environments. Because of the increasing demand for responsive and interactive software, edge-enabled mobile VR alleviates the latency issues that are otherwise associated with cloud-based VR applications. This reduction in latency not only boosts the factor of immersion by delivering more timely feedback but also facilitates smoother interactions required for user satisfaction. As consumers seek more interactive experiences, operators must recognize that investing in edge computing infrastructures will become increasingly crucial to meeting these demands. The potential for delivering heretofore unseen immersive experiences heightens the stakes, pushing operators to consider new business models in the context of such advanced technologies, a development observed in recent studies of 5Gs impact on market forces (Cuevas et al., 2017). The education industry will also stand to gain significantly from richer user experiences in edge-backed mobile VR. With uses ranging from medicine to engineering, the immersive quality of VR environments offers specific advantages for experiential learning. Virtual reality and augmented reality technologies, for example, are being used in medical schools for simulation training and skill development. These applications highlight VRs potential for enhancing learning outcomes, since immersive experience imbues a context that encourages greater retention of knowledge. More specialized applications in specialized fields, like dermatology, illustrate the versatility of VR instruments in the classroom, emphasizing their growing applicability (Dellavalle et al., 2020). With edge computing, instructors can build real-time engagements responsive to several different needs of learning, thus making VR an important ally in pedagogical innovation in various domains. Furthermore, the effect of enriched user experiences in edge-based mobile VR extends to the consumer marketplace, where the need for leading-edge applications continues to grow. With ever-more capable hardware on mobile devices, consumers are seeking out experiences that balance entertainment with utility. At this intersection lies new opportunity for use cases such as virtual tourism, which offers new means of exploration with less spatial constraint. To leverage these opportunities, mobile operators must embrace edge computing advantages, which facilitate low-latency interaction critical to maintaining user interest and satisfaction. As the demand for compelling content grows, stakeholders in the VR world must collaborate to explore new forms and experiences that are enriched with edge-supported technologies, ultimately enhancing the mobile virtual reality entertainment environment (Cuevas et al., 2017) (Figure 6.8).

Figure 6.8. The role of edge ML in virtual reality.

Source: https://aicompetence.org/edge-ml-seamless-latency-free-ar-vr-experiences/.

6.3.1. Factors Influencing User Experience in Mobile VR

Mobile virtual reality (VR) user experience is significantly affected by a number of interrelated variables, the most prominent among them being connectivity and media delivery dynamics. In the course of interacting in virtual environments, their quality of experience relies on the convergence of networked media comprising text, audio, and images. The ability of mobile VR environments to draw upon solid connections—such as high-speed internet and sophisticated wireless protocols—makes it possible to deliver immersive content with low latency. The connectivity is necessary because more users are generating and distributing content in these environments. Evolution in internet usage with over one billion users of digital media contributes to even greater expectations for a best quality experience, which demonstrates the industrys need to keep pace with the rapid rate of technological and content delivery innovation as discussed in Aggoun et al. (2008). Therefore, the understanding of such dynamics is critical in enhancing user satisfaction and use of VR platforms. Another fundamental aspect influencing user experience in mobile VR is user interface design and interaction models. A well-designed interface plays a pivotal role in ensuring users have the ability to explore complex virtual scenes in a natural manner. Factors such as responsiveness, usability, and visual simplicity significantly influence a user's ability to engage fully with the VR content. Moreover, the use of sensory feedback components, such as haptic feedback and spatial audio, plays an essential role in providing a greater level of immersion. As mobile VR technology continues to evolve with more advanced tracking techniques, much like those applied in surgical skill assessment with laparoscopic devices, it may further augment user interactions and learning curves in virtual environments. These advancements are a good illustration of the potential of novel approaches to user interface design that have the capability to significantly enhance the way people perform tasks and accomplish things in mobile VR as presented in Chmarra et al. (2011) (Figure 6.9).

Figure 6.9. User experience in mobile VR.

Source: https://media.licdn.com/dms/image/v2/D4D12AQF3WnC_ftMb-g/article-cover_image-shrink_720_1280/B4DZWjFr3CHYAI-/0/1742197940951?e=2147483647&v=beta&t=7OufspDGH8xMwY0SJxSKPmICqyDic0wjBBkIm9I2k0c.

Finally, users' socio-cultural context is a key factor in determining their experiences in mobile VR environments. Users' cultural background, history of experience with technology, and history of experience with virtual worlds can generate varied routes to engagement and satisfaction. For instance, those who have extensive experience playing games will navigate these virtual worlds more efficiently compared to newcomers since they will be transferring competence from earlier situations to new ones. Furthermore, as VR-based applications are increasingly integrated within collaborative and social platforms, the ability to interact with others within these spaces becomes highly imperative. Perceptions of interaction, community, and shared experience on the part of users will necessarily continue to influence their overall satisfaction and adoption of mobile VR technology. By recognizing the interaction of such user-centric factors, developers are able to create tailor-made experiences that resonate with different segments of people, thereby leading to more engaging and inclusive virtual experiences.

6.3.2. Role of Latency and Bandwidth in User Satisfaction

Within the domain of Edge Assisted Mobile VR, comprehension of latency and bandwidth roles is most important to improving user satisfaction. Latency is the time period between a users action and system response, and this directly impacts the immersive experience sought by VR. Low latency is essential; even slight delays can impair interaction flow, causing an interrupted experience that decreases user engagement. Conversely, there exists large bandwidth that allows for the quick transmission of rich visual and sound data, enriching the VR experience. With seamless experiences becoming the expectation of users, it now forms a fundamental design problem to satisfy both latency and bandwidth. The intersection point of technology and user expectations raises the imperative of enhancing network parameters for a rewarding user experience in VR-based applications. Bandwidth is not a stand-alone variable; it is intrinsically tied with latency and overall quality of service in mobile VR settings. The ability to handle and render high-definition content in real time is paramount in the preservation of user satisfaction. With low bandwidth, there is an occurrence of compression artifacts or lag, which have negative impacts on the immersive qualities that users take pleasure in. Also, unreliable bandwidth can exacerbate the problems of consistent latency and making it unpredictable to ensure a better user experience. In this regard, the use of edge computing can help mitigate such problems by placing content nearer to users and hence optimizing bandwidth utilization and latency.

This is consistent with the requirements of today's era for individualized and quality delivery of media, affirming the relevance of robust network topologies in maximizing the satisfaction of users in mobile VR settings. In exploring further the complex dynamic interaction among latency, bandwidth, and user satisfaction, the use of digital twins (DT) technology for managing networks offers promising avenues. DTs offer an emulated model of network elements, with the capability of real-time monitoring and changes based on user experience and system performance. This dynamic organization allows not just better management of network resources but also adaptive strategies that adjust the user experience in VR solutions. With the assistance of DT-based methods, service providers are capable of optimizing latency and bandwidth in accordance with user demands and contextual need. Such advancements underscore the pivotal significance of investing in infrastructure that is technical in nature with an emphasis on user aspects affecting user satisfaction, a transition towards more responsive and user-centric virtual worlds, enriching ultimately the individual's immersed experience in edge assisted mobile VR (Charles et al., 2006; Hu et al., 2023).

6.3.3. User Feedback and Its Impact on Future Developments

User feedback is essential in iterative development of Edge Assisted Mobile VR applications. With emerging technologies, users' experiences are increasingly making contributions towards the functionality and architecture of virtual reality platforms.

User feedback collection and analysis assist developers in identifying repetitive issues and avenues for enhancement, which further affect future iterations of the technology. For instance, adopting user preferences can make significant contributions to usability and engagement improvement, therefore yielding a more engaging experience.

This type of information is particularly crucial in a high growth rate-dominated industry that is characterized by heavy technology involvement, where synchronizing product functionality with user needs is the success factor. The implications of user feedback extend beyond superficial visual tastes; they have the potential to directly influence business models and provision of services for Edge Assisted Mobile VR. As 5G networks become available, which provide ultra-low latency and high-speed data transport, users' needs need to be understood in order to capitalize on optimization of these improvements.

As highlighted by recent analysis, operators are considering ways of making investment in network infrastructure worthwhile through innovative applications addressing user comments. Such a trend offers a good opportunity for developers to capitalize on intelligence earned from consumers and consequently build experiences not only meeting existing demand but also anticipating future market requirements and innovation, positioning themselves ultimately more competitively in the market (Cuevas et al., 2017)

In addition, the intersection of user feedback and emerging technologies presents fertile ground for the development of serious games for cultural heritage contexts. As noted in the analysis of serious gaming technology, the deployment of user feedback can reinforce the education and engagement capabilities of Heritage VR applications.

With the deployment of feedback, producers can enhance channels of communication, interactivity, and visual representation, transforming the way cultural stories are engaged with. This evolution not only engages viewers with historical content but also addresses some of the issues recorded in existing literature on serious games. By an emphasis on end-user feedback during development, stakeholders ensures that applications of cultural heritage evolve to suit user expectations while providing an enriching experience that respects and conserves history (Lerner et al., 2010).

6.4. APPLICATIONS OF EDGE ASSISTED MOBILE VR

The integration of edge computing into mobile Virtual Reality (VR) experiences is a significant step towards addressing the challenges that mobile platforms have inherently dealt with. With the shift towards immersive technologies, low-latency and high-bandwidth data processing is increasingly important. Edge-enabled mobile VR takes advantage of locally available computing resources in order to significantly reduce latency, allowing for real-time data processing in proximity to the consumer. This setup enables seamless interaction in virtual environments, facilitating applications in gaming, education, and simulation training that require instantaneous response and feedback. Through edge computing platforms, developers will be in a position to optimize user experience and satisfaction and thereby expand the scope of mobile VR applications. The synergy between edge computing and mobile VR presents an opportunity for authors to author more interactive experiences that can target an expanding user base with different requirements, transcending the customary limitations of cloud-driven platforms. Edge-based mobile VR is an enabler for richer content creation and interaction within the Metaverse context. The creation of the Metaverse is based on immersive virtual experiences that can be designed and deployed successfully. With the application of a Mixture of Experts (MoE) model along with Generative Artificial Intelligence (GAI), developers can utilize the capabilities of edge computing to simplify data management and processing functions. This new approach not only improves the quality and reliability of video content production but also allows dynamic user interaction in the Metaverse. These advancements allow users to experience objects that are not only pleasing to the eye but also full of context, paving the way for new applications in social networks, virtual shopping malls, and collaborative workspaces. Besides, this convergence points to the potential of edge-assisted technologies to shift the content accessibility and production paradigm, thus unlocking the full potential of the Metaverse. Applications of edge-assisted mobile VR have extensions across sectors, highlighting its versatility and potential for change. In healthcare, for instance, mobile VR can be used to conduct remote consultations, training, and surgical simulations so that professionals can conduct complicated operations without being physically present in a surgery unit. Moreover, the interactive nature of VR enhances learning outcomes since it enables learners to assimilate complex information within simulation environments, enhancing the effectiveness and enjoyment of learning. Also, industries such as tourism and real estate are enhanced by portable VR through immersive property tours and virtual vacations. Applications are also enhanced by the reduced latency and greater processing offered by edge computing, which supports efficient rendering of high-definition visual and audio content. Overall, the merging of mobile VR with edge computing not only drives innovation but also improves user experience across industries across the board, indicative of the long-range implications of this merging (Figure 6.10).

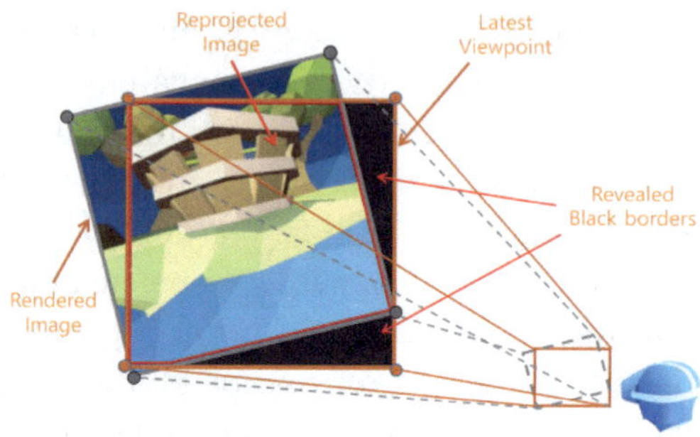

Figure 6.10. VR image reprojection and resulting black borders.

Source: https://encrypted-tbn0.gstatic.com/images?q=tbn:ANd9GcR0PXafqzmxKA8g0_AN7avLa8rST4eynUtyRQ&s.

6.4.1. Use in Gaming and Entertainment

The advent of edge-enhanced mobile virtual reality (VR) is revolutionizing the world of gaming and entertainment through more immersive experiences with significantly lower levels of latency. Traditional gaming platforms are marred by latency that can compromise the user experience, particularly in competitive settings. Edge computing addresses these issues through data processing in close proximity to the user and elimination of latency that can lead to cloud-based systems. This technology innovation not only guarantees smoother gaming but also facilitates complex interactions within massive virtual worlds. With games depending more and more on real-time response for immersive experiences, the use of edge assistance becomes inevitable, allowing developers to design new game mechanics and narratives that were unimaginably complicated due to latency constraints. The shift towards instant responses is changing user experience and redefining limits in gaming worlds. Also, edge-assisted mobile VR extends beyond the usual gaming and penetrates into cultural and educational growth. Through recent studies, as illustrated, the merge between learning content and gaming technology has rolled out a tapestry of possibility for playful learning. The entertainment game principles can also be applied to more serious gaming applications, which are increasingly being used to enable greater engagement in cultural heritage environments, such as museums or historical learning spaces. With real-time graphics and interactivity, edge-assisted mobile VR can create engaging narratives that draw users into learning, taking advantage of the strengths of gaming to support knowledge attainment and cultural understanding. Such convergence of entertainment and education reflects a growing recognition of gamings capability as a serious discussion and enrichment aid, a two-in-one capability which can revolutionize education models in the digital age (Lerner et al., 2010) (Figure 6.11).

Figure 6.11. The advent of edge-assisted mobile virtual reality (VR) is reshaping the landscape of gaming and entertainment.

Source: https://miro.medium.com/v2/resize:fit:1200/1*0zemDdWXlU-R6QK-t18OsXQ.png.

Insofar as market potential is concerned, the arrival of edge-enabled mobile VR provides developers and gaming industry players alike with a revenue-laden future. The extent to which operators can ride on these innovations depends directly on their ability to make changes in business models that weigh not only profitability but also enhanced user experience. As noted in recent analysis, the various applications envisioned for 5G technology on which such edge calculations are founded have the potential to disrupt traditional models of operation by enabling new sources of revenue. However, investments to upgrade infrastructure must be weighed against potential benefits, with evolving user expectations requiring higher performance and richer content experiences. Thus, businesses need to strategically position their products and services in conjunction with the possibilities provided by edge-assisted mobile VR in order to be competitive in a changing market that continues to prioritize interactivity and urgency in entertainment and gaming (Cuevas et al., 2017).

6.4.2. Applications in Education and Training

Application of Edge Assisted Mobile Virtual Reality (VR) in schools offers groundbreaking opportunities for learning through immersive VR. Instructors can create simulations that reflect real realities through the application of VR, leading to greater student attention and comprehension. Medicine as a course of study can be enhanced by VR application that allows students to practice procedures in a secure environment. Remarkably, the potential of VR in dermatology has been underemphasized, yet it can provide naturalistic visualizations and interactive experiences that can enhance medical education at an intrinsic level.

Figure 6.12. Edge assisted mobile virtual reality (VR) in educational settings offers transformative opportunities for immersive learning experiences.

Source: https://external-content.duckduckgo.com/iu/?u=https%3A%2F%2Fimageio.forbes.com%2Fspecials-images%2Fimageserve%2F60fa55b0bb0508f4ac956653%2F0x0.jpg%3Fformat%3Djpg%26width%3D1200&f=1&nofb=1&ipt=58b031094fbb4d27956abdb475762121c5f6369e00fe9204261fa28251cc7dc3.

The application of VR is capable of facilitating learning by providing real-time feedback and enabling deep examination of complex subjects, ultimately bridging the gap between theory and practice (Dellavalle et al., 2020). Apart from traditional learning environments, Edge Assisted Mobile VR also has great potential in the area of cultural heritage education. The immersive experience of VR can take the learner back in time to historical monuments or recreate critical moments in the past, making learning more in-depth and meaningful. Serious games, utilizing sophisticated VR technology, provide new avenues to engage students in cultural heritage, making history real and interactive. This approach not only enhances information retention but also contributes to critical thinking and collaborative skills. The benefits of serious gaming applications, as identified through research, are that they can make communication and collaboration among participants more efficient, thereby complementing the factors of engagement crucial in learning environments (Lerner et al., 2010). Last but not least, individualized learning paths enabled by Edge Assisted Mobile VR can address different styles and needs of learning. This flexibility enables students to learn at their own comfort level, experiencing tailored experiences that maximize their learning to its optimal level. The capacity of VR to offer virtual space where learners can experiment and explore without risk is of unique value in vocational training. For example, exposure to dangerous environments, say, combat or construction, can be simulated, allowing students to confront and resolve challenging situations without the actual risk. Thus, this new process of training not only prepares individuals for their work but also instills a culture of readiness and safety essential in various fields of work (Dellavalle et al., 2020; Lerner et al., 2010) (Figure 6.12).

6.4.3. Potential in Healthcare and Therapy

The integration of Edge Assisted Mobile Virtual Reality (VR) in hospitals has revolutionary potential for both patients and practitioners. In the past, medical education was rooted primarily in theoretical knowledge and minimal practice-based knowledge. With the advent of VR technology, however, came the prospect of simulation that mirrors real medical conditions with immersive training for both medical students and professionals. For instance, Medicine Meets Virtual Reality 22 conference showed the capability of VR tools, which simulate patient experiences and predict health outcomes, thus enhancing learning. This is crucial because it makes it possible to perform the learning process with virtual patients, learning beneficial skills without direct exposure to real procedures, eventually producing more qualified healthcare professionals in the long run (Myers et al., 2017). Also, mobile VR apps can play a significant role in therapeutic treatment, particularly in patients with chronic pain, anxiety, or post-traumatic stress disorder (PTSD). By using immersive settings, patients are transported into calming or therapeutic contexts that can significantly reverse symptoms. For example, VR exposure therapy has been shown to facilitate gradual desensitization to feared stimuli in a secure and controlled manner. The interactive nature of mobile VR enables individualized treatment interventions, with exposure designed to suit the unique needs of the patient. As technology continues to improve, haptic feedback and real-time data integration will increasingly create even more immersive experiences for therapy, ultimately contributing to improved patient outcomes and treatment satisfaction (Myers et al., 2017). Moreover, the integration of the Internet of Things (IoT) and mobile virtual reality (VR) is paving the way for breakthroughs in healthcare practice that are truly revolutionary. This combination makes seamless integration of disparate data sources possible, enabling real-time monitoring of states of patients and customization of treatment experiences. To illustrate, the emergence of autonomous healthcare systems assists in the detection of patient-specific needs on time, and treatment planning can be optimized accordingly. As indicated by the increasing demand for personalized care solutions, the utilization of Edge Assisted Mobile VR with IoT technologies can promote consolidated and responsive systems of care. This ecological convergence not only supports patient engagement but also contributes towards collaboration among healthcare professionals, ultimately resulting in a better and superior healthcare setting.

6.5. FUTURE TRENDS AND INNOVATIONS

As technology continues to evolve, the fate of Edge Assisted Mobile Virtual Reality (VR) is heavily vested in network development, particularly with the rollout of 5G networks. These ultra-high-speed networks will dramatically reduce latency, thereby increasing the bar for the immersive experience of mobile VR applications. The capability to handle vast amounts of data at the network edge opens up new scenarios that were previously unachievable. For example, real-time decision-making is made possible with 5G technology for use cases that require immediate response, such as gaming or telemedicine. However, this transition away from legacy networks to 5G also has drawbacks, for example, the pressure on telecommunication companies to deal with the expense of large-scale infrastructure investment. The benefits of these innovations would allow operators to take advantage of new business models and market opportunities, making them remain relevant in a fast-moving online world (Cuevas et al., 2017). Least among these is the role of design in the future of Edge Assisted Mobile VR. As technology becomes more embedded in user experiences, involving design ethics in the creation of VR is an important consideration. Emerging paradigms of design thinking encourage developers to emphasize moral responsibility as much as innovation and encourage a user-focused approach with maximum participation. Team projects and workshops may help students and practitioners build consciousness of these ethical issues while embracing technologies that facilitate learning and intra-personal interaction. Through involving diverse voices in the design, the subsequent innovations have the capacity to reflect on a more diversity of human experiences and needs, thus making mobile VR inclusive and accessible. This will be crucial in enabling us to navigate the challenges of future technological landscapes and advance responsible design practices (Abbey et al., 2019). Blending Edge Assisted Mobile VR with artificial intelligence (AI) will be a possibility in the future that can reshape user interaction paradigms. The integration of AI capabilities may enhance dynamic content generation, personalization, and real-time adaptation of user behavior. For instance, AI analytics may enable apps to modify their environments or game levels more smoothly, thus continuing to engage and interest users in the long term. Furthermore, as these technologies advance, new types of interactive and narrative experiences would be created, leading to new possibilities for new educational applications and therapeutic applications. But this future also calls for a sensitivity to ethics in data use, privacy, and user agency. By addressing these areas with care, developers can utilize AIs potential to the fullest while upholding user agency, making Edge Assisted Mobile VRs a driving force of technological innovation in cyberspace (Cuevas et al., 2017; Abbey et al., 2019) (Figure 6.13).

Figure 6.13. The future of edge assisted mobile virtual reality (VR).

Source: https://external-content.duckduckgo.com/iu/?u=https%3A%2F%2Fwww.adorama.com%2Falc%2Fwp-content%2Fuploads%2F2022%2F10%2Farchitecture-mockup-vr-headsets.jpg&f=1&nofb=1&ipt=18a3227a64a082090130a679f757c4bffc6a7a76f7d0a3e90d450e9c52e53264.

6.5.1. Predictions for the Evolution of Mobile VR Technology

With the advancement of mobile virtual reality (VR) technology, edge computing integration is going to revolutionize the user experience. This transition will cut latency issues significantly and enhance the response of VR applications, making interactions more immersive and interactive. With the advent of 6G wireless communication networks, the experts envision a potential for pervasive high-speed connectivity necessary for real-time services such as VR games and virtual meetings. These networks will employ machine learning (ML) for optimizing various layers of communication, drastically improving performance and reliability. The ability to process huge amounts of data on edge servers close to users will enable smoother experiences with the removal of delay that is usually characteristic of mobile VR devices. The breakthrough in ML and network optimization will, in turn, lay the basis for revolutionary achievements in mobile VR technology, opening the door to future developments in this field (Abbas et al., 2020). Besides, new business models will support the evolution of mobile VR technology with greater connectivity. With the rollout of 5G technology, it is anticipated that there will be numerous applications demanding ultra-low latency, primarily in entertainment and simulation. The operators will need to invest in robust infrastructure to cater to these applications' demands, with opportunities and challenges that come with it. Some of the service providers' investments may appear daunting, but the additional capabilities they produce may be worth their cost. Operators may be able to diversify their revenues by offering advanced VR services that capitalize on the enhanced network capabilities. These future developments of business models will affect the mobile VR ecosystem and create rich possibilities for venturing into new markets and applications, thereby enhancing the end-user experience and propagating the use of the technology further (Cuevas et al., 2017). Moreover, the integration of mobile VR technology with edge computing promises a future where content personalized by artificial intelligence pervades everywhere. When individuals engage in VR experiences, ML algorithms would learn about their interaction and preference, optimizing content delivery in real-time. This personalized approach will not only reward the users more but also encourage more extensive use of VR in fields like education, healthcare, and distant collaboration. Edge computing in combination with state-of-the-art ML techniques will enable convergence of VR systems towards more interactive and adaptive environments. As these technologies become combined, we can anticipate a substantial increase in the performance of mobile VR applications and stimulate innovation across industries and ultimately change the way people interact with digital spaces. This promising avenue for mobile VR serves to highlight the imperative need for ongoing investment and research in subsequent wireless generations (Abbas et al., 2020; Cuevas et al., 2017).

6.5.2. Emerging Technologies That May Influence Mobile VR

Marriage between mobile edge computing (MEC) and mobile virtual reality (VR) is a significant step towards enhanced functionality and experience of VR applications. The combination offers low-latency access to the compute resource, which is essential within immersive VR environments where lag by even milliseconds would shatter user immersion. MEC offers support for actual proximity to precious computing resources, overcoming issues of being limited by device processing power. It is apt to note that the use of user-centric energy-aware mobility management schemes optimizes both radio access and computation latencies, which makes an optimal user experience possible. They allow VR applications to maintain high performance irrespective of natural constraints found in mobile devices. This efficiency urge is important, particularly as simulation outputs convey the potential of the algorithm to handle different network conditions, thereby reflecting the context-based demands of mobile VR users who ask for seamless continuous interactions and timely surroundings (Sun et al., 2017).

The impending advent of 5G technology is yet another technological upheaval that guarantees to hugely impact mobile VR surroundings. 5G is characterized by its ultra-low latency and high processing capacities for data, which are essential in delivering high-quality VR experiences. This network evolution supports new applications that demand responsiveness in split seconds, potentially revolutionizing how individuals use VR for gaming, training, and other sectors. The deployment of such comprehensive capabilities, however, requires enormous investments from operators as they need to redesign their networks to address these high requirements. Thus, operators stand to gain from finding practical business models that leverage these innovations. The evolving 5G power opens up opportunities for venturing into new market segments, which could enable providers to strengthen their position in more competitive markets by offering more sophisticated services that capitalize on the speed and efficiency of mobile VR solutions (Cuevas et al., 2017). Furthermore, the relationship between emerging technologies like AI and ML with mobile VR is expected to revolutionize interactions between users in virtual environments. AI can customize user experience and optimize content delivery by analyzing user behavior and preferences in real-time. For instance, using predictive analytics, AI can dynamically personalize VR interactions for optimal relevance and engagement levels. This tailored experience not only enhances user satisfaction but also encourages longer use of VR applications. Further, with more intelligent and networked gadgets, such as smart TVs or beam-forming smartphones, these can facilitate shared experiences in VR to create group interactions more coordinated and immersive. The convergence of AI, ML, and VR offers a fertile platform for innovation that marks the dawn of uses unforeseen heretofore, thus indicating the vast scope of these emerging technologies in defining mobile VR's future (Sun et al., 2017).

6.5.3. The Role of 5G in Enhancing Edge-Assisted Mobile VR

The advent of 5G technology is a turning point in the evolution of mobile virtual reality (VR), particularly when combined with edge computing platforms. By being able to deliver ultra-low latency and high data rates, 5G not only enhances the user experience but also supports advanced computing to be run closer to the user at the network edge. This proximity mitigates the load on individual devices and localizes processing tasks to nearby edge servers, thus facilitating improved graphics and interactive features in mobile VR applications. As stated, new business models are emerging, driven by the deployment of low latency services, which enable improved operational capabilities of mobile VR. Therefore, 5G's enabler role is crucial in realizing the full potential of edge-assisted mobile VR, offering access to immersive applications in every aspect of life, from entertainment to training simulations (Cuevas et al., 2017). Furthermore, coupling machine learning with 5G enhances edge-assisted mobile VR capability significantly. With continued evolution toward 6G wireless communication, machine learning innovation will be instrumental in improving network performances and end-user experience in mobile VR. With the immense data and computational capacity endowed by 5G networks, machine learning algorithms can personalize VR content transmission and customize users' experiences in real time. Such a feature enables environment sensing, avatar interaction, and adaptive rendering content, which delivers an uninterrupted virtual experience to end-users. Besides, machine learning can enhance zero-touch optimization in wireless networks in solving dilemmas such as bandwidth allocation and service prioritization that are the pillars of guaranteeing high-quality mobile VR experiences (Abbas et al., 2020). Hence, the convergence of machine learning and 5G technology makes edge-assisted mobile VR attain unmatched levels of performance and immersion. The scope for creative use cases in mobile VR helped by edge assistance is vast under the umbrella of 5G and edge computing synergy. In healthcare, education, and gaming, augmented experiences in VR have the potential to transform traditional practice through the provision of immersive visualization and interaction that hitherto were impossible. For instance, remote surgeries conducted under mobile VR can leverage edge-based real-time processing and analysis of data, significantly improving the quality of care. Similarly, schools can create interactive learning environments for students to learn subjects interactively from home. Its economic impact is immense, with space for operators to take advantage of new markets as they react to these ballooning application demands driven by 5G technology (Cuevas et al., 2017). Therefore, 5G's role in designing edge-assisted mobile VR is not merely post-technology but a new age in the way we interact with the digital world, with the potential to cause revolutionary social changes.

SUMMARY

The evolving situation of Edge Assisted Mobile VR isn't merely a technological revolution but also a radical transformation in how virtual reality experiences are presented and optimized. Using edge computing, this system eliminates latency and accelerates processing, enabling people to have the virtual reality experience like never before, at once immersive and utilitarian. As will be evident in many applications, the potential for Edge Assisted Mobile VR in changing fields such as education, training, and healthcare is enormous. This convergence of technology enables real-time data processing and analytics, which is vital for interactive and immersive environments to make them all the more relevant in a constantly evolving digital landscape. Moreover, Edge Assisted Mobile VR is not merely the height of enhanced user experience; it also addresses core issues of accessibility and scalability. The architecture allows efficient resource allocation so that high-quality VR content can be delivered on more devices, even on less computationally capable ones. This democratization of technology is in step with the direction of education and training today, where VR applications can be utilized across different populations. As the case with respect to specific industries has been discussed, the versatility of Edge Assisted Mobile VR can augment the effectiveness of training as well as retention, as illustrated through its use in medicine, where immersive spaces are utilized for surgical simulations as well as procedural training. Finally, the incorporation of Edge Assisted Mobile VR into other existing technologies emphasizes the potential and future use of this technology. The transition from traditional applications to more specialized uses, such as in surgery, is one demonstration of the momentum toward the incorporation of VR in professional instruction. The results of studies on the effectiveness of these technologies confirm the necessity to establish VR as a standard teaching tool, particularly in such specialized areas as dermatology, where innovative methods continue to be researched. As industries mature to suit the demands of today's society, the uses of Edge Assisted Mobile VR can only expand, with the potential to revolutionize user interaction and pedagogical methods for different disciplines. As recognized in the recent advances in surgical education, the convergence of VR and real-world application establishes a stronger basis for the sustainable growth and extensive incorporation of such technologies into widespread practices (TLoop et al., 2014; Dellavalle et al., 2020).

The Edge Assisted Mobile VR debate is about the most important advancements and knowledge shaping this new domain. The debate revolves around the way 5G and 6G technologies ensure the high bandwidth and low latency essential for a highly immersive virtual reality experience. The transition from 5G to 6G is paramount because it does not just ensure better speed but also capacity to support multiple connected devices simultaneously. This wireless communication system development simplifies the deployment of Edge computing paradigms, in which processing is done close to the end-user. As emphasized in the literature, this locality cancels out delay times and offers more favorable user experiences in various applications in mobile VR, thereby offering revolutionary possibilities for industries such as healthcare and entertainment (Cheng-Wang et al., 2023). Moreover, the foundational frameworks being established for 6G are not only addressing existing issues but also shaping future developments. In healthcare, Edge Assisted Mobile VR is emerging as an innovative tool enhancing patient care and training. The integration of the Metaverse with technology such as AI, virtual reality, and augmented reality unlocks new horizons for medical education and practice. Through the ability to immerse in simulations, healthcare providers can engage in realistic simulations that improve their capability in a controlled setting, resulting in better outcomes for patients. Additionally, patients have access to individualized and flexible approaches to care, which can actually improve participation and compliance with treatment regimens. The potential of these technologies bridging the gap between healthcare practitioners and patients places Edge Assisted Mobile VR in the spotlight of medical innovation (Chengoden et al., 2023). This system not only illustrates the role of immersive experiences in training but also portrays the importance of technology in reshaping healthcare paradigms. Finally, the key points addressed regarding Edge Assisted Mobile VR have far-reaching implications for industries other than healthcare, including entertainment, education, and telework. Combining Edge computing with mobile VR leads to more sophisticated real-time interaction that makes collaborative platforms ignoring geographical constraints possible. The technology is poised to transform traditional practices across industries, allowing for enhanced learning processes and innovative problem-solving techniques. The debates also mentioned challenges of putting these technologies into practice, including challenges over data security, interoperability, and accessibility. As the narrative of Edge Assisted Mobile VR goes along, addressing these matters will be essential to ensure wider adoption and acceptance. Ultimately, as practitioners, researchers, and technologists collaborate to innovate across this terrain, the implications for society at large will only be deep.

REFERENCES

1. Abbas, R., Ahmad, I., Ali, S., Amuru, S., et al. (2020). 6G white paper on machine learning in wireless communication networks. http://arxiv.org/abs/2004.13875 (accessed on 16th September 2025).
2. Abbey, B., Brown, B., Buijs, C., Candy, L., Csikszentmihalyi, M., Feland, J., et al. (2019). The ‘responsibility’ factor in imagining the future of education in China. https://core.ac.uk/download/237010983.pdf (accessed on 16th September 2025).
3. Aggoun, A., Amon, P., Arbel, I., Chernilov, M., et al. (2008). Multimedia delivery in the future internet. https://core.ac.uk/download/335423.pdf (accessed on 16th September 2025).
4. Al Sulaimi, R. A., & Tumati, R. (2023). The digital frontier: Exhibiting the transformative impact of technology on enhancing event attendees’ experiences in Oman. https://core.ac.uk/download/599817780.pdf (accessed on 16th September 2025).
5. Albanese, A., Fajardo, J. O., Giannoulakis, I., Kafetzakis, E., et al. (2016). System architecture and deployment scenarios for SESAME: Small cells coordination for multi-tenancy and edge services. https://core.ac.uk/download/46598382.pdf (accessed on 16th September 2025).
6. Allam, Z., Sharifi, A., Bibri, S. E., Jones, D. S., & Krogstie, J. (2022). The metaverse as a virtual form of smart cities: Opportunities and challenges for environmental, economic, and social sustainability in urban futures. *Smart Cities, 5*, 771–801. https://doi.org/10.3390/smartcities5030040 (accessed on 16th September 2025).
7. Bacciu, D., Bahr, R., Bröring, A., Cavallo, F., et al. (2017). Internet of robotic things: Converging sensing/actuating, hypoconnectivity, artificial intelligence and IoT platforms. https://core.ac.uk/download/84045908.pdf (accessed on 16th September 2025).
8. Baidya, S., Chen, Y., & Levorato, M. (2018). eBPF-based content and computation-aware communication for real-time edge computing. http://arxiv.org/abs/1805.02797 (accessed on 16th September 2025).
9. Buyya, R., Chi, Q., Mahmud, R., Toosi, A. N., et al. (2018). Management and orchestration of network slices in 5G, fog, edge and clouds. http://arxiv.org/abs/1812.00593 (accessed on 16th September 2025).
10. Charles, D., Ma, M., McDonough, S., McNeill, M., et al. (2006). Virtual reality games for motor rehabilitation. https://core.ac.uk/download/30733505.pdf (accessed on 16th September 2025).

11. Chen, K. C., Hanzo, L., Jiang, C., Ren, P., et al. (2019). Thirty years of machine learning: The road to Pareto-optimal wireless networks. http://arxiv.org/abs/1902.01946 (accessed on 16th September 2025).

12. Chengoden, R., Victor, N., Huynh-The, T., Yenduri, G., Jhaveri, R. H., Alazab, M., Bhattacharya, S., et al. (2023). Metaverse for healthcare: A survey on potential applications, challenges and future directions. *IEEE Access, 11*, 12765–12795. https://doi.org/10.1109/access.2023.3241628 (accessed on 16th September 2025).

13. Chmarra, M. K., Gómez Aguilera, E. J., Lamata de la Orden, P., Oropesa García, M., et al. (2011). Methods and tools for objective assessment of psychomotor skills in laparoscopic surgery. https://core.ac.uk/download/148661114.pdf (accessed on 16th September 2025).

14. Cuevas, M., Dohler, M., Laya, A., Lema, M., et al. (2017). Business case and technology analysis for 5G low latency applications. https://core.ac.uk/download/96762095.pdf (accessed on 16th September 2025).

15. Dellavalle, R. P., Obagi, Z. A., & Rundle, C. W. (2020). Widening the scope of virtual reality and augmented reality in dermatology. https://core.ac.uk/download/287622747.pdf (accessed on 16th September 2025).

16. Ding, A. Y., Liyanage, M., & Porambage, P. (2018). Five driving forces of multi-access edge computing. http://arxiv.org/abs/1810.00827 (accessed on 16th September 2025).

17. Dwivedi, Y. K., Kshetri, N., Hughes, L., Slade, E., Jeyaraj, A., Kar, A. K., Baabdullah, A. M., et al. (2023). Opinion paper: "So what if ChatGPT wrote it?" Multidisciplinary perspectives on opportunities, challenges and implications of generative conversational AI for research, practice and policy. *International Journal of Information Management, 71*, 102642. https://doi.org/10.1016/j.ijinfomgt.2023.102642 (accessed on 16th September 2025).

18. Hu, S., Huang, X., Shen, X., Yang, M., et al. (2023). Digital twin-driven network architecture for video streaming. http://arxiv.org/abs/2310.19079 (accessed on 16th September 2025).

19. Kadun, S., & Oktaviyanthi, R. (2025). Optimization of geometric thinking through interactive worksheets: A scoping review. https://core.ac.uk/download/649301926.pdf (accessed on 16th September 2025).

20. Leitão, R., Marcos, A., & Rodrigues, J. M. F. (2018). Mobile learning: Benefits of augmented reality in geometry teaching. https://core.ac.uk/download/156758190.pdf (accessed on 16th September 2025).

21. Lerner, A., Nareyek, A., Watt, A., Lintermann, B., Cruz-Neira, C., Jones, C., et al. (2010). Developing serious games for cultural heritage: A state-

of-the-art review. https://core.ac.uk/download/9599306.pdf (accessed on 16th September 2025).

22. Liu, G., Du, H., Niyato, D., Kang, J., Xiong, Z., Jamalipour, A., Mao, S., et al. (2024). Fusion of mixture of experts and generative artificial intelligence in mobile edge metaverse. https://www.semanticscholar.org/paper/7d377e2f1d41960ea62e0fd7bc5d0fa4db36cf78 (accessed on 16th September 2025).
23. Loop, C. T., Subsol, G., Westheimer, G., Dryden, I., Matalas, I., Canny, J. F., Koza, J. R., et al. (2014). Towards multiple 3D bone surface identification and reconstruction using few 2D X-ray images for intraoperative applications. https://core.ac.uk/download/29821931.pdf (accessed on 16th September 2025).
24. Myers, M. R. (2017). Trends in virtual reality technologies for the learning patient. https://core.ac.uk/download/211336430.pdf (accessed on 16th September 2025).
25. Sagar, S., Bhasker, V., Bhimanapati, R., Chhapola, A., & Jain, S. (2023). Optimizing performance in mobile applications with edge computing. *Universal Research Reports*. https://www.semanticscholar.org/paper/b0156bdc675cfbaf9bbe9d28d781eccb5e357974 (accessed on 16th September 2025).
26. Sun, Y., Xu, J., & Zhou, S. (2017). EMM: Energy-aware mobility management for mobile edge computing in ultra-dense networks. http://arxiv.org/abs/1709.02582 (accessed on 16th September 2025).
27. Wang, C. X., You, X., Gao, X., Zhu, X., Li, Z., Zhang, C., Wang, H., et al. (2023). On the road to 6G: Visions, requirements, key technologies, and testbeds. *IEEE Communications Surveys & Tutorials, 25*, 905–974. https://doi.org/10.1109/comst.2023.3249835 (accessed on 16th September 2025).

CHAPTER 7

SECURITY AND PRIVACY IN INDUSTRIAL EDGE COMPUTING

Contents

INTRODUCTION

The emergence of Industrial Edge Computing is a deep revolution in the world of technology, one where physical systems intersect with digital data processing. With this revolution comes a decentralized approach where processing occurs closer to the location of data generation, enhancing efficiency and responsiveness. But with this technology lies serious concerns for security and privacy. With these systems being integrated, Cyber-Physical Systems (CPS) and the Internet of Things (IoT), they become increasingly susceptible to cyber-attacks, whose target can extend beyond flaws in hardware even into software settings. Dynamic reconfiguration in real-time only makes it more difficult to monitor, the design teams relinquishing control over central components and their interconnections, eroding the very foundations of traditional engineering practice (Azorin-Lopez et al., 2018). This calls for a thorough investigation of the privacy and security implications in industrial settings. With information abundance from such networked systems, user privacy becomes a top issue. As information turns into a commodity that acts as a middleman between systems autonomously, maintaining the confidentiality and integrity of user behavior is vital. The combination of mechatronics and cloud computing technology poses the unique challenge of maintaining user trust in a system where the data is dynamically accessible and manipulable. The possibility of unauthorized eavesdropping and data tampering threatens not only individual privacy but also the integrity of the industrial systems reliant on this data stream. Hence, by addressing these challenges, a multi-dimensional strategy with robust security mechanisms and privacy measures appropriate to the subtleties of Industrial Edge Computing is needed. As observed in existing discourse, never before has the necessity for secure and private data handling methods been more crucial in the achievement of sustainable development and utilization of such technology (Dagstuhl et al., 2011). In addition, the convergence of emerging technologies also requires that current regulatory standards for industrial computing practices be reexamined. The regulators need to interact with representatives from all levels of technology developers to end users in an effort to create holistic guidelines that capture the intricacies of edge computing ecosystems. This should not only include addressing security loopholes but also ensure novel solutions that offer flexibility and decision-making capacity for users on the utilization of data. With edge computing restructuring industrial activities, due attention must be paid to the ethics of data handling and actors' roles in guaranteeing users' privacy. The interface between security and privacy in Industrial Edge Computing therefore demands ongoing research focus, requiring innovations that harmonize technical progress and the safeguarding of basic rights. The development of a secure, privacy-focused environment can ultimately make industrial use more dependable and effective at providing that the benefits of this technological growth are reaped without compromising user trust.

Definition of Industrial Edge Computing

Industrial Edge Computing represents a paradigm shift in data processing and management in manufacturing and industry. By locating computational resources close to the sources of data origin—i.e., IoT devices and sensors—

organizations are able to reduce latency as well as bandwidth utilization while enhancing real-time decision-making capabilities. Such proximity does not just optimize system response time but also lightens centralized cloud infrastructure loads, which otherwise clog under data burden. The combination of IoT and fog computing is also becoming the standard in this context because it opens up the possibilities for more efficient data management solutions that are precisely tailored to address individual problems that arise within industrial processes (Butun et al., 2018). Therefore, Industrial Edge Computing is a technological basis that enables the next stage of smart manufacturing and digitalization. As the importance of Industrial Edge Computing is enhanced further, security and privacy concerns are extensive. Data processing at a local location keeps the risks in transmitting data over extensive networks within bounds but does not eliminate them entirely. There may be security vulnerabilities at the edge, which would require strong cybersecurity controls specifically designed for such environments.

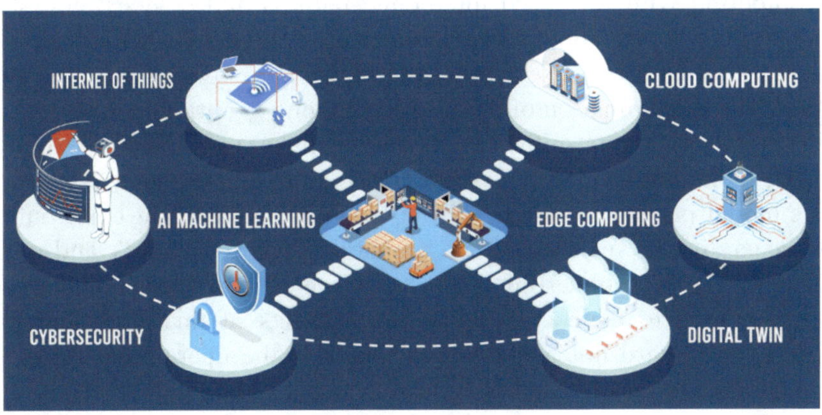

Figure 7.1. Industrial edge computing.

Source: https://external-content.duckduckgo.com/iu/?u=https%3A%2F %2Fieb-media.com%2Fwp-content%2Fuploads%2F2024%2F07%2FIndustrial-Edge-1.png&f=1&nofb=1&ipt=dee41254ff593bba48eb284c2b987083b7419677a75bb69fc33923667ad873b9.

For example, the use of IoT in industrial environments creates numerous points of entry for cyber-attacks, which may compromise valuable operational data and intellectual property. This fact all the more calls for formulating end-to-end security policies that reflect the unique vulnerabilities posed by edge infrastructures, particularly with interdependent device deployments (Butun et al., 2018). As industries shift to digital platforms, it is essential to secure this new computing environment. Industrial Edge Computing privacy also calls for equal seriousness, particularly with data being increasingly traded in open data markets. The concept of an open data market allows for trading of data collected by IoT devices, where customers and data owners can negotiate access to data. While it is useful for innovation and of potential business value, it simultaneously raises important privacy concerns. Data collected using IoT devices can be extremely sensitive, and therefore implementation of rigorous privacy-preserving measures must be employed to prevent potential breaches and misuse. It is essential that the benefits of data exchange are weighed against stakeholder privacy. Thus, industries must be keen to implement strict privacy controls to ensure that data utilized in such ecosystems is not shared with unprivileged stakeholders (Figure 7.1).

Importance of Security and Privacy

Security and privacy emerged as key concerns in the context of industrial edge computing with increased interconnectedness and devices' complexity. As industrial systems adopt edge computing approaches, which allow for data processing closer to its location of origin, the exposure to cyberattacks increases. The dissemination of devices across long geographic distances, with limited resources and intermittent connectivity, makes one vulnerable to a range of threats, including Denial of Service (DoS) and Data Integrity Attacks. The analysis model presented within existing work is an excellent contribution to the understanding of such weaknesses, enabling one to quantify and mitigate risks accurately. By underlining the requirement for end-to-end security solutions tailored to edge computing, the findings of this study emphasize the need to safeguard not just the data, but also the operational integrity of Internet of Things (IoT)-based industrial systems (Abdildayeva et al., 2025). Additionally, as industrial enterprises become more data-driven in decision-making processes, the value of privacy is greater. The opportunity for data to reveal personal information extends beyond ordinary operational facts; it involves personal and proprietary information that needs to be protected by organizations. In open data markets, where data scraped from IoT devices is exchanged, the activity of negotiation between consumers and owners of data raises serious privacy concerns. The risk escalates when data can be unpicked to offer highly personalized insight into individuals' habits and inclinations. In response, stakeholders must put focus on privacy-protecting measures that will facilitate the exchange of data. Current privacy-preserving models, aimed at providing a balance between the explanatory capacity of data markets and the safeguarding of stakeholders, are imperative in creating a viable environment under which companies can thrive without undermining user trust (Perera et al., 2015). The confluence of security and privacy across industrial edge computing impacts not only operational performance but also customer confidence as well as compliance legislations. As businesses navigate through this complex predicament, the formulation of effective security controls becomes imperative. These controls must address not only security defense against external threat but also controls to ensure that data is handled in line with progressively stringent privacy legislations. The analysis model presented in recent research emphasizes paying attention to specific vulnerabilities and developing personalized defenses to secure critical infrastructure in the best manner. Consequently, enhancing security not only limits the possibility of cyber-attacks but also enhances the organization's reputation in the marketplace. A live security and privacy strategy will not only safeguard business information but will also ensure that consumer and stakeholder confidence is not wasted, thereby ensuring business continuity and growth in the rapidly evolving industrial industry.

7.1. SECURITY THREATS IN INDUSTRIAL EDGE COMPUTING

The rapid integration of Industrial Edge Computing (IEC) into manufacturing systems has introduced a range of security threats that need careful consideration. With industrial processes increasingly interconnected via the Internet of Things (IoT), industrial environments are exposed to emerging and special cyberattack threats. Cyberattacks can exploit vulnerabilities in networked sensors and actuators utilized to observe and control critical processes in factories. For instance, actuator attacks would violate the functional integrity of the equipment and lead to severe safety risks along with potential material damage. Dependent on low-power wireless networks for communication, the integrity of the transfer of data is no less important. This overall apprehension highlights the necessity of robust security frameworks capable of mitigating such weaknesses in industrial settings as embodied within ongoing discussions on inter-networking vital industrial components in a secure manner (Frey et al., 2018). Improvements in security methodologies, such as Information Centric Networking (ICN), provide prospective avenues for enhancing security against ongoing threats in IEC. ICN offers a content-centric approach that significantly fortifies Denial of Service (DoS) attacks resilience, thereby ensuring industrial service availability even under malicious conditions. Further fortification of the data protection of integrity and confidentiality can be achieved through the use of layering security protocols, in addition to resource-efficient encryption techniques. As industrial surroundings are likely to be harsh in nature, the remarks on the usability of using ICN for safety-critical applications become increasingly significant. Comparisons of performance with more traditional IP-based approaches like CoAP and MQTT show that ICN can provide a safer ground for the complexity of device interconnecting in industrial settings and thus pave the way for secure industrial operations (Frey et al., 2018). Despite the growing complexity of attack vectors used on IEC, the majority of experts are optimistic for the continued expansion of the IoT and, by extension, IEC. As previously mentioned, the interconnectedness of machines and their alignment with human operators presents positive resources and services that enhance productivity and innovation. Growth has to occur, however, in tandem with efforts on hardening security procedures and practices. Organizations must be proactive in their approach to cybersecurity, not only to prevent potential breaches but also safeguard confidential data from privacy violation. These risk management practices are the mainstay in guaranteeing stakeholders' trust and error-free operation of industrial systems. And even as threats can seem imminent, a unison and watchful endeavor can keep risks in check and realize the complete potential of Industrial Edge Computing.

7.1.1. Types of Cybersecurity Threats

The cyber threat environment is becoming increasingly more complicated, especially with regard to industrial edge computing. Especially noteworthy, Denial of Service (DoS) attacks are at the top of the threat list, incapacitating network availability by flooding devices and servers with excessive requests. In industrial settings, such disruptions can shut down production lines, resulting in massive loss and inefficiency in operations. The vulnerabilities of Industrial Internet of Things (IIoT) devices are further augmented by their generally diminished security capabilities, making them extremely vulnerable to attacks. As specified in recent studies, the uptick in DoS attacks highlights the urgent necessity of sophisticated cybersecurity solutions that are specifically tailored for edge computing environments in order to safeguard the integrity and availability of high-value industrial processes (Zhukabayeva et al., 2025). Another ubiquitous type of threat to industrial edge computing environments includes ransomware, a malicious software that encrypts an organization's data and then demands payment to decrypt the data. Deployed in industrial environments, ransomware is a serious threat not just to data integrity but also to the safety and security of physical processes. Ransomware attacks can cause critical infrastructure to come to a standstill, leaving systems inoperable for extensive periods with significant recovery costs. The integration of IIoT devices contributes to the intricacy of the threat landscape since the majority of these devices lack strong protection capabilities against such sophisticated attacks. Therefore, organizations must highlight the adoption of strong cybersecurity practices like incident response plans, regular security audits, and staff training to avert the risk of ransomware invasions into their operations (Okunlola et al., 2025) (Figure 7.2).

Figure 7.2. Types of cyber security threats.

Source: https://media.licdn.com/dms/image/v2/D5612AQHLm4yKAnkdVA/article-cover_image-shrink_600_2000/article-cover_image-shrink_600_2000/0/1688146396949?e=2147483647&v=beta&t=GWLIbUskarbxJx8FoumuPjPv_73wf4UXZpOGxj1Td_4.

Furthermore, Man-in-the-Middle (MITM) attacks are also a significant cybersecurity concern within the field of industrial edge computing. Through these attacks, attackers are able to intercept and even alter communications between devices and networks, which leads to compromised data integrity along with unauthorized access to sensitive information. The intercommunicative aspect of IIoT systems offers sufficient scope for attackers to exploit unsecured channels, especially in environments where encryption is not applied appropriately. These vulnerabilities highlight the importance of employing encryption protocols and security communication standards in protecting data in transits, such as Transport Layer Security (TLS). Addressing such primary vulnerabilities empowers organizations to improve their cybersecurity position and minimize the potential impacts of MITM attacks threatening their industrial processes (Zhukabayeva et al., 2025).

7.1.2. Vulnerabilities in Edge Devices

The introduction of edge devices in industrial settings has revolutionized the landscape of data processing, enabling real-time analytics and instant decision-making. The innovation, however, has introduced significant vulnerabilities that undermine the integrity and security of such systems. Edge devices run in distributed environments that may lack proper security measures, leading to a broadened attack surface. The built-in resource constraints of edge devices then also contribute towards these vulnerabilities, since their limited processing capabilities can hinder the enforcement of end-to-end security controls. Moreover, most edge devices are mounted in physically accessible locations, making them susceptible to physical attacks, which can compromise their functionality and data integrity. Since more organizations are embracing edge computing solutions in their operations, awareness and mitigation of such vulnerabilities are paramount to safeguarding industrial environments against potential cyber-attacks (Abdildayeva et al., 2025). Relying on continuous connectivity and network communications within edge computing systems introduces additional threats. Data integrity of communications between edge devices and the outside world is threatened by many cyberattack vectors including man-in-the-middle attacks and denial-of-service (DoS) attacks. These compromise communication links, leading to data loss or corruption that can impair mission-critical business functions. A study established that edge devices in industrial settings are likely to face a wide range of attacks, which requires further embedding of more robust security controls to mitigate the most dangerous attacks (Abdildayeva et al., 2025) (Figure 7.3).

Figure 7.3. Vulnerabilities in edge devices.

Source: https://www.kratosspace.com/-/media/k/co/24/isac/edge-device-cybersecurity.jpg.

In addition, making communications secure becomes more and more problematic because of the diversified technology environment with various producers using systems that operate on non-uniform security rules, rendering it even more challenging to fight threats effectively. Apart from network and physical threats, edge devices are also exposed to software and informational threats. The heterogeneity of the applications running on these devices can create vulnerable weaknesses, especially if they are compromised software or unpatched weaknesses. In a smart grid context, for instance, the addition of edge devices for communications has opened possible avenues for cyberattackers, and therefore energy infrastructure vulnerabilities have been created as a result that can be exploited to bring about widespread disruptions. As edge computing continues to evolve within industrial spaces, organizations must guarantee an end-to-end security structure addressing physical and digital space alike. This is imperative not only for protecting the edge devices but also for securing the integrity of the industrial system as a whole so that infrastructures become resilient to future cyber-attacks (Abdildayeva et al., 2025).

7.1.3. Impact of Security Breaches on Industrial Operations

Industrial operation security violations can have far-reaching effects, leading to enormous monetary loss and service interruption. When cyber vulnerabilities are exploited, as is the case in industries that are more reliant on inter-connected systems like the smart grid, the impacts are catastrophic (Qian et al., 2012). Cyber intruders can manipulate operation controls, leading to equipment failure, plant shut-downs, and potential safety hazards. The effects not only address the short-term capacity for operations but can have a knock-on effect along supply chains, leading to extended downtime and increased costs. On top of that, organizations are likely to suffer from regulatory fines and compensations while they are trying to cope with increased oversight following a breach. Hence, the immediate cost is complemented by long-term reputational harm, impacting stakeholder trust and consumer confidence. In industrial edge computing, the complexity of the systems exacerbates security breach risks. With increasingly ubiquitous Internet of Things (IoT) devices, data quantities generated need to be processed by strong and secure mechanisms. New vulnerabilities caused by IoT technologies, which pose available tools for criminals, are brought in when they are integrated (Abdolee et al., 2019). A satisfactory compromise would expose confidential operational information and potential intellectual property, which would lead to competitive losses. Moreover, the dynamic nature of cyber-attacks necessitates organizations to maintain a pro-activeness in dealing with cybersecurity by performing high-level protocols and solutions that confront specific vulnerabilities triggered by interconnected industrial environments. The challenge lies not just in identification, but to create end-to-end frameworks that are indicative of realistic security solutions. The consequences of security breaches transcend immediate operational inefficiencies, affecting industrial dynamics and strategic decision-making on a larger scale. With organizations confronting the consequences of cyberattacks, they are compelled to rethink their infrastructures, investing in stronger technologies and improved security features. This transition has the potential to fuel innovation but also challenges budgetary abilities, particularly for small and medium-sized businesses that may lack the funds for necessary upgrades. Further, it is increasingly difficult to manage the regulatory landscape as governments themselves more often enforce tougher cybersecurity laws, requiring organizations to adapt at a rapid rate or face being taken to court. In this rapidly developing technological landscape, maintaining a secure and resilient operating space remains essential to safeguarding not only individual companies but the overall integrity of industries themselves.

7.2. PRIVACY CONCERNS IN DATA HANDLING

In industrial edge computing, data processing privacy concerns are highlighted by the rapid expansion of connected systems and devices. As more organizations adopt edge computing to enhance operational efficiency and reduce latency, the volume of sensitive data generated is large. The data often holds personal information, confidential algorithms, and even intellectual property and therefore its protection is imperative.

Figure 7.4. Privacy concerns in data handling.

Source: https://imageio.forbes.com/specials-images/imageserve/633b2a0572c7c1953d93dbab/Data-protection-and-secure-online-payments--Cyber-internet-security-technologies-and/960x0.jpg?height=473&width=711&fit=bounds.

The largest problem here is when one thinks of the processing and transmission of data on the edge. Insecure communication systems have the potential to expose users' sensitive information to cyber-attacks, causing unauthorized access and data breaches. The repercussions of such breaches extend beyond monetary losses in the short term but also harm organizations' reputations and destroy consumers' trust. Thus, establishing robust security arrangements is required to minimize threats to data privacy in industrial applications. Further, the transition to smart solutions via edge computing solutions poses significant privacy issues that must be addressed. The installation of Internet of Things (IoT) devices within industrial sectors creates a vast ecosystem where data exchange freely between edge hardware and cloud central systems. Nevertheless, the union of cloud, fog, and edge computing models incites criticism of data manipulation tendencies. Although it offers new avenues to innovate and improve efficiency, it also presents challenges in upholding user privacy. As outlined in earlier discussions, tracing and safeguarding data transactions between other devices remains a tall order that demands revolutionary security models. In addition, having specific data governance policies is necessary to define data usage limits as well as data compliance with privacy legislation. These actions are crucial to ensure the ethical handling of sensitive data utilized in industrial purposes (Figure 7.4). Lastly, the moral implications of data privacy in industrial edge computing environments warrant special attention. With companies employing data analytics to streamline operations and project maintenance needs, there exists an underlying responsibility to protect the data of individuals and institutions. Companies must balance crossing the threshold of using data for the sake of operational gain with not compromising user privacy. Transparency in data management, for example, open consent mechanisms and user rights, can encourage a more ethical approach to data management. Since these issues of privacy become increasingly acute more frequently, effective risk management strategies have to evolve with technological advances. Application of safe communication protocols that can guarantee data integrity, along with good privacy policies, will be essential in safeguarding industrial edge computing systems against cyber attacks. The challenges are not compliance issues, but inherent aspects of building sustainable and ethical digital environments where business and consumers can thrive.

7.2.1. Data Collection Practices

Data collection approaches with regard to industrial edge computing have drastically shifted since the emergence of Cyber-Physical Systems (CPS) and Internet of Things (IoT). Traditional data collection approaches usually allowed for engineering teams to have control over system elements and by extension their implications at the design level. However, dynamism and intricacy resulting from the integration of IoT devices make control challenging to enforce. These devices provide data perpetually, with high-frequency real-time reconfigurability based on context and user demands, making traditional paradigms for data collection intricate. Consequently, data can immediately get commodified, leading to unforeseen trespasses upon user privacy. Thus, organizations must reassess their data collection procedures to ensure operational effectiveness while addressing the demand for adequate security practices, ensuring that user-specific data is protected in a varying technological environment. The integration of edge computing and cloud technologies adds complexity to the practice of data gathering and associated risks of security and privacy. With the services being executed nearer to where data originates, there is a shift towards a new paradigm where significant operations can be performed on edge devices, meaning response time is enhanced and delay minimized. But this shift requires a subtle touch when working with data because data is not only collected but also processed and stored locally before being relayed to centralized clouds, if that is indeed the case.

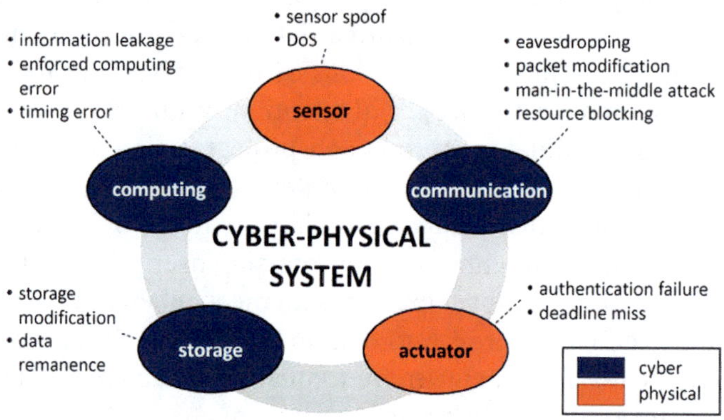

Figure 7.5. Attack surface of cyber-physical system (CPS).

Source: https://www.researchgate.net/figure/Attack-surface-of-Cyber-Physical-System-CPS-24_fig1_332826219.

As mentioned, where CPS overlaps with intelligence in collecting and processing data, there are questions of ownership and data integrity. Organizations must remember these concerns and implement end-to-end data governance frameworks that outline standards for where and how data are to be employed, with regulation compliance maintained without a loss of user privacy (Azorin-Lopez et al., 2018). Emerging trends in data collection also must consider the implications of fog computing, where distributed architecture facilitates streamlined sharing of data among edge nodes and the cloud. This model emphasizes the need for strong coordination of data traversing nodes of different nodes in the network, whose direct consequences are data security and privacy. With edge devices possessing more and more sophisticated capabilities, including decision-making and data sharing, managing such systems becomes much more complex. Organizations therefore have to create multi-layered architectures that place highest priority on the success of secure processing of sensitive data in multiple environments. The edge computing and fog advances demonstrate a promising possibility of enhanced data collection efficiency but naturally increase the threats of unlawful access and data leakage, hence necessitating ongoing debate and invention in privacy-safe protocols (Jukan et al., 2016) (Figure 7.5).

7.2.2. User Consent and Data Ownership

The issue of user consent and ownership of data has emerged as a critical element in the security vs. privacy debate in industrial edge computing. With more businesses rolling out edge computing, they must know how to get informed consent from users regarding collection and utilization of data. This includes not only open communication around what data are being collected but also uses and risks of that information. Denying adequate information to users can lead organizations to step over ethical lines and violate legal standards, inviting potential backlash and loss of trust. Also, as the ownership of data gets watered down in collaborative edge domains, transparent governance guidelines and policies are necessary to retain control for users of their personal data while allowing organizations to interpret and utilize such data safely and ethically. In industrial edge computing, the risks of data transmission and processing call for sensitive handling of user consent. Organizations must use secure device pairing (SDP) schemes to improve smart devices' communication channels and protect user data. Recent research shows that existing SDP schemes possess dominant systemic security flaws that can be targeted by hackers (Fomichev et al., 2017). Bolstering the incorporation of privacy specifications in the development of such schemes is important in regaining users' trust in data management procedures. Promoting a security culture that emphasizes user consent can potentially enable organizations to not only comply with existing legislation but also enjoy a good reputation in data protection and ethics obligations. Additionally, the increasing application of large data mining with the aim of exploring socio-economic problems evinces the need to uphold user consent and ownership rights. While the applications of creative data analysis are immense, they must be followed in a manner that respects personal privacy and is not eager to undercut democratic principles (Barabasi et al., 2011). As organizations tap the potential of big data through their working frameworks, open practices in regard to how data is collected, analyzed, and communicated are crucial. Developing robust legal principles and institutional mechanisms to govern this ecosystem will allow users, securing their rights amidst evolving technological advancements. In everything, balancing the worth of big data against the need to uphold user consent and privacy is a fundamental challenge for organizations involved in industrial edge computing (Figure 7.6).

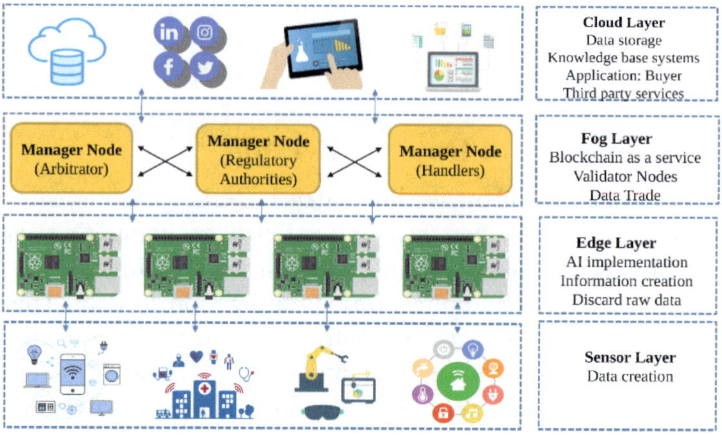

Figure 7.6. Architecture of EdgeBoT, a distributed P2P data trade and fair access network model based on the Ethereum platform.

Source: https://www.mdpi.com/sensors/sensors-20-03965/article_deploy/html/images/sensors-20-03965-g001.png.

7.2.3. Regulatory Compliance and Privacy Laws

Under the emerging industrial edge computing world in the developing world, privacy laws and regulatory requirements are now the center of data protection as well as secure operation. Organizations using edge computing technologies are under an array of regulations, including the General Data Protection Regulation (GDPR) and the Health Insurance Portability and Accountability Act (HIPAA), which require rigorous norms for collecting, storing, and processing personal data. The challenge is more in articulating technological solutions in terms of compliance requirements rather than understanding these regulatory frameworks. Non-compliance carries significant financial cost as well as damage to reputation. Therefore, companies need to have effective compliance regimes involving regular audits and risk assessment to ensure their compliance with privacy law, ensuring that all data handling practices are in conformity with pre-defined legal standards. Also, with the Internet of Things (IoT) expanding its forays into industrial settings at an increased rate, the regulatory compliance ramifications are vast and intricate. The intersection of IoT and edge computing poses unique challenges with regard to cybersecurity and data privacy. For example, IoT devices, commonly characterized as decentralized, can make organizations susceptible to attacks that regulatory efforts aim to counteract. Its implementation has emerged as a viable solution to the challenge of securing IoT through providing a decentralized means of securing communication and data integrity. However, such technologies must be integrated with extreme care based on their computational requirements and potential to influence compliance with existing privacy regulations (Abdolee et al., 2019) (Figure 7.7).

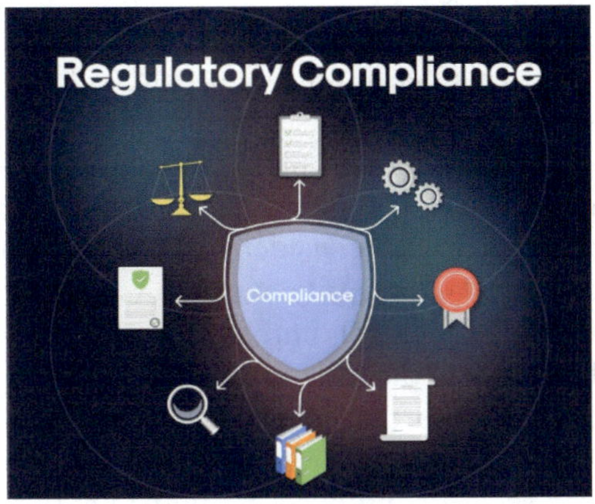

Figure 7.7. Regulatory compliance and privacy laws have taken center stage in ensuring data protection and secure operation.

Source: https://cdn.prod.website-files.com/5ff66329429d880392f6cba2/672a127a161566bbd8a51e0b_1%20-%202.11-min.jpg.

Hence, organizations must deal with a complex web of regulatory obligations while ensuring their technological implementations do not weaken compliance activities. Finally, the smart grid example denotes the regulatory issues in edge computing environments. As these networks evolve to be integrated with next-generation communications technologies, compliance with cybersecurity regulations becomes critical. The smart grid employs electronic communication media that must be safeguarded from data breaches that will impede service and breach consumer information (Qian et al., 2012). Regulatory guidelines are needed to lead the deployment of the security requirements, ensure a culture of responsibility among stakeholders. Additionally, the increased adoption of smart grid technologies requires the reforming of existing laws in a bid to address emerging vulnerabilities. Managing regulatory compliance in industrial edge computing early on will not only protect organizations from future liabilities but also support the sustainable growth of new technologies in the industrial market. Thus, managing regulatory compliance in industrial edge computing is not only a necessity; it is a critical component of maintaining trust and security in the digital economy.

7.3. SECURITY MEASURES FOR EDGE COMPUTING

The application of edge computing in industrial environments has effectively reshaped the operational efficiency but, simultaneously, has also augmented security threats. The devices of edge computing are typically deployed in resource-constrained environments with devices dispersed over large geographical distances. This decentralization extremely changes the security paradigm, leading to amplified attacks via an expanded attack surface. The problem of periodic connectivity and physical security attacks necessitates a robust framework for the security of the edge devices and confidential data they process. Successful strategies must consider possible IIoT threats like Denial of Service (DoS) attacks and data integrity attacks. As explained in Abdildayeva et al. (2025), the analytical model introduced addresses these challenges, categorizing typical attack patterns and proposing concrete measures to improve the IIoT system defenses with the enhancement of edge computing. While developing a security framework unique to edge computing, organizations must ensure a multi-layered security approach. It entails physical security, network security, and application-layer security, so that all parts of the infrastructure are fortified. Implementing advanced encryption protocols will protect data at rest and in transit, reducing the risk of improper access. In addition, employing real-time monitoring and anomaly detection appliances can significantly contribute to the detection of threats and acting on them.

The dynamic nature of threats implies that organizations are required to maintain their security posture in a constantly updated form. The integration of concepts from future technologies, such as Artificial Intelligence (AI) and machine learning, can support predictive analytics capability, whereby preventive measures against future attacks are feasible. These integrations are emphasized in the discourses on 6G communications and its integration with edge computing, as emphasized in Askar et al. (2024). It is also important to establish a security-conscious culture among employees when dealing with securing edge computing environments.

Employees must be trained in device management best practices, password hygiene, and phishing detection. An effective training program can instill a vigilant eye at the workforce, significantly eliminating the human factor in security incidents. Scheduling regular security audits and penetration testing also helps to proactively uncover vulnerabilities, allowing organizations to shore up defenses before threats materialize. Such measures are in line with findings of (Abdildayeva et al., 2025), which confirm that both technology and human dimension combined efforts are required to make edge computing a reality in IIoT environments. Overall, an across-the-board security plan encompassing technological, procedural, and human dimensions is required for organizations keen on protecting their assets in the age of a burgeoning digital landscape (Figure 7.8).

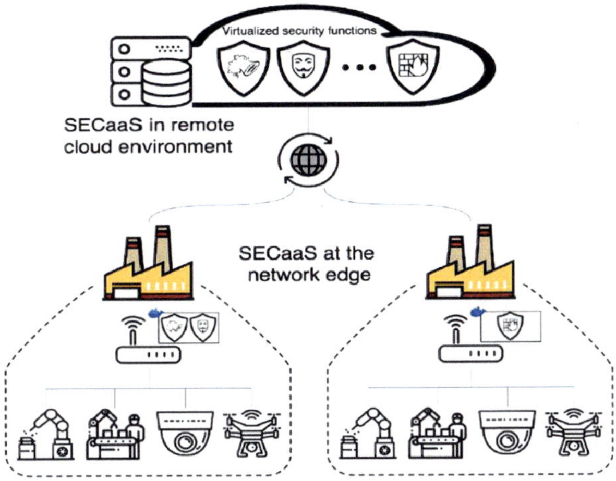

Figure 7.8. Security-as-a-service in industrial edge scenarios.

Source: https://in.element14.com/edge-computing-security-risks-and-solutions-trc-bl?srsltid=AfmBOorA3EMbD87qlRFCc8w015WkgPxQNbJnkFY8FB1fPbCYf1RWpIjG.

7.3.1. Encryption Techniques

Encryption techniques play a critical role in ensuring that data security and confidentiality of industrial edge computing is enhanced. With increased integration of systems and devices, sensitive information shared also rises significantly. Without the right encryption mechanisms, the information can be readily accessed and breached, undermining the integrity of industrial processes. Techniques such as symmetric and asymmetric encryption provide ways of securing data at rest and in transit to ensure that only approved parties can access sensitive information. Through the use of strong encryption protocols, organizations are capable of protecting their data from danger and establishing confidence in their business processes, remaining compliant with regulatory frameworks governing data protection. Under industrial edge computing, where data is generated and calculated at the point of origin, deployment of cryptography technologies must be particularly designed to meet specific operational needs. For instance, the use of lightweight cryptography algorithms may enhance the performance of edge devices that usually have constrained processing capability. There is a need to balance encryption security against performance, especially where latency and efficiency are a problem. Secondly, the integration of encryption into wider paradigms such as open data markets involves the consideration of mechanisms through which data can be securely traded and accessed. Privacy and security necessities are similarly echoed in arguments surrounding value generated from aggregated data as well as in the openness required to protect personal data in such marketplaces (Perera et al., 2015) (Figure 7.9).

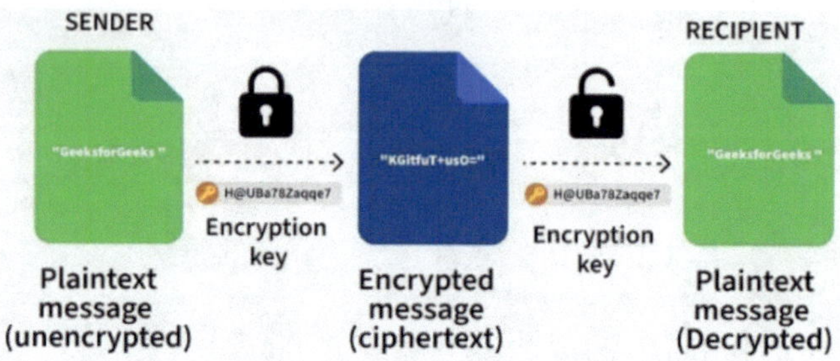

Figure 7.9. Data encryption.

Source:https://media.geeksforgeeks.org/wp-content/uploads/20241216211708228659/How-data-encryption-works.webp.

Further, the progress made in smart grid technology is a classic illustration of the need for robust encryption schemes to address the different cyber issues entailed in digital communication. Since smart grids employ sophisticated networks of sensors and equipment for resource allocation, any security failure can be disastrous for consumers and producers alike. This presents a unique challenge in employing strong encryption techniques that are able to counter the elevated level of cyber-attack sophistication. Tailored solutions need to be developed, integrating encryption into communications protocols to safeguard confidential data against potential breaches. By understanding and addressing the vulnerabilities of smart grid communications, stakeholders are able to create stronger infrastructures capable of operating securely in increasingly interconnected environments (Qian et al., 2012).

7.3.2. Access Control Mechanisms

Access control systems are at the forefront of protecting data and privacy in Industrial Edge Computing. Access control determines who can utilize what assets, maintaining the confidentiality of sensitive information from unauthorized use. Through the application of both authentication and authorization processes, access control ensures that only authorized users will interact with crucial industrial systems and data. With increasingly dynamic industrial settings employing sophisticated technologies such as the Internet of Things (IoT), the demand for efficient access controls that can readily support multifarious user roles and privileges grows more urgent. Apart from addressing the insider threat, this helps in the facilitation of accountability and traceability in organizational activities, which ultimately enhances the overall security posture necessary in today's industrial applications. The incorporation of access control systems must also contend with the specific vulnerabilities of the connectivity infrastructures involved in contemporary industrial applications. As pointed out by cyber security concerns in smart grids, weak security in communication channels can expose systems to threats and vulnerabilities, rendering them susceptible to attacks undermining both data integrity and operational reliability (Qian et al., 2012). Thus, it is essential to come up with access control methodologies that are not just proactive but also robust, able to defend against expected and emergent security threats. In addition, such mechanisms need to be constantly evaluated and revised to stay abreast with the fast pace of cyber threats so that industrial systems continue to be shielded from misuse by malicious players. In an open data economy, where data harvested by IoT sensors is available for sale, access control systems gain a further level of complexity. Data privacy becomes the prevailing concern, since the risk of sensitive personal data being sold makes ethical and security concerns highly important. The market players are compelled to tread a thin line between data sharing for business benefit and upholding the right to privacy of individuals (Perera et al., 2015). Rigorous access controls ensure that owners of data are in command of who their data will be accessed by and thereby forestall unauthorized exploitation. Establishing the data governance frameworks with clear parameters for access is essential in creating trust among the users and enabling the safe utilization of data in a more connected world.

7.3.3. Intrusion Detection Systems (IDS)

IDS are essential in safeguarding industrial edge computing environments, where the convergence of networking and computing resources presents new vulnerabilities. As IoT devices have proliferated, more data is being created and transferred around, providing potential avenues for attackers to weaponize these systems. Intrusion Detection Systems are designed to monitor network traffic and system behavior to identify potential malicious or unauthorized activity. Through the integration of IoT and fog computing, challenges emerge through the complex architecture of a number of devices and streams of information. More important is the necessity for robust IDS, as such systems need to be able to analyze huge amounts of data in real time with minimal latency, and this is especially crucial in an industrial setting where timely responses to threats are critical (Butun et al., 2018). In the context of industrial edge computing, security implications of IoT integration must be tackled from an overall perspective. Existing research points to numerous security issues entailed in integration, and this necessitates sophisticated IDS solutions. These systems, apart from detecting intrusions, must ensure confidentiality, integrity, and availability of sensitive data. As the discipline evolves, the development of adaptive IDS that can learn from evolving patterns of attack will be essential. This flexibility will guard against increasingly sophisticated threats to industrial systems, enabling organizations to maintain their continuity of operations. Key considerations regarding the convergence of IDS technology and industrial applications continue to inform best practice and innovative approaches to further enhancing security interventions (Derhab et al., 2020).

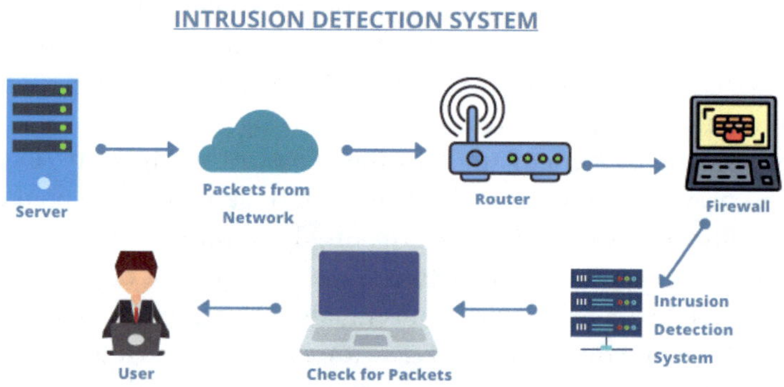

Figure 7.10. Intrusion detection systems in industrial edge computing.

Source:https://networksimulationtools.com/wp-content/uploads/2020/12/Intrusion-Detection-System-Projects.png.

In spite of the creation of Intrusion Detection Systems, there exist problems. The extremely dynamic nature of industrial settings has a tendency to produce false negatives and positives, which would undermine the efficiency of an IDS. Therefore, it is essential to maximize the accuracy of these detection systems for their successful implementation. Existing research focuses on the creation of systems that combine traditional detection algorithms and machine learning mechanisms. This integration provides the IDS with a constant ability to adjust by sensing and reacting to emerging forms of attacks. More than that, the shared architecture of IoT devices necessitates a more collaborative approach to cybersecurity, where information and insight gathered from one device can be used to improve the overall security posture within the network. Hence, persistent research and innovation in creating advanced IDS solutions are still the high priorities to ensure effective security and privacy in industrial edge computing (Butun et al., 2018) (Figure 7.10).

7.4. PRIVACY-ENHANCING TECHNOLOGIES (PETS)

The advent of PETs is becoming increasingly significant in the realm of Industrial Edge Computing. Through the installation of cyber-physical systems (CPS) and the Internet of Things (IoT), the privacy and security of data get reshaped at a highly rapid pace, necessitating the incorporation of PETs. PETs are made to protect user privacy while not putting functionality and efficiency of interlinked systems at risk. In recognizing their importance, it is necessary to consider the adaptive character of system configuration in the context of CPS environments, where reconfiguration in real-time based on context and user needs may obscure traditional understandings of control of data. The use of PETs therefore becomes a necessity in ensuring the privacy and security of user data in being up to date with the changing environment of IoT and CPS interactions (Azorin-Lopez et al., 2018). As businesses rely increasingly on data-driven decision-making, PETs' adoption also serves as a critical reaction to consumers' heightened concern about privacy invasions inherent in data commodification within the IoT setting. The high rates of produced data by many devices can potentially expose weaknesses that can be exploited by malicious actors, thereby putting sensitive information at risk. Hence, privacy-enhancing technologies are significant for the establishment of customer trust and for a secure context for data exchange. Applying various PETs, including data anonymization and encryption, as well as decentralized frameworks, organizations are able to protect against threats of data breaches and misuse. Not only do these technologies protect users, but they are also in accordance with regulation, promoting responsible data management in industrial settings (Mercadé et al., 2020). While in the case of innovation encouragement among small and medium-sized enterprises (SMSTEs), PETs adoption is also highly significant. Since these organizations have the goal of adopting emerging technologies without violating user privacy, adopting PETs can be regarded as a strategic enabler in the encouragement of innovation. With the triplex of governance, technology, and sustainability aspects, there is a system whereby the privacy element is treated alongside efficiency of operations. By implementing PETs in their technology stack, SMSTEs both satisfy compliance and ethical needs as well as enhance their competitive advantage in the marketplace. Ultimately, as industrial edge computing continues to evolve, prioritizing privacy-enhancing solutions will be key to ensuring user trust as well as driving innovation across sectors (Azorin-Lopez et al., 2018; Mercadé et al., 2020).

7.4.1. Anonymization and Pseudonymization

In industrial edge computing, anonymization and pseudonymization play a critical role in ensuring the privacy and security of the data. Anonymization refers to the process of altering identifiable data so that one cannot be identified, basically disconnecting the data from the user. This process is vital in the industrial context where firms collect vast volumes of operating data from network devices. By employing anonymization, business organizations can utilize data analysis without violating the privacy of employees or customers. For example, a manufacturing organization can contrast machine performance data without revealing identifiable information about the operators or maintenance staff. This central approach resonates with mounting demands for data ownership principles, emphasizing the requirement for transparent, governed frameworks that facilitate personal information security without precluding positive insights from data analysis (Mayer et al., 2018). On the other hand, pseudonymization maintains data utility and offers an added layer of safeguard against data breaches. In contrast to anonymization, which irrevocably wipes out identifiable parts, pseudonymization replaces them with synthetic identifiers or pseudonyms, allowing the tracing of data without revealing personal details. The technique can be particularly useful in scenarios where re-identification ability is essential for conformity or operational purposes, i.e., clinical research or predictive maintenance in industries. Pseudonymization finds a balance between data privacy and accessibility to cater to the growing demand for strong privacy controls as well as operational effectiveness. Additionally, with industries adopting the Internet of Things (IoT), using pseudonymization methods can assist in protecting sensitive data gathered from numerous sensors and devices, reflecting the spirit of privacy protection in the midst of technological growth (Dhinakaran et al., 2024) (Figure 7.11).

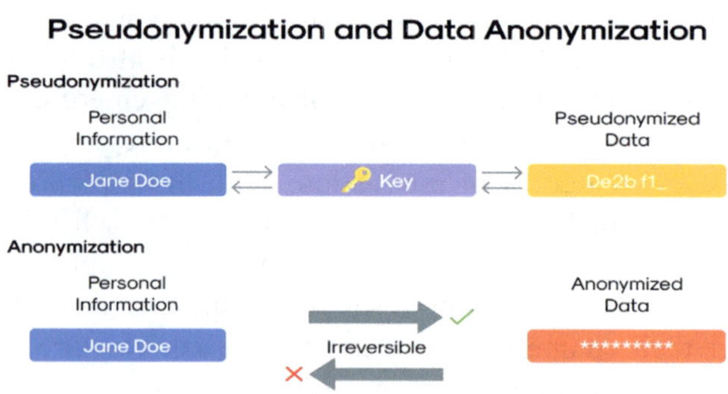

Figure 7.11. Anonymization and pseudonymization.

Source: https://cdn.prod.website-files.com/5ff66329429d880392f6cba2/6671c6cd7d0289631ae2d890_9%20-%2018.06-min-2.jpg.

Anonymization and pseudonymization are both crucial components of strong data governance initiatives in industrial edge computing. With businesses having to handle increased risks to data privacy, government requirements, and ethical concerns, these practices provide real-world means of avoiding data exposure risks. Their use escalates with the shifting dynamics of digital data that require agile and secure options. Including these strategies not only helps organizations comply with data protection regulation, but also helps to create consumer trust as consumers become more and more concerned with the way that their data is being collected and utilized. Accordingly, anonymization and pseudonymization use shall be a premise for enhancing security measures and establishing data rights within the complex connection between new technologies and privacy preservation in industry settings (Mayer et al., 2018; Dhinakaran et al., 2024).

7.4.2. Secure Multi-Party Computation

In the rapidly evolving industrial edge computing world of the present times, data security and privacy are of the highest concern. Secure Multi-Party Computation (SMPC) is the key approach in such a scenario in which two or more entities can compute a function on their inputs collaboratively without disclosing their inputs. This joint requirement for collaboration and secrecy is particularly crucial in environments where sensitive data is being processed, such as manufacturing processes involving intellectual property algorithms or confidential trade secrets. SMPC enables industrial organizations to conduct data analysis and machine learning processes without revealing individual data sets, hence facilitating innovation under the constrain of privacy (Figure 7.12).

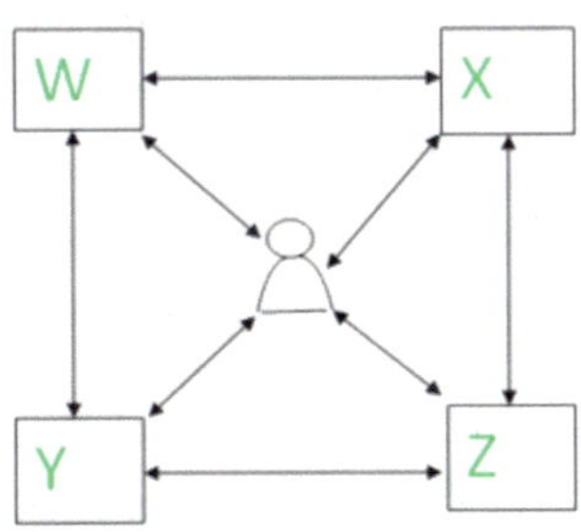

Figure 7.12. Multiparty sharing data among each other with any third party using a specified protocol.

Source: https://www.geeksforgeeks.org/blogs/what-is-secure-multiparty-computation/.

The effects of SMPC extend beyond just confidentiality of data; it optimizes trust between partners within co-working industrial environments. When different organizations are able to co-work on projects, the assurance that sensitive information will not be leaked inspires investors to trade data and information. In presence of SMPC frameworks, industries can mitigate risks related to data leakage and illegal access, which leads to more secure security policies compliant with regulatory standards. The use of such privacy-enhancing techniques promotes a scenario where competitive organizations are able to function together in perfect harmony, allowing IoT applications and smart manufacturing innovations. Additionally, the integration of SMPC in the Cloud of Things (CoT) architecture offers a complementary remedy for resolving the heterogeneity issue brought about by connected devices. Since there are so many IoT devices generating enormous amounts of data, protecting processing of this data is a serious challenge. Middleware solutions can be used to make communication between various systems easier and accommodate SMPC procedures effectively. Such a mix, in addition to enhancing operational efficiency, also sets the stage for the introduction of sophisticated analytics in edge computing environments, thereby transforming raw data into smart insights while having strict security controls as seen in the growing body of literature connected with middleware technologies for CoT (Farahbakhsh et al., 2017; Farahbakhsh et al., 2017).

7.4.3. Blockchain for Data Integrity

The combination of blockchain technology and industrial edge computing provides a groundbreaking opportunity for the optimization of data integrity. As industries move towards edge computing, data volumes produced in the periphery of the network grow exponentially. The scaling of data creates gargantuan challenges with regard to security and privacy, specifically data stream integrity. Blockchain's decentralized and immutable nature provides a robust foundation for addressing these challenges. With the application of cryptographic techniques, blockchain ensures that information fed into the system cannot be altered or deleted without consent, maintaining its integrity. It is especially important when there is a requirement for real-time processing of information to contribute to operational decision-making and the tampering of data may lead to improper outcomes or security breaches. Furthermore, the privacy concerns in industry IoT applications point towards the needs of safe handling of data mechanisms. As indicated by recent studies, there exist diverse threat models that target aspects of data privacy and integrity in the IoT network. These threats can not only destroy individual devices, but they can even attack the entire networks reliability. Blockchain technology emerges as a prime candidate to mitigate such risks through a clean record of all transactions, accessible to legitimate users but not to others. Increased security from blockchain can instill greater levels of trust among the stakeholders, thereby promoting cooperation and operational efficiency in industrial ecosystems. Blockchain for data integrity is particularly relevant in sectors such as agriculture, where data-driven decision-making is crucial for sustainability and productivity (Derhab et al., 2020). However, there are issues with the integration of blockchain technology, such as those concerning scalability and computational complexity in IoT environments. The restrictions which blockchain protocols impose, such as high computational overhead and potential latency, demand utmost care to avoid introducing fresh vulnerabilities. Research bears out that blockchain has the potential to significantly enhance data integrity but must be tuned to the individual needs of edge computing structures. When companies are looking for blockchain solutions, they need to balance that trade-off between security dividends and resource to achieve optimal performance. Moreover, the adoption of consensus algorithm can have a huge impact on the efficiency of industrial data integrity processes (Abdolee et al., 2019). Therefore, an in-depth knowledge of the both pros and cons of blockchain is needed to design safe and privacy-accepting industrial edge computing environments (Figure 7.13).

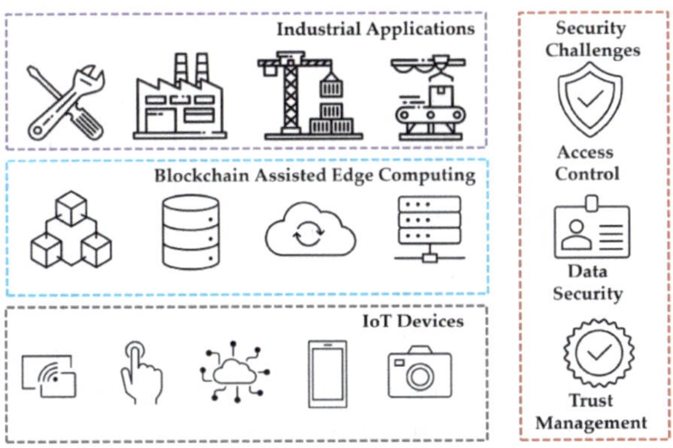

Figure 7.13. Blockchain technology within industrial edge computing.

Source: https://www.nature.com/articles/s41598-025-00337-3.

7.5. CASE STUDIES OF SECURITY AND PRIVACY IMPLEMENTATIONS

In exploring the area of security and privacy implementations under industrial edge computing, several case studies reveal the necessity of such aspects in safeguarding confidential information. The case study of a manufacturing plant is one such instance where they applied fog computing for optimizing its operational efficiency with data integrity ensured. By using edge devices-powered real-time analytics, the company was able to collect and process data locally, reducing exposure to potential breaches that typically happen when passing data to the cloud. This deployment showcased the interoperability between proximity and security, proving the effectiveness of edge computing in mitigating threats from centralized cloud architectures. The findings of these studies underscore the importance of context-based security frameworks adapted to the very specific needs of industrial environments. More research into IoT and fog computing architectures has uncovered the potential for even stronger privacy protections through adaptive security. In a case study, a smart city app showed how decentralized fog computing might promote enhanced privacy through data processing and sharing limitations at the local level. The data of citizens was accorded high confidentiality, since system design made use of localized processing facilities to anonymize users' data before mixing it with cloud services. This type of approach shielded not only the personal data but also promoted the building of trust among the users because they were assured that their information was not going to be unnecessarily revealed. These examples illustrate the revolutionary capability of industry-specific architectures to address at once security, privacy, and operational effectiveness in intelligent environments. Additionally, edge computing has paved the way to novel security strategies, particularly for mitigating threats from an increasing array of IoT devices. In one recent study, an international energy company implemented a fog-to-cloud security design with multiple layers, which significantly improved cybersecurity resilience. By employing an extensive network of interconnected fog nodes, the company developed a system that continuously sensed and responded to real-time threats against vulnerabilities. The adaptive approach not only improved security for critical infrastructure but also facilitated proactive management of security controls based on emergent threats. With advancements in industrial edge computing, the use of such layered controls for security, as illustrated through the case studies, will be instrumental in development and deployment strategies to counter increasingly sophisticated attacks (Carpio et al., 2019; Jukan et al., 2016).

7.5.1. Successful Security Frameworks in Industry

The increased application of information and communication technologies (ICTs) within industries generates the demand for successful security frameworks that can manage new security threats. A good security framework effectively consolidates disparate technologies and policies into a single defensive barrier against threats. Above all, these frameworks need to incorporate not only technical elements but also organizational designs that enable collaboration and innovation among industry stakeholders. As highlighted in recent discourse around intelligent cities, the same extends to industrial edge computing, whereby ICTs are applied to enable data-driven decisions through collective information. The dynamic nature of industrious environments demands flexible responses to security initiatives such that a proactive, as opposed to reactive, response is employed to fortify defenses against potential intrusions that could threaten both operational integrity and public confidence (Stahl et al., 2017). Sound security frameworks must also address the specific threats present in industrial scenarios, particularly in Industrial Internet of Things (IIoT) environments. As the field of green IoT-based agriculture demonstrates, threat identification and classification are most critical. Threat models can be classified into those addressing privacy, authentication, and data integrity. Thus, companies must develop tailored strategies to combat these vulnerabilities and comply with new legislation. By applying a broad taxonomy of threat models and advanced security techniques, industries can better position themselves to address both existing and anticipated threats. Therefore, investment in developing secure IoT frameworks that are privacy and integrity centered will benefit not just individual enterprises but the industrial ecosystem as a whole (Derhab et al., 2020). Furthermore, robust security models also need to adopt new technologies such as blockchain to further secure industrial edge computing ecosystems. The versatility of the blockchain technology allows privacy-oriented solutions to be implanted in existing infrastructures to provide more security guarantees. Decentralized data handling methods, as such, not only promise better integrity and availability but also allow organizations to have sole control over sensitive information. With industries increasingly embracing automation, as well as collaborating on information, incorporating innovative approaches with an emphasis on security will be critical. Guidelines for future research should seek to develop these technologies to address the unique security challenges posed within industrial settings, resulting in secure and sustainable development amidst more ever-changing digital environments (Derhab et al., 2020).

7.5.2. Lessons Learned from Security Breaches

The security incidents have important implications that can be applied to strengthen the privacy and security architecture of industrial edge computing. One of the key lessons is to utilize comprehensive threat models that conceptualize a number of types of attack vectors and vulnerabilities. Organizations can learn from previous incidents through an analysis of trends in cyber-crime. For instance, Cyber-crime Science methods emphasize empirical security mechanism testing highly and suggest that Information Security strategies must be subject to continuous evaluation and improvement based on real findings

(Hartel et al., 2010). This dynamic process encourages constant attention and proactive measures, enabling organizations to cultivate good security procedures that adapt to threats. Another essential security incident lesson involves the open information management principle. With industrial edge computing, information responsiveness and accessibility have major effects on security resilience. As noted by Diana Manderson from the Digital Connections Council, openness in processes can aid in driving innovation and making defenses more resilient against cyber-attacks (N/A, 2008). By making systems and data transparent but also enveloped in well-documented protocols, organizations can provide for cooperative operations that improve threat detection and response. Transparency, however, is only made possible by balancing it with stringent control over privacy to protect sensitive information, indicating the necessity of addressing security through a two-faceted approach to attempt to allow for collaboration as well as confidentiality. Lastly, the integration of user training into security controls presents itself as a prime takeaway from more recent attacks. Human error is still a root cause of exposures, and it is imperative that industrial edge computing organizations invest in awareness and training initiatives. Security controls are only as effective as the people who implement them; thus, heightened user sensitivity can significantly alleviate risk associated with security failures. This is in line with Crime Science practice values, whereby understanding human behavior and how it can cause security breaches is vital (Hartel et al., 2010). Informing users of their possible weaknesses and the importance of their input towards protecting security can result in an engaged and knowledgeable workforce, which can ultimately make the security framework better in industrial edge environments.

7.5.3. Comparative Analysis of Different Approaches

The industrial edge computing environment is filled with diverse techniques that try to enhance security and privacy. Among them, the convergence of fog computing with IoT provides opportunities and risks. Through distributing storage and processing of data, fog computing tries to avoid the latency of cloud computing. However, as is apparent in present studies, this transition involves complex security concerns that must be analyzed and prepared for with immense care. Conjoining fog computing and IoT can lead to robust cybersecurity protection; however, it also demands an intensive study of potential vulnerabilities born out of increased data generation and bandwidth usage in these combined platforms (Butun et al., 2018). It is significant to realize these implications since researchers seek to find means of capitalizing on the advantages of such integration without risk of threats due to security breaches. When sensor networks are applied in industry, how the connected systems are secured is a critical part in securing operational integrity. Traditional sensors and actuators, that form the basis for monitoring processes, are becoming more integrated using low-power wireless networks to cloud platforms, thus presenting potential vulnerabilities. New technologies like Information Centric Networking (ICN) have also been found to be robust contenders for enhancing security in these setups. ICN's content-oriented approach to security brings the promise of improved denial-of-service attack resistance, something which is of particular interest in industrial settings where safety is paramount. Such an approach contradicts common practices such as CoAP and MQTT, which have established that new paradigms can offer improved protection mechanisms suited for the hostile conditions of industrial IoT environments (Frey et al., 2018). Comparisons between these approaches can highlight their strengths and shortcomings, guiding deployment decisions in emergency scenarios. Furthermore, comparative analysis of the different security frameworks determines that no one solution is available to combat all forms of threats posed by industrial edge computing. Each method has its advantages as well as disadvantages, thus necessitating the need for a tailor-made solution based on specific operational demands and regulatory landscapes. With more industries adopting sophisticated edge computing models, an understanding of the differences between many different technological frameworks is paramount. For instance, while fog computing avails proximity and reduced latency, its distributed nature can complicate security protocols as well. Conversely, adopting only traditional cloud-based solutions might lack immediate processing requirements (Butun et al., 2018). Hence, a hybrid solution, balancing the immediacy of edge computing with the strength of cloud capabilities, would perhaps best balance security without sacrificing the integrity of industrial processes. Only through such detailed evaluation and judicious deployment can businesses possibly excel in the intricate security landscape of industrial edge computing.

SUMMARY

Security and privacy concerns in industrial edge computing are important because the technology trend continues to evolve. Devices at the edge gather and process a lot of information, and there is a higher probability of exposure to various threats and vulnerabilities. The integration of Internet of Things (IoT) technologies worsens this issue, since recent studies have shown that the proliferation of IoT devices not only leads to more data generation and bandwidth usage but also to unprecedented security challenges. Indeed, while the integration of fog computing and IoT creates possibilities for enhancing cyber-security offerings, it also creates challenges that can potentially nullify data integrity and user privacy. Safeguarding sensitive information in such a fast-paced environment must remain at the top of all stakeholders that implement industrial edge computing solutions for long-term operational practices. When handling issues of security and privacy, which are intricate in nature, one has to understand the system dynamics of industrial edge computing ecosystems. With the advent of CPS and IoT, comes a new paradigm where system components are not guaranteed to be controlled. Instead, real-time adjustments per user needs complicate how engineers can meaningfully control security. As well, since information is used as a commodity that passes from system to system autonomously, user privacy becomes paramount. The intersection of cloud technology with mechatronics also raises noteworthy issues about function allocation and safeguarding user information, demonstrating an irreducible intertwining of changing technology and user security requirements that must be met (Azorin-Lopez et al., 2018). Lastly, the setting for industrial edge computing security and privacy is one of constant conflict between technological progress and changing threats. Industry players must adopt co-operative initiatives to build comprehensive strategies that address such challenges from a whole-of-government approach. Solutions must be crafted not just to prevent unauthorized access and data breaches but also to build security awareness culture among operators and users. In light of the possibilities of cataclysmic consequences arising from security breaches, it is critical to give top priority to comprehensive security models. After some time, with the appropriate thought and proactive measures, the benefits of industrial edge computing can be harvested and the attendant risks mitigated optimally (Butun et al., 2018). Such an endeavor calls for constant research, development, and investment in security solutions aimed at taking into account the unique character of edge computing environments.

Industrial edge computing convergence presents indisputable advantages, particularly in optimizing operations performance and processing real-time data. However, as organizations increasingly rely on these technologies, the resulting security and privacy concerns become the focal point. A centrally relevant problem is how exposed communication infrastructures that drive such communication systems are. This is a particularly challenging problem in environments like smart grids, which must both have very high operational reliability and cyber resilience. Emerging research indicates that cyber-attacks can result in huge economic costs and operational downtime, further emphasizing the importance of a robust set of security frameworks tailored to meet the unique needs of edge computing. These frameworks must deal with the variability of vulnerability of distributed communications and pervasive computing in order to sustain the integrity and reliability of mission-critical industrial systems (Qian et al., 2012). The architectural complexity of Cyber-Physical Systems (CPS) integrated with the Internet of Things (IoT) also adds an extra layer of security issues. Compared to traditional systems, design teams no longer possess end-to-end control over any given piece, as dynamic forces may change setup in real-time based on user needs. This calls for a new understanding of security mechanisms able to track the flexible characteristics of modern industrial systems. In addition to this, the commodity of information in smart IoT environments raises significant privacy issues, which may threaten user data as it is autonomously transferred between systems. Hence, security protocol design and deployment need to be adaptive in a bid to effectively manage not only data integrity but user privacy as well within ever-changing conditions (Azorin-Lopez et al., 2018). Simply put, the balance of increased operational capability in the background of growing security and privacy concerns articulates the imperative conversation of industrial edge computing. Organizations must navigate the complexities of combining cutting-edge technologies while preserving system integrity and user confidentiality against inherent threats. The integration of robust security measures is essential not only for protecting the infrastructure but also for building trust among users and stakeholders of the ecosystem. As industrial environments continue to advance, emphasis on robust privacy and security measures will be the key to driving sustainable and secure technological advancement (Qian et al., 2012; Azorin-Lopez et al., 2018).

REFERENCES

1. Abdildayeva, A., Adamova, A., Karabayev, N., Zhukabayeva, L., et al. (2025). Evaluating an analytical model of cyberattack effects on an IIoT system with edge computing capabilities. https://core.ac.uk/download/665436712.pdf (accessed on 16th September 2025).
2. Abdolee, R., Maroufi, M., & Tazekand, B. M. (2019). On the convergence of blockchain and Internet of Things (IoT) technologies. http://arxiv.org/abs/1904.01936 (accessed on 16th September 2025).
3. Anderson, J., & Rainie, L. (2017). The Internet of Things connectivity binge: What are the implications? https://core.ac.uk/download/89472988.pdf (accessed on 16th September 2025).
4. Askar, S., Shukur, H. M., & Zeebaree, S. R. M. (2024). The utilization of 6G in Industry 4.0. https://core.ac.uk/download/617929879.pdf (accessed on 16th September 2025).
5. Azorín-López, J., Bradley, D., Hehenberger, P., Milne, A., et al. (2018). Mechatronics & the cloud. https://core.ac.uk/download/228178466.pdf (accessed on 16th September 2025).
6. Barabási, A., Diekmann, A., Halevy, A., Monreale, A., Szalay, A., Vespignani, A., et al. (2011). From social data mining to forecasting socio-economic crisis. http://arxiv.org/abs/1012.0178 (accessed on 16th September 2025).
7. Butun, I., Sari, A., & Österberg, P. (2018). Security implications of fog computing on the Internet of Things. http://arxiv.org/abs/1809.10492 (accessed on 16th September 2025).
8. Carpio, F., Dizdarevic, J., Jukan, A., Masip Bruin, X., et al. (2019). A survey of communication protocols for Internet of Things and related challenges of fog and cloud computing integration. https://core.ac.uk/download/187266039.pdf (accessed on 16th September 2025).
9. Derhab, A., Ferrag, M. A., Maglaras, L., Shu, L., et al. (2020). Security and privacy for green IoT-based agriculture: Review, blockchain solutions, and challenges. https://core.ac.uk/download/288345720.pdf (accessed on 16th September 2025).
10. Dhinakaran, D., Raja, S. E., Sankar, S. M. U., Selvaraj, M., et al. (2024). Privacy-preserving data in IoT-based cloud systems: A comprehensive survey with AI integration. http://arxiv.org/abs/2401.00794 (accessed on 16th September 2025).
11. Farahbakhsh, R., Farahzadia, A., Rezazadeh, J., Shams, Z., et al. (2017a). Middleware technologies for cloud of things: A survey. http://arxiv.org/

abs/1705.00387 (accessed on 16th September 2025).

12. Farahbakhsh, R., Farahzadia, A., Rezazadeh, J., Shams, Z., et al. (2017b). Middleware technologies for cloud of things: A survey. https://core.ac.uk/download/333623071.pdf (accessed on 16th September 2025).
13. Frey, M., Gündoğan, C., Kietzmann, P., Lenders, V., et al. (2018). Security for the industrial IoT: The case for information-centric networking. http://arxiv.org/abs/1810.04645 (accessed on 16th September 2025).
14. Hartel, P., Junger, M., & Wieringa, R. (2010). Cyber-crime science = Crime science + Information security. https://core.ac.uk/download/pdf/11476794.pdf (accessed on 16th September 2025).
15. Jukan, A., Marín Tordera, E., Masip Bruin, X., Ren, G., et al. (2016). Foggy clouds and cloudy fogs: A real need for coordinated management of fog-to-cloud computing systems. https://core.ac.uk/download/81582274.pdf (accessed on 16th September 2025).
16. Mayer, A., & Ritter, J. (2018). Regulating data as property: A new construct for moving forward. https://core.ac.uk/download/213019991.pdf (accessed on 16th September 2025).
17. Mercadé Melé, P., Molina Gómez, J., & Sousa, M. J. (2020). Technology, governance, and a sustainability model for small and medium-sized towns in Europe. https://core.ac.uk/download/322918717.pdf (accessed on 16th September 2025).
18. Okunlola, O. A., Olaoye, J., Okunlola, O. S., Okunlola, A. O., & Alao, O. (2025). Cybersecurity solutions for industrial Internet of Things–Edge computing integration: Challenges, threats, and future directions. *International Journal of Future Engineering Innovations*. https://www.semanticscholar.org/paper/84b10b67caaf2d1fd6dc59684bab2c9e9caf466b (accessed on 16th September 2025).
19. Perera, C., Ranjan, R., & Wang, L. (2015). End-to-end privacy for open big data markets. https://core.ac.uk/download/327950102.pdf (accessed on 16th September 2025).
20. Qian, Y., Sharif, H., Tipper, D., Yan, J., et al. (2012). A survey on cyber security for smart grid communications. https://core.ac.uk/download/12211131.pdf (accessed on 16th September 2025).
21. Schloss Dagstuhl, Leibniz-Zentrum für Informatik. (2011). *Dagstuhl Reports: Volume 1, Issue 2, February 2011*. https://core.ac.uk/download/14522611.pdf (accessed on 16th September 2025).
22. Stahl, E., & Dupuis, N. (2017). Trends in smart city development. https://core.ac.uk/download/83111937.pdf (accessed on 16th September 2025).

23. Zhukabayeva, T., Zholshiyeva, L., Karabayev, N., Khan, S., & Alnazzawi, N. (2025). Cybersecurity solutions for industrial Internet of Things–Edge computing integration: Challenges, threats, and future directions. *Sensors (Basel, Switzerland), 25.* https://www.semanticscholar.org/paper/7238333f6e734e5380ed9e802fa02ac46ed8d852 (accessed on 16th September 2025).

CHAPTER 8

RELIABILITY, FAULT TOLERANCE, AND RESILIENCE IN EDGE COMPUTING

Contents

INTRODUCTION

With the rapidly evolving environment of technology, edge computing appears as a prominent paradigm to facilitate data processing around the source. This paradigm improves latency and bandwidth utilization in line with the requirement of modern applications, particularly in the field of the Internet of Things (IoT) and real-time analytics. But as it goes large with deployment and grows more complex, reliability, fault tolerance, and resilience become important. Edge computing systems are normally deployed in a distributed manner, with numerous devices and sensors that communicate and cooperate. Such configurations expose the systems to a myriad of challenges including hardware malfunctions, network failures, and environmental factors capable of resulting in data loss and unavailability. In addressing these vulnerabilities, a comprehensive understanding of the topic principles of reliability is required and the formulation of matching strategies for guaranteeing system operation in the face of adversities. To properly mitigate failures in edge computing systems, measures of resiliency should be introduced. These are a number of techniques such as redundancy, replication of data, and self-recovery mechanisms to exist so that service is not disrupted. Reliability is more of an issue regarding how systems should function correctly under stated conditions for a given duration. Fault tolerance deals with how systems can continue running even when faults do. This is particularly critical for edge computing, where quick response can make a significant difference in decision making in mission-critical applications. Using the integration of advanced methodologies, edge computing structures can be built that are robust enough to withstand unforeseen disruptions. As seen in high-performance computing environments, brute system complexity calls for systematic approaches to fault tolerance, and hence an adaptation need has been realized for edge environments as well (Jinsuk et al., 2017). Along with this, new resilience techniques are essential to push edge computing architectures. Rising component failure rates in big systems, as exhibited in high-performance computing applications, necessitate robust defense mechanisms. Innovative developments, including adaptive control loops for fault recovery, show the prospect of constructing more resilient edge computing environments. The above methods not only recover existing faults but also optimize resource utilization during recovery processes. The ability to cooperate computations between faulty and healthy components, minimizing waste as much as possible, paces the way for paradigms in changing fault tolerance and reliability (Huber et al., 2018). Thus, with growing emphasis on edge computing, designing resilient systems is a primary factor to maximize performance as well as reliability in diverse applications.

Importance of Reliability in Edge Computing

With the rapidly evolving nature of edge computing, dependability is now more crucial than ever. After deployment, edge computing systems process enormous volumes of data closer to where it is indeed produced, thereby enhancing responsiveness and efficiency. However, such systems have inherent susceptibility to various types of failures, from hardware malfunctions to unpredictable network dynamics. Reliability becomes essential as the slightest break can lead to subpar service performance, not just impacting the user but rendering the operation inefficient as well. This reliability is particularly important in real-time data processing systems such as driverless vehicles and manufacturing automation. With the shift in infrastructure, the understanding of the revolutionary nature of decentralized computing—rather than the traditional data centers—is essential to addressing these reliability problems in edge computing systems (Buyya et al., 2017). Along with that, fault tolerance is inevitably intertwined with the reliability of edge computing. Fault tolerance mechanisms ensure the operationality of the systems under less-than-ideal conditions, such as component faults or unpredictable interference in communications networks. Particularly in wireless sensor networks (WSNs) in which nodes would be prone to failure as a result of unreliable connectivity, it is crucial to develop systems with a native resilience against such challenges. This resilience not only supports uninterrupted service but also enhances the self-healing capacity of the network. For instance, rendering a WSN k-connected guarantees that it will remain operational even after the failure of more than one node without any compromise to connectivity. Therefore, the incorporation of fault tolerance techniques with strength in edge computing systems is essential to ensure operating reliability (Huang et al., 2015). Ultimately, resilience in edge computing is a comprehensive problem that includes reliability and fault tolerance under a single operational model. An edge computing system with resilience can adaptively react to failure and variation without disrupting service. The path to achieving this resilience is highlighted by the need to overcome several challenges such as network topology control and optimizing resources. By realizing the interaction between reliability, fault tolerance, and resilience, developers can build stronger edge computing systems. Additionally, the current architecture is being developed with these considerations in mind, with the possibility of revolutionizing the way computing resources are leveraged. When the future of edge computing comes to light, ensuring reliability will be key in harnessing the true potential of such new technologies (Buyya et al., 2017).

Overview of Fault Tolerance and Resilience

Fault tolerance and resilience are most critical in the context of edge computing, particularly because these kinds of systems are increasingly being utilized in mission-critical applications. Fault tolerance refers to the behavior of a system to operate normally even if it has faults or errors. This is a critical behavior in the context of edge computing, as the resources are dispersed in many locations, causing component failure to be more likely. Fault-tolerant system design generally involves various strategies such as error detection and redundancy to minimize the impact of failures on system performance. With the incorporation of these techniques, edge computing systems are able to ensure higher reliability, thus providing uninterrupted service to users while ensuring peak efficiency and resource utilization. Resilience, on the other hand, identifies the capability of a system to recover following disruptions and accommodate changing conditions. This not only includes the technical mechanisms through which systems are capable of tolerating faults but also variability- and uncertainty-accepting approaches that are associated with edge computing settings. As numerous devices are networked and offering dynamic conditions, designing for resilience is becoming more complex. For instance, as revealed through research on high-performance computing systems, the intricacy and sheer quantity of components and their interactions necessitate a comprehensive strategy for resilience with focus on codified design habits and established patterns for faulting mastery (Jinsuk et al., 2017). These practices are able to help system designers create solutions prioritizing robustness and adaptability in handling failures. With the growing size and complexity of edge computing systems, the need for new resilience techniques becomes more imperative. New algorithms leverage the principles of fault tolerance as they adapt to rectify specific challenges posed by exa-scale systems. For example, adaptive control loops can facilitate real-time recovery processes by reconstructing solutions in faulty regions while also allowing healthy parts of the system to proceed with computations (Huber et al., 2018). These measures do not just enhance system reliability but also optimize overall efficiency by eliminating wasteful computation. With the deep understanding and combining of both resilience and fault tolerance, edge computing systems can ensure stable operation and optimal performance, ultimately benefiting a wide variety of applications that depend on their reliability in todays fast-paced technology landscape.

8.1. UNDERSTANDING RELIABILITY IN EDGE COMPUTING

Reliability in edge computing requires a comprehensive examination of the way distributed systems perform under stress and failure. With the paradigm shift to progressively decentralized models, with tasks of processing done closer to the data source, there is a greater likelihood of all types of failures. This is due to the heterogeneous nature of the hardware and software elements involved, which are bound to have unforeseen vulnerabilities. Hence, enhancing reliability to be more mature is important in particular because such systems form the basis of critical applications in real time like self-driving cars and IoT devices. Additionally, reliability encompasses both the accuracy of outputs and ensuring that services keep operating even in case of hardware failure or network breaks, making it an advanced task in edge computing scenarios. One of the most important aspects of reliability is the use of fault-tolerant components that will respond to failure when it occurs. Edge computing demands that methods used not just fix existing faults but also plan for future system performance in a distributed architecture. For instance, taking cues from high-performance computing methodologies, creating resilience solutions is paramount in maintaining computational integrity under stress. The complexity of inter-device, inter-network, and inter-application communication requires disciplinized approaches such as design patterns to facilitate efficient fault handling. This can involve the use of well-documented methods from HPC settings, as discussed in current studies, which emphasize the demand for tailored solutions for resilience that involve various layers of the system architecture, hence allowing edge computing systems to efficiently sustain functionality on component failure (Jinsuk et al., 2017). Aside from that, there must be continuous research in creating new resilience techniques that can keep up with the ever-changing nature of the system architecture. For instance, the recent development of algorithm-based recovery technologies as a demonstration of how systems can be ensured to have operation continuity even when portions thereof can be rendered inoperative by faults. The adaptability of these methods, particularly in managing computations within both the normal and error-prone parts of the system, is crucial in minimizing computational redundancy as well as enhancing time-to-solution. They are strongly applicable in large-scale deployments where the danger of component failure is exaggerated; offsetting such dangers is of central importance in moving toward edge computing reliability (Huber et al., 2018).

8.1.1. Key Metrics for Measuring Reliability

Reinforcing reliability in the edge computing context is crucial due to the distributed architecture, which naturally has multiple providers and varying degrees of service quality. Since more and more organizations base their operations on varied cloud infrastructures, the metrics of reliability become essential tools for measuring system performance. Of these metrics, Mean Time Between Failures (MTBF) and Mean Time To Repair (MTTR) provide quantitative baselines that reveal the total resilience of a system. MTBF measures the average time executed in operation between failures, accounting for how often system downtime occurs, while MTTR includes the average time taken to repair such failures. Together, they inform stakeholders about expected system performance, eventually influencing maintenance policies toward growing operation reliability in edge environments. The rapidly changing environment of upcoming technology necessitates a complex handling of such measures, taking into account the need for their inclusion in comprehensive reliability models (Buyya et al., 2017). As a supplement to MTBF and MTTR, availability measurement, the proportion of time for which a system is available for immediate use and usable, is a central measure. In edge computing, where devices communicate to dispersed systems, availability becomes even more important. High availability ensures continuous delivery of services, critical for applications dealing with real-time data and requiring instant response. However, traditional availability metrics might not fully encapsulate problems encountered in edge settings, where local outages and transient connectivity are the usual case. This requires the utilization of advanced measurement techniques, such as Service Level Agreements (SLAs), which define detailed reliability expectations between providers and consumers. The greater complexity of cloud infrastructures heightens the stakes of creating robust metrics to effectively handle expectations and deliver credible services in a wide range of contexts, but further emphasizes the requirements of stringent measurement practices in this evolving environment (Estrada-Galiñanes et al., 2018) (Figure 8.1).

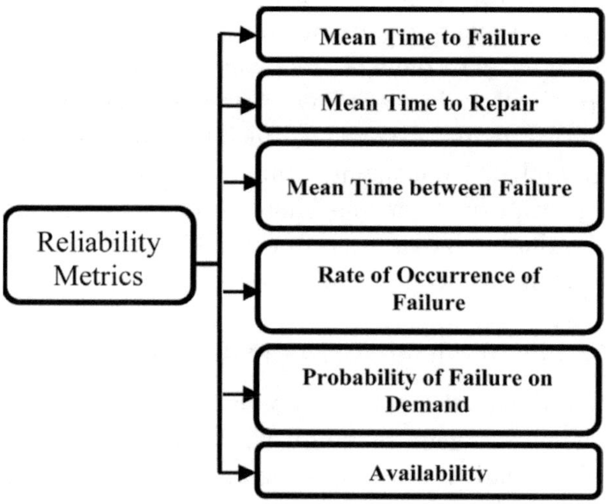

Figure 8.1. Software reliability metrics.

Source: https://www.researchgate.net/profile/Kavyashree-Nagarajaiah/publication/353853402/figure/fig1/AS:11431281161382058@1684991386646/Software-Reliability-Metrics-7.ppm.

Additionally, redundancy programs are another key measure that impacts the reliability of edge computing systems to a great extent. They offer protection against failure, sustaining data and services from potential failure, thereby ensuring that systems remain operational in adverse environments. Various strategies of redundancy such as replication and erasure coding ensure that systems become more resistant by maintaining replicas of critical information across nodes or creating a virtual layer of cross-linked storage devices. Interestingly, alpha entanglement codes introduce a new way of measuring redundancy and fault tolerance, enabling more data availability and longevity in distributed systems. These codes are robust to varying needs and constraints of resources and offer plenty of flexibility to trade between security and performance. Thus, with edge computing increasingly being used by organizations, understanding and knowledge of such redundancy factors are vital in achieving optimal reliability and resilience for their technological systems (Estrada-Galiñanes et al., 2018) (Figure 8.2).

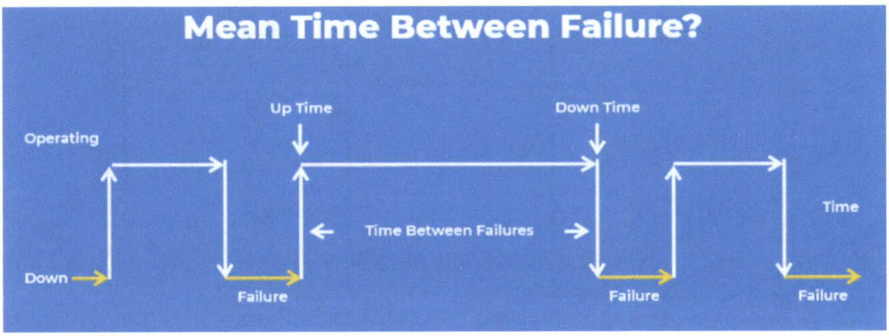

Figure 8.2. Mean time between failure.

Source: https://terotam.com/blog/what-is-mean-time-between-failure.

8.1.2. Factors Affecting Reliability

The reliability of edge computing can be greatly impacted by a range of issues, from quality hardware to system design and environmental variables. Quality hardware components with robust performance requirements reduce the likelihood of edge device failure as they are typically deployed in varied and often harsh environments. With greater demand for edge computing, added complexity in hardware configuration increases the likelihood of component failure. This calls for the incorporation of more advanced fault tolerance techniques, which can regenerate functioning without significant downtime. A case in point is the application of algorithms governing dynamics between sound and deteriorating subsystems in a way capable of optimizing problem-solving in real-time, hence enhancing reliability (Huber et al., 2018). Preserving hardware integrity and tightly designing system architectures are thus critical to creating strong reliability measures. The other important factor that shapes the reliability of edge computing systems is software executed in these systems. Software defects, particularly in advanced applications, lead to system failure and decreased performance. This is amplified in edge computing due to the fact that devices are self-sufficient and often have significant tasks to perform. The use of error detection mechanisms, such as Error-Detecting Codes (EDCs), can guard against control logic and data path failures in edge computing-implemented cryptographic circuits. While the focus has traditionally been on protecting data, loss prevention methods need to be applied to control logic so that weaknesses in the total reliability of the systems are prevented (Gaubatz et al., 2007) (Figure 8.3).

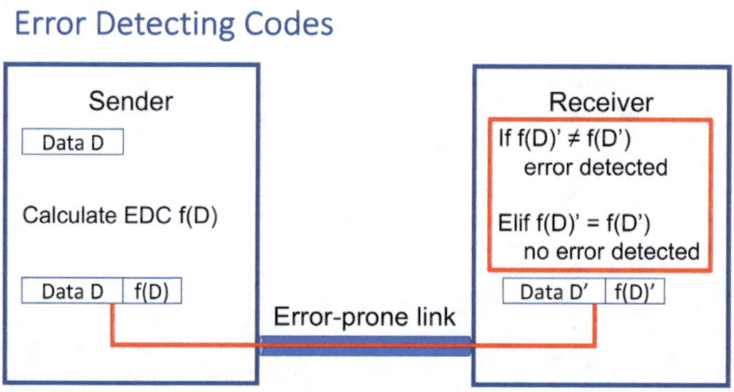

Figure 8.3. Error-detecting codes (EDCs).

Source: https://external-content.duckduckgo.com/iu/?u=https%3A%2F%2Ftse2.mm.bing.net%2Fth%2Fid%2FOIP._1xR4yQ4Bon52-WXm3p1JQHaEK%3Fpid%3DApi&f=1&ipt=dcfe727b48c2df9afe63c86848757c487dbe69c0376173870383460d2056984a.

Therefore, robust software testing and the integration of sound safeguards are needed to make edge computing applications more reliable. Finally, environmental factors become a significant component of reliability for edge computing systems. As these systems are mostly deployed within uncontrolled environments, i.e., geographic locations or cities with strong electromagnetic interference, they can get exposed to many external stresses. Temperature fluctuations, humidity, and dust deposition have the potential to induce hardware wear and failure. Hence, prevention and mitigation of such environmental factors are important to maintain the integrity of edge devices. Resilience design must also consider these extrinsic factors so that there are no gaps in functioning and system stability under adverse conditions. By maintaining both internal system configurations and external environmental factors, a comprehensive reliability model can be established that strengthens edge computing deployments against various types of failures, ensuring constant performance and consumer confidence.

8.1.3. Techniques to Enhance Reliability

Reliability should be optimized in edge computing to enable systems to work under varied conditions and potential failures. Perhaps one of the key ways of accomplishing this is redundancy measures, which can impact greatly on limiting the impact of component failures. Redundancy can broadly be categorized into hardware and software redundancies. Hardware redundancy entails the utilization of multiple physical units of critical components, such that if one fails, others automatically replace it. Software redundancy, on the other hand, generally results from employing diverse algorithms that, when executed in parallel, can check outputs against each other and therefore ensure data consistency and integrity. These methods are especially required in edge environments, where proximity to data sources necessitates the timely recovery from errors without compromising on service quality. As illustrated by initiatives like LEGaTO, the application of redundancy onto heterogeneous hardware can provide compelling energy savings together with system reliability enhancement (Alvarez et al., 2018). Moreover, embedding fault-tolerant design techniques into edge computing is also a crucial approach towards guaranteeing reliability. The field of fault-tolerant computing focuses considerably on system architectures that are immune to errors but not completely fail. One of the most cited techniques is error detection and correction codes able to detect and correct faults in real time, especially in those applications subject to external interference. Applying such codes not only isolates the data path but also addresses the critical need for control logic protection. For instance, more recent advancements propose multifault-resistant sequential control logic from traditional Error-Detecting Codes (EDCs) with large minimum distances to enhance cryptographic circuit tolerance further against potential attacks. Control logic is particularly focused upon because it is currently an unmitigated vulnerability in fault-resistant cryptography (Gaubatz et al., 2007). Finally, regular monitoring and adaptive recourse considerably enhances edge computing system reliability. Monitoring involves regularly analyzing the performance indicators of the systems with the aim of identifying possible failure points before they result in significant downtimes. Adaptive methods, such as dynamic resource allocation and load balancing, allow the systems to proactively respond to changing conditions or operations demand. By reallocating resources according to real-time data analytics, edge computing infrastructures are able to maintain optimum operations despite setbacks. In addition, delineating strict maintenance protocols and periodic update schedules can anticipate weaknesses, thus improving system longevity and dependability. These practices in aggregate form the basis of a strong foundation that not only improves dependability but also edge computing systems that are robust, making them capable of being able to satisfactorily meet evolving user and application needs in an evolving computing environment.

8.2. FAULT TOLERANCE MECHANISMS

Fault tolerance mechanisms are especially critical in the case of edge computing to maintain system reliability and availability, particularly given the geographically distributed location of edge devices. Fault tolerance mechanisms allow systems to keep running despite errors or component faults, which can have critically affecting consequences on user experience and service delivery. Redundancy is one of the basic methods employed in fault tolerance; it involves the replication of important elements or services so that when failure occurs, there is always another one available to resume seamlessly. The method is particularly vital in edge computing setups because latency and real-time processing demands create a peculiar challenge. By integrating redundancy, organizations can render their edge computing frameworks not just fault tolerant but also capable of handling user requests even with partial system failure, ultimately resulting in better system performance and user experience. The second most significant aspect of fault tolerance mechanisms in edge computing is the integration of sophisticated predictive analytics. These analytics use machine learning algorithms to predict potential failures based on history and current system performance metrics. By allowing systems to anticipate faults, organizations are able to avoid unplanned failures and implement corrective actions before faults are encountered. This proactive action goes a long way in improving operational efficiency and service continuity. Moreover, the incorporation of predictive analytics in fault recovery processes enables edge devices to self-heal automatically, dynamically responding to failure events and minimizing downtime. As systems get more advanced with more complex interconnected devices, the need for predictive models that can be highly fault-tolerant grows increasingly important, further necessitating the use of end-to-end fault tolerance mechanisms in modern edge computing systems (Oloruntoba, 2025). Consensus algorithms' operation serves to further underscore the importance of fault tolerance mechanisms within distributed edge computing systems. Because nodes operate collectively, ensuring consistency in data integrity and working state becomes vital, particularly when the system is faced with faults. Consensus protocols such as Practical Byzantine Fault Tolerance (PBFT) and Proof of Work (PoW) provide frameworks that enable distributed systems to remain consistent and reliable even when there are possible adversities such as node failure or malicious attacks. These algorithms allow the system to reach an agreement on the network state independently of faulty nodes, effectively adding to the robustness of edge computing applications. With increasing reliance on distributed architectures, the development and optimization of consensus protocols for edge environments will become essential to ensure continuous fault tolerance and operational resilience (Kumar et al., 2025) (Figure 8.4).

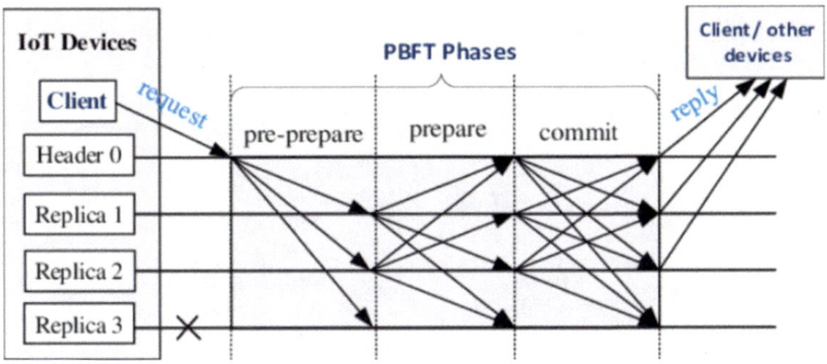

Figure 8.4. Normal case operation of the practical byzantine fault tolerance (PBFT) network.

Source: https://www.researchgate.net/figure/Normal-case-operation-of-the-Practical-Byzantine-Fault-Tolerance-PBFT-network-6_fig5_334612877.

8.2.1. Types of Faults in Edge Computing

In edge computing, there are several types of faults that can occur depending on the peculiar architecture and operating environment of distributed systems. Hardware failure is one of the typical faults that may happen in several forms, for instance, malfunctioning sensors, network interface cards, or even entire nodes. Such types of failures result in severe communication and data handling disruption, and thus impact service availability and reliability. In addition, software faults, including bugs or application vulnerabilities executed at the edge, further complicate system dependability. Since edge devices often operate in unstable environments, i.e., remote locations or harsh physical conditions, these hardware and software malfunctions may arise at an alarming rate, implying the requirement for robust fault tolerance capabilities tuned to address these special problems (Jinsuk et al., 2017). Another significant category of faults in edge computing relates to network instability. Because edge devices rely on communication with central cloud infrastructures or device-to-device communication to perform tasks, issues such as latency, packet loss, or network failure can potentially significantly impair performance. This is especially important in applications that require real-time data processing, such as autonomous vehicles and industrial automation (Figure 8.5).

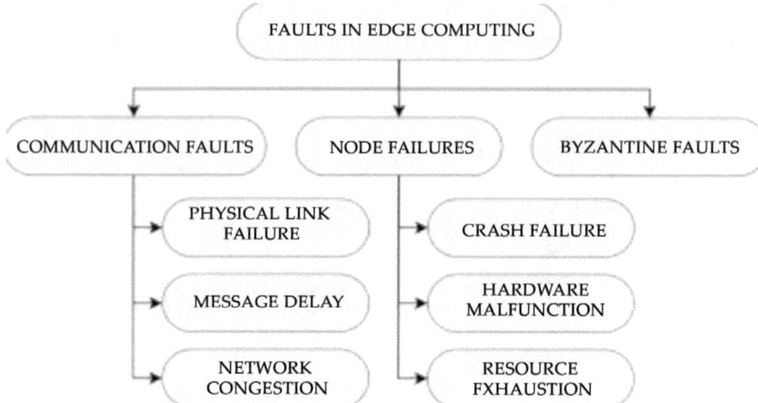

Figure 8.5. Types of faults in edge computing.

Source: https://ars.els-cdn.com/content/image/1-s2.0-S1389128624006352-gr3.jpg.

Network failure not only impacts data speed and reliability of delivery but can also cause cascading failures in the system. Resilience measures must be considered for these network-type failures through the application of redundancy, dynamic routing protocols, and dynamic reconfiguration mechanism to lessen interruption and ensure continuity (Huber et al., 2018). Data inconsistency faults are also a significant concern in edge computing configurations. Because these systems are distributed, information that is generated at different locations can end up being inconsistent due to variations in synchronization, which could lead to erroneous decision-making or system responses. This can be complicated by the constant update and continuous generation of data which edge applications are likely to provide, as this can lead to conflicts if not managed. In order to overcome this, one needs to take stringent data consistency procedures and fault detection with the quick detection and immediate remediation of mismatches. Employing new methodologies, like those derived from high-performance computing patterns of resilience, can be utilized in order to advance the ability to ensure the integrity of data, thereby enhancing both fault tolerance and reliability of edge computing systems (Jinsuk et al., 2017).

8.2.2. Strategies for Implementing Fault Tolerance

In edge computing, fault tolerance demands careful planning involving emphasis on resilience and reliability. One of the strategies is to build comprehensive fault detection mechanisms that can identify anomalies in real-time. By monitoring system performance and resource usage constantly, such mechanisms can actively notify operators of the potential failures before they become critical issues. This proactive strategy facilitates rapid response, minimizing downtime and ensuring system integrity. The addition of automated recovery processes makes this strategy even better, as the system can recover automatically after fault detection. This strategy not only makes operational performance easy but also reduces the need for human intervention, releasing organizations from the capability of undertaking other functionalities important for edge computing advancement. Another important strategy relies on the use of redundancy in edge computing systems. Through the use of redundant parts—either hardware duplication or duplication of data—it is made easy for the condition where, in the event of one component failure, others take over without disrupting service continuity.

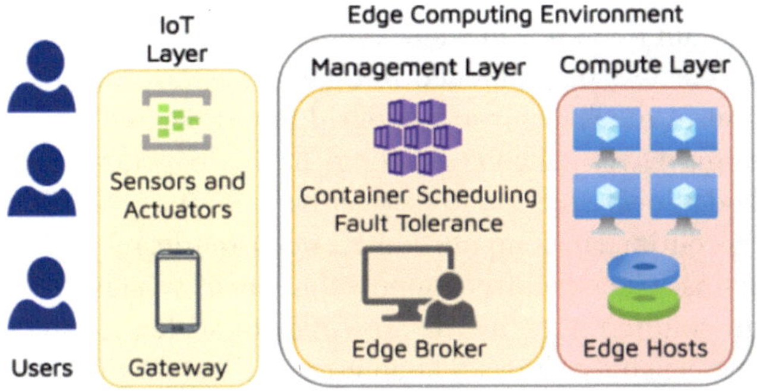

Figure 8.6. Implementing fault tolerance necessitates a strategic approach that prioritizes resilience and reliability.

Source: https://external-content.duckduckgo.com/iu/?u=https%3A%2F%2Fd3i71xaburhd42.cloudfront.net%2F4c82f091a264ca4826536efe114d2930d7e9dc96%2F3-Figure1-1.png&f=1&nofb=1&ipt=31b82b5934cd242146f67a1f28f6b82978c266608d9132490436799ee6ac854b.

This is particularly important as edge computing systems are usually distributed in nature, with components being prone to localized failure. Moreover, as emphasized in the design patterns methodology developed for high-performance computing systems, organizing redundancy in separate patterns allows effective control over complex systems (Jinsuk et al., 2017). This imposes ordered implementations that may be modified to specific fault models. Lastly, redundancy not only supports operational reliability but also trust in the systems capability to withstand unexpected faults while retaining performance. Finally, the use of advanced programming models can significantly enhance fault tolerance on edge computing systems. Initiatives like the LEGaTO project are a great representation of recent work streamlining heterogeneous hardware platforms with goals toward minimal power consumption yet high performance using task-based programming models (Alvarez et al., 2018). These programming models provide flexibility in task distribution over multiple computing elements, enabling better fault isolation and recovery techniques. By dynamic workload balancing and resourcing in response to faults that have been identified, these models contribute to the overall resilience and adaptability of the systems. This design coding confluence that happens on purpose provides developers greater ability to construct more resilient applications capable of sustaining function even under adverse conditions, opening the door to a new era in reliability with edge computing (Figure 8.6).

8.2.3. Case Studies of Fault Tolerance in Practice

The research of fault tolerance in edge computing results in a set of case studies that illuminate the use of resilience mitigations. One such case is utilizing an adaptive control mechanism in multigrid iterations and has proven highly promising in high-performance computing. In this paper, a novel algorithmic recovery method allows a system to recover from faults by making sure that the functional parts continue to compute while, concurrently, rebuilding solutions in the faulty domains. The concurrent approach reduces wastage of resources and reduces time-to-solution, thereby maximizing exa-scale system computational efficiency. The case study shows that an error estimator within mathematics is needed to control local recovery and re-coupling direction effectively, again demonstrating how advanced recovery mechanisms can increase the reliability of edge computing (Huber et al., 2018). The second very solid example of fault tolerance appears in the LEGaTO project environment, an EU consortium to integrate heterogeneous hardware into a single homogeneous software environment. This research highlights the importance of robust programming models that can be dynamically remapped onto different computational platforms, from CPUs and GPUs to FPGAs. Task-based programming paradigms enable applications to manage failures in a cost-effective way while simultaneously minimizing energy consumption. Significant energy reduction is what the work aims for, while further reinforcing that fault tolerance can be inherently linked to computing sustainability initiatives. In the process, the field of edge computing not only addresses the issue of reliability but also ensures its innovations become compatible with environmental ends, which is proof of the convergence between technology and ecological responsibility (Alvarez et al., 2018). All these case studies cumulatively illustrate the diversified approach to realize effective fault tolerance in edge computing systems. They highlight how new algorithms, in combination with visionary project models, can significantly enhance reliability and resilience, particularly with growing system complexities. The future development of edge computing largely depends on continued research on various fault recovery techniques. By seeing these practical applications, researchers better comprehend the dangers of system failure and can develop better techniques to combat their consequences. In the long run, the experiences gained through such case studies will guide subsequent computing infrastructures to become robust and efficient as they scale up to handle increasing pressures.

8.3. RESILIENCE IN EDGE COMPUTING

The resilience principle in edge computing is paramount to delivering untainted service and top-tier performance in more decentralized architectures. With the proliferation of edge computing environments, these environments are subjected to extraordinary exigencies, such as heterogeneous network reliability and opportunities for hardware failure due to more extensive deployment within physical locations. This mandates imposing sophisticated resilience methods that can keep up with the shifting conditions prevalent at the edge. Design patterns, such as those in high-performance computing (HPC) systems, enable programmers to architect error detection and recovery strategies in methodical manners. These strategies enable edge devices to continue running effectively even with local disruptions, thereby helping overall reliability and service continuity that edge computing applications demand. The collaboration between hardware reliability and software resilience then forms a significant subfield in building resilient edge systems. In failures management, edge computing edge control mechanisms can significantly enhance resilience by dynamically managing resources and fault recovery procedures. For instance, algorithmic deployment to guide recovery operations at the local levels instantaneously reacts to an identified failure within specific nodes or components. These procedures can enhance computational efficiency by maintaining the operation of healthy subdomains while rebuilding faulty ones simultaneously. Essentially, this adaptive framework guarantees that both active and passive fault tolerance techniques are being effectively implemented, thus ensuring overall system performance increase. As one can notice with respect to HPC systems, resilience simply cannot be a secondary consideration; rather, it must be integrated into the system design itself right at the onset. Therefore, resilience of edge computing would then be a matter of aligning performance demands with unpredictability of system faults. Moreover, constant evolution of edge computing means constant innovation in approaches to resilience, as much as system complexities rise. With increasingly more devices processing gargantuan amounts of data at the edge, probabilities of encountering faults will likely rise, consistent with experience in exa-scale computing scenarios. This is the truth behind searching for new recovery technologies, such as algorithm-based recovery technologies, to emphasize error-free recovery at the expense of no waste of resources. Effective resilience systems must be capable of avoiding under-solving and over-solving by local recoveries because inefficiencies within these will result in tardiness in service provision. Error estimation techniques as applied in HPC start becoming relevant in spurring local recoveries in edge environments. Therefore, developing resilience methods becomes crucial in strengthening edge computing against the inevitable attacks caused by hardware and network weaknesses (Figure 8.7).

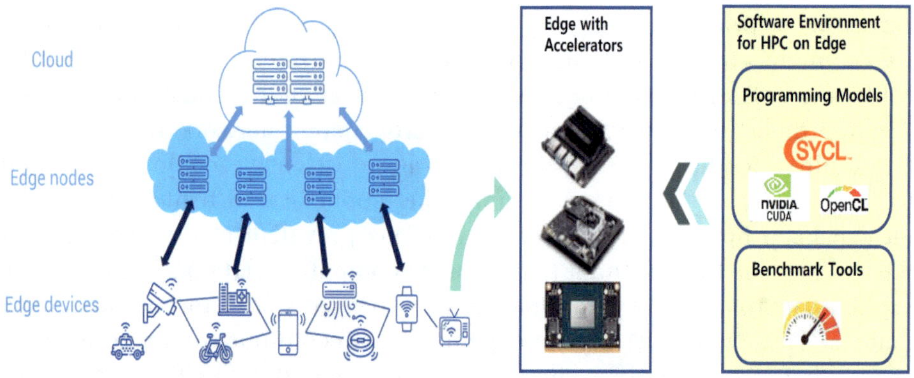

Figure 8.7. High-performance computing on edge accelerators.

Source: https://www.mdpi.com/mathematics/mathematics-11-01055/article_deploy/html/images/mathematics-11-01055-g001.png.

8.3.1. Definition and Importance of Resilience

Resilience, as used in the context of edge computing, is typically defined as the ability of a system to withstand and recover from unexpected disruptions or failures without sacrificing functional integrity. The characteristic becomes of especially important prominence as reliance on distributed computer infrastructure increases, particularly when processing data is conducted closer to data sources. The value of resilience transcends mere recoverability; it also encompasses the proactive design and operating practices that enable systems to anticipate, absorb, and accommodate various kinds of challenges. Consistent with this, resilience not only ensures protection for uninterrupted availability of services but also is an important factor in establishing trust among users who depend on the dependability of such computational platforms. Realization of resilience in this multi-dimensional setting is vital in the formulation of resilient systems that will have the ability to operate effectively under different operating conditions. The importance of resilience is all the more significant considering the unusual requirements imposed by edge computing environments. Unlike common data centers, edge environments will often operate in uncontrolled settings where physical resources are limited and susceptibility to environmental factors is higher. Modular data centers (MDCs), designed to be more robust, are a good example of this principle.

Figure 8.8. Modular data center.

Source: https://www.green4t.com/wp-content/uploads/2021/09/mdc-650x650.jpg.

They are not just constructed for operational efficiency; rather, they are constructed to perform optimally even in harsh conditions, thus ensuring system longevity. Through their modularity features, MDCs offer the ability to scale simply and service without any chances of obsolescence or failure due to static infrastructure. Such design paradigms highlight how resilience is crucial to guaranteeing data security and service continuity, especially when highlighted together with reliability and fault tolerance requirements in edge computing contexts (Asghari et al., 2017). Integrating resilience methods is not a last-minute arrangement to mitigate potential failures but also a proactive measure to enhance system performance. Advanced techniques such as multifault-resistant control logic in cryptographic systems serve to underscore the necessity of robust designs with minimal weaknesses (Gaubatz et al., 2007). By incorporating error detection and redundancy, they are able to ensure operational integrity in the face of multifaceted attacks. Reliability, fault tolerance, and resilience therefore converge to form an integrated platform for edge computing infrastructure development. As such technologies continue to advance, the worth of resilience will increase all the more, driving innovation and enhancing user experiences on millions of applications while paving the way for more resilient tech ecosystems (Figure 8.8).

8.3.2. Resilience vs. Fault Tolerance

The two words resilience and fault tolerance, although popularly used interchangeably, refer to distinct approaches to fault management in edge computing systems. Fault tolerance refers to the ability of a system to function as expected in spite of faults through mechanisms like redundancy, error detection, and recovery processes.

Figure 8.9. The overlap between resilience and fault tolerance.

Source: https://www.ufried.com/blog/resilience_vs_fault_tolerance/.

For instance, for fault-tolerant cryptographic systems, security is primarily focused on maintaining data integrity during processing. Techniques such as N-modular redundancy and complex error-detecting codes are being designed to enhance fault tolerance of critical functions, illustrating how robust fault tolerance can significantly enhance system operation in adverse conditions (Gaubatz et al., 2007). This emphasis on defensive tactics is reflective of a deterministic approach, where specified procedures regulate response to specific failure modes, thus ensuring continuity of operation. Resilience, conversely, characterizes a broader set of capabilities that allow systems to respond and adapt to unforeseen disruptions and maintain necessary functions. Resilient edge computing systems don't just intend to be able to withstand failure but to be able to learn from it as well, for allowing proactive changes and adjustments to be made in the future. Modular data centers, for instance, are examples of resilient design where flexibility and self-healing are combined to enable them to operate effectively even in the face of environmental challenges or resource shortages (Asghari et al., 2017) (Figure 8.9). Focus on flexible infrastructure, as a matter of contrast to mere redundancy additions, reflects a systemic reliability strategy that promotes sustainability and operational efficiency. This flexibility allows organizations to deploy ICT infrastructure in hostile environments, thereby making resilience a critical component of computing solutions currently. Resilience and fault tolerance are all part of the reliability equation for edge computing in the end, but they fulfill complementary purposes. While fault tolerance is the first line of defense against some failures through systematic recovery, resilience enlarges the dialogue to include the systems general capacity for adaptation to unanticipated changes and duration in the face of those changes. By the organizational culture of ongoing improvement, organizations can leverage both to construct more robust architectures that not only limit risk but also capitalize on opportunities from operational upset. As edge computing technology advances, it will be important to comprehend and harmonize these two models in the development of effective, future-proof systems that are both trustworthy and adaptive enough in an increasingly complex digital world.

8.3.3. Approaches to Building Resilient Systems

Edge computing resilient system design involves a multi-disciplinary approach with emphasis on reliability and fault tolerance. Admitting that edge devices are likely to operate in an environment that is equatable to resource scarcity and communication challenge, architects are compelled to integrate mechanisms with the ability to manage failures. Redundancy is one possible way, which not only involves duplicating necessary components but also function diversification across the nodes within the edge. This multi-faceted redundancy can minimize single points of failure, significantly enhancing overall system resilience. Through comparison with traditional fault-tolerant designs and emerging edge computing breakthroughs, it is clear that an even more integral design paradigm—beyond hardware and software design—can significantly enhance system reliability while accommodating the idiosyncratic demands of edge deployments. Synthesizing advanced error detection and recovery functions forms the core of resilient system designs. For instance, in fault-tolerant cryptography, efforts have traditionally been focused on data path protections, but upcoming research puts weaknesses in control logic under the spotlight. With the rise of guidelines that leverage Error-Detecting Codes (EDCs) in sequential control logic, researchers have demonstrated an effective path towards improving reliability on edge computing platforms. The provided techniques not only improve resistance to potential attacks but also provide scalable solutions without compromising performance. The success of EDC-based approaches showcases how innovative approaches can address past shortcomings, enabling more powerful and stable edge computing frameworks that are imperative in mission-critical tasks. In dynamic environments, such as wireless sensor networks (WSNs), connectivity under failure is an overwhelming concern for resilience. The k-connectivity is most applicable since it is the ability of a WSN to endure node failure without breaking operation continuity. The answer to this lies in robust topology control and multi-path routing that adaptively navigate their way through the complexities of real-time data transmission. Existing research illustrates how theoretical progress in topology control is capable of rendering networks robust against various deployment phases, from pre-deployment to re-deployment. By implementing these controls, system designers can develop resilient architectural solutions that are not only resistant to physical interference but also dynamic in response to changing requirements and threats, thereby enhancing overall system reliability in edge computing applications.

8.4. THE ROLE OF DISTRIBUTED SYSTEMS

Distributed systems are of utmost significance in edge computing to enhance reliability and fault tolerance. Such systems, involving an interconnected network of nodes that share communication and process information in concert, enable localized processing close to the point of data origin. This architectural advantage not only reduces latency but also diffuses the risk of single points of failure. The distributed nature of such systems enables automatic data rerouting and jobs from failed nodes to operational nodes, which is paramount in guaranteeing service continuity. Further, with the extensive use of edge devices, hardware failure is very likely. Thus, building fault-tolerant distributed systems that can adapt automatically to the failure of components is more critical in the aspect of ensuring uninterrupted service as well as the optimal utilization of resources. In addition to enhancing reliability, the deployment of distributed systems contributes to fault tolerance via multiple resilience mechanisms. Design patterns are one of them, which is achieved by using design patterns to promote the development of fault-tolerant systems, so developers can do something about possible faults in advance. Encapsulating decades of acquired best practices, patterns offer a clearly defined process of managing faults in edge computing. For instance, during system failures, reliable patterns facilitate quick recovery, as introduced in high-performance computing approaches (Jinsuk et al., 2017). Implementing such patterns not only minimizes the service disruptions but also optimizes the performance of the whole system through efficient use of resources even when the hardware is degrading. Besides, research on adaptive recovery and control algorithms within distributed systems significantly enhances their operational robustness.

Recent advances provide insights into how algorithmic recovery processes can adaptively adjust according to various fault states in such a way that even during failures, operations can be ensured (Huber et al., 2018). Through the use of an asynchronous online process of recovery, healthy subsystems can maintain operation while recovering lost computational tasks from failed nodes. Such an approach focuses on coordination within distributed architecture to avoid wastage of resources as well as use of optimal time-to-solution. With advancing distributed systems in edge computing, their ability to implement such adaptive strategies will grow increasingly important, making it an important cornerstone in achieving strong fault-tolerant computer frameworks (Figure 8.10).

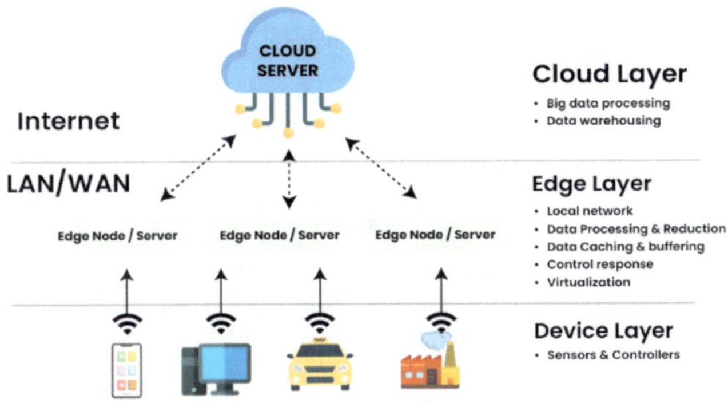

Figure 8.10. Edge-cloud architecture in distribution system.

Source: https://www.geeksforgeeks.org/system-design/edge-cloud-architecture-in-distributed-system/

8.4.1. Characteristics of Distributed Edge Systems

The essential characteristics of distributed edge systems rely on their unique structure, which offers processing as well as storage facilities close to the data source. This structural element eliminates latency and enhances performance, particularly for time-sensitive applications such as IoT devices and real-time analytics. By decentralization of processing, edge systems can operate in a fault-tolerant manner compared to the traditional centralized systems, with local decision-making ability and prevention of overloading central servers. Furthermore, the distributed nature promotes redundancy, as nodes can share in processing data and hence increase fault tolerance. Edge devices' connectivity also provides collaborative processing, significantly reducing the waste of resources. As such, distributed edge system architecture therefore facilitates smooth operation alongside reinforcing their inherent capability to offer reliability and resilience within dynamic environments. Reliability of distributed edge systems usually occurs through redundancy and failover deployment. Many nodes operational within the systems create a redundancy buffer against the failure of individual components given that several nodes have a tendency to provide duplicated functions or responsibilities. Such redundancy ensures that even when one of the nodes fails, they can be replaced without a break, thus ensuring uninterrupted delivery of service. In addition, distributed systems benefit from the principle of localized healing; when a fault is discovered, recovery actions can be applied with minimal effect on the overall performance of the network.

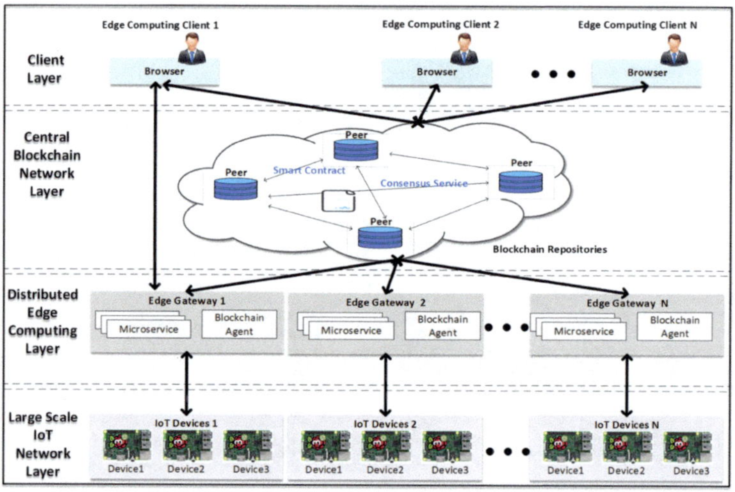

Figure 8.11. Proposed IoT architecture based on distributed secure edge computing.

Source: https://www.mdpi.com/actuators/actuators-10-00197/article_deploy/html/images/actuators-10-00197-g001.png.

This design paradigm is in keeping with escalating demands for systems that will run continuously in mission-critical applications, from healthcare to industrial automation industries. As a result, the average reliability of edge systems is a key factor in their overall approach towards fault tolerance and resiliency. Apart from fault tolerance and reliability, resilience in distributed edge systems can be largely enhanced through adaptive learning capabilities and intelligent resource management. Through the integration of machine learning algorithms, such systems can monitor trends in failures and workloads, allowing them to predict maintenance needs and proactively distribute resources. Such an ability not only enhances efficiency in operations but also optimizes the potential of the systems to self-tune into dynamic environments and unexpected failure. The case of wireless sensor networks (WSNs) illustrates this adaptability, where edge node deployment is informed by real-time feedback from the environment, illustrating a demand-driven model of resource management (Anda et al., 2012). This adaptability is beneficial in facilitating the general theme of resilience in edge computing in that systems are able to respond dynamically to duress and continue to deliver solid service under varying conditions. Thus, characteristics of distributed edge systems collectively form a paradigm shift in how edge computing can achieve high reliability and resilience (Figure 8.11).

8.4.2. Impact of Distribution on Reliability

In edge computing, system reliability depends heavily on the availability of computational resources. The greater the demand by applications for more performance and less latency, the greater the tendency is to share processing workload across multiple nodes. However, such a sharing can introduce complexity factors that affect reliability, including potential hardware faults and network condition heterogeneity. Though failures in a distributed configuration are to be expected, strong architectures can manage such failures efficiently to maintain continuity of work. Modern research identifies that as the number of compute elements is increased, the failure rate also increases, thereby necessitating new resiliency methods. Through algorithmic recovery mechanisms wherein the parts of the system can continue functioning while reforming the solution in failed domains, reliability can be immensely enhanced (Huber et al., 2018). Further, network architecture choice within distributed systems profoundly influences their reliability as a whole. Modular data centers, for example, have been the essential design that provides edge computing with greater resilience by making easier deployments even in hostile environments. Data centers are resilient in the sense that they can withstand failures without constant on-site maintenance, hence increasing operation uptime. Their performance is based essentially on the integrity and robustness of their fabric of networks. If even a minimal component, for example, a network switch, fails, it has the capacity to collapse the entire system unless architecture is carefully established. Failure analyses such as those employing Monte-Carlo simulations have thus become essential in evaluating the performance and dependability of various topologies of networks based on component failure (Asghari et al., 2017). In addition, the distribution implications go beyond mere reliability; they also include fault tolerance and resilience of the system. Spreading resources geographically across locations can counteract the effects of localized failures, thus improving resilience. For example, in case one edge node is down, the computing load can be moved automatically to an alternative node without affecting service availability. But such nimble movement requires advanced monitoring and control functions to proactively fix possible downtimes. As shown by studies, applying adaptive control systems in a distributed environment can be utilized to maximize the recovery process in a manner that solutions are rebuilt while maintaining computation loads maintained across healthy nodes. What is ultimately crucial is to understand the distribution-reliability relationship with the aim of formulating robust edge computing solutions that can efficiently operate under unavoidable adversity (Huber et al., 2018).

8.4.3. Challenges in Managing Distributed Systems

Distributed systems pose a multi-dimensional set of issues that significantly impact their reliability, fault tolerance, and resilience, particularly with regards to edge computing. As the architecture progresses toward multiple providers and decentralized computing resources, consistency management among nodes becomes increasingly difficult. The dynamic nature of cloud infrastructures, having transitioned from the traditional centralized data center setup to more decentralized configurations, requires organizations to shift their methods of monitoring systems and managing data. Without a single mechanism to manage synchronization issues and data coherence, the risk of data inconsistency grows with a high likelihood of system failure and user mistrust. These problems must be realized in the context of fault tolerance and reliability because solving these problems is key to realizing the full benefit of next-generation cloud systems that enable dynamic computing demands (Buyya et al., 2017). Moreover, the employment of microservices supports more modular system design but also introduces its own challenges to distributed environments. Microservices architecture, while enabling scalability and making the service more resilient, also complicates handling those services that tend to become interdependent. All the issues of service granularity, inter-service communication, and fault isolation have to be addressed with utmost care to provide system robustness. Microservitization is a process that not only involves migrating to microservices but also redefining the technical activities enabling this architectural shift. This kind of complexity calls for a serious understanding of how to design the various microservices in an efficient way and keep them resistant to failure, ultimately impacting the reliability expectations that come with modern distributed systems (Andrawos et al., 2019). Last but not least, the edge computing environment also has its particular issues that further speed up the management of distributed systems. With increasing use of IoT devices and requirement for real-time processing of data, edge deployments have to perform heavier workloads with high reliability while remaining efficient. The challenge lies in balancing local processing capability with connectivity to the central resources since non-persistent connectivity can lead to loss of data as well as interruption in operations. Secondly, the decentralized setting of edge computing has a tendency to result in lack of balance in resource availability and computation power, thus rendering fault-tolerance methods difficult to implement. Overcoming this is essential in enhancing resilience in distributed systems as organizations try to deploy solutions that are capable of functioning in such conditions, ensuring lasting service availability and performance integrity despite potential failure (Buyya et al., 2017; Andrawos et al., 2019).

8.5. SECURITY CONSIDERATIONS

In the new world of edge computing, securing strong security is paramount with the characteristic vulnerabilities of this architecture. Unlike traditional central architectures, edge computing involves dispersing loads across numerous devices and networks with diverse points of attack. The more endpoints—smart devices, sensors, and local processing nodes—the larger the problem grows, as each device represents a potential entry point for perpetrators. Moreover, the dynamic edge environment is prone to triggering insufficiently secured devices and infrastructure, which upon hacking can lead to unauthorized access and exploitation. To this concern, developers and engineers have to deploy robust security measures across the systems lifetime in an effort to guarantee data integrity and confidentiality is maintained even in decentralized systems. One of the important factors in achieving good security in edge computing lies within fault-tolerant mechanisms that are aimed at protecting data and control logic. Although much effort has been focused on securing the data path in cryptographic circuits, a clear void lies in protecting the control logic against fault attacks. As underlined by current writing, particularly the findings of current studies, defenses made by conventional approaches often overlook this critical dimension, leaving systems vulnerable to advanced attacks. The arrival of multifault-resilient sequential control logic, supported by conventional Error-Detecting Codes (EDCs), offers a possible remedy. Such a strategy offers enhanced defense against potential exploitation, allowing edge systems not only to detect faults but also to mitigate the threats introduced by control path vulnerabilities effectively and therefore enhance overall security. Additionally, as cloud infrastructure is undergoing a revolutionary shift toward decentralization, security implications must keep pace with this altered setting. The utilization of multiple cloud providers offers a more robust architecture but introduces complexities in the aspect of securing across heterogeneous environments. With increased data transfer between edge devices and cloud services, having one system of security ensures sensitive information remains protected. Research indicates that as cloud frameworks evolve to meet decentralized frameworks, a multi-dimensional security strategy will be critical in addressing emerging threats and vulnerabilities. The problems mentioned here must be assigned top priority, and an aggressive roadmap for the deployment of these new security frameworks can greatly enhance the dependability and resilience of systems that make use of edge computing facilities as noted in the ongoing debate concerning cloud systems in the future (Buyya et al., 2017).

8.5.1. Security Threats in Edge Computing

The arrival of edge computing has induced a greater interest in the possible security threats involved in its adoption. Edge computing systems, inherently, are distributed rather than being centralized, which creates inherent vulnerabilities. The decentralized structure offers an entry point to several various forms of attacks like data breaches, denial-of-service (DoS) attacks, and physical modification. With growing closeness of processing and storage to the data source, devices at the edge, being often constrained by limited resources and processing capacity, may not have robust security. Hence, attackers are able to exploit these vulnerabilities to violate data integrity and availability. The complexity of the security of a number of edge devices introduces issues outside traditional data center security controls, highlighting the need for elastic and pervasive security policies crafted for the edge computing scenario. Among the most important facets of countering security issues in edge computing is addressing interdependencies in an organization's IT infrastructure. Current risk assessment practices typically do not work, as they are poor at capturing the intricate interactions between edge system components. This failure complicates the assessment and mitigation of potential availability risks, which impacts reliability and fault tolerance. In a bid to overcome these limitations, organizations must adopt more sophisticated risk mitigation techniques that take into account the dynamic nature of edge computing environments. Incorporation of tools designed for thorough risk analysis can help companies identify vulnerabilities and recommend best-in-class countermeasures. With added focus on such interdependencies, companies will be able to protect their edge computing systems in a more secure manner against all forms of security attacks, making the operation framework sound. Moreover, with edge computing integrating multimodal artificial intelligence (AI) systems, the security landscape is rendered more complex but promising. Decentralized systems reduce the exposure of single points of failure along with enhancing the resilience of AI applications overall by distributing control across multiple nodes. Along with securing security more strongly, it also facilitates easier processing of multiple types of data, contributing to the resilience of multimodal AI solutions. However, their integration is challenging in maintaining security systems that can be compatible with both edge computing frameworks and the complexity of AI. Future research should look into doing good things when merging decentralized systems with multimodal AI to tap their advantages while overcoming inherent weaknesses. Exploring these intersections will open up novel applications in many areas, including healthcare and autonomous systems, where security is a concern paramount (Bolzoni et al., 2007; Saad et al., 2024) (Figure 8.12).

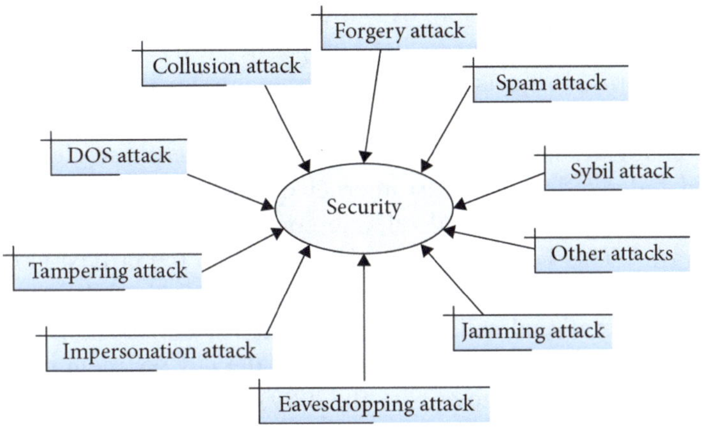

Figure 8.12. Security threats in edge computing.

Source: https://www.researchgate.net/figure/Security-threats-in-edge-computing_fig1_343715115.

8.5.2. Relationship Between Security and Reliability

In edge computing, security and reliability become a pressing issue to system developers and architects. Reliability refers to the guaranteed system performance that enables systems to function in the correct manner under various conditions and interruptions. This property is inherently intertwined with security because security threats may disturb reliability by opening unauthorized accesses or breaching system integrity. For instance, a security violation may lead to corruption of data or denial of service, lowering the edge devices' trustworthiness. Hence, the enhancement of security controls not only protects sensitive systems and information but also enhances the trustworthiness of operations to create confidence among stakeholders and users of edge computing. Fault tolerance is equally a significant element that relates security and trustworthiness in edge computing systems. Fault tolerance is the ability of a system to continue operating normally in the event of failures or errors, and it is a subset of reliability as well as security. When a security attack induces disruption of normal business processes, it has the potential to induce cascading failure in systems that are interdependent, thus making them unreliable. Conversely, fault-tolerant designs can counteract effects of such security attacks. The experiences from models like the Army Fault Tolerant Architecture (AFTA) emphasize the necessity to incorporate good maintenance approaches in an effort to enhance not just fault tolerance but also system reliability, illustrating the complementary characteristics of security and reliability in technology infrastructures (Alger et al., 2025). Additionally, ongoing evolution of the Future Internet emphasizes the need to design architectures that complementarily integrate security and reliability concerns. Projects to build next-generation internet infrastructures highlight the importance of service-aware network designs that emphasize resilience, reliability, and safe data processing. Research strategies that promote parallel and federated methods to internet development suggest mechanisms that natively support secure and reliable communication across an extensive set of platforms. This holistic perspective is vital to the provision of enabling edge computing systems to respond effectively to both the cybersecurity threat challenge and operational reliability requirements, emphasizing that security and reliability must evolve in tandem towards the development of strong edge computing solutions (Abramowicz et al., 2009).

8.5.3. Best Practices for Securing Edge Environments

In addressing the complexities inherent in edge computing, the implementation of best practices in edge environment security is of utmost concern. Given the distributed nature of edge computing where devices are located far from the main data centers, exposures are simply unavoidable. Therefore, a multi-layered security approach is required with interventions such as encryption, access controls, and endpoint security that protect devices from unauthorized access and data loss. Moreover, a robust identity and access management system is crucial to being able to authenticate users and devices consistently. Through the implementation of such practices, organizations can enhance the reliability and integrity of edge environments and thereby reduce risks associated with more exposure to potential cyber threats. Furthermore, the dynamic nature of edge computing demands continuous assessment of security protocols and practices. With changing technologies come the evolution of techniques employed by hackers, and organizations have to adapt their security measures as a result. Software and firmware patching and upgrades can help significantly ensure edge devices are protected against what is known, and monitoring systems and threat detection can facilitate responses to security violations in a timely fashion. Such looking-forward behavior contributes to not just fault tolerance but overall resilience in edge environments. The process can further be complemented with the inclusion of artificial intelligence (AI) in security infrastructures to provide predictive abilities that foresee possible vulnerabilities in advance prior to them being exploitable, as required in continuity of operations in edge computing designs (Firschein et al., 2025) (Figure 8.13).

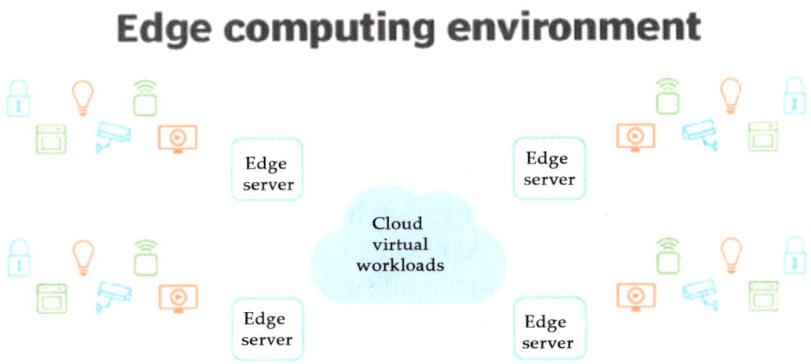

Figure 8.13. Securing edge environments.

Source: https://www.techtarget.com/rms/onlineimages/iota-edge_computing_environment-f_mobile.png.

In addition to these technical measures, building a security-aware culture in organizations is no less crucial towards the goal of securing edge environments. Employees need to be aware of the threat environment and trained for optimal practices in identifying and responding to security incidents. By means of extensivtraining mechanisms, the staff can become cognizant of the importance of data privacy and security in edge computing and fortify the organization's defense system. Additionally, verifying and complying with industry standards and regulations can bolster the security stance of the edge environment. These will assist in creating a resilient infrastructure that can effectively address emerging challenges as they occur, finally facilitating the overall objectives of reliability and fault tolerance in edge computing systems (Derhab et al., 2020).

SUMMARY

The topics of reliability, fault tolerance, and resilience are of top priority in the context of edge computing, serving as the foundation for robust systems that can survive failure and continue to function effectively. As complexity in edge computing environments comes out through distributed architecture and heterogeneity of devices, dependable data processing is confronted with escalating issues. The integration of advanced fault tolerance mechanisms allows for such systems to provide service continuity even during node failures or communication link outages. Such adaptability is important not only for providing operational effectiveness but also for maintaining user trust and satisfaction in edge-controlled applications. Additionally, studies on resilience strategies, especially in the context of wireless sensor networks (WSNs), highlight overarching strategies in coping with network failures and steady availability of service. Since WSNs are implemented in possibly fault-causing surroundings, connectivity through k-connected structures is one clear use of resiliency principles. By focusing on both topological management and multi-path routing, scholars have observed methodologies that make such networks more self-healing, based on current research findings, which investigate ways to fortify connectivity at different deployment stages (Huang et al., 2015). Such research not only gives emphasis to the role of resilience in edge computing but also provides a roadmap for future developments in this technology. Finally, the examination of the practical applications of such ideas in industries such as aviation further emphasizes the need for reliability and resilience. According to research conducted at NASA Langley Research Center, the combination of research programs with industry demands is essential to creating fault-tolerant systems. Recommendations for improved resource allocation readily concentrate on areas of priority, placing emphasis on ongoing adaptation and evolution of hardware and software systems (Dunham et al., 2025). By establishing an innovation culture and adaptive design within edge computing infrastructures, stakeholders can unite with the objective of creating more robust and resilient solutions that evolve to meet the evolving needs of technology and society.

In the context of edge computing, the interplay between fault tolerance, reliability, and resilience is a cornerstone upon which efficient and resilient systems are built. With the march of technology towards extreme-scale HPC, the need for resilient architectures has become increasingly fundamental. The sheer size of such systems, which comprise millions of interacting components, presents unbridgeable hurdles in ensuring reliable behavior. Fault events can trigger extreme failures such as incorrect computation or unexpected termination of critical applications. Therefore, it is imperative to develop techniques that will improve edge computing platforms' resilience. Techniques such as employing design patterns are essential since they enable practitioners to structure solutions for resilience in an effective way while accommodating the vast variety of fault models encountered within intricate computing environments (Jinsuk et al., 2017). Additionally, the employment of Wireless Sensor Networks (WSNs) further proves the necessity of fault tolerance and resilience for edge computing. These networks are most vulnerable to failure because of weak links, environmental influences, and limited resources. The k-connectedness of a WSN is an important concept in this context that describes the networks capability to keep functioning even after the failure of $k - 1$ nodes. This functionality makes WSNs connected and functional while highlighting the need for edge networks that typically operate under adverse environments to be resilient. The integration of strong topology control and multipath routing techniques plays an essential role in delivering the self-healing functionality of WSNs, ensuring that the networks can heal dynamically and effectively from faults and thus improve their reliability and performance (Huang et al., 2015). In summary, ensuring reliability, fault tolerance, and resilience in edge computing is a multi-faceted approach solving the unique challenges of technology innovations at the edge. The methods being developed, particularly in HPC systems, illustrate the need for engineered resilience solutions that dynamically adapt to faults without compromising system integrity. Moreover, the data obtained through research of WSN architectures provides further knowledge of resilience principles that can be used for most edge computing models. With further advancements in the edge computing environment, increased research and innovative practices will be important towards creating resilient systems capable of accommodating the complexities of present-day computing demands and environmental changes and ultimately creating stronger and more secure technology.

REFERENCES

1. Abramowicz, H., Brunner, M., Chemouil, P., Galis, A., et al. (2009). Management and service-aware networking architectures (MANA) for future internet position paper: System functions, capabilities and requirements. https://core.ac.uk/download/pdf/11476514.pdf (accessed on 16th September 2025).
2. Alger, L. S., Babikyan, C. A., Butler, B. P., Friend, R., et al. (2025). Advanced information processing system: The Army fault tolerant architecture conceptual study. Volume 2: Army fault tolerant architecture design and analysis. https://core.ac.uk/download/pdf/42811477.pdf (accessed on 16th September 2025).
3. Alvarez, C., Bautista, L., Becker, T., Billung-Meyer, M., et al. (2018). LEGaTO: First steps towards energy-efficient toolset for heterogeneous computing. https://core.ac.uk/download/224976296.pdf (accessed on 16th September 2025).
4. Anda, M., Goodfield, D., Lee, K., Murray, T., et al. (2012). Experiences and issues for environmental engineering sensor network deployments. https://core.ac.uk/download/30649493.pdf (accessed on 16th September 2025).
5. Andrawos, M., Aßmann, U., Bass, L., Behara, D. G. K., Betts, T., Bianco, P., Bryant, D., et al. (2019). Microservice transition and its granularity problem: A systematic mapping study. https://core.ac.uk/download/426749569.pdf (accessed on 16th September 2025).
6. Asghari, V., Cheriet, M., Lemieux, Y., Moghaddam, S., et al. (2017). A Monte-Carlo approach to lifespan failure performance analysis of the network fabric in modular data centers. http://arxiv.org/abs/1401.7528 (accessed on 16th September 2025).
7. Bolzoni, D., Etalle, S., Salvato, M., Zambon, E., et al. (2007). Model-based mitigation of availability risks. https://core.ac.uk/download/pdf/11470647.pdf (accessed on 16th September 2025).
8. Buyya, R., & Varghese, B. (2017). Next generation cloud computing: New trends and research directions. https://core.ac.uk/download/96664300.pdf (accessed on 16th September 2025).
9. Chung, J., Mohror, K., & Saridakis, T. (2017). A pattern language for high-performance computing resilience. http://arxiv.org/abs/1710.09074 (accessed on 16th September 2025).
10. Derhab, A., Ferrag, M. A., Maglaras, L., Shu, L., et al. (2020). Security and privacy for green IoT-based agriculture: Review, blockchain solutions,

and challenges. https://core.ac.uk/download/288345720.pdf (accessed on 16th September 2025).

11. Dunham, J. R., & Siewiorek, D. P. (2025). Assessment team report on flight-critical systems research at NASA Langley Research Center. https://core.ac.uk/download/pdf/42816904.pdf (accessed on 16th September 2025).
12. Estrada-Galiñanes, V., Felber, P., Miller, E., Pâris, J. F., et al. (2018). Alpha entanglement codes: Practical erasure codes to archive data in unreliable environments. http://arxiv.org/abs/1810.02974 (accessed on 16th September 2025).
13. Firschein, O., Georgeff, M. P., Kautz, W. H., Levitt, T., et al. (2025). NASA space station automation: AI-based technology review. https://core.ac.uk/download/pdf/42844682.pdf (accessed on 16th September 2025).
14. Gaubatz, G., Savaş, E., Sunar, B., et al. (2007). Sequential circuit design for embedded cryptographic applications resilient to adversarial faults. https://core.ac.uk/download/pdf/11739420.pdf (accessed on 16th September 2025).
15. Huang, Y., Martínez Ortega, J. F., López Santidrián, M. L., Sendra Pons, A., et al. (2015). Resilient wireless sensor networks using topology control: A review. https://core.ac.uk/download/pdf/148680234.pdf (accessed on 16th September 2025).
16. Huber, M., Rüde, U., & Wohlmuth, B. (2018). Adaptive control in rollforward recovery for extreme scale multigrid. http://arxiv.org/abs/1804.06373 (accessed on 16th September 2025).
17. Kumar, A., Bhardwaj, D., Nayak, P., Parashar, J., & Kumar, D. (2025). Optimization of fault tolerance in distributed systems via consensus protocol. *Advances in Nonlinear Variational Inequalities*. https://www.semanticscholar.org/paper/f18aff6a0c3ac469c287a36298037b06f98a6c0a (accessed on 16th September 2025).
18. Oloruntoba, O. (2025). Architecting resilient multi-cloud database systems: Distributed ledger technology, fault tolerance, and cross-platform synchronization. *International Journal of Research Publication and Reviews*. https://www.semanticscholar.org/paper/766f2fa099eef97018168af819b5ac320e619547 (accessed on 16th September 2025).
19. Saad, A., & Mostafa, K. (2024). Optimizing decentralized systems with multimodal AI: Advanced strategies for enhancing performance, scalability, and real-time decision-making in distributed architectures. https://core.ac.uk/download/620852566.pdf (accessed on 16th September 2025).

CHAPTER 9

INTEGRATION WITH CLOUD AND LEGACY SYSTEMS

Contents

INTRODUCTION

The arrival of cloud computing has revolutionized organizational data management and application deployment processes. In the background of the current digital transformation, the union of cloud and legacy systems has emerged as a realm of greatest significance for organizations looking to induce operational efficiency and maintain competitive advantage. This convergence allows companies to leverage the cloud's scalability and flexibility while maintaining the comfort of their current legacy systems, which can store valuable data and functionality. While companies navigate these waters, a smooth integration method becomes inevitable in order to maximize the benefits of each environment, enhance productivity, and unlock new opportunities for innovation and growth. Awareness of problems related to integration with current systems is essential to practical implementation. Organizations could encounter problems in data silos, compatibility, and the need for massive retraining of personnel familiar only with traditional infrastructures. Furthermore, issues of security and compliance could also pose challenges towards integration since sensitive data must be handled carefully in order to comply with regulatory needs during migration to the cloud. To address these, firms can adopt end-to-end approaches through the utilization of middleware products to bridge the interoperability gap between systems and APIs to enable more smooth data exchange. These approaches not only facilitate interoperability but also allow firms to phase out legacy programs step by step with no interference with current operations. Moreover, the relevance of this integration extends beyond business activities; it can greatly impact business process sustainability. Industry 4.0 technologies that are speeding up their emergence further underscore the importance of cloud-legacy integration because they enable organizations to utilize data analytics and real-time processing in making decisions that support sustainability goals. By balancing smart processes and legacy systems, organizations can achieve maximum use of resources, reduce waste, and achieve environmental compliance more effectively. They thus have the potential to propel more ambitious sustainability objectives, with organizations leveraging technological innovations not only for profit but to make social and environmental responsibility, assisted by suggestions such as those of the United Nations Sustainable Development Goals (Harris et al., 2020; Bai et al., 2020).

Definition of Cloud Systems

Cloud systems are a paradigm shift in data storage, processing, and management that relies on the use of the internet as a medium for the provisioning of resources on-demand. In broad terms, cloud systems enable the sharing of computing resources—servers, storage, databases, networking, software, and analytics—within the cloud, and anyone can access them anywhere. This paradigm shift transfers the burden of managing infrastructure away from individual organizations and onto expert service providers. The inherent scalability of cloud infrastructure ensures that organizations can scale their usage of resources on-demand, coupling costs to usage. Consequently, companies are able to achieve significant levels of enhancement in operational efficiency and flexibility and therefore identify cloud systems as an intrinsic building block in contemporary IT solutions which aspire to offer integrations with current legacy systems as well as support future technological innovations. Moreover, cloud infrastructures are characterized by their multi-tenancy model, in which several customers can be installed on a given set of computational resources in secure and efficient fashion.

Figure 9.1. Cloud systems represent a transformative approach to data storage, processing, and management.

Source: https://external-content.duckduckgo.com/iu/?u=https%3A%2F%2Fwww.logosglobaltech.com%2Fwp-content%2Fuploads%2F2020%2F09%2FItem-13_iStock-1137011043-scaled.jpg&f=1&nofb=1&ipt=567d0a1b55456217030087b390b8bcbeb42a3463f59b13083618512d2ce9017c.

This model reduces the waste of resources and optimizes performance through load balancing and resource pooling. In the combination of cloud functionality with legacy systems that may not be built to handle such efficiencies, understanding the implication of multi-tenancy is crucial where organizations go for cloud solutions. In addition, security is also a critical concern during times of transitioning to cloud environments. Implementing sophisticated encryption techniques and access controls can mitigate the risks of data breaches and misuse. This emphasis on effective, scalable, and secure use of resources causes organizations to consider their operating models in a different way, ensuring that legacy systems adapt or can integrate effectively with cloud-based architectures. The convergence of cloud infrastructure with legacy technology means there are also special challenges and opportunities for organizations engaged in optimizing their IT environments. For instance, cloud-based integration can provide enhanced data analytics, so that organizations can derive actionable insight not available from the traditional legacy environment alone. But as documented in studies, providing traceability and safety between combined systems demands strict systems engineering solutions for both cloud and legacy components. By embracing formal models describing the interaction between heterogeneous systems, organizations can better manage complexities such as emergent behavior and data interoperability. Therefore, successful integration requires a strategy framework that, in addition to meeting legacy constraints, capitalizes on cloud advantages and, thereby, improves overall functional capability and propels organizations forward for long-term growth and innovation (Jackson et al., 2008; et al., 2019) (Figure 9.1).

Definition of Legacy Systems

Legacy systems are outdated computer systems or programs which still exist because they perform important functions well although they are less technologically capable than modern systems. Legacy systems usually get embedded into organizational processes so replacing or upgrading them poses a risk to affect operations. Their design usually includes older programming languages, hardware, and database technologies which can be unsupported by vendors. This complexity presents special integration challenges with modern cloud offerings, which stress flexibility and agility. To remain competitive in the international marketplace, the complexities of legacy systems must be understood in making informed technology adoption decisions as well as digital transformation strategies. Imperfect as they may be, legacy systems hold valuable business logic and data that businesses rely on day in and day out. Transition from these systems towards cloud-based systems has to be done with utmost care that usually involves determining the effects of integration and migration. There can be a selection of a hybrid solution where the old and new systems can exist side by side for a while as a risk-aversion measure for outright replacement of the systems. The process can also be complicated further by current security stances and compliance mandates, which can have additional resource and expertise needs. It is pertinent to observe the manner in which these complicate the overall enterprise architecture and design of information systems as the companies attempt to leverage modern technologies despite having the constraint posed by their legacy infrastructure. The integration of cloud technologies with legacy systems calls for an intimate knowledge of both operating models. Since enterprises are increasingly looking for innovative application of emerging technologies to achieve competitive advantage, consolidation of legacy applications and cloud can result in increased efficiency and innovation (Mehnen et al., 2013). For example, technologies such as Software Defined Networking (SDN) and Network Function Virtualization (NFV) have had the ability to mitigate some of the complexity brought about by aging systems by providing dynamic management capabilities that did not exist within traditional legacy infrastructures (Aghvami et al., 2018). But integration is not without its hassles; organizations must contend with data compatibility issues, user training, and the constant need for flawless system performance. These issues underscore the complexity of legacy systems in a world where business survival hinges on agility and transformation (Figure 9.2).

Figure 9.2. Legacy systems.

Source: https://acropolium.com/img/articles/what-are-legacy-systems/img01.jpg.

Importance of Integration in Modern IT Environments

With present IT systems, integration of legacy systems with the cloud is very crucial in order to boost operational efficiency and data accessibility. Organizations are hindered with numerous technological platforms with varied objectives in various departments. Without any integration, the systems are isolated and ultimately affect cooperation and cause delay in decision-making. An integrated strategy not only makes data sharing in real time between platforms easier but also provides for leverage on existing resources as they move to the latest cloud solutions. An example can be seen in energy management in schools, where open-source solutions combined with proprietary systems enable institutions to measure and control energy efficiency efficiently across buildings (Akrivopoulos et al., 2017). These initiatives are a classic example of integration as a means of driving innovation and sustainability in today's IT environments. Additionally, integration of cloud and legacy systems is necessary to cater to evolving end-user needs, especially in sectors such as education and healthcare. With advancing technology, user expectations of students, caregivers, or patients evolve towards more intuitive without altering already-entrenched habits.

Older users will only accept new technologies if the systems are designed to be unobtrusive and intuitive. By being embedded in existing formats, like health monitoring and family communication, elder care systems can provide critical services and enable their adoption (Chatzigiannakis et al., 2017). Therefore, creating an integration-focused culture not only improves user experiences but also aligns technology innovation with user needs, emphasizing the importance of prudent integration. Lastly, the intricacy of today's IT environment requires strategic emphasis on integration to fuel innovation as well as reduce risks linked with technological fragmentation. As organizations adopt a hybrid IT infrastructure model—combining varied cloud-based resources with traditional systems—new concerns arise, such as security risks and data integrity issues. An integrated approach enables organizations to establish robust architectures that can secure sensitive information and facilitate operational agility. For example, imposing a uniform data protocol across systems allows for integrity of data to be upheld and adherence to regulations. This double emphasis on innovation and security reflects the pivotal position of integration in coping with the realities of the IT environments of today, further consolidating the argument that successful integration plans are key to organizational survival and growth.

9.1. BENEFITS OF CLOUD INTEGRATION

The transformation toward cloud integration provides ample benefits that can potentially make organizations' operating efficiency affluent too. Cloud technology provides the opportunity for organizations to achieve enhanced resource management, which allows for more effective allocation and utilization of IT resources. One of the major strengths is the possibility of smooth data migration from legacy environments to cloud environments, which allows for more flexibility in addressing business needs. This dynamic scalability enables firms to expand or contract resources in proportion to existing demand, thus minimizing operating costs. As firms grow and become established, this flexibility is crucial to competitiveness in a dynamically changing world. Further, integration can de-risk the risks of data silos, such that information flows freely throughout the firm and enhances collaboration between departments and teams. Additionally, cloud integration facilitates enhanced security and compliance with data, which are crucial elements for modern organizations. With the application of cloud services, business firms can utilize advanced security features that are not available to typical legacy systems. Cloud service providers spend a great deal of money investing in cutting-edge security technologies that are capable of safeguarding sensitive information from cyber threats in response to regulatory requirements. Besides, cloud allows for centralized management of security policies such that organizations are able to monitor and control data in a more efficient manner. Such an integrated security strategy not only protects against unauthorized access but also assists in enabling regulatory compliance and industry standards. Emphasizing the significance of cloud installations, businesses can leverage continuous integration and continuous deployment (CI/CD) practices in such a way that they can implement security more into their process, building a security-first culture into their operating system. Cloud integration provides the flexibility to enhance innovation and operating flexibility as well. Using a cloud-based model, organizations can prototype and launch new applications in a very short time, thereby compressing their time-to-market. This capacity to innovate rapidly enables companies to remain ahead of the competition in a continuously changing environment, where technological progress can determine leadership in the marketplace. In addition, tools such as EbbRT demonstrate the synergetic interaction between legacy systems and cloud applications through the ability to develop applications that take advantage of the scalability and elasticity of cloud platforms. EbbRTs approach highlights the manner in which integration of domain-specific application-specific software with cloud functionality empowers organizations to enhance core capabilities while optimizing developer productivity. With organizations still driving the dividends of digital transformation, integration through the cloud emerges as a prime innovator and strategic enabler, shaping the future of operational success in a networked world (Aghvami et al., 2018; Appavoo et al., 2015) (Figure 9.3).

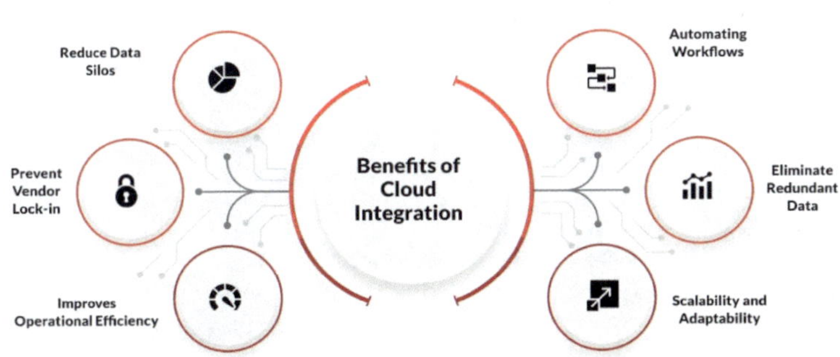

Figure 9.3. Benefits of cloud integration.

Source: https://i2.wp.com/apptread.com/wp-content/uploads/2022/06/Benefits-of-CLoud-Integration.jpg.

9.1.1. Scalability and Flexibility

The interfacing of cloud technologies with legacy systems points to the critical need for scalability and flexibility in organizational infrastructures. As more businesses transition to cloud environments, there is a greater need to modify resources dynamically. Scalability ensures that systems can support growth, whether in terms of handling larger amounts of data or serving more concurrent users without a reduction in performance. This is particularly relevant in contexts such as Software Defined Networking (SDN) and Network Function Virtualization (NFV), in which companies need to transform their radio access networks. Migrating to a full SDN-based RAN is particular about the scalability issues, as most companies still grapple with legacy infrastructure alongside emerging technologies. Therefore, organizations must consider not only technically but also strategically how to align legacy solutions with scalable cloud solutions (Aghvami et al., 2018). In addition, the fluidity of cloud environments allows organizations to adapt well to changing demands and shifts in operations. By leveraging hybrid solutions, firms can leverage the consistent performance of on-premise infrastructure for predictable workload and the elasticity of cloud resources for peak usage. This dual-pronged approach is the most vivid example of the intrinsic flexibility cloud solutions offer, allowing organizations to optimally control cost and resource allocation. High Performance Computing (HPC) clouds, for instance, are a quickly developing trend in this arena, which facilitates the execution of computationally demanding applications and offloading the performance load from internal clusters. These models give a variable technology stack where organizations can transform and reallocate resources as needed, enhancing overall efficiency and responsiveness of operations (Buyya et al., 2018) (Figure 9.4).

Figure 9.4. Scalability and flexibility of cloud integration.

Source: https://solutiondots.com/wp-content/uploads/2018/03/Cloud-Scalability-and-Flexibility.jpg.

The convergence of flexibility and scalability in legacy and cloud integration systems not only determines the operational dynamics but also holds critical competitive advantages. Companies that can leverage this synergy are more likely to innovate, as their IT infrastructures can accommodate new applications and services without significant refits. Also, with the changing business landscape in terms of the increasing age of big data and artificial intelligence, companies need flexible and scalable systems to propel growth and productivity. By investments in bringing cloud capabilities into place in current systems, organizations can ensure agility and competitiveness while capitalizing on future trends. Lastly, realizing solutions to the scalability and flexibility challenges will define the fate of companies in navigating the intricate landscape of today's digital transformation (Buyya et al., 2018).

9.1.2. Cost-Effectiveness

Cloud and legacy systems convergence offers companies a means to enhance cost-effectiveness without compromising operational efficiency. Legacy systems tend to utilize a lot of money in maintenance expenses and are supported by constant investment in hardware and software upgrades. Utilizing cloud technology, companies can eliminate some of these expenses because cloud providers offer infrastructure maintenance as well as scalable resources according to organizational needs. Furthermore, the pay-as-you-go aspect of cloud service pricing helps businesses reduce the cost outlays by paying only for what they use, benefiting the most businesses that have changing demands. This shift will ultimately lead to a reduced total cost of ownership since businesses can direct financial resources toward innovation and growth rather than system maintenance. Also, cloud integration gives the access to cutting-edge technology not present in legacy infrastructure and, therefore, enhances the competitive edge of a company. An example is the adoption of cloud testing tools in a hybrid setup that can immensely ease the development of applications, improving quality and time-to-market with cost management. As indicated, cloud testing reduces the need for significant capital expenditure on expertise-based hardware and software through providing on-demand resources as a service. This flexibility, aside from cost savings, also establishes a more vibrant development culture that can respond to changes in market dynamics. Through the use of cloud testing capabilities, business organizations can achieve more efficient development cycles and enhance their service capacity at low costs without the high cost of experiencing prolonged testing infrastructure (Lněnička et al., 2013). Finally, the combination of cloud technology with conventional systems has the ability to address particular solutions for challenges in heritage and historical data management with other cost-reduction measures. Examples, such as the application of Building Information Modeling in Durham Cathedral, show that the need for tailored information requirements for management of heritage assets can lead to improved efficiency and lowered operational complexities. This does not only facilitate improved asset management but also complies with existing data practices, allowing organizations to maintain historic integrity while benefiting from new technologies. By the acknowledgment of these special requirements and bringing them together into a single cost-effective strategy, organizations can successfully overcome cloud solution convergence with legacy challenges, with the resulting effect being an enhanced sustainable and economically efficient operational model (Charlton et al., 2020).

9.1.3. Enhanced Collaboration and Accessibility

The transition to cloud-based systems has been the driving force behind substantive improvements in collaboration across various domains, particularly education. By utilizing cloud technology, institutions facilitate real-time communication and collaborative work among students, teaching staff, and administrators. Integration not only facilitates easy sharing of resources but also enhances the ability to work collaboratively on projects in spite of distance. In this context, enriched publications, as defined in Hochstenbach et al. (2008), thrive due to interoperability standards managed by cloud systems. These models enable individuals to access and provide input into shared digital repositories seamlessly, thereby ensuring a platform conducive to innovative scholarly work and collaborative scholarly interactions. Accessibility, as an integral feature of contemporary digital trends, has transformed the way individuals engage with learning material and collaborative resources. Cloud-based systems offer varied points of entry, ensuring availability for users of different abilities. Inclusive design principles embedded in these systems are likely to accommodate broad sets of learners, providing equal access to information and shared space. For instance, initiatives outlined in Alevizou et al. (2010) demonstrate use of Web 2.0 tools to facilitate sharing and discussion between teachers, prioritizing ease of use and function. Such innovations underscore the importance of accessible technology in ensuring equity in opportunities for participation, consequently improving the collaborative process and broadening the access horizon of education. In addition, successful integration of cloud and legacy systems assists in extending institutional flexibility, further entrenching collaboration and accessibility. This integration assists in maintaining existing legacy infrastructures while embracing flexibility provided by cloud environments. Thus, institutions can revise their workflows without forfeiting valuable information or functions embedded in legacy systems. Such flexibility in such integrations provides an open forum where different teams can share ideas and best practices freely. Case studies referenced in Hochstenbach et al. (2008) illustrate how such synergy has created new academic spaces to work with, whereby the promise of further collaborations through a shared interest towards fusion of both innovative and conventional systems in academic environments is strengthened.

9.2. CHALLENGES OF LEGACY SYSTEMS

The integration of cloud computing and legacy systems also presents numerous challenges that can hinder organizational innovation and efficiency. With a desire to remain competitive in the dynamic technological landscape, businesses find themselves managing legacy infrastructure that is incapable of accommodating new applications and processes. Legacy systems are typically not scalable to address new cloud environments, hence restraining organizations from fully leveraging the benefits of cloud services. This inflexibility not only complicates system connectivity but also increases the cost of doing business since companies must maintain both new and old solutions simultaneously. Therefore, lack of smooth migration to cloud architecture is a major barrier to technology innovation and business responsiveness. The other major characteristic of legacy systems is their embedded security vulnerabilities that would potentially be aggravated through integration with cloud offerings. The majority of legacy systems were created without modern security controls in effect, which left them vulnerable to various forms of cyber-attacks. As companies attempt to combine these outdated systems with new cloud environments, they inadvertently put themselves at risk. Mixing vintage and new technologies has the potential to create security vulnerabilities that can be exploited by hackers to access a network. In addition, network softwarization, although promising in terms of efficiency and manageability, improves these vulnerabilities because older systems may not be able to support advanced security mechanisms (Aghvami et al., 2018). It is thus crucial for organizations in their quest to protect their data and offer regulatory compliance to cover the security challenge of legacy systems. Cloud technology implementation also necessitates reworking existing business processes that have been built upon legacy systems. As many businesses find, their models of operation are founded on past practices that are not synergistic with the agile development practices encouraged by cloud computing. This lack of synergy may lead to inefficiencies that hamper digital transformation efforts and prevent organizations from being capable of realizing the full potential of cloud integration. Moreover, as companies shift towards new production paradigms, such as Cloud Manufacturing, they have to encounter the hurdle of adapting their existing systems to these newer network technologies (Mehnen et al., 2013). Failure to tackle these challenges not only lags the implementation of more efficient systems but also compromises the competitive edge of an organization in the global market. Thus, organizations need to design end-to-end strategies to converge legacy environments with their business process modernization initiatives to make the shift to cloud more seamless (Figure 9.5).

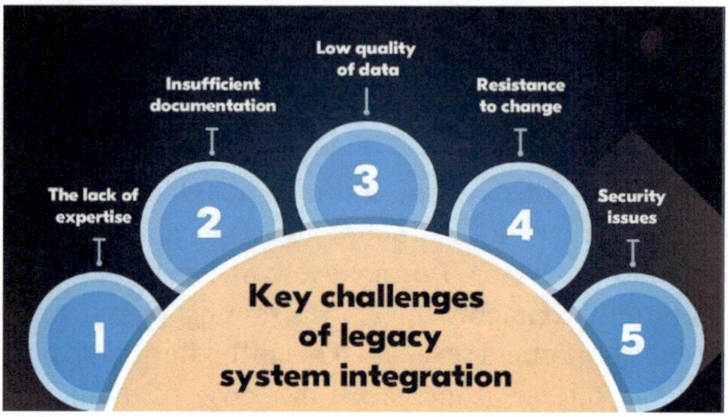

Figure 9.5. Key challenges of legacy system integration.

Source: https://acropolium.com/blog/legacy-systems-integration/

9.2.1. Technical Limitations

Cloud system integration with the legacies requires a vast array of technical limitations that have to be addressed by organizations. One of the most significant challenges is created by the native incompatibility between next-generation cloud solutions and legacy, as the latter work on diverse protocols, architectures, and data formats. It can result in inefficient data transfer protocols, and as a result, latency and reduced performance. While technologies such as Software Defined Networking (SDN) are capable of providing new kinds of solutions, these are unlikely to be extendable to all the various legacy environments. What the current situation suggests is that rather than having a fully integrated SDN-enabled radio access network (RAN), corporations will ultimately be installing piecemeal solutions that are not holistic in scope when addressing the broader integration problems (Aghvami et al., 2018) (Figure 9.6).

Thus, organizations are grappling with limitations by not merely technology but by the need for common strategies encompassing both systems. Yet another major technical limitation is legacy application scalability in the hybrid cloud paradigm. Hybrid clouds have been constructed to take advantage of the best of on-premise infrastructure and cloud platforms so that organizations can efficiently manage workloads. Legacy applications, however, were typically built without scalability in consideration, thus leading to performance challenges under full loads. It may be challenging for businesses to relocate resource-intensive programs from on-premises data centers to scalable public clouds without sacrificing performance (Buyya et al., 2018). Furthermore, the variability of resources available across diverse environments makes real-time data processing and analysis difficult, particularly for operations that require sustained levels of high-performance computing. With the increase in this legacy versus new systems technology gap, the need to bridge these limitations becomes increasingly evident. Finally, security risks are a significant technical limitation in legacy and cloud system integration. As businesses transition to cloud infrastructures, the threat of cyberattacks enters the picture when legacy systems are in use that may not have been updated to current security standards. The transition to cloud services can set the stage for legacy software to become susceptible to new avenues of attack, especially when dealing with sensitive data. That sits atop the need for compatibility across different security measures that can create holes in defenses. For instance, when an organization migrates to a cloud environment, it may require the reevaluation of access controls and data protection mechanisms that inadvertently lead to more exposure during migration (Aghvami et al., 2018). Therefore, organizations must concentrate on establishing robust security frameworks that can bridge these gaps effectively between legacy and cloud environments while ensuring data integrity and compliance in a constantly evolving digital landscape.

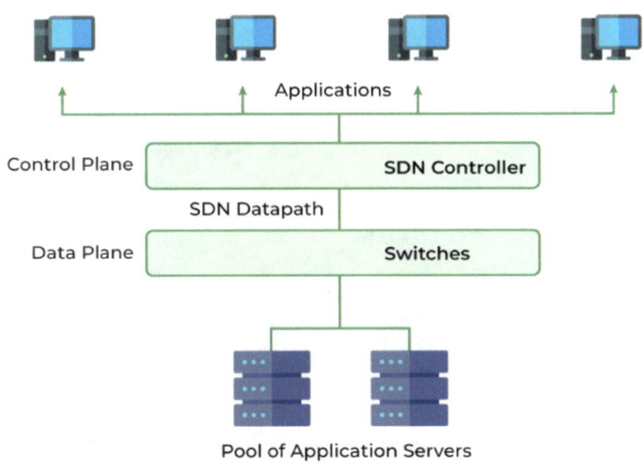

Figure 9.6. Software defined networking (SDN).

Source: https://media.geeksforgeeks.org/wp-content/uploads/20230405132159/Software-Defined-Networking.png.

9.2.2. High Maintenance Costs

High maintenance costs are the greatest challenge to cloud and legacy system integration. When companies transition to modernize their IT systems, they typically experience the financial burden of sustaining older technologies. Legacy systems, while functional, require constant maintenance, patching, and monitoring so that they function at their peak performance levels. These ongoing costs not only strain budgets but also divert resources that can otherwise be used for innovation and strategic initiatives. Moreover, the complexity of integrating these ancient systems to newer cloud-based alternatives makes maintenance even more expensive since specialized skills may be needed to ensure both systems are run and maintained well. Such a dichotomy can lead to inefficiencies and added costs, which highlight the need for an organization to adopt a holistic approach towards IT management that addresses legacy system maintenance as much as cloud integration. Migration to cloud platforms has the potential to bring down the cost of operations through increased efficiencies and flexibility; however, hidden high maintenance costs have a tendency to emerge once this migration occurs (Figure 9.7).

Figure 9.7. High maintenance costs present a significant challenge in the integration of cloud and legacy systems.

Source: https://www.cloud-kinetics.com/wp-content/uploads/2023/06/Enterprise-Cloud-Cost-Management-6-Steps-To.jpg.

Companies may also first underestimate the total cost of ownership of cloud integration, particularly with legacy systems that will not readily fit into new ones. Special accommodations, such as the use of middleware or custom APIs, are commonly required to provide interoperability between legacy and cloud applications. Accommodations not only incur additional costs but also create an increased operations footprint, thereby further complicating maintenance. Here, a thorough cost-benefit analysis becomes important before embarking on any large-scale integration efforts since it allows organizations to make strategic decisions with respect to future maintenance-related costs and align them with long-term objectives. Additionally, to preclude unimaginably high maintenance expenditure during integrating legacy and cloud-based systems, organizations must analyze the potential of adding innovative frameworks for ensuring performance and maintainability enhancement. For instance, application-specific operating system progress over the years, including EbbRT, show how specialized solutions can incrementally contribute to efficiency and reduce overhead. EbbRT allows programmers to build specialized library operating systems for distinct workloads, thus making it easier to maintain and enhancing the system overall. Organizations can achieve substantial latencies and resource reductions using these types of frameworks. Such a culture not only reduces the burdens of some of the legacies but also fosters a responsive and adaptive IT culture conducive to continuous improvement and cost savings. As firms navigate the complexity of system integration, focus on state-of-the-art solutions will become key to alleviating the consequences of runaway maintenance expenses (Casey et al., 2025; Appavoo et al., 2016).

9.2.3. Security Vulnerabilities

The converging of legacy infrastructure and cloud systems introduces critical security threats that need to be handled with caution. When organizations transition their infrastructures into the cloud, security measures applied in legacy systems prove ineffective. SDN and NFV, for instance, introduce complexities that will likely create unforeseen vulnerabilities, particularly in data flow through interdependent networks. While such technologies promise increased management and operational efficiencies, they also expose new attack surfaces under which adversaries can attack. The most urgent issue here is that security controls catch up with such developments by laying emphasis on the defusing of risks involved with legacy frameworks and adding robust, adaptive security features in moving from them (Aghvami et al., 2018). Along with this, cloud deployment of services is dealing with massive amounts of sensitive data dispersed across numerous systems, which poses additional security challenges. Not only does a data breach in cloud infrastructures compromise organizational integrity, but it also puts customer information at risk. While organizations onboard existing infrastructure that lacks the newest security elements that new cloud infrastructures possess, there is more possibility of exploitation. Solutions like OpenStack, offering an attractive platform for cloud integration due to the fact that they are open source and adaptable, may also pose vulnerabilities unless secured appropriately. For instance, putting a multi-node cloud infrastructure such as BradStack into productive use without thorough penetration testing leaves security vulnerabilities that are easily found and exploited by attackers, hence necessitating thorough evaluation of all the components used in the integration process (Al-Shaidy et al., 2017). Lastly, remediation of security vulnerabilities requires organizations to approach the management and evaluation of risk in an integral manner. This involves not only investing in the newest security technology but also a security-aware culture among employees who work with these systems. Security training needs to be provided in identifying potential threats and what their consequences are for cloud and legacy systems. Organizations also need to remain conscious of the evolving landscape of cybersecurity threats and adapt their strategy accordingly. The complexity of merging heterogeneous systems underscores the importance of regular collaboration between decision-makers, security professionals, and IT to develop effective procedures and policies that work in the best interest of security without stifling innovation. Failure to do so might result in huge reputational damage and business interruptions (Al-Shaidy et al., 2017).

9.3. CASE STUDIES OF SUCCESSFUL INTEGRATION

The convergence of cloud solutions with traditional systems has yielded a number of case studies highlighting successful migrations that fuel operational efficiency and innovation. A prime example is a top financial institution facing issues with its aged mainframe systems. In order to remain competitive and gain access to up-to-date analytics tools, the organization embraced a hybrid cloud system to allow its legacy systems to exist side by side with cloud applications. This strategy enabled the bank to phase out critical applications and data without much disruption. With the adoption of software-defined networking (SDN) principles, as clearly elaborated in Aghvami et al. (2018), the business achieved improved data flow and reduced latency, which eventually resulted in improved customer service. The project also emphasized the importance of thorough planning and stakeholder engagement to facilitate migration with minimum hitch and associated risk of legacy integration. The second fascinating case study comes from a major healthcare provider that sought to improve interoperability across its various departments, with each department working with dissimilar legacy systems. With the need to access patient records in real time and newest medical data, the company implemented an integration platform in the cloud. The platform allowed disparate legacy applications to communicate productively with each other while providing a unified repository for data analytics. The consolidation added operational efficiency as well as patient care through the ability to access critical medical information immediately. The project success demonstrated strategic benefits of using cloud technology in filling the existing system gaps, which equated to cooperative tenets of SDN and network function virtualization as quoted in Aghvami et al. (2018). Lastly, a global manufacturing company proved the advantage of cloud and legacy system integration by transforming its supply chain management. The company began with a group of isolated legacy systems that were stifling efficiency as well as visibility of data. With the help of cloud-based platforms for real-time tracking and analytics, the company consolidated its supply chain operations into a single platform. This shift not only made processes effective but also provided flexibility in accommodating market requirements. Greater visibility into the operations allowed for greater decision-making leading to cost reduction and effective utilization of resources. This case study highlights how strategic integration, enabled by robust technologies as outlined in, can lead to staggering competitiveness and operational sustainability enhancements.

9.3.1. Example of a Financial Institution

Banks and financial institutions have discovered increasingly cloud computing solutions to raise their operational productivity and responsiveness in an increasingly evolving scenario. An instance is a worldwide bank that has successfully merged its legacy systems with cloud services. The bank discovered the imperative of modernization in order to remain competitive and opted for a hybrid cloud strategy. With the cloud facilities, the bank achieved easy scalability, reduced operational costs, and increased data accessibility for customers and workers. However, the challenge of integrating new cloud offerings with existing legacy systems, characterized by outdated technologies, had to be strategized and implemented. Ultimately, such integration enabled the organization to leverage sophisticated analytics and customer relationship management applications, significantly enhancing its customer satisfaction and service levels. Despite the advantages, financial institutions face numerous challenges when integrating cloud solutions and legacy systems. The complexities in legacy infrastructures usually equate to enormous compatibility issues and increased security threats. For example, traditional banking applications may not seamlessly interact with modern cloud-based platforms, with extensive customizations and middleware solutions. In addition to that, regulation and compliance requirements provide yet another layer of complexities, requiring institutions to take on strict security measures and data management. According to research, cloud deployments have become a critical component for institutions seeking to incorporate cutting-edge technologies alongside compliance with industry standards (Al-Shaidy et al., 2017). As banks and other financial institutions are in this hard work, the emphasis on creating a successful and secure integration plan gets more in focus. The development of cloud manufacturing teaches valuable lessons that can be extended to these financial institutions in the same process. The shift towards services-oriented models of manufacturing, enabled by technology innovations in the form of cloud computing, is an indication of the challenges banks face when attempting to innovate service delivery. Through it, there is increased collaboration, savings, and efficiency in productivity for stakeholders (Mehnen et al., 2013). As finance institutions adopt cloud manufacturing models, they tend more and more to use end-to-end solutions for consolidating disparate systems, automating workflows, and answering customer needs more effectively. The successful integration of cloud and legacy systems not only propels finance institutions towards enhanced functional competences but also positions them in a competitive space in the rapidly moving digital space.

9.3.2. Example of a Healthcare Provider

Healthcare professionals are significantly affected by the union of legacy and cloud environments, with far-reaching effects on patient care and operating effectiveness. For instance, a healthcare professional who employs cloud-based clinical applications, such as Software as a Service (SaaS), reduces clinical workflow significantly. By maintaining electronic health records (EHRs) in a cloud environment, providers can exchange patient information instantly from various locations, improving healthcare team collaboration. As noted, growing popularity of cloud computing options has prompted different institutions to explore their potential uses and adaptability for the health sector (Mangiuc, 2025). The trend not only supports timely decision-making but also supports reducing operational costs through a limitation in the requirement of massive on-site infrastructure. Furthermore, the creation of a patient-driven model, specifically through the development of Personal Health Records (PHRs), addresses another component of this integration. Patients are empowered by healthcare professionals by providing access to medical information directly to the patient and thereby allowing more control within their own care procedure. MyPHRMachines are a new model that allows patients to take control of their records via a cloud-based model centered on interoperability (Comuzzi et al., 2012) (Figure 9.8).

This model allows patients to share records with healthcare providers easily without compromising data privacy or security. Therefore, this integration not only enhances the patient experience but also allows providers to deliver personalized care based on complete health information. Lastly, the combination of cloud technologies and legacy systems can also be viewed from the aspect of advanced data analysis and predictive modeling in healthcare. By the integration of legacy EHR systems with advanced cloud-based analytics solutions, clinicians are able to draw on vast reservoirs of data in order to identify patterns and guide clinical care. This can have the potential to revolutionize population health management by enabling proactive methods for anticipating disease outbreaks or enhancing chronic care management. To this end, the creation of cloud-based solutions is a response to the necessity for healthcare providers to catch up with changing paradigms in technology to ensure they are competitive and patient-focused in the context of an increasingly digitalized world. The ongoing innovation in this respect is a revolutionary chance for an increase in healthcare delivery.

Figure 9.8. Cloud and legacy systems in electronic health records (EHRs) and personal health records (PHRs).

Source: https://www.ayamahealth.com/blog/wp-content/uploads/2024/02/Nov-blog.png.

9.3.3. Example of a Retail Company

In the current retail context, companies are confronted more and more with the challenge of integrating cloud technology with historical systems. An example case in point is that of the well-known retailing behemoth Target, which has made significant strides in adopting cloud solutions to enhance efficiency in operations. Target previously had relied on a large portfolio of historical systems that helped its supply chain as well as stock management. But growing the demand for real-time processing of data and logistics effectiveness resulted in a change strategy with a heading of cloud integration. Besides streamlining its operations, such a transition allowed Target to introduce a modular architecture that boosts flexibility and allows for innovation, aligning with the findings outlined in Bonina et al. (2014). Such updates become critical for retail companies to achieve competitiveness in an ongoingly changing marketplace. Also, the shift to cloud architecture brings into focus the need for a robust partner ecosystem that moves beyond core strengths. Initially, several retailers, such as Target, opted to leverage vertically integrated solutions, which suppressed responsiveness and adaptability to changing market forces. However, when market dynamics changed, it became apparent that building on core capabilities while enabling feasible collaboration with third-party partners fostered a more responsive strategy (Aulkemeier et al., 2015). Through the implementation of a service-oriented architecture, Target has been able to integrate various software solutions and applications to enhance customer experience, enhance logistics, and optimize inventory management. This collaborative approach allowed the company to achieve flexibility and responsiveness to customers' needs, a best example of the potential benefits from re-engineering retail operations through cloud and legacy system integration. Although finally integrating cloud and legacy systems is not free of challenges, particularly in relation to data interoperability and security, for a company such as Target's, uniform integration among dissimilar information systems is paramount. Moving to a cloud environment means overcoming barriers related to legacy system constraints while maintaining secure customer information. Cloud technologies offer advanced data management and analytics features, which are crucial to ensure compliance as well as win customer trust. As discussed in Bonina et al. (2014) and Aulkemeier et al. (2015), successful adoption of cloud solutions is capable of helping a retailer overcome complex operations problems and drive overall business performance. Hence, ongoing innovation and integration of cloud services with legacy systems are prime drivers that will form the cornerstone of retail business success in the future.

9.4. BEST PRACTICES FOR CLOUD AND LEGACY SYSTEM INTEGRATION

Incorporation of legacy systems with cloud services is a daunting exercise for organizations in the current technology environment. Although organizations continue to move in the direction of embracing cloud-based solutions, one must realize the complications of legacy systems. The best practices in such integration start off with a comprehensive study of current legacy systems and their functionalities. Such an assessment should describe the way in which various components of the legacy system can integrate with cloud solutions in the best possible manner without affecting performance or security. Insights through interviews with HR executives suggest that it is important to assess which processes can be easily transitioned to the cloud while upholding the integrity of legacy functionalities (Collier et al., 2017). Having clear goals and intended results at the onset of integration allows groups to develop specific strategies that enhance functional effectiveness and create organizational adaptability. In addition, creating a robust data management strategy is also essential for integration success. Data silos must be avoided, and data exchange between cloud and traditional environments should be seamless. This includes the implementation of middleware systems capable of translating and mapping data formats between various systems. By using such technologies, organizations can offset compatibility issues and ensure data integrity during integration. HR leaders' insights reveal that decision-making competency across cloud and legacy systems can further be aided through the use of data analytics tools. This integrated approach enables organizations to drive knowledge from diverse data sources, drive innovation, and improve performance as a whole (Collier et al., 2017). In essence, a considered data strategy is the key to unlocking the benefit of cloud as well as legacy infrastructures. In terms other than technicalities, another important best practice of cloud and legacy system integration lies in building the spirit of collaboration among IT teams. It assists in creating constant communication between team members who possess multi-skilled talents and knowledge in areas, thereby enhancing the efficiency of problem-solving. Regular training and workshops will help eliminate the gap in knowledge between the new cloud technologies and introduce legacy system experts to cloud capabilities and vice versa. Moreover, as the IoT ecosystem is growing, service developers are faced with a mixture of connectivity options and communication protocols, complicating integration. A cloud-based platform that is able to accommodate these various devices and protocols has the potential to significantly ease the integration process. With collaboration among teams as the priority and through the use of cutting-edge integration platforms, organizations can optimize their ecosystem for today's as well as tomorrow's technology advancements.

9.4.1. Ensuring Data Consistency

Data consistency is a top concern in cloud and legacy system consolidation. The architectural differences and data management techniques applied by modern cloud-based platforms versus traditional legacy systems can lead to data inconsistency, which significantly jeopardizes the operational efficiency. Data is generally scattered in cloud environments and is therefore vulnerable to synchronization problems to which legacy systems are not typically exposed. Moreover, the static schema of legacy databases can result in inconsistencies in data updates and versions, thereby further complicating reporting and analytics issues. In order to resolve such issues, organizations must adopt good data governance models that enable real-time data validation processes so that these can be integrated seamlessly with minimal errors. One such effective data consistency-fostering approach is to leverage advanced technologies such as ontologies and semantic enrichment frameworks, which have appeared in modern intelligence data consolidation activities. By mapping data from distinct systems into a common semantic framework on a standardized basis, organizations are able to minimize the risk of stovepiping in which different sets of data remain disconnected from one another.

Figure 9.9. Ensuring data consistency is a paramount challenge when integrating cloud and legacy systems.

Source: https://media.licdn.com/dms/image/v2/D4E12AQFS-8F1tuD9cg/article-cover_image-shrink_720_1280/article-cover_image-shrink_720_1280/0/1707680484932?e=2147483647&v=beta&t=1HPkV0WWxjCBM8jBq3HvtfUrnVbJCuNPkL2oHj-p7IM.

This hybrid strategy enhances data interoperability and eases data management on cloud and legacy systems. Specifically, the use of well-defined ontologies can enable contextual understanding that leads to better data cleaning processes and validation checks. As is discussed in the study on the Distributed Common Ground System Standard Cloud (DSC), applying this approach can make information more credible and of better quality to be utilized in life-or-death decision-making (Fu et al., 2012). Besides, consistency in data transcends technical implementations; it must be a cultural necessity for organizations. Training of teams and continuous professional education of data management practices can foster a culture of best practices and awareness of data quality. This change of culture is felt through more coordination among the IT teams and end-users, both of whom must understand the implications of inconsistent data. Organizations can also leverage continuous monitoring and audit processes that identify inconsistencies in advance, allowing for immediate corrective action. Such a proactive strategy is significant in environments with dynamic and multi-faceted data storage, like those in smart grid infrastructures whose integrity for operation relies significantly on safe and trustable communications (Qian et al., 2012). These multi-faceted strategies not only enable organizations to deliver data consistency but also enhance overall system resilience while blending cloud and legacy systems (Figure 9.9).

9.4.2. Implementing Robust Security Measures

The convergence of cloud environments with legacy technology raises critical security concerns that call for the implementation of sound security practices. The revelation of sensitive information in migration from traditional systems to cloud infrastructure is among the primary concerns in the integration. As companies relocate their businesses, threats may originate from legacy systems that may not have modern security features and cloud infrastructure, which, while naturally secure, are still vulnerable to external threats. There needs to be a battle against such threats through a multi-level security framework comprising encryption, access control, and real-time monitoring systems. With the help of these measures, organizations can provide assurance that sensitive information is secure and the possibilities of unauthorized access or data breach are reduced, while allowing the advantages of cloud integration not to be negated by compromised security. Furthermore, the evolution of industrial systems highlights the need for end-to-end security solutions as organizations are moving toward increasingly integrated environments. Industrial control systems were traditionally implemented on air-gapped, stand-alone networks, limiting their exposure to external threats. This trend is slowly reversing as businesses seek to eliminate inefficiencies and enhance communication using Internet of Things (IoT). As pointed out, "the increasing range and scope of these interconnections raise additional security issues" where safety-critical systems are concerned (Evangelopoulou et al., 2017). In order to combat such challenges, laying down robust security measures such as intrusion detection systems, regular security audits, and employee training becomes a necessity. These processes not only safeguard operational technology (OT) but also improve overall organizational resilience against potential cyber-attacks on integration loopholes. In addition, ensuring appropriate data privacy management is a large part of implementing robust security measures in integrated cloud and legacy systems. With educational organizations increasingly leveraging big data to evaluate and enhance operational efficiency, it is crucial to put student privacy on par with system efficiency (Berendt et al., 2017). Ensuring adherence to proper data protection regulations and adopting transparent practices as a core principle of data management can go a long way in minimizing the chances of security breaches. Sound security practice should involve periodic checking of data access policies and user rights to avoid access by unauthorized users. Through the establishment of a security-conscious culture and promotion of ethical use of data, organizations can reconcile utilizing data to realize institutional growth while simultaneously upholding ethical use and ensuring individual rights to privacy online.

9.4.3. Training Staff for New Systems

Successful integration of legacy systems and cloud is based on well-specified training programs for the employees. As organizations move towards newer technologies, the necessity for in-depth training becomes critical. Not only does training recognize the gap between legacy procedures and new cloud applications but also facilitates easier resistance to changes within the employees. Effective training efforts need to be structured to address certain operational needs and need to employ diverse learning methods considering variables like employee learning style and previous technology experience. By equipping employees with the necessary skills and information, organizations can achieve higher user adoption levels, ultimately leading to more productivity and functionality in the organization when new systems are introduced. Moreover, stakeholder engagement is a significant aspect of the training process. Engaging employees in training material development can make the process ownable and confidence-increasing, eliminating anxiety regarding changes in technology. Through learning about insights through interviews with Human Resources executives across various industries, organizations can discover best practices and useful training models. These models can be modified to fit individual business settings so that employees are encouraged to feel confident and comfortable with the new systems. It has been established through studies that firms that focus on such in-depth training methods are likely to achieve smoother transitions and operational outcomes, a phenomenon experienced in different industries (Collier et al., 2017). Big data analytics included in training programs is also likely to have significant benefits. By applying knowledge gained from big data, organizations can optimize their training processes and customize them to suit the changing needs of their employees. For example, data can expose patterns in employee performance, identify areas where skills are lacking, and determine the best training methods for certain teams or positions. Such data-driven approach not only enhances the effectiveness of training but also ensures it to be aligned with the general objective of integrating cloud and legacy systems. With the emphasis on evidence-based policymaking in both educational and organizational environments increasing, the use of big data can help bring about more logical decision-making and better utilization of resources in employee trainings (Berendt et al., 2017).

9.5. FUTURE TRENDS IN INTEGRATION

As more companies embrace cloud technology alongside their existing legacy environments, integration's future is already well on its way to being radically changed. At the center of that revolution are the uses of Software Defined Networking (SDN) and Network Function Virtualization (NFV) as enablers. These technologies have the potential to make it easier to manage network resources, addressing some of the remaining issues concerning integration, particularly in high-efficiency and highly dynamic environments. But the ambitious goal of full integration of SDN-based RAN with 5G capability is faced with great challenges. The likelihood of half-way solutions in this direction, rather than end-to-end one, serves to reinforce the ongoing need for focused research and development on SDN architectures. These innovations will not only simplify interactions between cloud-based and legacy systems but also offset any latency and security challenges associated with the softwarization of networks (Aghvami et al., 2018). The expansion of the Internet of Things (IoT) has far-reaching implications for future integration directions since it emphasizes the need for having harmonized service architectures that can operate across multiple domains. As IoT ecosystems become more complex, there are millions of devices and communication protocols, leaving developers with the task of managing these heterogeneous networks, which is a herculean one. Integration strategies in the future will need to therefore emphasize creating strong platforms that can support many IoT devices seamlessly across varying communication modes. By making use of cloud-based products that have been specifically designed for this purpose, organizations can simplify service development and deployment. This approach, apart from improving efficiency, also accelerates the realization of IoT's full potential, outlining how integration is able to merge disparate systems effectively for improved operating cohesion. Cloud platforms facilitating smooth interactions between resource-constrained IoT devices will surely be on the forefront of this integration trend (Demeester et al., 2015). In the future, the interrelation between legacy systems and emergent cloud technologies will be guiding the paradigm shift in organizational integration. New trends will be more adaptive, elastic solutions that can transform according to changing business requirements and still maintain business continuity. Integration of Artificial Intelligence and Machine Learning with cloud and legacy systems will also be at the forefront, offering predictive analytics that can optimize resource utilization and reduce complexity. This integrated strategy by intelligence enables organizations to leverage data better, drive decision-making, and maximize service delivery. As businesses aspire to build better infrastructures, the convergence of legacy and emerging technologies will not only redefine integration best practices but also lay the ground for next-generation solutions able to cope with the evolving nature of a digital world. Through these advancements, the future of integration promises to be dynamic and indispensable for organizational success (Figure 9.10).

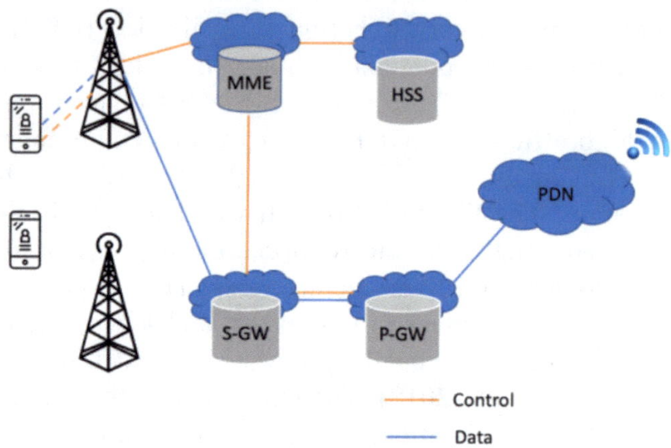

Figure 9.10. Radio access network.

Source: https://ars.els-cdn.com/content/image/1-s2.0-S1084804522001382-gr3.jpg.

9.5.1. Rise of Hybrid Cloud Solutions

The trend of hybrid cloud technology is transforming the enterprise IT environment, providing businesses with a flexible platform to integrate legacy and cloud infrastructure in a seamless manner. With businesses increasingly seeing the limitations of the on-premise model and the growing need to scale, hybrid clouds present themselves as a compelling strategy. This approach enables companies to maintain sensitive workloads on private servers but utilize the elastic capacity of the public cloud for variable needs. The integration thus makes room for rapid data processing and efficiency in operations, which are most crucial in today's fast-paced digital era. In addition, hybrid solutions provide a viable line of transition for those organizations that are hesitant to abandon their legacy systems entirely, thereby enabling a more step-by-step approach to IT modernization and business continuity. As the hybrid cloud idea takes off, its implications are felt far beyond basic operational efficiencies. One of the primary advantages is optimization of resource allocation, whereby firms can react admirably to variable demands without incurring a treasure in doing so. The model enables sensitive workloads to be run on-premises and provides a secure environment through the use of public cloud resources for peak utilization in a pay-as-you-go manner. This capability becomes extremely important for high-performance computing (HPC) environments, where resource-intensive applications are able to leverage hybrid solutions for scientific and business analytics use cases. A proper understanding of how to balance these on-premises and cloud resources is evolving, as businesses seek the best performance out of hybrid configurations while addressing critical considerations such as pricing mechanisms and operating sustainability. Further, the evolution of hybrid cloud solution is fraught with problems to be addressed to realize their full potential. Security threats and regulatory issues remain at the top of corporate agendas with regards to adopting these systems. Specifically, the integration of software-defined networking (SDN) in these infrastructures presents challenges that need robust management processes and mechanisms. As has been reported in recent polls, there is much research that exists around the fluctuating landscape of SDN and its application to refining the radio access network (RAN), as well as questions regarding its further applicability within hybrid architectures. By eliminating these hurdles, organizations are able to create a more efficient, secure, and resilient hybrid cloud infrastructure that can facilitate innovation and respond to heightened demands for IT agility in the growing data-driven world (Aghvami et al., 2018; Buyya et al., 2018) (Figure 9.11).

Figure 9.11. The rise of hybrid cloud.

Source: https://www.telecomreviewasia.com/wp-content/uploads/2023/09/The_Rise_of_Hybrid_Cloud-01.jpg.

9.5.2. Increased use of APIs

The increased use of Application Programming Interfaces (APIs) is the most important feature for cloud and legacy system integration. APIs are middle-layer software that enables different applications, services, and platforms to communicate with each other. When organizations shift to cloud-based solutions, it is mostly a challenge to integrate these services with existing legacy systems. These are augmented by the realization that APIs developed by other clouds are usually proprietary and this makes them hard to integrate. Integration involves comprehension of APIs in question and their roles to a larger degree. This implies that organizations need to invest in training and staff so they can conduct such integrations seamlessly, with the aim of having proper communication among heterogeneous systems. Within the context of the general trend towards a more integrated technological environment, the deliberate use of APIs is a critical element in achieving seamless integration (Abramowicz et al., 2009). Additionally, the development of APIs is a continuous process. The upcoming internet architecture, in particular, Management and Service-aware Networking Architectures (MANA) design, is depicting an unmistakable movement toward the proliferation of interoperable APIs particularly designed for cloud environments.

As indicated by the latest research, the ongoing global efforts aimed at creating a new generation of the internet emphasize the necessity to provide new-generation networking capabilities that sustain extensive ranges of applications and legacy infrastructure. These cloud-based API frameworks are designed to facilitate integration and lower interoperability issues between separate cloud applications. With the use of such developments, organizations can not only streamline their internal processes but also enhance their capacity to handle emerging marketplace demands. The increased use of solid APIs thus directly aligns with current needs as well as future needs in the new IT integration environment (Abramowicz et al., 2009). Last but not least, the increased application of APIs is a revolutionary approach in solving integration issues faced by companies. The quantitative study of 114 companies confirms that as companies shift to cloud-based systems, they face integration issues that, in the majority of cases, lead to the utilization of proprietary APIs. This can result in the situation where companies face "vendor lock-in," limiting their capacity to switch or migrate to alternative systems. Tackling these issues requires a strategic focus on interoperability, and this is why software architects and developers design applications with adaptable, standard APIs. Prioritizing interoperability and standardization allows companies to construct a more agile and responsive architecture that enables maximum efficiency in operations while integrating cloud-legacy systems effortlessly. This kind of strategy ensures that the substantial investments in digital change yield maximum returns and strengthen resilience in the face of rapid technological change (Opara-Martins et al., 2015).

9.5.3. Adoption of Artificial Intelligence in Integration Processes

The integration of artificial intelligence (AI) into existing and cloud systems represents a shift in operational capacity and data handling capability. In pursuit of improving service delivery, AI serves as a facilitator of process automation that was typically fraught with inefficiencies. By applying machine learning algorithms and predictive analytics, organizations not only improve decision-making but also optimize the deployment of resources in their existing infrastructures. Deployment of AI technology into the systems enables adaptive responsiveness to shifting market needs and thus an environment that is more agile. Furthermore, the use of AI tools promotes peaceful coexistence among systems of heritage and newer cloud-based designs that facilitate smooth transition and integration of mutually incompatible technologies in an integrated way. Merging AI into integration processes also involves associated challenges and issues. Organizations will need to battle with the complexity of ensuring compatibility between newer AI solutions and heritage systems that are themselves defined by outdated technologies. This will need a careful review of existing infrastructures to identify where potential integration points and areas for improvement might be required. Moreover, from the security and data privacy point of view, combining AI modules needs an efficient framework for secure management of sensitive information. As theorized within the evolving reality of the Internet of Things (IoT), the networked and dynamic nature of AI products and emerging technologies puts additional requirements on integration without disruption, particularly in the context of problems such as interoperability and data integrity within cloud and legacy worlds (Bacciu et al., 2017). Thus, businesses are going to need to be prepared to invest as much in strategy as technology in order to deal with these challenges. Effective use of AI in integration processes radically alters the company's working landscape. With added analytical capability and automation, companies are better able to react to customers and thus provide competitive advantage. Layered software architecture for interoperability among multiple tools, both new and old, is thus essential to encapsulating this change. This architecture lends itself to real-time data processing and efficient communication between various systems, which eventually leads to a computer-integrated factory system that is suitably aligned with the needs of the market (Consoli, 2025). With AI adoption by companies, there is also the possibility of a flexible and agile structure, so in addition to increased operating efficiency, they can also shift course based on evolving threats and opportunities within the tech industry. Aligning these new frameworks with current business operations has the potential to foster an atmosphere conducive to continued growth and better customer satisfaction.

SUMMARY

The conclusiveness of the essay on Integration of Cloud and Legacy Systems highlights the significance of coordination between contemporary cloud systems and old legacy systems. As organizations strive to optimize operations and enhance delivery of services, integration of both varied environments turns into a vital issue. The complexities introduced by heterogeneous network connectivity options and legacy system communication protocols pose a need for strategic solution accommodating the interoperability and compatibility challenges. Cloud platforms, by virtue of their extremely accommodating nature of being flexible, can bridge these challenges, as evidenced by the ability to offer a consistent environment with various IoT devices and services. Proper integration of these systems is crucial not only for operational efficiency but also for tapping the innovative capabilities of next-generation technology. Of particular importance highlighted in the conclusion is the actual benefit of employing cloud-based solutions in consolidating legacy systems. By bridging the gap between new cloud applications and old infrastructures, organizations can capitalize on enhanced data analytics, scalability, and flexibility. This blend also provides an opportunity for better service deployment, particularly when used in IoT applications where heterogeneous devices have a tendency to be challenges for service developers. The outcomes depicted in this paper validate that cloud platforms do have the ability to simplify greatly the tasks left to service developers, rendering the development process simpler while ensuring robust performance across various applications. These advances are key as businesses strive to maintain competitive advantages in an increasingly digital environment, as the emphasis on innovative solutions for efficient integrations remains high. Finally, studies on cloud and legacy system integration reveal broader implications for the future of technology advancement. With increasing organizations adopting practices like Software Defined Networking (SDN) and Network Function Virtualization (NFV), the process of softwarization comes across as a catalyst for innovations ahead in the management of these integrated setups. The process of transitioning toward a fully SDN environment, particularly with regard to radio access networks, reveals the complexities involved in integrating legacy with the latest technologies. As cloud technology keeps improving, organizations need to be on the watch for potential weaknesses in dealing with this softwarization. Last but not least, a profound understanding of how cloud services are engaged with legacy systems will be essential in order to design solid, adaptive infrastructures capable of responding to the requirements of an ever-evolving technological landscape, as also indicated by the identified gaps in existing research activity (Demeester et al., 2015; Aghvami et al., 2018). The integration of cloud and legacy systems is a key area for organizations to enhance operational efficiency and responsiveness. As more businesses tap into the cloud, it is necessary to comprehend the interactions between the emerging architecture of the cloud and existing legacy systems. Legacy systems have essential data and workflows that, if left unmerged, will create silos and hamper progress. This integration smoothens workflows by enabling legacy systems to leverage cloud resources, hence enabling real-time access to data and enhanced scalability. Organizations are able to benefit from this convergence in order to enhance customer experiences and operational processes, eventually creating a more agile business climate. However, this integration is not without challenge, in the form of data safety issues, system compatibility, and potential disruptions during the course of the transition, which will have to be carefully addressed to make for an effective rollout of hybrid technologies. Additionally, the ethical and practical challenges of integrating cloud technologies with legacy systems are of paramount concern in the digital landscape of today. While businesses leverage sophisticated artificial intelligence technology to automate their cloud operations, they must address the intricacies of automated process risks of bias and disinformation. A study highlights the need for careful research into the use of generative AIs with an admonition against rigorous scrutiny of the training data that supply such devices (Yogesh et al., 2023). Stakeholders must also be vigilant for the privacy and security ramifications of digital transformation. Developing governance frameworks will be key to managing these risks, as unchecked technology can lead to unforeseen consequences. Not only do such measures assist in safeguarding sensitive information, but they assist in promoting trust in the technological infrastructures more and more organizations rely upon in order to attain success in their operations. Finally, greater awareness of the development of the technological ecosystems, particularly regarding the advent of the Metaverse, can provide valuable insight into future integration methodologies. The current iteration of the Metaverse is a revolutionary shift in the way humans interact with virtual spaces, driven by Generation Zs demand for seamless online and offline experiences. With cloud and legacy systems beginning to adopt elements of the Metaverse, companies need to rethink their approach to integrating technology. That includes not only adopting bleeding-edge hardware and software technologies but also reimagining user interaction and application definition (Park et al., 2022). Through these trends, companies can develop immersive spaces that amplify user experiences and tap the full potential of combined legacy and cloud infrastructure. Ultimately, adopting such master strategies will be crucial to organizations hoping to succeed in an increasingly complex digital landscape.

REFERENCES

1. Abramowicz, H., Brunner, M., Chemouil, P., Galis, A., et al. (2009). Management and service-aware networking architectures (MANA) for future Internet position paper: System functions, capabilities and requirements. https://core.ac.uk/download/pdf/11476514.pdf (accessed on 16th September 2025).
2. Aghvami, H., Dohler, M., Fletcher, S., Friderikos, V., et al. (2018). Will SDN be part of 5G? https://core.ac.uk/download/157863188.pdf (accessed on 16th September 2025).
3. Agono, F., Misra, S., & Odun-Ayo, I. (2018). Cloud migration: Issues and developments. https://core.ac.uk/download/157741092.pdf (accessed on 16th September 2025).
4. Akrivopoulos, O., Amaxilatis, D., Chatzigiannakis, I., Mylonas, G., et al. (2017). An IoT-based solution for monitoring a fleet of educational buildings focusing on energy efficiency. https://core.ac.uk/download/158327961.pdf (accessed on 16th September 2025).
5. Alevizou, P., & Conole, G. (2010). A literature review of the use of Web 2.0 tools in higher education.
6. Allen, L. E., Blake, G. A., Boogert, A. C. A., Bourke, T. L., et al. (2003). From molecular cores to planet-forming disks: An SIRTF legacy program. https://core.ac.uk/download/10211246.pdf (accessed on 16th September 2025).
7. Al-Shaidy, A. N. M. K., Kamala, M. A., Kinteh, S., Kiran, M., et al. (2017). Technical report on deploying a highly secured OpenStack cloud infrastructure using BradStack as a case study. http://arxiv.org/abs/1712.09152 (accessed on 16th September 2025).
8. Appavoo, J., Cadden, J., Dong, H., Krieger, O., et al. (2016). EbbRT: A framework for building per-application library operating systems. https://open.bu.edu/bitstream/2144/21780/1/2016-002-ebbrt.pdf (accessed on 16th September 2025).
9. Appavoo, J., Cadden, J., Krieger, O., Schatzberg, U., et al. (2015). EbbRT: Elastic building block runtime–Case studies. https://open.bu.edu/bitstream/2144/21765/1/2015-006-ebbrt-case-studies.pdf (accessed on 16th September 2025).
10. Aulkemeier, F., van Hillegersberg, J., Iacob, M. E., Paramartha, A., et al. (2015). A pluggable service platform architecture for e-commerce. https://core.ac.uk/download/pdf/31155617.pdf (accessed on 16th September 2025).

11. Aurich, J. C., Davis, S., Jacques, J. J., McDonough, W., Piller, F. T., Pine, B. J., & Toffler, A. (2012). Sustainable product development strategies: Business planning and performance implications. https://core.ac.uk/download/20089599.pdf (accessed on 16th September 2025).
12. Bacciu, D., Bahr, R., Bröring, A., Cavallo, F., et al. (2017). Internet of robotic things: Converging sensing/actuating, hypoconnectivity, artificial intelligence and IoT platforms. https://core.ac.uk/download/84045908.pdf (accessed on 16th September 2025).
13. Bai, C., Dallasega, P., Orzes, G., & Sarkis, J. (2020). Industry 4.0 technologies assessment: A sustainability perspective. *International Journal of Production Economics, 229*, 107776. https://doi.org/10.1016/j.ijpe.2020.107776 (accessed on 16th September 2025).
14. Barbosa, J., Cachada, A., Leitão, P., Pires, E. J., et al. (2017). Petri nets approach for designing the migration process towards industrial cyber-physical production systems. https://core.ac.uk/download/153416859.pdf (accessed on 16th September 2025).
15. Barnholtz-Sloan, J. S., Basu, A., Borowsky, A. D., Bui, A., et al. (2020). Cancer informatics for cancer centers (CI4CC): Building a community focused on sharing ideas and best practices to improve cancer care and patient outcomes. https://core.ac.uk/download/288432567.pdf (accessed on 16th September 2025).
16. Berendt, B., Blakemore, M., Kern, P., Littlejohn, A., et al. (2017). Big data for monitoring educational systems. https://core.ac.uk/download/131316813.pdf (accessed on 16th September 2025).
17. Bonina, C. M., Elaluf-Calderwood, S., & Liebenau, J. (2014). Modularity and network integration: Emergent sustainable services in mobile payment systems. https://core.ac.uk/download/35437024.pdf (accessed on 16th September 2025).
18. Buyya, R., Calheiros, R. N., Cunha, R. L. F., Netto, M. A. S., et al. (2018). HPC cloud for scientific and business applications: Taxonomy, vision, and research challenges. http://arxiv.org/abs/1710.08731 (accessed on 16th September 2025).
19. Casey, T., & Enqvist, H. (2025). Mobile communications industry scenarios and strategic implications for network equipment vendors. https://core.ac.uk/download/pdf/6605800.pdf (accessed on 16th September 2025).
20. Charlton, J., Greenwood, D., Kelly, K., Moreton, R., et al. (2020). The complexities of managing historic buildings with BIM. https://core.ac.uk/download/323307080.pdf (accessed on 16th September 2025).

21. Chatzigiannakis, I., Amaxilatis, D., Vasileiou, E., Irene, D., et al. (2017). Delivering elder-care environments utilizing TV-channel based mechanisms. https://core.ac.uk/download/98343525.pdf (accessed on 16th September 2025).
22. Collier, D., & Schallenbach, C. (2017). HR shared services (HRSS): Model and trends. https://core.ac.uk/download/219376958.pdf (accessed on 16th September 2025).
23. Comuzzi, M., Soda, P., Tortorella, F., Van Gorp, A., et al. (2012). MyPHRMachines: Lifelong personal health records in the cloud. https://core.ac.uk/download/29017368.pdf (accessed on 16th September 2025).
24. Consoli, D. (2025). A layered software architecture for the management of a manufacturing company. https://core.ac.uk/download/pdf/6673186.pdf (accessed on 16th September 2025).
25. Demeester, P., Hoebeke, J., Moerman, I., Van den Abeele, F., et al. (2015). Integration of heterogeneous devices and communication models via the cloud in the constrained internet of things. https://core.ac.uk/download/55746971.pdf (accessed on 16th September 2025).
26. Dwivedi, Y. K., Kshetri, N., Hughes, L., Slade, E., Jeyaraj, A., Kar, A. K., Baabdullah, A. M., et al. (2023). Opinion paper: "So what if ChatGPT wrote it?" Multidisciplinary perspectives on opportunities, challenges and implications of generative conversational AI for research, practice and policy. *International Journal of Information Management, 71*, 102642. https://doi.org/10.1016/j.ijinfomgt.2023.102642 (accessed on 16th September 2025).
27. Ernst, R., Nolte, M., & Schlatow, J. (2019). Controlling concurrent change – A multiview approach toward updatable vehicle automation systems. https://core.ac.uk/download/190382646.pdf (accessed on 16th September 2025).
28. Evangelopoulou, M., Johnson, C. W., & Pavlova, T. (2017). Applying lessons from cyber-attacks on Ukrainian infrastructures to secure gateways onto the industrial Internet of Things. https://core.ac.uk/download/111557942.pdf (accessed on 16th September 2025).
29. Fu, C., Malyuta, T., Mandrick, W. S., Parent, C., et al. (2012). Horizontal integration of warfighter intelligence data: A shared semantic resource for the intelligence community. https://core.ac.uk/download/223236027.pdf (accessed on 16th September 2025).
30. Harris, C. R., Millman, K. J., van der Walt, S., Gommers, R., Virtanen, P., Cournapeau, D., Wieser, E., et al. (2020). Array programming with NumPy. *Nature, 585*, 357–362. https://doi.org/10.1038/s41586-020-2649-2 (accessed on 16th September 2025).

31. Hochstenbach, P., Elbaek, M. K., Russell, R., Schmelz Pedersen, B., et al. (2008). DRIVER technology watch report. https://core.ac.uk/download/55769861.pdf (accessed on 16th September 2025).

32. Jackson, B., Delfosse, X., Gorda, S. Y., Hut, P., Naef, D., Greenberg, R., Barnes, R., et al. (2008). Tides and the evolution of planetary habitability. http://arxiv.org/abs/0807.0680 (accessed on 16th September 2025).

33. Lněnička, M. (2013). Cloud based testing of business applications and web services. https://core.ac.uk/download/14742035.pdf (accessed on 16th September 2025).

34. Mangiuc, D. M. (2025). Enterprise 2.0–Is the market ready? https://core.ac.uk/download/pdf/6261799.pdf (accessed on 16th September 2025).

35. Mehnen, J., Shehab, E., & Yadekar, Y. (2013). Challenges of cloud technology in manufacturing environment. https://core.ac.uk/download/42143894.pdf (accessed on 16th September 2025).

36. Opara-Martins, J., Sahandi, R., & Tian, F. (2015). Implications of integration and interoperability for enterprise cloud-based applications. https://core.ac.uk/download/42142796.pdf (accessed on 16th September 2025).

37. Park, S., & Kim, Y. G. (2022). A metaverse: Taxonomy, components, applications, and open challenges. *IEEE Access, 10*, 4209–4251. https://doi.org/10.1109/access.2021.3140175 (accessed on 16th September 2025).

38. Qian, Y., Sharif, H., Tipper, D., Yan, Y., et al. (2012). A survey on cyber security for smart grid communications. https://core.ac.uk/download/12211131.pdf (accessed on 16th September 2025).

CHAPTER 10

APPLICATIONS OF EDGE COMPUTING IN INDUSTRIAL SECTORS

Contents

INTRODUCTION

The advent of edge computing has revolutionized the industrial landscape, serving as a premise for the evolution of technologies in various industries. With companies endeavoring to optimize performance, reduce latency, and improve data processing capabilities, edge computing has emerged as a critical asset. Through the processing of data close to the point of origin, organizations are able to capitalize on real-time analytics, thus driving efficiency and innovation.

This aligns with the Industry 4.0 premises where networked services and digital manufacturing are central to competitiveness. Companies are now relying more on edge computing to visualize manufacturing data in an efficient manner, as according to studies emphasizing its use to provide In-Transit Analytics essential for Industrial Internet of Things (IIoT) applications (Ali et al., 2017). Therefore, a deeper understanding of edge computing applications is necessary in driving industrial productivity and innovation. Beyond processing data, however, the implications of edge computing are far-reaching, essentially redefining decision-making across industries. Through edge-based data collection and analysis, organizations can make well-informed, real-time decisions that minimize operational downtime and optimize responsiveness. This capability is particularly relevant in constantly evolving environments where speed and adaptability take precedence. To illustrate, predictive maintenance uses is increasingly reliant on edge computing to facilitate data collection from machines, enabling timely detection of oncoming failures. This shift not only maximizes uptime but also conserves enormous amounts of capital associated with unplanned downtime. Thus, the implementation of edge computing in industrial settings facilitates a transition to more intelligent operations, justifying that empowerment of real-time decision-making is essential to ensuring industrial competitiveness within an ever-evolving marketplace landscape (Ciarli et al., 2019). In examining the applications of edge computing in industrial sectors, it is important to determine the paradigmatic change this technology achieves on various operation models. From manufacturing to supply chain management, edge computing fuels pivotal innovations, enabling industries to tap into the promise of data-driven insight. Crucially, through the ability to constantly monitor systems and processes in real-time, companies are able to respond rapidly to anomalies and optimize performance metrics. Edge computing also promotes collaboration between previously isolated departments, enabling them to address challenges within organizations more holistically. As industries become more inclined towards digital transformation, understanding these applications will become inevitable for both stakeholders and professionals. In a bid to guarantee ongoing growth, embracing edge computing not only streamlines operations but also provides the foundation for upcoming developments in industrial practices, hence highlighting its significance in the current debate on technological advancements in the industrial sector.

Importance of Edge Computing in Industry

The advent of edge computing has been a game changer in various industrial sectors by meeting the urgent need for real-time data processing. The traditional cloud computing models often suffer from latency, which is detrimental to industries that require instantaneous decision-making, i.e., manufacturing and logistics. With the deployment of edge computing solutions, organizations can process data at its source, leading to reduced latency and enhanced operation efficiency. This trickles down, allowing industries to respond in a timely fashion to changing situations, improve automation capabilities, and maximize the utilization of resources. As businesses strive to stay competitive, edge computing integration is essential in fully leveraging the data generated by IoT sensors and devices in fluid environments, rendering the technology more vital to the modern industrial landscape. Further, edge computing enhances data security and privacy, a vital concern for data-driven businesses today. By processing sensitive information locally rather than transferring it to distant cloud facilities, businesses are able to neutralize the risk of data theft and hacking. This distributed computing trend not only protects confidential data but also complies with increasingly stringent data privacy laws across jurisdictions. The services industry, for instance, would stand to benefit immensely from such a strategy because it intertwines data management with regulatory requirements. With the economy moving further towards becoming a postindustrial economy based on digital platforms and networked services, the security dividends offered through edge computing cannot be exaggerated in terms of instilling confidence among consumers and stakeholders. Therefore, businesses are going to adopt edge solutions to maintain the integrity of their data while also enhancing operational agility (Britchenko et al., 2018). Moreover, the influence of edge computing is also going to fuel new business models across industrial sectors. There are new emerging start-ups that leverage edge computing to fuel service delivery and customer experience. These companies are not only adopting edge technologies; they are rebuilding their operational models around them. With edge real-time data, businesses are better placed to develop customized solutions to meet specific customer needs, strengthening the connection between product offerings and consumer needs. Such disruptive impact serves to emphasize shifting business dynamics driven by technological advancements. The findings from the case studies reveal how businesses utilize edge computing to enhance significant activities, increase customer segmentation, and strengthen value propositions, thereby building long-term competitive edge in the midst of rapid commercial change (Bala et al., 2018). Hence, embracing edge computing is critical to not just enhancing operational efficiency but also to driving innovation across sectors.

10.1. MANUFACTURING

The industry of manufacturing is going through a paradigm shift with the arrival of edge computing technologies, which bring with them enormous opportunities for real-time processing of data and decision-making. With Industry 4.0, manufacturers are opting in large numbers for digital solutions that enable machines and services to converse with each other easily. This integration makes it easy to monitor and analyze manufacturing processes in real-time, leading to a data-driven environment necessary for innovation. According to Ali et al. (2017), manufacturing data visualization is the foundation on which insights that enhance competitiveness are developed. As businesses leverage this capability, they can enhance performance, reduce downtime, and enhance product quality, eventually leading to enhanced efficiency and productivity in the manufacturing sector.

Figure 10.1. Manufacturing industry is experiencing a transformative shift with the advent of edge computing technologies.

Source: https://community.connection.com/wp-content/uploads/2021/05/1330121-Edge-Compute-BLOG.jpg.

The integration of innovative technologies, such as nanomechanical relay (NEM relay) circuits, goes on to illustrate the pivotal role that edge computing plays in the manufacturing sector. These NEM relay circuits, known for their stability under harsh conditions, are a valuable option for applications based on edge processing. NEM relays can, as stated in Bleiker et al. (2024), work effectively in harsh conditions without consuming power during standby mode and therefore prove suitable to notably resource-constrained manufacturing environments. The use of these technologies allows for the deployment of edge computing solutions that support such mission-critical features as predictive maintenance and real-time quality control. NEM relay circuits can be used by manufacturers to realize dramatic enhancements in operational efficiency and reliability. Furthermore, the relevance of edge computing extends beyond such near-term operational gains, revolutionizing the strategic outlook of manufacturing firms.

The shift towards manufacturing paradigms that are data-driven allows for a culture of iterative innovation and continuous improvement. With access to real-time analytics on their data, organizations are not only able to refine their existing processes but are also able to prototype new manufacturing processes and technologies. These innovations are critical to maintaining competitive edge in a rapidly changing marketplace. As such vendors integrate these edge computing capabilities into their tactical offerings, they position themselves to seek out new business models and markets, paving the way for sustainable growth and resistance against challenges in the industry (Figure 10.1).

10.1.1. Real-Time Data Processing

The advent of real-time data processing represents a turning point for the climate of industrial environments, driven by the rising demand for efficiency and speed. Close on the heels of this comes edge computing, enabling data processing to occur closer to where data originates rather than relying too heavily on cloud-based centralized models. By employing local computing resources, companies can reduce latency significantly, facilitating instantaneous decision-making that is critical in functions such as predictive maintenance, quality assurance, and supply chain operations. This enhanced immediacy not only increases the effectiveness of operations but also facilitates a higher degree of responsiveness to market needs, a key factor in the context of Industry 4.0 initiatives. Thus, data processing in real time in edge computing becomes a prominent feature in gaining competitive advantages in industrial environments (Ali et al., 2017). Additionally, data processing in real time has a revolutionary effect in the Industrial Internet of Things (IIoT) where devices connected to the internet generate tremendous volumes of data to be processed in real time. It is made possible by the application of edge computing, which enables In-Transit Analytics, where data is processed and analyzed as it traverses the network. Due to this capability, organizations are able to view critical manufacturing information in real-time, thereby fostering decision-making and even creative changes in operation processes. Real-time visibility enables businesses to capitalize on breaking trends, minimize downtimes, and significantly enhance overall productivity. The convergence of IIoT and edge computing offers a dynamic framework where real-time data processing is not only of value but a necessity within the industrial field to achieve efficient operations and sustainable growth (Ali et al., 2017). Finally, advances in technology within communications, that is, integration of millimeter-wave (mm-wave) technologies, drive real-time data processing within industry applications. As companies are already increasingly depending on robust connectivity to facilitate edge computing, the coming of 5G networks also promises reduced latency and higher data rates. This facilitates rapid data transmission of numerous connected devices so that the processed data reaches the decision-makers instantaneously. Network architecture functional splits envisioned for 5G make it possible to provide effective signaling channels and facilitate the collection of context information at the networks' edge. All such advancements not only dispel access delays but also improve data transmission stability, thereby the performance of real-time data processing applications. Therefore, the implementation of such technologies places real-time data processing at the forefront of industrial innovation and efficiency gains (Figure 10.2).

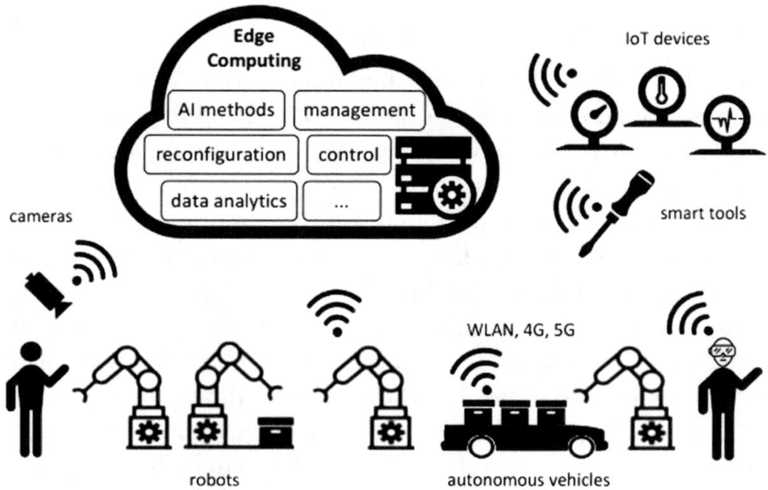

Figure 10.2. Real-time data processing at the edge.

Source: https://5ghub.us/wp-content/uploads/2023/11/Image2-1-jpg.webp.

10.1.2. Predictive Maintenance

In industrial industries, predictive maintenance is one of the most popular applications of edge computing, which allows businesses to automate their maintenance and maximize operational efficiency. With the application of real-time data analytics in the edge, businesses can monitor equipment condition in real time without the latency of cloud computing. This just-in-time access to information enables faster and better decision-making, converts to downtime savings, and ultimately to cost savings. With industries embracing this digital revolution, data visualization of manufacturing has become a necessity. The coming together of predictive maintenance aligns well with Industry 4.0's emphasis on integrated capabilities and real-time information driving innovation and competitiveness (Ali et al., 2017). To that end, the advent of advanced

Information and Communication Technologies has also revolutionized the maintenance approach in industrial environments. Predictive maintenance runs hand-in-hand with concepts such as Prognostics and Health Management (PHM), providing a platform for equipment failure prediction before it occurs. By using data-driven methodologies for monitoring the condition of machines, predictive maintenance not only enhances reliability but also directs the creation of maintenance policies. This shift towards an active maintenance approach ensures effective resource distribution, minimizes the occurrence of unplanned outages, and supports long-term asset sustainability in industrial applications (Crespo et al., 2016) (Figure 10.3).

Figure 10.3. Predictive maintenance in industrial sectors.

Source: https://media.licdn.com/dms/image/v2/D5612AQFFeMG1Py8ALw/article-cover_image-shrink_720_1280/article-cover_image-shrink_720_1280/0/1689961052400?e=2147483647&v=beta&t=s8dyxfLN8WHMBk201FjF1SSnGP4BEFP2XC70gd_HDhg.

With advancing predictive maintenance technology, there is a vision for radical improvement in operating processes and equipment life. Integration with edge computing supports imperative functions such as condition-based monitoring and smart diagnostics. Businesses can impose tailored schedules for maintenance, based on real-time scrutiny of machine performance. This shift from traditional maintenance to a more dynamic approach indicates growing dependence on analysis of data for optimal industrial operations. With the competitive pressures in modern manufacturing, predictive maintenance, fueled by the promise of edge computing, will transform planning operations, ultimately resulting in increased productivity at reduced costs in diversified industrial segments (Crespo et al., 2016).

10.1.3. Quality Control Enhancements

In the industrial industries, advancements in quality control have increasingly been improved with the integration of edge computing technologies. This paradigm shift guarantees that information is processed in real-time at the point of event occurrence, thereby allowing organizations to make immediate quality decisions rather than waiting for analysis to occur. By positioning computing power closer to the plant floor, companies are able to implement more effective monitoring of production processes, which will enable anomalies to be identified sooner. These developments promote a proactive approach to quality assurance and diminish defects before they get beyond control. Furthermore, edge computing-induced ultra-low latency provides quality parameters to cut-time update, so enterprises can cut-time make data-driven decisions that optimize production efficiency and product reliability and hence propel overall market competitiveness, as stated by Cuevas et al. (2017). Another primary attribute of quality control enhancements is cut-time performing predictive analytics by leveraging the synergy between edge computing and advanced machine learning algorithms. By continuously monitoring data from multiple sensors and devices during production, organizations can identify patterns and potential quality failures in advance. Not only does this predictive capability reduce waste and operating costs, but it also accelerates the feedback cycle for on-time process adjustments in manufacturing. As industries increasingly adopt this technology, it is imperative that operators redefine traditional models and implement sophisticated practices that leverage real-time insights for continuous improvement. This shift in strategy is highlighted by the potential of new technologies, aligning with (Department of Innovation et al., 2025) to prioritize research infrastructure facilitation of such innovation. Additionally, the introduction of 5G technology also increases the scope of edge computing in providing quality control capabilities in industrial sectors. With the urging of manufacturers to integrate more advanced, automated systems, there is a greater demand for reliable connectivity and ultra-low latency service. Convergence with edge computing strategically enhances the speed and reliability of data transmission, which is critical in determining quality measurements performed in real time. Consequently, companies can use more adaptive production processes and quickly respond to variations in quality measures. This innovation development forms new business models upon improved service delivery and operation effectiveness, as suggested in Cuevas et al. (2017). Ultimately, the application of edge computing technologies will transform quality control processes to be stronger and more responsive to the dictates of a more competitive market.

10.2. ENERGY SECTOR

The energy industry with its unique challenges and opportunities stands at the crossroads with the integration of innovative digital technologies like edge computing. This digital age enhances operation efficiencies considerably and facilitates real-time data processing, ultimately leading to smarter energy management systems. Through decentralized computing power close to the source of data, edge computing facilitates timely decision-making processes. This is particularly beneficial in monitoring and managing energy distribution networks, where quick response to fluctuating demand and immediate sensing of anomalies can significantly prevent wastage and enhance the reliability of services. The more dynamic the energy environment gets, the more critical it is for these smart systems, particularly in the guise of renewable sources of energy whose fluctuating supply conditions must be balanced through responsive, flexible management. Also, the intersection of edge computing with the power sector is a good example of the broader implications of Industry 4.0 technologies on working spaces. The integration of such digital technologies enables not only more control of energy flow but also room for developing more sophisticated predictive analytics solutions. Such instruments utilize massive amounts of data generated within the sector, thereby forming the basis of maintenance strategies, grid optimization, and peak load management. According to the postulates expounded in Prieto et al. (2019), academic work towards advancing understanding of such technologies is of utmost priority. For instance, institutions that incorporate experiential learning through Industry 4.0 laboratories can train a workforce well-set to lead the complexities ushered by such innovations. This synergetic bond permits theoretical knowledge to be supplemented by experiential insights, driving the energy sector towards increased sustainability. Lastly, edge computing also provides an entry point for further optimizing the deployment of Internet of Things (IoT) devices in the energy sector, permitting improved data collection and analysis. Due to local processing capabilities, edge devices are able to analyze energy consumption patterns, enabling more accurate information regarding user activity and enabling dynamic balancing of loads. This local approach not only maximizes energy usage but also enhances the dependability of the energy source by minimizing the impact of outages. Coupled with the fifth-generation network's communication functionalities, as discussed in Li et al. (2018), the application of cognitive content-centric networking platforms can be the source of innovative solutions, such as personalized energy management applications. These advancements underline the radical potential of edge computing in redefining business models within the energy industry, eventually leading to a more robust and efficient energy grid (Figure 10.4).

Figure 10.4. Edge computing for the energy sector.

Source: https://developer-blogs.nvidia.com/wp-content/uploads/2022/01/Energy-Featured-Image-2.png.

10.2.1. Smart Grid Management

Smart grid integration into energy business is a watershed towards enhancing the efficiency and dependability of power systems. The traditional power grids with uni-directional flow of energy and limited communications have failed to meet contemporary needs such as increasing energy demands and security concerns. The shift towards Smart Grids (SGs) enables bi-directional energy exchange between consumers and providers and thereby real-time observation and control of energy resources. The shift is greatly reliant on Internet of Things (IoT) devices that are utilized mainly to monitor, analyze, and manage grid systems. Through the use of these technologies, smart grids can regulate power generation, transmission, and distribution more effectively, ultimately leading to better energy consumption and wastage minimization, facilitating more environmentally friendly industrial processes (Copeland et al., 2019). Development of smart grid management systems also connects importantly to edge computing innovations that enhance data processing nearer to where data are being produced. In use cases where latency and real-time responsiveness are critical, edge computing is a valuable paradigm by allowing real-time processing of data. This is particularly useful in rural distribution networks, as traditional infrastructure often lacks efficiency in operation. A novel architecture which has been developed for rural distribution networks combines edge computing for the purpose of uniting telecommunication benefits with novel power electronics technologies. By decentralizing control systems and enhancing the management of real-time data, this approach makes it possible for operators to manage low-scale electrical storage effectively, thereby maximizing the integration of distributed energy resources and overall grid resilience (Díaz et al., 2018). In addition, smart grid management implications extend to environmental sustainability and energy conservation and redefine industrial processes in various industries. With the adoption of smart grid principles, industries can reduce their carbon footprint by optimized management of energy resources and increased use of renewable sources. The shift not only helps meet global sustainability goals but also boosts economic competitiveness by reducing operational costs associated with the consumption of energy. With industries opting for smart grid technology, they are also embracing advanced technology that supports predictive maintenance, load forecasting, and increased demand response capabilities. Thus, the combined impact of edge computing and smart grid management fosters a more environmentally conscious industrial setting, allowing stakeholders to counter the twin challenge of eco-responsibility and energy efficiency in an increasingly interdependent world (Copeland et al., 2019) (Figure 10.5).

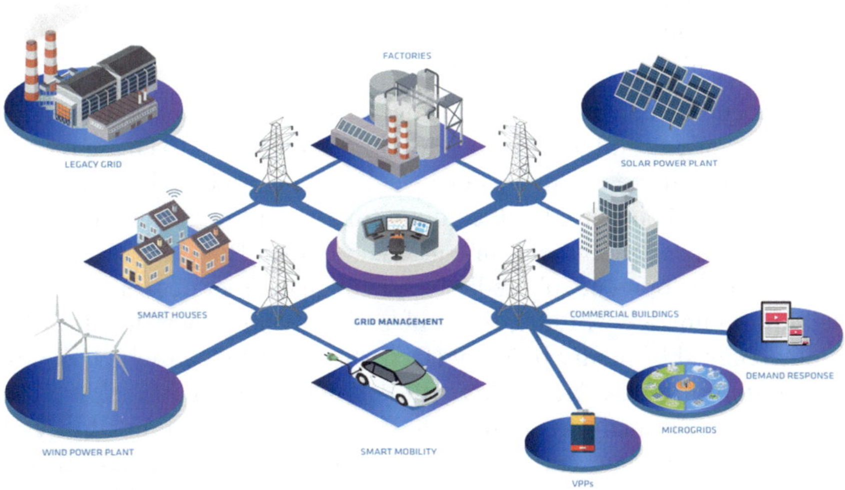

Figure 10.5. The integration of smart grid management.

Source: https://media.licdn.com/dms/image/v2/D5612AQGvqvZn1R9irw/article-cover_image-shrink_720_1280/article-cover_image-shrink_720_1280/0/1709631633037?e=2147483647&v=beta&t=kGXXPtabKCKG8E0BBl8WMbI9iN6QnWxY_bF0Ds-Siw0.

10.2.2. Renewable Energy Integration

The incorporation of non-traditional sources of power into present power systems has become an immediate necessity in order to enhance sustainability and reduce climate change. This transition requires an upgrade of traditional power grids to Smart Grids (SGs), which provide bi-directional power exchange between producers and consumers. Smart Grids rely on a variety of advanced technologies, the most significant being the Internet of Things (IoT), to facilitate monitoring, analysis, and control of power distribution. Smart sensors and meters as components of IoT devices enhance connectivity and enable real-time data collection, which is essential in optimizing energy use and energy management.

Because renewable energy generation is variable and dependent on the changing availability of resources, these technologies enable the ability to react more dynamically towards energy demands, culminating eventually in higher reliability and efficiency in grid operation. Mitigation of the challenges entailed in the integration of renewable sources is central in ongoing endeavors for enhanced energy security and waste minimization (Copeland et al., 2019). Furthermore, strategic use of edge computing plays a pivotal role in integrating renewable energy systems into industrial processes. By processing data closer to where the generation takes place, edge computing has the capacity to significantly reduce latency, making decision-making processes faster and optimizing the efficiency of operations.

This decentralized processing of data method allows real-time analytics, which is especially useful in situations where fast responses to changing energy supply and demand are essential. For instance, industrial settings where solar or wind energy is being used, edge computing can allow for automatic shifts in energy use depending on real-time grid conditions. Besides, this integration supports the development of predictive maintenance strategies that employ IoT data to minimize downtime, thus enhancing overall operational resilience within the renewable energy industry (Department of Innovation et al., 2025). The integration of renewable energy will definitely continue to evolve further as technologies and methods continue to be improved. As outlined in various strategic plans, including national research infrastructure roadmaps, there is a need for robust policy frameworks to ensure alignment of sustainable approaches to industrial application. Aside from improving innovation, these frameworks stress research into areas of capability that optimize the adoption of renewable systems across various industries. By aligning research frameworks with real-time data processing power, industries can implement improved mechanisms for aggregating renewable energy sources. Over the long term, the convergence of edge computing and renewable energy initiatives can significantly contribute to revolutionizing the production, utilization, and management of energy in industrial contexts, towards a brighter and cleaner future (Copeland et al., 2019).

10.2.3. Monitoring and Optimization of Resources

With the introduction of edge computing, the method through which industries tackle the critical issue of resource monitoring and optimization has become altered. Traditional systems are weighed down with latency and bandwidth issues, especially in situations that require real-time data processing. With edge computing, industries can greatly enhance their operational efficiency by localizing data processing to the network's edge. This real-time visualization of data enables manufacturers to track machinery and processes around the clock, enabling timely maintenance and reducing downtime. As implied by Industry 4.0 principles that emphasize interlinked services for increased manufacturing perspectives, edge computing is key to fulfilling these goals, enabling the infrastructure required for In-Transit Analytics that can unleash new competitive benefits through data visualization (Ali et al., 2017). Besides, application of edge computing in resource monitoring develops superior decision-making abilities in various industrial processes. With the use of data at the edge, companies get to reveal patterns and anomalies hidden within aggregate data analyses performed in centralized environments. Optimization develops proactive management strategy in allocation of resources, hence easing operations. For instance, edge computing can be used to integrate IoT devices that record real-time equipment performance data so companies can fine-tune resource allocation dynamically. This adaptive approach reduces waste and optimizes use of resources while enhancing further operational resilience in an increasingly dynamic industrial context. In terms of energy management, edge computing also presents huge opportunities for optimizing resources in smart grid infrastructures. The architecture of the smart grid, particularly in rural environments, allows for improved resource management via decentralization that increases response and efficiency. With the convergence of power management and telecommunications technology, the suggested frameworks allow for distributed energy resources to be used without affecting grid stability. As elaborated through various studies, including Intelligent Distribution Power Routers, this combination of edge computing and novel paradigms for energy management empowers operators to optimize the use of resources in real time, thus transforming traditional energy networks into more resilient systems that can cater to variability in needs (Díaz et al., 2018). This revolution plays a central role in enabling sustainable industrial processes in the energy sector (Figure 10.6).

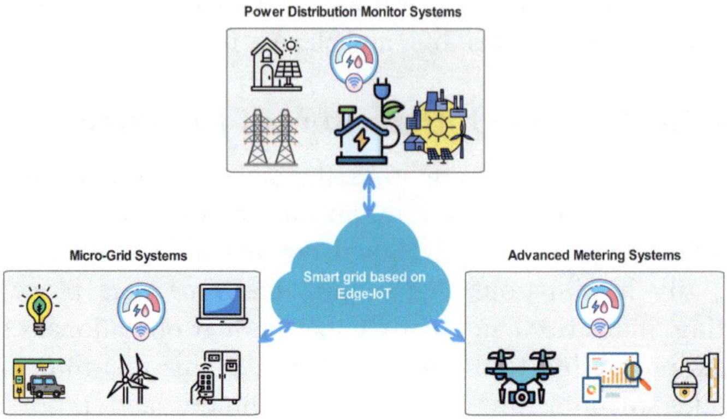

Figure 10.6. The three key services of IoT-based smart grids.

Source: https://www.mdpi.com/energies/energies-15-06140/article_deploy/html/images/energies-15-06140-g002.png.

10.3. TRANSPORTATION AND LOGISTICS

Integration of edge computing into transportation and logistics is revolutionizing responsiveness and efficiency of the supply chain. With the industry still requiring real-time data and fast response times, edge computing is a winner that enables nearer data processing to the point of origin. This is proximity to latency, which is removed, and enables real-time decision-making, something that is highly critical in real-time logistical settings where there is a requirement to deliver products to customers very fast. Besides, technologies such as RFID have a focal point in enhancing supply chain management by providing a way of enhanced visibility and tracking of commodities. To a large degree, effective use of RFID demonstrates the adoption process of technology spurred by customer needs and organizational innovativeness, demonstrating how technology and operational efficiency are co-dependent in logistics (Johnson et al., 2008). In addition, the role of edge computing can be better understood in the broader context of the services sector, which contributes significantly to economic development. With transport and logistics becoming increasingly integrated with the growth of technology, the sector is evolving into a hyper-sector that not only facilitates but also drives economic growth. Edge computing implementation allows logistics firms to analyze and react to market trends at velocity, thereby enhancing service quality and operational efficiency. In the focal point with edge computing, firms are adequately positioned to construct capital and drive customer satisfaction, which is essential as the global economy evolves increasingly towards a service-oriented model (Britchenko et al., 2018).

On top of this, edge computing offers revolutionary solutions for inventory management and resource allocation in transport and logistics. With real-time data analytics, businesses can optimize routing, reduce the usage of fuel, and reduce delivery tardiness. With the ability to process information at the edge, preventive measures can be taken, e.g., modulation of logistics based on real-time traffic flows or customer orders. Consequently, the anticipated benefits of edge computing technology adoption underscore its value in achieving cost-saving and increased service levels. Through this technology innovation, the logistics and transportation sectors are not only addressing current challenges but also preparing for future needs, ensuring a robust and sustainable working model that synchronizes with industry expectations (Johnson et al., 2008) (Figure 10.7).

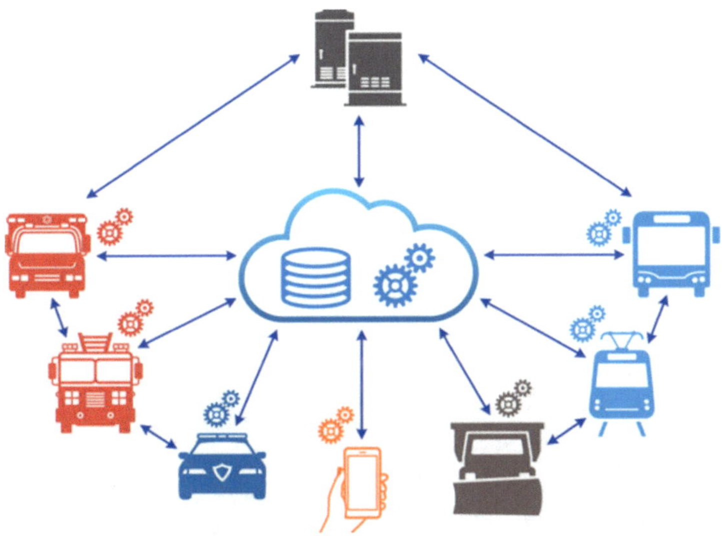

Figure 10.7. Edge computing for transportation.

Source: https://www.emtracsystems.com/wp-content/uploads/2021/04/diagram-edge.jpg.

10.3.1. Fleet Management Solutions

The implementation of Fleet Management Solutions (FMS) into industrial processes showcases the revolutionizing potential of edge computing. By leveraging localized processing power, organizations are able to enhance the management of their fleets with real-time data analysis. Using this approach, latency is minimized to its lowest by instantaneous processing of critical data regarding vehicle performance, location, and driver behavior, thereby enabling decisions on better insights. The advent of the Internet of Things (IoT) has further evolved FMS, where a network of connected vehicles continues to feed information into centralized platforms. Based on current literature on IoT capabilities, enhanced computing and sensing capacities enable cars to perform sophisticated maneuvers based on real-time information, where data-driven insights play a central role in operational efficiency and safety (Baaziz et al., 2015). Apart from this, edge computing helps Fleet Management Solutions achieve big data analytics effectively. By integrating vehicle-high-resolution data streams with machine learning algorithms, predictive maintenance and fleet optimization are achieved. Analyzing past and real-time data, companies can find patterns and trends and rectify impending issues proactively before they disrupt operations. The shift toward proactive practices of maintenance not only extends the life of vehicles but also suppresses operating costs significantly. Industry analyses identify that the use of big data analytics in fleet operations is a significant enabler for companies that aim to uprise their operations based on a more lean and reactive logistical framework (Baaziz et al., 2015) (Figure 10.8).

Figure 10.8. Fleet management solutions.

Source: https://fms-tech.com/wp-content/themes/fms-tech/assets/img/FMS-Tech-Fleet-Management-System-and-Technology-Software-Solutions.jpg.

In addition, the concept of intelligent transportation systems is well suited to Fleet Management Solutions' goals, particularly as industries shift to more intricate city settings. Smart city initiatives utilize information and communication technologies (ICTs) that aggregate data from various city services and offer insights to improve fleet routing and management. Through collaborative organizational designs that foster innovation, FMS can address public issues in an efficient way, enhancing sustainability and reducing congestion on the roads by maximizing vehicle flow and use of resources. These synergies create a connected world in which vehicles do not only operate in silos but contribute to wider urban dynamics, creating a path towards a sustainable future. This integration is a milestone in using edge computing in industrial settings, particularly with the growing calls for efficiency and sustainability.

10.3.2. Traffic Management Systems

Traffic Management Systems (TMS) is one of the primary applications of edge computing in urban infrastructure, enhancing traffic efficiency and safety by a considerable amount. Processing data at the network edge, TMS can rapidly analyze current traffic conditions and dynamic response to congestion, accidents, or other incidents possible. The integration of such systems helps to collect valuable information from sources such as cameras, sensors, and networked vehicles that can then be utilized to guide not only traffic signal control but also long-term city planning. Additionally, the shift towards edge computing enables it to reduce latency in processing data so that time-critical information can be accessed almost in real time, and thus overall efficiency of traffic control and travel through cities is enhanced. The advent of 5G technology has gone on to revolutionize Traffic Management Systems with the ability to enable ultra-low latency communication that is essential for real-time applications. According to literature, the investment in sophisticated network capabilities is essential in satisfying the requirements of new applications for TMS (Cuevas et al., 2017). The application of millimeter-wave technologies, even though it is complicated by propagation constraints, introduces higher bandwidth and supports a variety of connected devices. These innovations enable safe data to be shared, making it feasible for TMS to take advantage of contextual information related to traffic patterns and user insights. This innovation has the possibility to greatly improve smartphone-based navigation devices and other connected services, eventually making the commuter lifestyle and traffic system more efficient. To optimize the performance of Traffic Management Systems, it becomes essential to have traditional systems intertwine flawlessly with advanced edge computing architecture. With the use of context information gained through user movements and traffic flow, cell discovery processes can be made more efficient and can help support the quick adjustment of traffic signals, as per latest studies (Capone et al., 2017). With the utilization of geo-located databases having historical traffic data, prediction analysis can also be valuable, thus supporting pro-active traffic management programs. This integration allows urban traffic systems to forecast and adapt to changing conditions significantly reducing the incidence of bottlenecks and accidents. Through the adoption of such innovative methods, Traffic Management Systems become a central asset towards the creation of smart cities and overall city mobility (Figure 10.9).

Figure 10.9. Traffic management systems (TMS) represent a pivotal application of edge computing in urban infrastructures.

Source: https://media.licdn.com/dms/image/v2/D4D12AQHViMCn0YGTLw/article-cover_image-shrink_600_2000/article-cover_image-shrink_600_2000/0/1690488585929?e=2147483647&v=beta&t=tW2M6QKuaTfpvSA0Pkpc7X1Kzr8Aok4issK4O7owAR8.

10.3.3. Supply Chain Optimization

In the background of industrial sectors, supply chain optimization is a vital component in order to enhance operational efficiency and competitiveness. The use of edge computing in supply chain operations makes it possible to analyze data in real time, thereby facilitating businesses to respond to dynamic marketplace variations in real time. With edge data processing, companies are able to curb latency, improve decision-making, and reduce supply chain disruptions. Furthermore, the advanced operational research-based algorithms can also help in calculating right levels of inventories, demand planning, and resource allocation to allow firms to maximize operations and maintain costs at an optimum level. The ability to apply such insights in near-real time transforms traditional supply chain management into a dynamic model capable of adjusting to changes in market trends to ultimately provide greater customer satisfaction and loyalty. Further, edge computing technology significantly enhances the performance of supply chain management through its capability to enhance adaptive and automatic manufacturing systems. With Industry 4.0, businesses can leverage new technologies such as additive manufacturing (AM) in a bid to create highly tailored products on demand. This transformation means that supply chains are not just reactive but also proactive with an emphasis on efficiency and waste reduction. For instance, the integration of AM processes allows localized manufacturing, hence lowering transportation expenditure while production flexibility improves. As companies proceed in accordance with intelligent manufacturing concepts, data-based decision-making even increases. The integration of supply chain optimization and edge computing, here, offers an environment where companies can innovate without compromising operational efficiency or sustainability, showcasing a required change in industrial practices (Dehghanghadikolaei et al., 2019). Supply chain optimization with edge computing also promotes transparency and collaboration across the value chain. By making stakeholders accessible at points of touch such as suppliers, manufacturers, and shipping partners, companies can consolidate and make their operational framework more cohesive. By doing so, this transparency not only boosts partnership trust, but also foster cooperative problem-solving. For instance, predictive analytics fueled by edge computing may detect potential disruptions because of supply chain congestion or fluctuating demand patterns. The end result is a longer-lasting supply chain that can adapt rapidly to unforeseen setbacks. Therefore, with industries still spending in technologies that enhance connectivity and utilization of data, the role of edge computing in supply chain optimization will continue to grow, leading to sustainable business practices in line with today's economic and environmental agendas (Darby-Dowman et al., 2002).

10.4. HEALTHCARE

The advent of edge computing has transformed the healthcare sector by enabling simpler data processing at the point of origin, rather than relying on central cloud resources. This model of technology addresses principal issues such as latency, bandwidth constraints, and security, significantly improving the operational efficacy of health systems. Edge computing supports real-time analytics on data, providing real-time patient monitoring and prompt decision-making essential to critical care environments. Furthermore, edge computing enabled devices can operate without dependence on the central systems and ensure consistent performance in spite of network failure. Hospitals and clinics, therefore, can provide improved quality care by processing large amounts of data without overwhelming central systems. This efficiency not only benefits patient outcomes but also optimizes resource use, encompassing the central principles of modern healthcare delivery (Britchenko et al., 2018). In addition to facilitating care delivery, edge computing enhances patient empowerment and individualization of healthcare services. Through wearable health technology and mobile health apps, patients have timely access to their health data, enabling them to make well-informed care decisions. Edge computing processes such information at the edge, providing timely insights to patients and providers while maintaining information private and secure. Communication between edge devices and central systems provides the correlation of diverse health data that is critical in the development of individualized treatment plans. Through active patient involvement in their own care, providers are able to attain improved adherence to treatment guidelines, which is critical in achieving desirable clinical outcomes.

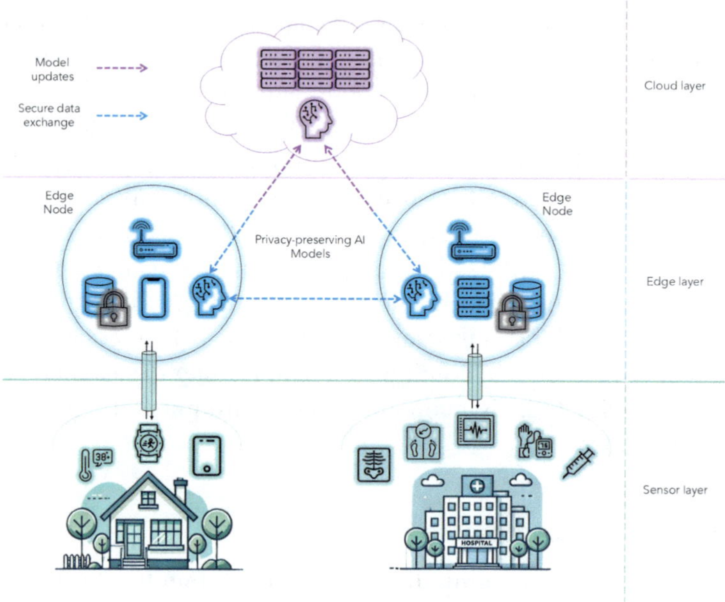

Figure 10.10. Overview of edge computing in healthcare.

Source: https://www.mdpi.com/futureinternet/futureinternet-16-00329/article_deploy/html/images/futureinternet-16-00329-g003.png.

This transformation towards patient-centered care is in line with current trends in healthcare, encouraging a more comprehensive style of managing health (Cuevas et al., 2017). Additionally, the application of edge computing to healthcare also has enormous economic consequences, especially in an environment where technology is becoming more dependent. The minimization of operational expenses related to managing data is among the most prominent economic advantages. By minimizing the reliance on centralized cloud infrastructure, health organizations are able to optimize their investment in processing and storing data. Edge computing facilitates hospitals to focus their resources only on patient care and not IT overhead, leading to an overall improvement in the efficiency of service. Additionally, with healthcare systems still evolving, the future integration of technologies such as artificial intelligence and machine learning through edge computing will open up new sources of revenue. Such technologies have the potential to facilitate revenue generation in the context of new healthcare models, thus contributing to the sustainability and resilience of healthcare organizations in a financially stressed environment (Britchenko et al., 2018) (Figure 10.10).

10.4.1. Remote Patient Monitoring

The integration of Edge Computing into healthcare simplifies the deployment of Remote Patient Monitoring (RPM), a groundbreaking use case within the industry. With RPM, clinicians can collect, analyze, and monitor patient data in real-time, facilitating better clinical decision-making and personalized treatment. By processing information in nearer proximity to the point where it's collected, Edge Computing lowers the delay, allowing for real-time data handling and reducing the bandwidth required to transmit large volumes of data to central cloud servers. The capability is particularly vital during emergencies, where reaction times must be quick so that lives can be saved in certain situations. The shift towards RPM not only enhances patient outcomes but also optimizes the use of resources in health facilities, showing how Edge Computing can redefine operational efficiencies in health settings. Edge Computings role also becomes critical when faced with chronic diseases because it presents constant monitoring of health outside of traditional clinical settings. For patients with diseases such as diabetes or heart disease, wearable devices for real-time monitoring of vital signs prove to be useful since early intervention in the care of their health is possible. These use cases require very low latency to deliver adequate data processing, which is a prerequisite for ultra-low latency services in fields such as healthcare. As mentioned in Cuevas et al. (2017), investments to construct robust network infrastructure facilitating such innovative applications can lead to new business models in healthcare. Therefore, RPM not only enhances patient engagement and adherence to treatment plans but also opens opportunities for healthcare providers to migrate toward value-based models of care, focusing more on quality rather than volume. Furthermore, economic advantages of Remote Patient Monitoring enabled by Edge Computing go beyond the level of patients individually to the overall healthcare system. By reducing hospital readmission and easing the burden on healthcare facilities, RPM is capable of initiating substantial cost reductions. Higher efficiency through real-time access to information allows healthcare providers to make decisions on resource and patient management confidently. This validates strategic frameworks to boost research outputs in health care, as shown in Department of Innovation et al. (2025). With ongoing investments by health care organizations in RPM technologies, they open the door to a new paradigm for healthier sustainable health care practices and improved patient experiences, spotlighting the capability of Edge Computing to redefine industrial applications across sectors (Figure 10.11).

Figure 10.11. Remote patient monitoring devices in healthcare.

Source: https://external-content.duckduckgo.com/iu/?u=https%3A%2F%2Fstatic.wixstatic.com%2Fmedia%2F40d6e1_717fa90656ed412e953325774bbb5228~mv2.jpg%2Fv1%2Ffill%2Fw_823%2Ch_502%2Cal_c%2Cq_85%2F40d6e1_717fa90656ed412e953325774bbb5228~mv2.jpg&f=1&nofb=1&ipt=221018d1712ec639e871423c4765eb2cd085a2f0263a04996613c97cb9f4dc81.

10.4.2. Data Security and Privacy

The implementation of edge computing across industrial domains has transformed data handling and processing, especially with regards to data security and privacy. Decentralizing the processing of data and localizing it near the point of origin enables industries to ensure that they do not fall victim to unprecedented data breaches. This change underscores the importance of real-time data processing, as sensitive information never has to go too far from its point of origin, thereby curbing exposure to outside threats. Moreover, edge computing makes it possible to have more tailored security measures that can be tweaked in accordance with the specific needs of different industrial settings. This adaptability is especially critical in situations where it is necessary to secure data integrity and confidentiality to ensure operational success and compliance with industry regulations. Data protection under edge computing also raises serious issues in terms of establishing secure communication paths, particularly under the stress of evolving cyber threats. Recent research indicates a recent sharp rise in pre-attack cyber-attacks, which call for robust protection against malware and command-and-control (C2) techniques used to search for vulnerabilities in the edge. These developments underscore the need for strengthened security measures that go beyond endpoint protection to incorporate real-time monitoring and anomaly detection to avoid probable intrusions. Machine learning and artificial intelligence can further support such defenses, enabling systems to learn about emerging threats and adapt security strategies accordingly, securing industrial processes increasingly based on networked devices and data streams (Cova et al., 2014).

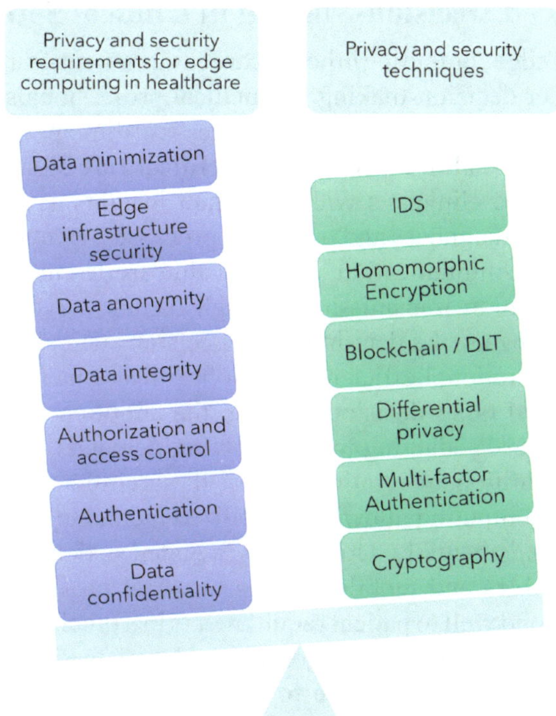

Figure 10.12. Security and privacy requirements in edge computing-enabled healthcare.

Source: https://www.mdpi.com/1999-5903/16/9/329.

Privacy concerns also loom big in the debate regarding the application of edge computing within industrial settings. As businesses amass huge repositories of personal information, particularly in sectors such as manufacturing and healthcare, the ethical handling of the information becomes front and center. The preservation of data acquisition methods in compliance with regulation stipulations such as GDPR puts organizations in the position of implementing rigorous controls that guarantee user privacy while benefiting from the advantages of edge computing. Besides, establishing a culture of transparency in utilizing data enhances stakeholders' and customers' confidence. As industries move towards adopting new technologies, an integrated framework that deals with both data protection as well as privacy must be established, such as governance, technology solutions, and staff learning, to successfully counter threats and foster innovation (Mercadé et al., 2020) (Figure 10.12).

10.4.3. Enhanced Decision-Making in Clinical Settings

The application of edge computing in healthcare environments is a groundbreaking move toward better decision-making for medical professionals. By processing data close to the source, edge computing makes real-time patient data analysis possible, which is crucial in emergency and critical care situations. This level of proximity provides clinicians with important insights at the point of care, which leads to faster diagnoses and treatment processes. Better data availability translates to better communication within healthcare teams, which omits the time lost in information transmission through distant servers. Consequently, healthcare workers can make data-informed decisions that significantly impact patient care and operational efficiency. With healthcare facilities relying more on data merging and rapid decision-making, the adoption of edge computing is a vital move towards adapting to the evolving demands of modern medical environments. In addition, integrating state-of-the-art infrastructural technology by means of edge computing allows personalized medicine to revolutionize the care of patients fundamentally. Utilizing aggregated patient data from various sources like wearables and mobile devices, medical professionals can create decisions that respond well to patient requirements in a precise way. Personalized treatment not only optimizes engagement and satisfaction among patients but also enhances patient adherence to treatments and preventive measures. Besides, with on-premises examination of vast data sets, clinicians can identify trends that can be utilized to inform population-level health initiatives. Such examination can detect underlying health inequalities that can be effectively controlled proactively. The combination of healthcare practitioners and data scientists with IT specialists based on the power of edge computing guarantees comprehensive knowledge of patient care, which is effective and innovative (Consulting et al., 2016). The integration of edge computing solutions into clinical settings also brings with it a vital layer of security and compliance, increasingly necessary in the data-centric healthcare landscape of the day. As patient data is private and under strict regulatory oversight, having patient data remain secure is imperative. Edge computing enables improved cybersecurity best practices by retaining patient data locally, reducing exposure to transmitting private data over possibly insecure networks. Furthermore, contextual real-time actions provided by edge devices help to quickly identify and respond against unauthorized access or data intrusion. This proactive security stance not only protects patient confidentiality but also builds credibility within the health environment. As clinical environments continue to advance, safe utilization of edge computing, therefore, appears to be an important consideration in optimizing decision-making processes with an emphasis on efficacy and safety for patients (Debackere et al., 2025).

10.5. AGRICULTURE

Application of edge computing technology in agriculture is a new way of optimizing farm productivity and management. With decentralization of computation and data processing closer to where data is generated, edge computing makes it possible to do real-time analysis and react accordingly. This immediacy is critical in agriculture as timely decisions can have a great impact on crop output and utilization of resources. For instance, edge devices with sensors can monitor soil water content, weather, and plant health and allow farmers to make informed decisions on irrigation, fertilization, and pest management. As farming activity moves towards precision agriculture, the role of edge computing increases by many leaps and bounds in helping farmers properly use their resources and enhance their capabilities in order to enhance an approach to food production that is sustainable. In this case, the agricultural services industry is at the forefront of developing the economy through increased productivity and efficiency brought about by technology application. Relying on advanced data analysis facilitated by edge computing is consistent with the shift towards a postindustrial economy where strategic management of agriculture practices is critical. As highlighted in the service sector debates, agriculture's value creation potential is colossal when innovative technology is utilized effectively. Being able to quickly process data from numerous sources allows farmers to take proactive measures that can mitigate the risks that come with climate change and market volatility. Further, with the world population on the rise, pressure toward sustainable food production demands an agricultural system that embraces technological innovation, thus enabling overall economic stability within developed economies, such as the case has been for the services sector (Britchenko et al., 2018). As countries move toward a knowledge economy, agriculture is also at the forefront of such a revolution, triggered by the embrace of cutting-edge technologies. The deployment of edge computing is a perfect illustration of the potential of skills and knowledge to enhance farm productivity significantly, highlighting the importance of having a skilled workforce that is knowledgeable in technological abilities. This alignment not only enhances the process of farming but also makes nations competitive in the world market where food production is highly valued to be efficient. The sophisticated mutual dependency of technology innovation and labor skill mirrors the requirement for continuing education and training in agriculture, establishing a culture of elevating the proficiency of the workforce. Ultimately, the integration of edge computing and agriculture is likely to revolutionize the sector, triggering economic and sustainability results in a more and more dynamic world context (Kelly et al., 2002) (Figure 10.13).

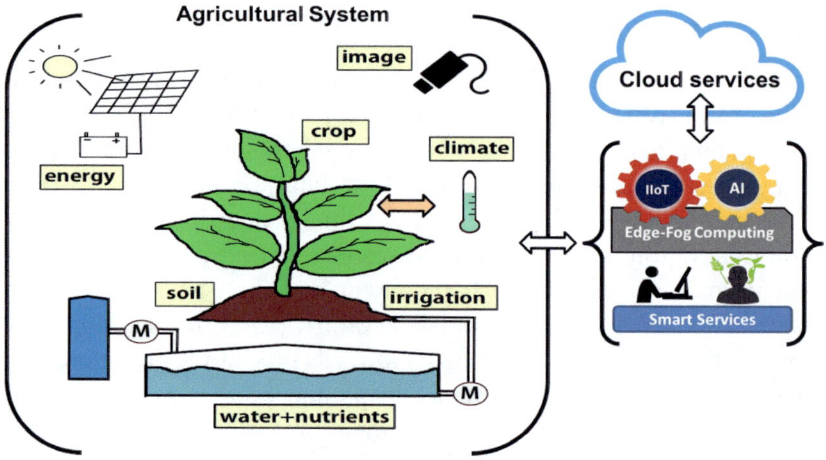

Figure 10.13. Edge computing in agriculture.

Source: https://media.licdn.com/dms/image/v2/D5612AQE8rzIcX3ddTg/article-cover_image-shrink_600_2000/article-cover_image-shrink_600_2000/0/1715943806516?e=2147483647&v=beta&t=opxke_z2Wg0Ymz8U2n4fUW9kd8q7fYVl-GYvZuFFuSe8.

10.5.1. Precision Farming Techniques

The incorporation of precision farming techniques into modern agriculture has been significantly enhanced with advancements in edge computing, which facilitates real-time processing of information at or near the source where information is in the process of being generated. This paradigm shift allows for better monitoring and management of agricultural activities using sensors and IoT devices deployed in the field. For instance, soil moisture sensors provide real-time feedback on irrigation needs so that farmers can best use water while ensuring maximum crop yields. Moreover, data collection and analysis through edge computing minimize latency and bandwidth needs, which are critical for timely decision-making. With precision agriculture continuing to evolve, the use of low-cost sensor networks is revolutionary since it makes access to advanced farming technologies available to all, hence more widely practiced and improving productivity within the sector (Derhab et al., 2020). Moreover, the security and privacy issues associated with integrating Internet of Things (IoT) technologies into agriculture cannot be overlooked.

Figure 10.14. Precision farming techniques.

Source: https://www.lingayasvidyapeeth.edu.in/sanmax/wp-content/uploads/2023/08/precision.jpg.

Device connectivity results in serious issues related to data integrity, privacy, and possible cyber-attacks. It is essential to attain a complete understanding of such vulnerabilities so that strong security frameworks can be formulated to safeguard the sensitive data obtained through precision farming techniques. For this purpose, it is important to explore next-generation security models, particularly those for green IoT agricultural applications. By mixing blockchain technology with other security mechanisms, farmers are able to protect their data more securely from unauthorized use and alteration. Not only is the agricultural data made secure but also confidence among the stakeholders is gained, thereby enabling new technology to be adopted in agriculture (Derhab et al., 2020). Furthermore, the use of edge computing in precision agriculture extends beyond mere data handling to encompass more sustainable farming practices. Through real-time analysis, edge computing helps farmers make data-informed decisions whose impact directly influences productivity as well as environmental conservation. An example is machine-to-machine communication that facilitates timely action in controlling pests and diseases, reducing the application of chemical inputs by significantly large amounts. The result is a cleaner style of farming that minimizes ecological footprints yet maintains high levels of productivity. Additionally, information based on data can lead to enhanced resource utilization, with a reduction in wastage and inefficiencies. As precision farming techniques are becoming increasingly advanced, the value added by integrating sustainable practices will be key to achieving long-term agriculture sustainability and resilience (Ferrandez-Pastor et al., 2016) (Figure 10.14).

10.5.2. IoT Integration for Crop Management

The application of the Internet of Things (IoT) in crop management is a big advance in agriculture that promotes precision agriculture and increased productivity. With the application of connected devices and sensors, farmers can monitor soil moisture, weather, and crop health in real-time. The data-driven approach allows for efficient management of resources with room for targeted irrigation, fertilization, and pest control, thus saving resources and preventing environmental degradation. Besides, IoT devices can forward valuable data to edge computing platforms that process data locally in aid of real-time decision-making. This renders farmers capable of making appropriate decisions that optimize yield and reduce operation costs, proving how modern technology can reshape traditional farming methods in the background of rising global food demands and environmental sustainability. Edge computing enhances the effectiveness of IoT deployment in crop management significantly by enabling quick processing and eliminating latency. By processing data close to the point of origin—i.e., on the farm field and not relying entirely on cloud computing—stakeholders in farming can respond to real-time inputs that are vital in decision-making. The real-time nature is especially critical in the determination of growth phases where conditions rapidly change, influencing crop health and yields. Utilization of edge computing in IoT systems enables a holistic evaluation of most agricultural parameters, including weather predictions and soil quality readings. By the utilization of these aspects, stakeholders in the agricultural sector are able to implement timely interventions, thus optimizing resource management and crop production. Technology integration is evidence of the necessity to modernize agriculture practice in order to meet the demands of food output in contemporary society. Apart from that, the combination of IoT technologies and edge computing supports ecologically friendly agricultural practices in harmony with global initiatives towards green agriculture. Traditional agriculture has a tendency to rely on one-size-fits-all approaches, which can lead to overuse of resources such as water and fertilizers, with an eventual toll on the environment. In contrast, IoT-based crop management systems provide precise, context-aware suggestions by analyzing data in real-time. For instance, irrigation times can be programmed to satisfy the specific water needs of crops, as picked up by soil moisture sensors. The integration also helps promote biodiversity through the ability of farmers to monitor the health of various plant species and act strategically in controlling their cultivation. With these technologies, not only can agricultural producers expand their output, but they also play a very vital role in environment conservation, as demonstrated through the increasing recognition of agriculture as a component of sustainable development policy in most countries (Britchenko et al., 2018; Ewart et al., 2019).

10.5.3. Livestock Monitoring Systems

Livestock monitoring systems are one of the key intersections of edge computing and agri-tech, with the potential for future gains in productivity and animal welfare. The systems use various sensors and devices located at the farm level to track real-time information on climatic conditions, diet, and animal health. Farmers can make efficient decisions to enhance operational efficiency based on these inputs. With the application of edge computing, processing is done closer to the source, reducing latency and allowing real-time analysis—essential for timely intervention in animal health. Given that livestock farming is more susceptible to climate change and its low resources, the application of advanced technologies is essential. Thus, the application of edge computing in livestock monitoring systems is a perfect example of a paradigm shift towards sustainable agriculture with a balance between traditional practices and modern technological capability, in an effort to build a stronger food production system. The operational functionalities of livestock monitoring systems are followed by seamless integration with Internet of Things (IoT) devices. With such devices, farmers are able to monitor animals on an individual basis, tracking feeding patterns, behavioral activity, and physiological indicators. This is a high level of monitoring, which can detect early disease signs and enable quicker action that can better reduce veterinary costs as well as improve livestock welfare. Besides, data collected through such systems may also be analyzed in the long run to have an even better understanding of trends and forecast the future and hence optimize herd management methods. Edge computing allows for such analyses to be conducted locally, so that critical processing of information isn't dependent on sometimes flawed cloud resources. Hence, cattle monitoring systems aided by IoT capabilities and edge computing facilitate a more efficient and adaptive agricultural framework, illustrating the pivotal function of technology in modern farming practices. Moreover, the impact of cattle monitoring systems is not confined to real-time improvement. Strategic implementation of these technologies can lead to higher compliance with animal care and food safety regulations. By maintaining extensive records of animal wellbeing and farm practices, farmers can provide open data to stakeholders, including consumers and regulators. Transparency will foster consumer confidence and satisfaction, which is more crucial in today's marketplace where ethics drive consumer purchasing behavior. Additionally, better livestock monitoring systems are also synergistic with national and global initiatives of promoting agricultural sustainability measures. As noted in recent strategic research and innovation plans, the only way the challenges facing the agricultural sector can be overcome is through the integration of quality research with application (Chrousos et al., 2014). Lastly, computerized livestock monitoring systems with sophisticated technology are at the center of instilling sustainable practices, thereby guaranteeing long-term business sustainability (Abba et al., 2017).

SUMMARY

The advent of edge computing is a critical change in industrial markets, simply revolutionizing how data is processed and accessed. With businesses depending increasingly on networked devices and automated processes, the capacity to evaluate real-time data at the network's edge is critical. This strategic action not only enhances operational efficiency but even enables businesses to leverage insights for new-age solutions. At the heart of this is the use of In-Transit Analytics-supporting technologies, which is vital in obtaining actionable insights from manufacturing data. Such technology allows companies to gain a competitive edge and enhance process and product innovation, hence addressing the principles of Industry 4.0 as outlined in the discourse on digital manufacturing (Ali et al., 2017). Furthermore, the integration of edge computing with emerging technologies such as 5G further adds to its utility in industrial applications. Millimeter-wave technology applications in 5G networks are a classic example of the ways enhanced connectivity can support rapid and reliable information exchange between devices at the edge. These developments enable more efficient cell discovery with less access latency that is related to backward propagation conditions. Through the use of context information, industrial operators can optimize their operation plans, enhancing the responsiveness and flexibility of their systems. Such convergence of 5G architectures and edge computing not only streamlines workflow but also provides the gateway for new innovation in industrial applications that can lead to transformative productivity and service delivery improvements (Capone et al., 2017). Ultimately, edge computing applications in industrial environments are innovative and multifarious in nature and hold promise for a paradigm shift in operational efficiency. As companies embark on furthering their investigations of the synergies between edge computing and other digital technologies, they are sure to be faced with new opportunities disrupting established business models. The benefits of edge processing are numerous and varied, from reduced latency, better resource utilization, and enhanced decision-making authority. With industries striving to keep improving and becoming more competitive, effective utilization of edge computing will play a crucial role in attaining the full potential of the Industrial Internet of Things (IIoT) and developing an innovation culture. This promising direction calls for further research and development aimed at realizing the potential of edge computing to optimize industrial growth and efficiency.

Industrial applications dramatically boost operation efficiency and processing capacity for data. By decentralizing data processing and moving it closer to the location of data origin, edge computing eradicates latency and reduces bandwidth requirements. Those sectors that exploit these functionalities enjoy improved real-time decision-making, which is crucial when handling shifting environments such as manufacturing and logistics. For instance, in a factory, edge devices can process equipment data in real-time to deliver predictive maintenance that minimizes downtime while optimizing productivity. This move from traditional cloud-based computation to edge-based platforms is an answer not only to efficiency but also to the emerging need for real-time analytical response in competitive markets, again emphasizing the relevance of edge computing in modern industrial application, for example, in projects like those described in the new partnership proposals for next-generation industries in New Hampshire (Consulting et al., 2016). Second, edge computing encourages stronger data security and control over privacy, an area of high interest in industries that handle sensitive information. By processing data locally rather than sending it along long networks, organizations have more protection from cyber-attacks. Particularly in industries such as healthcare and finance, being compliant with stringent regulations is an essential requirement. In such scenarios, edge computing allows secure transfer and analysis of data without exposing it to potential breaches in transmission processes. Furthermore, with industries increasingly embracing Internet of Things (IoT) technologies, the capability to process and secure large volumes of data collected from devices becomes crucial. The rapid reaction provided by edge computing not only enhances operational security but also underpins broader goals of innovation and technology-driven development, as in initiatives to bring together sophisticated research and industrial uses (Misuraca et al., 2013). The versatility of edge computing extends its applications beyond traditional manufacturing and cyber-security. Emerging fields like smart agriculture and autonomous vehicle technology are directly helped by edge computings capability. For example, edge computing devices in smart agriculture can monitor current environmental conditions to enable data-based choices that optimize yields and efficiency of resources. Similarly, autonomous cars apply edge computing to process large amounts of sensory data immediately to ensure safe travel and real-time adaptability to changing conditions. These applications highlight the potential of edge computing to revolutionize numerous sectors, providing new avenues for economic development and sustainability. The ongoing evolution of such technologies underscores the necessity for robust policies and convergent action to achieve the whole spectrum of innovations edge computing promises to industrial applications of the future (Consulting et al., 2016; Misuraca et al., 2013).

REFERENCES

1. Abba, M. K., Abdalla, K., Abubaker, M., Abuzukhar, S., et al. (2017). SPARC 2017 retrospect & prospects: Salford Postgraduate Annual Research Conference book of abstracts. https://core.ac.uk/download/96619994.pdf (accessed on 16th September 2025).
2. Ali, M., Anjum, A., Devitt, J., Hill, R., et al. (2017). Towards in-transit analytics for Industry 4.0. http://arxiv.org/abs/1710.04121 (accessed on 16th September 2025).
3. Baaziz, A., Kleiner, A., Feigelson, E. D., Waller, M. A., Boyd, S., Vandermerwe, S., & Zhou, Z. (2015). Big data and the Internet of Things. http://arxiv.org/abs/1503.07092 (accessed on 16th September 2025).
4. Bala, D., D'Ascenzo, F., Ruggieri, R., Savastano, M., et al. (2018). The impact of digital platforms on business models: An empirical investigation on innovative start-ups. https://core.ac.uk/download/195776530.pdf (accessed on 16th September 2025).
5. Bleiker, S., Kulsreshath, M. K., Li, Y., Marot, M., et al. (2024). Hardware platform for edge computing based on nanoelectromechanical relays. https://core.ac.uk/download/646018330.pdf (accessed on 16th September 2025).
6. Bolfek-Radovani, J., Briscoe, G., Dima, M., Fogg, R., et al. (2014). London creative and digital fusion. https://core.ac.uk/download/30697507.pdf (accessed on 16th September 2025).
7. Boujemaa, N., Compañó, R., Dosch, C., Geurts, P., et al. (2009). CHORUS Deliverable 3.4: Vision document. https://core.ac.uk/download/11434795.pdf (accessed on 16th September 2025).
8. Britchenko, I., Cherniavska, T., & Machashchik, P. (2018). New trends in development of services in the modern economy. https://core.ac.uk/download/323058294.pdf (accessed on 16th September 2025).
9. Bunte, F. H. J. (2025). Thought for food: The impact of ICT on agribusiness. https://core.ac.uk/download/pdf/6689732.pdf (accessed on 16th September 2025).
10. Capone, A., Devoti, F., Filippini, I., Sciancalepore, V., et al. (2017). Fast cell discovery in mm-wave 5G networks with context information. http://arxiv.org/abs/1705.07291 (accessed on 16th September 2025).
11. Chrousos, G., Dafermos, C., Featherstone, K., Haliassos, M., et al. (2014). National strategic framework for research & innovation. 2014–2020. https://www.econstor.eu/dspace/bitstream/10419/102713/1/798025204.pdf (accessed on 16th September 2025).

12. Ciarli, T., Coad, A., & Moneta, A. (2019). Exporting and productivity as part of the growth process: Causal evidence from a data-driven structural VAR. https://core.ac.uk/download/305117939.pdf (accessed on 16th September 2025).
13. Copeland, R., Crespi, N., Rehmani, M. H., Saleem, Y., et al. (2019). Internet of Things-aided smart grid: Technologies, architectures, applications, prototypes, and future research directions. http://arxiv.org/abs/1704.08977 (accessed on 16th September 2025).
14. Cova, M., Gardiner, J., & Nagaraja, S. (2014). Command & control: Understanding, denying and detecting–A review of malware C2 techniques, detection and defenses. http://arxiv.org/abs/1408.1136 (accessed on 16th September 2025).
15. Crespo Márquez, A., Guillén López, A. J., Gómez López, F. J., Macchi, M., et al. (2016). On the role of prognostics and health management in advanced maintenance systems. https://core.ac.uk/download/190375225.pdf (accessed on 16th September 2025).
16. Cuevas, M., Dohler, M., Laya, A., Lema, A., et al. (2017). Business case and technology analysis for 5G low latency applications. https://core.ac.uk/download/96762095.pdf (accessed on 16th September 2025).
17. Darby-Dowman, K., & Wilson, J. M. (2002). Developments in linear and integer programming. https://core.ac.uk/download/333433.pdf (accessed on 16th September 2025).
18. Debackere, K., Monard, E., Raspoet, D., Ratinckx, B., et al. (2025). Technologie en innovatie in Vlaanderen: Prioriteiten. https://core.ac.uk/download/pdf/6468460.pdf (accessed on 16th September 2025).
19. Dehghanghadikolaei, A., Emamian, S. S., Fotovvati, B., Gisario, A., et al. (2019). The potential of additive manufacturing in the smart factory industrial 4.0: A review. https://core.ac.uk/download/231748826.pdf (accessed on 16th September 2025).
20. Delgado Prieto, M., Fernández Sobrino, Á., Fibla Biosca, P., Romeral Martínez, M., et al. (2019). Active learning-based laboratory towards engineering education 4.0. https://core.ac.uk/download/294830056.pdf (accessed on 16th September 2025).
21. Derhab, A., Ferrag, M. A., Maglaras, L., Shu, L., et al. (2020). Security and privacy for green IoT-based agriculture: Review, blockchain solutions, and challenges. https://core.ac.uk/download/288345720.pdf (accessed on 16th September 2025).
22. Díaz González, F., Gallart, R., Girbau Llistuella, F., Heredero Peris, D., et al. (2018). Smart grid architecture for rural distribution networks: Application

to a Spanish pilot network. https://core.ac.uk/download/157811722.pdf (accessed on 16th September 2025).

23. Ewart, P. (2019). A comparison of processing techniques for producing prototype injection molding inserts. https://core.ac.uk/download/322841895.pdf (accessed on 16th September 2025).
24. Ferrandez-Pastor, F. J., García-Chamizo, J. M., Mora Pascual, J. M., Mora-Martínez, J., et al. (2016). Developing ubiquitous sensor network platform using Internet of Things: Application in precision agriculture. https://core.ac.uk/download/32327272.pdf (accessed on 16th September 2025).
25. Johnson, M., White, A., & Wilson, H. (2008). RFID in the supply chain: Lessons from European early adopters. https://core.ac.uk/download/140499.pdf (accessed on 16th September 2025).
26. Kelly, U., Marsh, R., McLay, D., McNicoll, I., et al. (2002). Defining and identifying the knowledge economy in Scotland: A regional perspective on a global phenomenon. https://core.ac.uk/download/9016138.pdf (accessed on 16th September 2025).
27. Li, G., Li, J., & Wu, J. (2018). Fog-enabled edge learning for cognitive content-centric networking in 5G. http://arxiv.org/abs/1808.09141 (accessed on 16th September 2025).
28. Mercadé Melé, P., Molina Gómez, J., & Sousa, M. J. (2020). Technology, governance, and a sustainability model for small and medium-sized towns in Europe. https://core.ac.uk/download/322918717.pdf (accessed on 16th September 2025).
29. Misuraca, G., & Stewart, J. (2013). The industry and policy context for digital games for empowerment and inclusion: Market analysis, future prospects and key challenges in videogames, serious games and gamification. https://core.ac.uk/download/28977794.pdf (accessed on 16th September 2025).
30. N/A. (2016). New Hampshire university research and industry plan: A roadmap for collaboration and innovation. https://core.ac.uk/download/215517669.pdf (accessed on 16th September 2025).
31. N/A. (2025). 2011 Strategic roadmap for Australian research infrastructure. https://core.ac.uk/download/pdf/30672610.pdf (accessed on 16th September 2025).
32. Stahl, E., & Dupuis, N. (2017). Trends in smart city development. https://core.ac.uk/download/83111937.pdf (accessed on 16th September 2025).

INDEX

E

F

G

H

I

L

M

N

O

P

Q

R

S

T

U

V

W